In the LIGHT of DAWN

In the LIGHT *of* DAWN

The History and Legacy of a
Black Canadian Community

MARIE CARTER

foreword by
DR. AFUA COOPER

University of Regina Press

Printed and bound in Canada. The text of this book is printed on 100% post-consumer recycled paper with earth-friendly vegetable-based inks.

Cover art:
Cover design: Duncan Campbell, University of Regina Press
Interior layout design: John van der Woude, JVDW Designs
Copyeditor: Rachel Ironstone
Proofreader: Rachel Taylor
Indexer: Patricia Furdek

Library and Archives Canada Cataloguing in Publication

10 9 8 7 6 5 4 3 2 1

University of Regina Press, University of Regina
Regina, Saskatchewan, Canada, S4S 0A2
TEL: (306) 585-4758 FAX: (306) 585-4699
U OF R PRESS   WEB: www.uofrpress.ca

We acknowledge the support of the Canada Council for the Arts for our publishing program. We acknowledge the financial support of the Government of Canada. / Nous reconnaissons l'appui financier du gouvernement du Canada. This publication was made possible with support from Creative Saskatchewan's Book Publishing Production Grant Program. / Initial development of the manuscript was supported by a generous grant from the Ontario Arts Council.

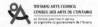

For the people of Dresden,
who inspired this book
and
for my husband, Jeff,
who believed I could write.

Contents

Foreword *by Dr. Afua Cooper* **xi**
Introduction **xv**

Chapter 1. Locating the Dawn Settlement in the Historical Landscape **1**
Chapter 2. Beyond the Underground Railroad: Migrations to the
       Dawn Settlement in the Fur Trading Era **19**
Chapter 3. The Shared Dream of Education:
       The Founding of the British American Institute **29**
Chapter 4. The Seeds of Discord:
       Exploring the Political Landscape of Dawn **39**
Chapter 5. The British American Institute:
       The Early Days of Success and Growth **49**
Chapter 6. Henson's Rising Star: Beyond the Fictional Uncle Tom **65**
Chapter 7. The Rev. John Scoble and the Decline of
       the British American Institute **77**
Chapter 8. "Who Has Not Heard of William Whipper?":
       Exploring the World of the Black Elite **87**
Chapter 9. "And Still They Come!":
       The Black Elite Migration to Dawn **99**
Chapter 10. The Intellectual Migration: The Ideas and Ideals
       of the Black Elite Come to the Dawn Settlement **111**
Chapter 11. "I Never Seen Greater Minds to Learn":
       Dawn's Missionary Influence **117**

Chapter 12. Dennis Hill and the Fight to
    Desegregate Common Schools 135

Chapter 13. Leaving the Promised Land:
    The Haitian Emigration Movement 145

Chapter 14. The Storms of War 155

Chapter 15. The Final Battle for the BAI:
    Brown and Scoble vs. Wright and Myers 163

Chapter 16. Restructuring the BAI to Serve a Changing Society 173

Chapter 17. A Time to Die and a Time to Mourn:
    The Fate of Dawn's Early Leaders 187

Chapter 18. Migration, Resistance, and Contribution
    in a New Century 199

Chapter 19. Answering the Call: Contributions
    to Community and Military 213

Chapter 20. The NUA Story: The Continued
    Resistanceto Segregation 223

Chapter 21. The Journey Towards a More Authentic History 243

  Afterword: The Road Ahead 255
  Acknowledgements 265
  Bibliography 269
  Notes 281
  Index 325

Foreword

It is fitting that *In the Light of Dawn* is the inaugural book for this series. *In the Light of Dawn* is a community study of one of the settlements in which Black freedom seekers from American slavery and racism established and lived and worked there with their families, and over the course of close to two centuries. Descendants of these community builders are still living in the area. The settlement is called Dawn and it was established in the southwestern area of the province of Ontario, and straddles what are now the counties of Lambton and Kent.[1]

In writing this history and telling this story, author Marie Carter is turning on its head the written and oral history of Dawn. Her work is a historiographical intervention, and a new history. Most of what we think about what we know the Dawn settlement, Josiah Henson, the British American Institute (BAI), and the Black history of Southwestern Ontario will be challenged upon reading this work. The received wisdom is that Dawn grew out of the BAI and both were associated with Black abolitionist and runaway slave Josiah Henson. In fact, in some texts Henson is credited with founding both Dawn and the BAI.

Another part of this "truth" is that the residents of Dawn were all African Americans who had fled American slavery to freedom in Canada, and that they all traversed the Underground Railroad in order to do so. While there are elements of veracity in these stories, Carter's book, based on new and ground-breaking research, indicates a more complex and exciting story about the origin, establishment, and history of the Dawn settlement.

The Dawn Settlement was not confined to the BAI and was not founded by Josiah Henson. In fact, the early history of Blacks establishing themselves in what became Dawn predates the establishment of the BAI, and the arrival of Henson to the region, and its geography and history extend beyond the BAI's territory and history. And while many of the Black residents were indeed fugitives from American slavery, many more were free people who left the United States because of proscriptions on their freedom. Additionally, these cohorts of persons had Canadian-born children. Furthermore, White and Indigenous families lived in the area, though within Dawn proper, the majority population were African-descended.

Josiah Henson himself is a towering figure in the Black history of Ontario and Canada as a whole. And in his time, he exerted influence at both the BAI and Dawn itself. But in the historiography his influence has been exaggerated.

Furthermore, contrary to what has come down to us in modern time, the Black community of Dawn was not comprised of a destitute band of fugitive who were dependent on White largesse. Black residents of Dawn and the neighbouring area owned farms, established businesses, and created schools and churches. They were intellectual and writers, industrialists, visionaries, investors, tradesmen, and community builders.

What Carter has done is to rewrite this history by going to the sources for the Dawn story, not only for Lambton County but also for Kent County, across whose boundaries the historic Dawn settlement currently lies, especially through maps and other primary documents. As a result, Carter has reconstructed a new, nuanced, and ground-breaking history and geography of Dawn.

By retelling the history of Dawn through a keen attention to primary documents, Marie Carter dismantles the dominant interpretation of the Dawn story through time and space.

But the history of Dawn is not only about what took place in the heroic 19th century of the Underground Railroad narrative, and the creation of Black spaces of freedom. There is also the legacy. This includes the layered story of Black civil and human rights activism which took place not only in Dawn but also in the surrounding areas like the town of Dresden. The legacy began with the work of abolitionists and freedom fighters like Henson and William Whipper, and in the mid-20th century, activists such as Hugh

Burnett continued the fight. The work of equality and justice that these Black activists pioneered was the groundwork for many pieces of progressive legislation that we now take for granted.

Marie Carter spent decades researching the history of Dawn, and consequently she has become the foremost expert of this story. Black Canadian history has taken a leap forward with publication of the *In the Light of Dawn*. We are thankful for the illumination Carter provides.

—DR. AFUA COOPER
Killam Research Chair in History, Dalhousie University

Introduction

The Dawn Settlement was established in the nineteenth century in and around what is today the community of Dresden (population 2,800) in the rural Municipality of Chatham-Kent (formerly Kent County) in South-western Ontario. I grew up here in the 1950s and '60s on what was then the Concession Three of Camden Gore (later named Uncle Tom Road and subsequently renamed Freedom Road). Our family's farm lay next door to what was then our neighbour Bill Chapple's relatively new museum, which he originally called "Uncle Tom's Home" (Fig. 1) and later, the Uncle Tom's Cabin Historic Site (now Josiah Henson Museum of African Canadian History). I have continued to live in and near Dresden for most of my seventy years, and it is from this vantage point and through my experience of this land and its people that I have come to question the authenticity of a long-accepted narrative of the Dawn Settlement as a failed utopian colony at the terminus of the Underground Railroad founded by Rev. Josiah Henson.

The heavy reliance on Josiah Henson's association with Harriet Beecher Stowe's protagonist in her landmark anti-slavery novel *Uncle Tom's Cabin* has led scholars to present Henson's case as an example of the "fictionalizing" of history.[1] Yet the Dawn Settlement and Henson were very real. But as I argue in this book, he is not the only important historical figure associated with the Dawn Settlement, nor, as is often assumed, was he the sole developer of the settlement.[2] The long shadow of "Uncle Tom" has often obscured Henson's real-life story: his association with the novel and his British trips which culminated in an audience with Queen Victoria, have served to make of Henson an exception in the minds of many Canadians. One recent biography of his life, for instance, extols him as a great man while characterizing the thousands of others who came to Canada as "abused, illiterate, uneducated, hungry former slaves" whose settlements were "like refugee camps... (lacking) a definite sense of permanency... And reliant for their existence on 'white outsiders.'"[3] As this book hopes to demonstrate, the Dawn Settlement was far from impermanent, and Henson's agency, ability, and contributions were not unique among his contemporaries at Dawn. This is not to diminish Henson's stature or accomplishments, which are considerable, but to more accurately place him within an often-forgotten community of Black leaders, whose presence has been lost in the long shadow cast by the "Uncle Tom" narrative.

Making of Henson and other iconic figures of the UGRR like Harriet Tubman has also had a tendency to freeze Black history in a nineteenth century context. Even outside of his Uncle Tom association, Henson's own story, published in 1849,[4] three years before Stowe's novel, is the quintessential slavery-to-freedom narrative, and these narratives had tended to reinforce what recent scholars have described as a "150-year fixation on a heavily romanticized view of the Underground Railroad" in Canadian consciousness, which has far-reaching implications.[5] They also tend to position Black Canadian settlements like Dawn at a *terminus* on the Underground Railroad, the end of a journey in search of freedom and equality. This "Promised Land" view of Canada assumes that Canadian society under British Law delivered on assurances of equal rights despite historical facts to the contrary.[6] As Deirdre McCorkindale argues, this narrative enables Canadians to claim a moral high ground in respect to our American cousins based on a faulty assumption that slavery and racism are not part of Canada's past and ongoing historical legacy.[7]

This book proposes a very different narrative, one in which Josiah Henson was not the first arrival in the Dawn Settlement, and in which the settlement was not exclusively a colony of formerly enslaved people of African descent, and where the fight for freedom and equality has continued through the resistance and contribution of the Dawn Settlement community—including both Black and white activists—throughout the nineteenth and into the twentieth and twenty-first centuries. At Dawn there existed a group of Black leaders of equal or greater stature to Henson, who had honed their political, organizational, and legal skills in the fight for equality in the US and formed their goals for their own advancement in the Black Convention Movement of the 1830s. They were part of an intellectual migration that informed and supported abolitionism and social activism in the Dawn Settlement and beyond, placing Dawn and other Canadian settlements with similar populations more squarely at the crossroads of Black thought and action in the nineteenth century. These Black elites often were also represented not as passengers but as activists in the William Still Underground Railroad. In Canada, as explored in Chapters 8, 9, and 10, these leaders settled in close proximity to one another, as they had in their previous homes, creating communities in which the ideas and ideals they had championed in Pennsylvania continued to be debated and continued to inform their activism. They supported these causes with all of their educational and monetary resources and their personal service on both sides of the US-Canada border.

In Canada, they also mobilized their education, activism, attitudes, knowledge, and resources to the fight for equal rights promised under British law, particularly in respect to education as is most dramatically seen in Dennis Hill's court case against segregated schools in Ontario, explored in Chapter 12. Dawn's inhabitants did not resist slavery from the relative safety of British soil in Canada West but remained willing to put their lives on the line for those they had left behind as demonstrated in their involvement with John Brown and their enlistment as soldiers in the American Civil War (explored in Chapters 13 and 14). Those who had been disappointed to find the promises of equality extended to them broken, would leave in significant numbers to pursue their dream of finding equity on more distant shores (Chapter 13). Others would remain to fight for their civil rights through successive generations throughout a two-hundred-year continuum of resistance. There was also a continuum of contribution which challenges the notion that early African-Canadian settlers were needy refuges who relied on the generosity of others to establish on Canadian soil. Rather, African-descent pioneers played an active part in building our communities and nation. Some built early infrastructure, others offered loans and mortgages to early white industrialists. These continuums of resistance and contribution run like a golden thread through the Dawn Settlement area's history, linking the vision and aspirations of past generations to those of the present day.

Much of our fractured understanding of the Dawn Settlement is rooted in the "confused and amorphous"[8] nineteenth-century contemporary reports of visiting investigators like Benjamin Drew[9] and the views of Mary Ann Shadd Cary, publisher of the *Provincial Freeman* newspaper, and her editors, like J.C. Brown and Rev. William P. Newman, who were passionate political opponents of Henson and the management of Dawn Settlement's manual labour school. Contemporary accounts of the nineteenth-century Dawn Settlement[10] tend to conflate it with the grandly named British American Institute of Science and Technology (BAI); yet the land record evidence (explored in Chapter 1) shows that the BAI was but one of the settlement's constituent parts. The Dawn Settlement's footprint on the landscape of the province of Ontario (Upper Canada from 1791 to 1841, and Canada West from 1841 to 1867)[11] encompassed the emerging community of Dresden and portions of the surrounding townships. As the field of Black history became more established in the mid-twentieth century, scholars like William and Jane Pease,[12] Robin Winks,[13] and Daniel G. Hill[14] relied heavily on contemporary visitors to Dawn, including Drew and others, even as they provided more detailed, nuanced, and contextualized examinations of the settlement. Descriptions given by these twentieth-century scholars continued to rely on these accounts which were mainly given during the 1850s and 60s when the BAI's management troubles had not yet been resolved, leading to a historical judgement that the school failed in its mandate of providing education to students of African descent; the perceived failure of the BAI has often led to the perception that the settlement as a whole "died out by the 1860s."[15] Records of land purchases at Dresden from 1853 to 1858 by the Black elite (see Chapter 8) were recovered as part of the Trillium Trail project in 2001.[16] By 2005 scholars such as Donald Simpson had begun to recognize that "it is necessary to distinguish between the failure of the British American Institute, and the success of individual blacks in the area."[17] Thus Dresden's rise is clearly positioned as a part of the Dawn Settlement story, and it is here in particular that the Black elite's presence can be found and their activities link Dawn's history to the global abolitionist movement.

Having made the startling discoveries of the Black elite in land record investigations for the Trillium Trail, I was inspired to further investigate the "disconnects" I had long felt between scholarly interpretations of the Dawn

Settlement and my lived experience of the land and the people who lived all around me in Camden Gore, Dresden, and Chatham Township, many of whom were descendants of its original settlers. A number of anomalous positionings of artifact buildings would also inspire further research on land records beyond the Trillium Trail area, and this led to the understanding that Black land ownership had not existed *on* the three hundred acres of the British American Institute but rather lay on its borders and extended outward from there in all directions (see Chapter 1). The clear evidence of Black settlement in Dawn Township prior to Henson's arrival, meanwhile, required a reassessment of the accepted timeline of the Dawn Settlement—traditionally 1841 to 1872, which mirrors the existence of the BAI and an extension of the timeline to both before and after the BAI's existence and Rev. Henson's lifetime. Extending the Settlement's timeline earlier than 1841 unsettled the notion that the Underground Railroad could explain the presence of all early-nineteenth-century Black settlements (see Chapter 2) and instead placed Dawn's narrative within the larger movements of Indigenous, white and African-descent peoples connected to the fur trade and other major movements of people in the Great Lakes region.[18]

Nina Reid-Maroney's work in *The Promised Land* and in her biography of Rev. Jennie Johnson, established the notion of an "intellectual migration," representing "the movement of ideas that changed as a result of that movement and in turn changed the world."[19] That understanding has been further expanded in this history's examination of the Black elite at Dawn, who embody this intellectual migration through the movement of ideas and ideals they formed in Pennsylvania in the Black Convention, Moral Reform, and early Women's Movements, and which continued to empower people in creating a society based on similar values through successive generations.

The first step in explaining this very different history of the Dawn Settlement, compared to the Underground Railroad narratives, has involved the creation of a map of the Dawn Settlement's geographic footprint (see Chapter 1). However, a second "mapping" that not graphically represented in this book needs to also be understood. This is an imagined map presented through the migration stories presented in the text and which is radically different from traditional maps of Underground Railroad routes which tend to show one way arrows with paths that originate in the US South and end at the Canadian border. The movement of people and ideas to and from Dawn, instead reveal more diverse origins and destinations and movements both ways across the Canada-US border, and along what Boulou de B'béri of *The Promised Land*[20] once termed "trajectories of Blackness" that astonishingly trace more ambitious journeys to and from Britain, the Canadian and American West, and the Caribbean.

At Dawn, often unexamined movements of people and ideas also manifest within the complex interrelationships *between* Canadian settlements. In Canada West, Black elites sometimes created communities that duplicated the close proximity of their homes to one another in their original communities. The Black elites like the family of William Whipper who invested heavily at Dawn, and A.D. Shadd, a leading resident of Buxton— had attended the same Black Convention and Moral Reform meetings in Pennsylvania and were part of the same UGRR networks in the US and on arrival here chose to live in close proximity to each other and be involved in similar political and social movements in the Kent settlements (including at in the Dawn Settlement, Chatham, Chatham Township, and Buxton).Understanding that these relationships existed necessitated a departure in this book from the tendency, particularly in the community histories of the 1970s and '80s such as *The Legacy at Buxton*[21] and *Seek the Truth*,[22] to divorce the histories of Kent's settlements from one another, with Rev. Josiah Henson seen as Dawn's story, Mary Ann Shadd Cary and the John Brown conventions as Chatham's, and A.D. Shadd and Rev. William King as Buxton's. Intertwining Dawn's history with that of other Kent settlements allows a better framing of Dawn's history within the larger international movements of people and ideas that travelled through this area and shows the extent to which Dawn's people were involved in initiatives begun in nearby communities, such as the Harpers Ferry quiet conventions at Chatham. Indeed, as Nina Reid-Maroney has stated, the "web of connection established a community stretched across a wide geographical area but held together by a broad set of ideological imperatives that made up the opposition in all of its varied expressions, to the institution of slavery."[23] In understanding these major local events as involving settlements beyond the ones where they took place, we begin to trace the more expansive joint efforts of people of African descent throughout Canada West. Dominant figures in Black Canadian history like Mary Ann Shadd Cary can also be better understood as having played key roles in the development of other settlements, such as in her intense involvement in the struggle to wrest control of the British American Institute from John Scoble (Chapter 7).

Dawn and the other Black Kent settlements reached their zenith in the nineteenth century, during a massive influx of thirty thousand people of African descent who came to Canada in the years leading up to the American Civil War. A tenth or more of this significant wave of migration is estimated to have settled in Kent's three major settlements: Chatham, Dawn, and Buxton. The Dawn Settlement lay along the navigable Sydenham River in the north of the county; Chatham was centrally located on the Thames River, the only other navigable river in the county; and Buxton's Elgin Settlement was located in the south. A number of other lesser-known Black settlements were established in the surrounding townships.[24] The mythologization of the Underground Railroad tends to present everyone involved in this migration as a homogenous group of people of African descent fleeing chattel slavery. Yet throughout this book, the astonishing diversity of settlements like Dawn in Canada West regarding racial, political, economic, and other factors is clear. These differences could unite communities but also result in conflict. The differing world views among leadership in the British American Institute, for instance, planted seeds of discord" that blossomed into a major impediment to the institute's advancement (see Chapter 4). Divisions between Tappan- and Garrisonian-aligned political camps also manifest themselves in the Dawn Settlement's leadership through conflicts—not only in North America but in Britain as in the example of Rev. John Scoble.

Understanding the interconnectivity of the Canadian Black settlements, as well as their diversity, also helps to unsettle the notion of these settlements as isolated "refuges" for the formerly enslaved and instead advance an image of them as vibrant and active centres of Black abolitionist thought and action. This interconnectedness is supported within the stories of many of Dawn's historical characters, including the white missionary Rev. Hiram Wilson, who emerges in this narrative as much more than "a clerical do-gooder"[25] and incompetent manager of the BAI, as he has sometimes been portrayed. Instead, Wilson's pioneering work in establishing the Canada Mission's twelve sites scattered across Southwestern Ontario (see Chapter 3) and his interactions with principal figures of the American Anti-Slavery Society, such as Lewis Tappan, and with the British and Foreign Anti-Slavery Society's secretary Rev. John Scoble underscore the international connections of the Dawn Settlement and its inhabitants—and shed light on Dawn's importance within the wider abolitionist world, as well as the importance of individual historical figures, including Henson. Henson's life is presented here in this larger context of the historically important figures at Dawn and aims to elevate our understanding of his life, beyond his fame as "Uncle Tom"; and to demonstrate that he was also a moral reformer in his own right and a brilliant promoter of the BAI's aims (Chapter 6).

Dawn's position within the larger map of North America was understood differently by mid-twentieth-century scholars like William and Jane Pease who saw Dawn merely as one of a number of planned colonies for manumitted people in North America. In their book *Black Utopia*, they lumped Dawn and settlements like those at Buxton, Lucan, and Essex County together with those developed in Antebellum America[26] as a solution to the "problem" of what to do with "free" people who were often not accepted within white society as equals.[27] Narratives such as *Black Utopia* have had a significant influence in interpreting the Black settlements in Canada West as planned utopian colonies at the terminus of the Underground Railroad, while urban centres like those in Chatham, Windsor, Toronto, and the Niagara Region have not been understood in this way. Chatham in particular has enjoyed a reputation as a Black mecca. The rural settlements, meanwhile (with the notable exception of Buxton's Elgin Settlement), have been, in this framing, largely understood as "failures." Modern scholars like Adrienne Shadd, who in her 2022 analysis of the Lucan Wilberforce Institute challenge this notion, pointing out that descendants still living on the land their ancestors first settled is clear evidence *against* the idea of failure. Shadd further argues that such settlements should not be judged against a utopian model but instead from the perspective of the settlers themselves who would have viewed their efforts in settling here as having "helped to strike a blow at the system of American slavery."[28] Descendants of Dawn's early settlers have similarly remained an enduring presence in the area, attesting to its success. African descent settlers cleared land and contributed to the establishment of farmland and introduced innovative crops like tobacco and hemp. African-descended investors like William Whipper developed infrastructure that supported both Black and white settlers. The activities of Dresden's Black elite and of the trustees of the Wilberforce Institute in surveying a large portion of Dresden's south-western quadrant and providing loans to white businesspeople at Dresden in the 1870s (Chapter 16) inspire an understanding of the role of the Black community as early developers of the townsite of Dresden.

This understanding of the Dawn Settlement as a success based]on new maps also lifts it out of its traditional confinement within a nineteenth century narra-tive and places it in a more expansive timeline that traces a two-hundred-year continuum of resistance and contribution by people of African descent. Along this timeline, we can watch the unfolding goals and actions of the Black elite; the agency of Dawn's people and their descendants to ensure the success of the BAI's educational mandate through restructuring (Chapter 16); the working for civil rights and resistance against racism (Chapter 20); and the restoration of authentic Black history (Chapter 21). Most dramatic is the hundred-year struggle to end school segregation, which began with Dennis Hill in 1853 and ended with the National Unity Association's significant role in the develop-ment of the *Fair Accommodations Practices Act* in Ontario in 1954 (Chapter 20). This continuum also manifests itself not only in the lives of the elite but those of ordinary men and women. Following Henson's "Rising Star" in Chapter 6, for instance, we can see that those who were formerly enslaved did not see themselves as limited by their former experiences but took the opportunities and resources they found in Canada to actively resist white society's efforts to limit their advancement, sometimes taking the fight against racism overseas. In the twentieth century, this sense of self-worth and personal agency manifested itself in the continued refusal of individuals to be excluded or diminished, as illustrated by the story of a Dresden house servant (Chapter 18) and in the contributions of those who gave exemplary service to the military and society (Chapter 19). A proud sense of personal, family, and community history also endured, and properly commemorating that history was felt to be an import-ant conduit through which respect of Dawn's descendants could be achieved. The continuum of this struggle is traced beginning with the story of the Rev. Jennie Johnson's 1948 lobbying of town council (Chapter 20), and through the story of Rosa Parks and the 1972 Masonic gatherings at Dresden (Chapter 21) and culminates in the renaming of the former Uncle Tom's Cabin Historic Site as the Josiah Henson Museum of African Canadian History.

The argument of this book then is twofold. Firstly, in the evidence outlined above, it proposes that Dawn was not a "failed Black Utopian colony" under the British American Institute's management, of which Henson was an exception as a leader. Rather, the Dawn Settlement was a successful and enduring community whose diverse population shared their ideals and actions with other Black settlements, placing them at the intersection of an international flow of people, ideas, and movements of their day. Dawn's early settlers were also contributors, economically and socially, to the building of local communities and Canadian society. Secondly, it proposes that Dawn's history represents a two-hundred-year continuum of resistance and contribution that continues to this day, particularly in respect to education, community service, anti-Black racism, and in the reclamation of authentic history. When the majority of the Black elite left the region during the era of American Reconstruction, they left behind their vision that Dawn could be a place of freedom and equality: they left an established community of people who retained much of their vision and world view and a culture of service and contribution whose spirit continued through successive generations.

Positionality and Conditionality

Arriving at this more complex and nuanced understanding of the Dawn Settlement has taken me a lifetime of questioning and twenty years of serious research that has involved a peeling away of layers of mythology and historical amnesia.[29] It is difficult to overstate how growing up literally next door to "Uncle Tom's Cabin" in the heart of the former Dawn Settlement has influenced my views on this history, in both positive and negative ways. On one hand, being exposed to Black history through a museum that often relied on the enduring popularity of *Uncle Tom's Cabin* to draw attention to Henson's story has meant I have at times viewed Black history through the lens of romanticized versions of the Underground Railroad, an approach that current scholarship rightfully criticizes for its negative impact. Yet, even the original developer of Uncle Tom's Cabin Museum would himself admonish visitors like me to learn the real name of "Uncle Tom" and to read about his real life. Consequently, I read Henson's slave narrative long before ever opening Harriet Beecher Stowe's *Uncle Tom's Cabin*. Still, Henson's slave narrative reinforced the notion that Dawn's original settlers shared a single migration story as passengers on the Underground Railroad. A positive impact of having the museum next door was that it ensured I would develop an early curiosity about what it represented and would be inspired to ask ongoing questions about the history of my neighbourhood.

The disconnect I felt between my own lived experience of the landscape and its people inspired questions from an early age. When I was just old enough to read, I struggled to decipher the rough black and white

The Henson Cemetery *(top)* and "The Home of Uncle Tom" *(bottom)* as they appeared in the early 1950s. *(Photos courtesy of the Dresden Archives)*

hand-painted signs that appeared on two ancient cemeteries along our concession road and posted in front of a weathered clapboard house on Chapple's property. When I asked my Flemish-immigrant parents what these meant, my father would tell me that "Uncle Tom" had been a character in *De Hut van Oom Tom* (the Dutch translation of *Uncle Tom's Cabin*), a book he had read in school. What this had to do with our neighbour's building—much less the man buried in the cemetery—I could not fathom. My father's explanation did not satisfy me, and one day, my mother, tiring of my ceaseless questions, pressed the quarter price of admission into my hand and sent me off in the company of my older brother to go ask Mr. Chapple for myself. During that first museum visit, Chapple placed a fragile artifact, a hand carved wooden butter bowl, into my hands. This not only sparked a lifetime love of museums and history, but his explanation that it had been made by the people who had once "lived all around here" instilled in me a particular perspective on the history that I have maintained to this day: that Black History was community history and not separate from other Canadian histories. Indeed, in those days, the notion that there was a need to explicitly study Black history was still over twenty years off. That this history was not represented in my grade six *Breastplate and Buckskin* textbook[30] seemed of little consequence as I happily accepted that history could be found in many places, including my own backyard.

My parents came to Canada on contract with the CPR (Canadian Pacific Railway) as agricultural workers and established their final home a mile outside Dresden next door to "the Cabin" during what was a particularly difficult time in that community's history—the final days of the National Unity Association's actions to desegregate privately owned businesses. It was a conflict I would not learn about until my teenage years, given that this politically charged and often personally painful conflict was never mentioned, particularly around children, in the years that immediately followed. My parents, for their part, long before Dr. Martin Luther King Jr. spoke of people being judged solely by the content of their character, unconsciously modelled this behaviour for my brother and me. As a consequence, our family was blessed with the presence of many people of good character who responded to us with neighbourly support, linking us to community networks and at times introducing us to aspects of Canadian culture. Marie McCorkle would arrive at our farm on the pretext of collecting for some neighbourhood appeal and would linger over coffee as she and mom talked about the kinds of things mothers with children of the same age and attending the same school tend to share. Through Marie, we kids were introduced to swimming lessons, trick-or-treating, and the taste of maple walnut ice cream. Bill Thompson similarly appeared at haying season with his tractor and baler, and after a day sweating in the field together Dad and Bill would enjoy a cold beer, the local news, and a few laughs while mom prepared them dinner. When another Chatham township farmer, Bruce Carter, became the first African-Canadian in Ontario to be awarded a seed corn dealership,[31] Dad switched from his usual brand to become Bruce's regular customer.

Years later Bruce's wife, Barbara Carter, then the site manager for Uncle Tom's Cabin Historic Site, invited me to join the museum's Community Advisory Board. My decade-long involvement introduced me to local Black historians Dorothy Shadd Shreve Segee and Gwen Robinson; through our conversations, I began to learn a very different perspective on our shared local history than the white-centric version I had grown up with. Through them I also came to understand that history was not simply a story about the past but had a role to play in the "uplift" of people of African descent. Shadd Shreve Segee would patiently answer all of my "fool questions" with good humour and together with Robinson would encourage me to develop a better knowledge of local families and to pursue original research using the diligent genealogical and land record techniques they often employed. Robinson's work to "twin" Chatham with Harpers Ferry, West Virginia, and her Chatham-Kent Black Historical Society's annual John Brown conferences impressed on me that the area had a significance that went beyond that of most local history.

With the land record discoveries of William Whipper and his colleagues at Dresden through the Trillium Trail Historical Walk[32] project, I embarked on twenty years of more serious inquiry and research into Dresden's Black history. During this time, I was invited to Buxton, where Bryan Prince, a prolific writer of meticulously researched Black history[33] and his wife, Shannon, then curator of the Buxton National Historic Site & Museum, introduced me to a congenial and supportive group of international researchers and historical writers—including Dennis Gannon, an expert on Rev. Hiram Wilson.

They and all the historians at the Prince's gatherings were generous in sharing their perspectives and research.

Beyond the discovery of Whipper's lands along the Sydenham River, the Trillium Trail Historical Walk[34] research had brought into sharp focus that the Dawn Settlement was much more than a "failed Utopian community" as I had learned in the mid-twentieth-century accounts then available. As a result of ongoing consultations with Gwen Robinson I was invited to become a co-investigator in the five-year Community-University Research Alliance Promised Land Project[35] where I would have my first experiences with academic discussion, presention and publication.[36] And even with the completion of this project, personal research continued.

It is with some trepidation that I've sought to pull together all of the findings of the past twenty years into this single volume. That trepidation stems from a recognition that my position within the community I am writing about presents some unique disadvantages. It requires above all, greater vigilance about personal bias as I attempt to walk the fine line of not wishing to be an apologist and at the same time not wishing to cause undue pain for neighbours and friends for whom these histories are personal and, in some cases, remain within living memory. As such I have endeavoured to present more recent events from a variety of different perspectives and within a context that hopefully achieves my aim of being accurate and balanced. For instance, in presenting the National Unity Association story, which has previously been told in *Season of Rage*[37] and in a 2022 presentation at the Chatham-Kent Museum, I have chosen to take the longer view of racism in Canada in hopes of instilling an understanding that this was not simply the "Dresden Story" as it was dubbed by the National Film Board but a part of Canadians' collective history. I have also brought to writing this book the perspective of having known some of those who are now judged as having been on the "wrong side" of history, and I have attempted to understand these individuals as people who sometimes struggled with conflicting values, or were simply ordinary people caught up in extraordinary times and not necessarily equipped by the times or personal formation to rise as champions of civil rights. Understanding their essential humanity has often challenged me to evaluate what my own response might have been in these circumstances— and how indeed I respond even today when faced with similar injustices.

Sometimes my close involvement in the community has provided me with a nuanced understanding of its history and local culture that might not be apparent to visiting researchers. In the seventeen years I worked at Leader Publications with editor and historian Don "Gummer" Spearman, his oral histories provided important insights into the sometimes complex interpersonal relationships that can exist in small towns—something which can be important to know about in analysis of seemingly contradictory and paradoxical attitudes of townspeople as noted by Sydney Katz in his 1949 article on Dresden's desegregation struggle.[38] Because I have known and interacted with local families over a lifetime, I often have been told intimate family stories—or stumbled onto inconvenient truths. In a number of cases, some family members are still reluctant to talk about these publicly. While some of these stories would have made powerful additions to this narrative, I have left them out because they are not my stories to tell. It is my fervent hope that those to whom they belong will eventually share them as they demonstrate the grace with which people have often borne great injustice.

Living in this place I have also been able to indulge in protracted searches of primary records, and as a community historian I have come across obscure local records not normally found among lists of Black history resources. These have sometimes yielded up small puzzle pieces that helped complete the historical picture. The Molly's Creek Women's Institute Tweedsmuir History, for instance, provided a frank glimpse into the strife around 1870s rural school integration, and Helen Burns's history of the local fire department told of the fiery end of Dresden's separate school. Having a community historian's knowledge of local leadership figures was helpful in recognizing the names of locally significant people like Alex Trerice, and by virtue of Trerice's role as the town's first mayor, to understand there was something more to the story of the BAI's land sales than a simple liquidation of assets.

As a local, I am also aware of the rich racial and cultural heritage of some of my neighbours, and this has inspired further examination of multiracial identities first begun by Handel Kashope Wright in the Promised Land Project.[39] As Wright points out, "we have inherited and been limited by the old racist obsession, with definitive racial identities [based on notions of] racial purity and definitive singular identity…based on which the vast majority including Blacks self-identity racially and assign racial identity to others."[40]

This tendency to assign a singular identity to what is in reality a diverse population has often served to limit understandings of the complexity of society at Dawn and of its people, their travels, influences, and abilities. Images of the Underground Railroad, such as the "running man," so often depicted in what were known as stereotype images in the nineteenth century—the equivalent of today's stock photo—have been overused, then in the many ads for "runaways" and now thanks to their use in promoting Black history sites, to the point that we tend to unconsciously identify nineteenth-century Black immigrants as a single homogenous group. Images in family photo albums, however, stand in stark contrast to the running man. While, as discussed by the scholars Thompson and Crooks, the images African-descent people created of themselves at times represent idealized images they nevertheless signal that the population at Dawn and elsewhere was more racially, culturally, and economically diverse than the stereotypical representations suggest.[41]

Coupled with census record information and family genealogies, family photos speak of complex interracial and intercultural relationships that

A 19th century printers' stereotype image of a "fugitive slave" (*left*) stands in sharp contrast to the portrait of a 19th century young woman who was a resident of the Dawn Settlement area, challenging us to think differently about our mental images of a "typical" Dawn settler. (*Photo from the Smith/Campbell family album, courtesy Calvin Shreve*)

in some cases can be traced back to the fur trade and which resulted in a cultural exchange or life experiences that led to the development of diverse skills, knowledge, and world views among people of African descent. While it would be wrong to deny that some of this complexity is the result of abuses of the slave trade, as discussed by Tiya Miles in *The Dawn of Detroit*,[42] it is also true that these unions were born of more positive interactions of the Middle Ground[43] period and hint at the often astonishing trajectories people continued to travel throughout the nineteenth century.[44] Don Juan Barrbero, for example, was a man of Spanish descent who came from South America in the late 1850s by way of Pennsylvania and settled at Dawn with his African-American wife and Ontario-born children.[45] Family genealogies like *Remnants of Forgotten Folk*,[46] *Planted by the Waters*,[47] and *Precious Memories*[48] show family roots that are profoundly intertwined with those of Indigenous people, and one story in the Hanson Cook family genealogy *Precious Memories* even claims a Malaysian ancestor.[49]

This makes it difficult at times to determine how individuals in the nineteenth century identified themselves or understood their identities. James Burns Hollensworth, for instance, has traditionally been understood as a Black man, but his death certificate describes him as a "white man of mixed race,"[50] and in the Census of Camden and Dresden between 1861 and 1881 he and his second wife are identified as Scots-Irish. In recognition of these complex racial and cultural identities, I have tried to use the term *African-descent* throughout this book. This has proved difficult to apply with consistency, however, and so the terms Black, African-American, and African-Canadian are also sometimes used, depending on the context. This identification recognizes the often-complex makeups and origins of Dawn's inhabitants and their descendants and acknowledges that we do not always know how individuals self-identified. In recognition of the primacy of Black experience in this history, I have also reversed the convention of most writing of not racially identifying whites while identifying non-white people; as such it should be assumed that where no racial identification is given, the person being discussed is of African descent. Indigenous groups are identified by the terminology they have chosen for themselves, and white people are identified either as people of European descent or by their country of origin. William Wright for instance, is described as Irish-born.[51]

Place names of communities and regions are identified by the terminology of the time period being discussed. Name changes to townships and roads should be particularly noted at Dawn after the Municipal Act of 1850 when the area of the Dawn Settlement is removed from its namesake township and becomes part of the Camden Gore, and the river that runs through the settlement changes from Bear Creek to the Sydenham River. Names of villages and towns, like McGees Ferry (now Kent Bridge), are similarly named to be consistent with the time period being discussed. The honorific "Rev." is placed before a person's name only at that point in the story where they become an ordained minister as in the case of Josiah Henson and William P. Newman, among others.

This book is not an exhaustive history of the Dawn Settlement area. Much further research remains as discussed in the afterword, and I have tried to avoid areas where I lack the cultural perspective to provide a credible analysis or any new insight such as family life, the Masonic order, and the role of the church in Black society. On the latter, Dorothy Shadd Shreve's *The AfriCanadian Church: A Stabilizer* provides greater insight than I could hope to impart.[52] I have also refrained from in-depth discussions of anti-Black racism for similar reasons and refer readers to the work of Funké Aladejebi, Michele A. Johnson, and others in *Unsettling the Great White North*. The twentieth-century Caribbean migration of temporary foreign workers to the Dawn Settlement area would also have fit well within this book's discussion of the continuum of migration, but my fifteen years as an organizer of outreach to migrant agricultural workers convinces me that I could not do justice to this subject within the limited space and particular focus of this text. It remains a topic for future work. While this is far from an exhaustive presentation of the Dawn Settlement's lost and forgotten history, I hope that what has been presented here is a worthy addition to current attempts to reclaim a more authentic history at the local and national levels.

Chapter 1

LOCATING *the* DAWN SETTLEMENT *in the* HISTORICAL LANDSCAPE

APS MATTER. WHEN ACCURATELY DRAWN, THEY ARE invaluable guides for negotiating complicated or unknown terrain. Historical maps are particularly useful for making the complexities of historical events simpler to understand. Maps of battlefields, for instance, make the movements of troops and changing geopolitical boundaries immediately clear. Examining maps can also show us how they have been used historically to justify or support political ends, as when school section boundaries in Kent County were redrawn to exclude racialized populations.[1] Historical maps can also be useful tools for historians in helping define the scope and size of an area of study.

Past studies of the Dawn Settlement have been greatly inhibited by the lack of an accurate map. Unlike the Elgin Settlement at Buxton, another Kent County settlement, Dawn has no maps or drawings clearly depicting its size and scope or the placement of its principal sites. The Elgin Settlement by contrast has a clearly defined boundary, and the locations of key structures like their church and founder Rev. William King's house are clearly depicted in sketches.[2] Compounding this lack of an accurate map of Dawn are the "amorphous and conflicting"[3] accounts of contemporary observers such as Benjamin Drew.[4] These suffer from a lack of understanding of the shifting geopolitical boundaries of the time.[5] From the outset, research of the Dawn Settlement for the creation of a new, more complete narrative then has rested on creating an accurate map of the settlement as it existed in the nineteenth century. This has been accomplished through an examination of land records within the former limits of Dawn Township in Lambton County and bordering areas of Chatham Township, Camden Township, and Dover Township in Kent County. Examining these records has not only helped to clarify where the Dawn Settlement lay, but has aided in identifying a number of constituent parts of the settlement beyond the British American Institute (BAI), including the emerging Town of Dresden, and has also surfaced the presence of significant Black abolitionists not previously known to have been associated with the settlement.

Ultimately, mapping settlement patterns has not resulted in a static map of the Dawn Settlement with clearly defined borders. Rather it demonstrates a concentrated area of settlement in and around what is today Dresden, Ontario, that extends out in all directions and has no clear end. Settlement rather becomes less concentred the farther we move away from the centre of concentration or sometimes stops only to reappear again in random pockets or blends into other settlement areas, particularly at the border between Camden Gore and Chatham Township. The size and scope of the settlement has also tended to evolve over time, rendering it impossible to create a single static map that represents once and for all time what the Dawn Settlement looked like. The exercise of mapping settlement patterns did, however, have value in helping negotiate the difficult terrain of the faulty historical descriptions which have contributed to the Dawn Settlement being falsely characterized as a failure. Discovering that there had been settlement from the time of the first land sales in Dawn Township also served to break the Dawn Settlement's history free of a constrictive framing within the timeline of the BAI—the famed three-hundred-acre manual labour school reputed to have been founded by Josiah Henson. Census documents and genealogies used to establish the racial identity of landowners also reveal that the

Dawn Settlement was not exclusively made up of formerly enslaved African-descent people but rather revealed a richly multicultural community, further challenging the characterization of Dawn as a planned colony for formerly enslaved people who came here exclusively from the US South—a presupposition that is rooted in a fixation on a romanticized Underground Railroad narrative.[6] What is revealed instead is a racially and culturally diverse settlement that included formerly enslaved people and freemen with diverse origins, many of whom possessed bi- and triracial identities and had diverse cultural influences and who were living among Indigenous and white people whose cultural identities and origins were also not homogenous. People of African descent, then, were revealed to have skills, education, and economic and other resources that challenge slavery-to-freedom narratives of how they came to the settlement and characterizations of them as "abused, illiterate, uneducated, [and] hungry former slaves."[7] This is a description they themselves resented, and which only burdens descendants with an image of their ancestors that is not flattering or helpful and, moreover, stands in the way of creating the more complex, nuanced, and accurate understanding of nineteenth-century Black history in Canada being called for by current scholars.[8]

Comparisons of Settlement Maps and Their Effectiveness

The lack of understanding of the Dawn Settlement's geography and a focus on the British American Institute's well publicized troubles has deeply impacted how the Dawn settlement was portrayed by contemporary investigators like Drew[9] and Howe[10] and in the Black abolitionist press by individuals like Samuel May.[11] Their confused descriptions have in turn influenced mid-twentieth century scholars like Pease and Pease, Hill, and Winks,[12] who have continued to centre their discussions of the settlement on the troubled history of the BAI and what is seen as Rev. Henson's leading role there. Rev. Henson himself is often a subject of controversy being seen at times as the Moses of his people,[13] and at others as the incompetent manager of the BAI's assets.[14] The BAI has further been charactered as controlling all the activity within the settlement, and this has tended to obscure other missionary activity and independent development that occurred there. It has often been assumed that the BAI's territory constituted the entirety of the Dawn

Settlement, and this in turn has perpetuated the notion that Dawn's settlers were reliant on the BAI for their survival. This land-based research approach in contrast shows that a number of settlers of African descent arrived, survived, and thrived through their own independent efforts, and that some were major contributors to the development of the Town of Dresden and farmland in the surrounding townships. The British American Institute (BAI) is further understood as a failed Black utopian colony rather than simply the manual labour school its land deed clearly defines it to be. The BAI was historically often referred to as the Dawn Institute, further blending its identity with that of the Dawn Settlement. In the geographic confusion the Dawn Settlement and the BAI often were not understood as having separate identities, and the notion that the settlement failed with the perceived failure of the BAI was consequently perpetuated. The legitimacy of this "failed" status is further challenged in current scholarship that suggests that Dawn and settlements like it, ought not to be judged by a utopian standard,[15] but by how those who settled there would have viewed them. Additionally, the status of the BAI as a failed educational institute is also challenged in Chapter 16 of this history through a re-examination of the context of the changing times that led to the liquidation of the BAI's land assets but not a termination to its educational mandate.

I became aware at an early age that the faulty interpretations of the Dawn Settlement's scope and nature that I encountered in early museum interpretations and various writings of local white historians such as Brandon, Spearman, and Lauriston[16] and academics like Pease and Pease,[17] Winks,[18] and Hill[19] did not match the familiar terrain of the neighbourhood where I lived or my experience of descendants of early settlers.[20] Our family's home farm lay literally next door to Uncle Tom's Cabin Museum, just outside Dresden, Ontario, and just down the road from the former BAI's three-hundred-acre site. As a youngster, there were no visual representations of the settlement available, leaving me with only a vague idea of where it had lain within my neighbourhood. As an eight-year-old, I was told by museum's owner-curator William Chapple that it had existed "all around here," leaving me to wonder if our farm had been part of it or if any of my neighbours were descendants of its early residents. Jack Thomson, who later owned an expanded version of Chapple's Museum, which he relocated farther down the road, would describe to me, when I was a teenager, that the Dawn Settlement lay between the Third Concession of what was then Camden Gore and the main thoroughfare of the Town of Dresden. This description matched Survey Map 133 of the British American Institute, which continued to be displayed at the museum under the ownership of the St. Clair Parkway Commission as the only representation of the settlement area. The 1871 survey map showed the three-hundred-acre BAI property laid out in a neat grid of streets with building and park lots, a market square, and cemetery ground.

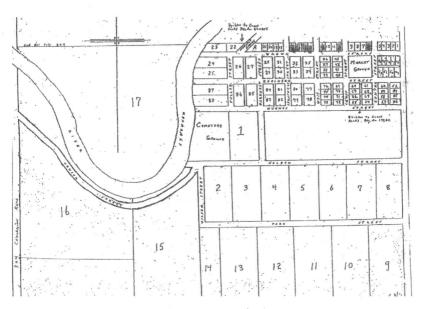

1871 Survey Map of the British American Institute. (*Map courtesy of Chatham-Kent Land Records Office*)

An Ontario Heritage Trust plaque erected at the museum site further described that the settlement had grown up around the BAI school. Combined with the displayed survey map, this reinforced the idea that the BAI and the Dawn Settlement occupied the same geographic space. That conclusion also seemed consistent with scholarly interpretations that said that all of the missions and infrastructure within the Dawn Settlement had been under the control of the BAI's management. The land around me seemed to whisper something very different. On it were key artifact buildings and sites that lay outside the boundaries of the institute's survey—like the burial ground across the road from the museum marked as the BAI Cemetery. A number of our neighbours of African descent also lived on multi-generational farms dating back to the time of the BAI that similarly lay well beyond the BAI's historic borders. There also remained key artifact buildings like original mission churches that were located just over the boundary of the former BAI grounds.

In the absence of an accurate map, the tendency has been to approach the Dawn Settlement's history almost exclusively through the life of its most famous citizen, Rev. Josiah Henson, long credited as the model for the protagonist of Harriet Beecher Stowe's landmark anti-slavery novel, *Uncle Tom's Cabin*. Henson's own biography, published before Stowe's book, embodies the quintessential slavery-to-freedom narrative—and has served to reinforce what current scholarship terms a "150-year fixation on a romanticized version of the Underground Railroad."[21] In turn, the focus on Henson's life has tended to reinforce a singular characterization of the Dawn Settlement as a terminus of the Underground Railroad—a community existing on the periphery of the larger struggle for freedom and equality. Scholars like Deirdre McCorkindale moreover maintain that Henson's association with Beecher Stowe's Uncle Tom has ensured Dawn's history has been heavily overshadowed by a "fictionalized" version of history which portrays residents exclusively as people escaping enslavement in the US South and, on arrival here needing the services of the BAI in order to survive. This tends to reinforce the notion that they settled on BAI land.

In 2001, while researching for the Trillium Trail Historical Walk project for our community, and in subsequent local research projects and the five-year international collaboration on the Promised Land Project—a Community-University Research Alliance Project—discoveries were made of prominent Black abolitionists and others who purchased large tracts of land on the borders of the BAI.[22] This added to my conviction that the traditional historical narratives were, at best, incomplete. Continued land record research also revealed a need to understand the evolution of Upper Canada to Canada West, with its evolving geopolitical boundaries that culminated locally in the Dawn Settlement being removed from its namesake Township of Dawn and led to the "amorphous and conflicting" historical descriptions of the settlement.[23]

Subsequent research showed that the 1871 BAI survey map was not a plan for the Dawn Settlement. Neither did the survey depict the settlement at the height of its development. Rather it represented a proposed plan for future development that included a surveyed grid of then non-existent roads and building lots on what was the largely undeveloped BAI property. The survey was completed and registered to facilitate the sale of the BAI's land assets and to pave the way for incorporation of much of its territory by 1872 within the boundaries of the newly incorporated Village of Dresden. Various accounts from historical observers like Benjamin Drew (author of a *Northside View of Slavery*), Rev. Hiram Wilson (co-founder of the British American Institute), court records, newspapers, and other nineteenth-century sources confirm that nothing like the development suggested by the grid of streets on the 1871 BAI survey map existed on the property at the time of its dissolution.[24] Even principle figures of the BAI's management, including Henson, Wilson, and others, lived outside the BAI on land they independently owned.[25] The division of its grounds for settlement of formerly enslaved people was also not part of the institute's mandate, but rather its deed specifies it was solely for the education of "Blacks, whites and Indians."[26] Indeed, establishing settlement on the site would have undermined the viability of the institution, that operated on the manual labour school model which required a large property where students worked part of their day in lumbering and farming in lieu of providing tuition. Their labour produced food for themselves and operating capital for the institution. Subdividing the BAI grounds for settlement would have diminished the land base on which its operation depended. Historic accounts provide additional evidence that no selling or letting out of the property at the scale suggested on the BAI survey map ever occurred. A court-filed affidavit of the institute's executive committee member George Cary notes only one farm existed on the institute property in 1871, consisting of four log buildings, a frame shanty, and a granary. The developer of this eighty-acre farm did not own it but rather was being charged $175 rent.[27] By contrast, the population of the Dawn Settlement by the mid-1800s is conservatively estimated to have been five hundred people. Faced with such incongruities, we must assume that the Dawn Settlement's population mainly lived outside the British American Institute survey's boundaries.

Geopolitical Boundary Changes

The Soutar's Kent County Directory of 1846[28] describes a large Black settlement along the banks of Bear Creek within what was then known as the Township of Dawn in Lambton County. It is highly likely that this area of Black settlement took its name from the Township itself, hence the Dawn Settlement. However, any association with its namesake township would end with changes to county boundaries that occurred just a decade after the founding of the British American Institute. In 1850, Kent County, which bordered Lambton to the south, annexed a portion of south Lambton. What had formerly been the southern portion of Dawn Township in Lambton County where the BAI had lain now became part of Camden Gore, Kent County, effectively divorcing the settlement from its namesake township and causing a great deal of confusion among visiting observers and later historians. At roughly the same time, the region's most defining geographic feature, its river, also underwent a name change from Bear Creek to Sydenham River. The familiar names of Dawn and Bear Creek continued in popular usage even after the township name changed to Camden Gore and the waterway name changed to Sydenham River. Yet land investors like William Whipper, a prominent Black abolitionist and Underground Railroad conductor from Pennsylvania, used the new, more correct terminology to locate his considerable land purchases, calling these properties his "lands along the Sydenham."[29] As a result, important abolitionists who settled and invested here were never understood as being part of the Dawn Settlement's history despite clear documentation existing in common historical references such as William Still's 1871 Underground Railroad history.[30]

The confusion over geographic place names appears to have strengthened the misconception that the British American Institute and Dawn Settlement were one and the same. The British version of Henson's biography even claims Henson founded the "town of Dawn"[31]. In reality, no such town ever existed. Rather it was the Town of Dresden that emerged out of the Dawn Settlement. When their report was reprinted in the *Chatham Daily Planet*, the, Daniel Van Allen, who was the founder of the original Dresden townsite fired off an indignant letter demanding a correction and saying "Henson never owned a square foot of the town, but I did."[32]

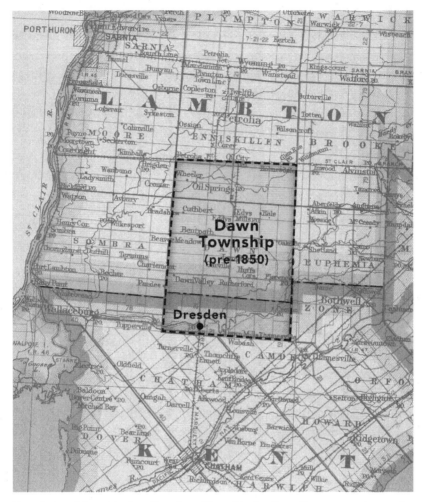

Boundaries of the original pre-1850 Dawn Township, Lambton County, superimposed on a post-1850 map. The Lower portion of Dawn became the Gore of Camden in Kent County. (*Graphics by D. Buchanan*)

Creating a New Map of the Dawn

Attempts to create a new map of the Dawn Settlement have involved searching land records and identifying landowners' cultural/racial identity through genealogy and primary and secondary historical sources. Property owners of African descent were identified in order to reveal settlement patterns that would define the Dawn Settlement's true scope and size. This methodology revealed a concentration of settlement in an area of pre-1850 Dawn Township, near what would later become the borders of the BAI school property, but which began at least twenty years before the institute's founding and Josiah Henson's arrival. This area of Black settlement did not have static or easily defined borders, but rather was a place of fluid and indistinct boundaries that changed over time. The settlement also did not abruptly fail with the

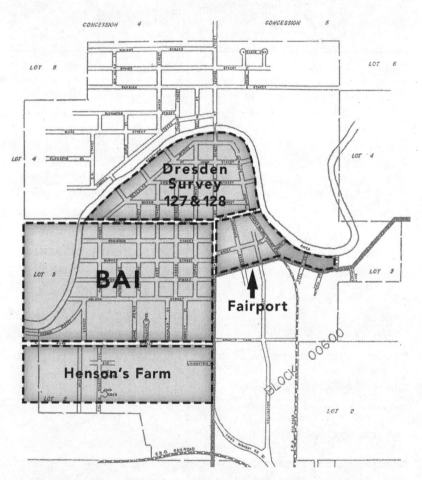

Map of Dresden's current townsite with historic areas of the British American Institute, Henson's farm, Dresden's original surveys (127 and 128), and the Fairport Survey. (*Map copyright M. Carter; graphics by D. Buchanan*)

dissolution of the BAI. African-descent ownership persisted on a large number of properties into the 1880s and although the population slowly and
steadily declined over time. Some descendants remain to the present day.
While the BAI remains an important constituent feature within the settlement area, its territory does not define its boundaries nor is the BAI the Dawn
Settlement's only important feature. Other constituent parts of the settlement
like its mission churches and land development and infrastructure created by
the Black elite in Dresden and farms in surrounding Camden Gore lie outside the school's property. Mapping these features of the settlement shows
the profound effect of early Black settlement had on shaping the landscape.

Survey 133 of the British American Institute emerged in this investigation
as a useful orientation tool for locating the Dawn Settlement's surviving features, including its two extant mission church buildings and cemetery, and to
determine where these lay in respect to BAI lands. The street names assigned
by the BAI trustees in its 1871 survey still appear on Dresden's street signs
today, making it easy for even the most casual observer to locate the historic
BAI property within the modern townscape and to determine where artifact
buildings lie in relation to that property. Because the institute was a central
feature of the Dawn Settlement, its survey map also provides a geographic
starting point for investigating land records to determine settlement patterns. And indeed, all around the BAI's three hundred acres, there are heavy
concentrations of African-descent ownership of land growing around the
borders of the BAI grounds and radiating outward in all directions from the
more or less central point. This is in contrast to the notion that the settlement
grew up on the BAI land around a school building.

Where the Dawn Settlement ended and other Black settlements began
is more difficult to determine. There are an astonishing number of properties owned by people of African descent in the wider region around the
core settlement area and in small, scattered pockets in neighbouring communities—including at Dawn Mills, upriver from Dresden, which served as
the area's postal village before Dresden assumed that role in 1854.[33] Similar
pockets existed in Euphemia Township, which neighbours Dawn Township
to the east, and there is a nearly unbroken concentration of properties that
extends into Chatham and Dover Townships to the south. While these
areas may not have been understood by their settlers as being constituent

parts of the Dawn Settlement, as the townsite of Dresden and the area of Dawn Township that became Camden Gore more surely were, the Dawn Settlement's missionary, social, and economic influences on these areas are apparent in historical accounts.

Settlement Patterns in and around the Dawn Settlement

The first landowners of African descent in the former Dawn Township officially registered their lands situated on the banks of Bear Creek in 1825.[34] In 1834 there were only a scant total of 353 people of all races in Lambton County with only a handful being of African descent.[35] By 1842, the Township of Dawn's population grew to 904 residents with an estimated fifty families believed to be of African descent.[36] By the late 1850s, five hundred people of African descent were reported living in the Dawn Settlement area, and these now represented the majority of landowners in the postal village of Dresden (defined by Surveys 127 and 128) and the western half of Camden Gore, south of the Sydenham River from roughly the first to the sixth concessions.

The first settlers officially established in 1823, on undeveloped lands they cleared on the banks of Bear Creek, immediately west of where the BAI

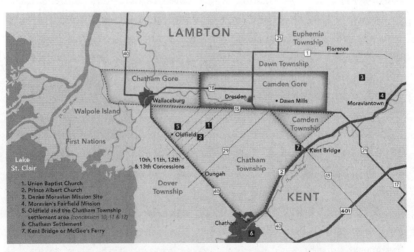

The Dawn Settlement in relationship to other settlements in North Kent and South Lambton, includes key mission outreach sites. *(Map copyight M. Carter, graphics by D. Buchanan)*

would later be established. Throughout the 1830s, settlement by African-descent and other non-Indigenous groups would remain sparse. The BAI's establishment in 1841 accelerated the settlement's growth. By the 1840s African-descent settlers developed farms to the south and west of the British American Institute, and many of these individuals had connections to the BAI. White missionary and BAI co-founder Rev. Hiram Wilson would purchase two hundred acres immediately south of the institute. Wilson resold one hundred acres of this land to the BAI's trustees, adding to the BAI's original two hundred acres, then sold portions of the remaining hundred acres to Josiah Henson and other early African-descent arrivals. George Cary, a BAI executive committee member, owned a small acreage on the institute's western border, and by 1838 trustee George Johnson had also settled nearby. This strong presence of British American Institute leadership just over the borders of the BAI's property seems to reinforce the notion that its management controlled all activity in the settlement, but this was not the case. These lands were independently purchased by the BAI leadership and were interspersed with properties of other individuals with no connection to the institute. John Myers, for example, independently developed a two-hundred-acre farm property on Lot 1, Concession 3 of Dawn Township, situated immediately south of the properties owned by Wilson and Henson. By 1861, the Myers farm was valued at $2,500—the second highest valuation of any farm in the neighbourhood, next to that belonging to white landowner Henry Sharp.[37] Myers had cleared fifty-four acres of bush and was nurturing a substantial acreage of hemp for rope production, wheat, livestock feed, vegetables, and tree fruits. The farm supported $520 of livestock production, including two oxen, four steers, two milk cows, seven horses, twenty-eight sheep, and twenty-two hogs.[38] Prosperous individual landowners like Myers played an important role in helping others to establish. The level of production on such farms as his would have required a great deal of manual labour, presenting an essential employment opportunity for new arrivals. Myers's large land holding also allowed him to sell parts of his property to other people of African descent, likely facilitating the purchase of land to this growing influx of new arrivals at a time when white landowners were becoming increasingly resistant to selling to them. There is evidence of such resales of sections of Myers's property, as seen in the two smaller acreages of one and forty acres that were divided off his main property and sold to other people of African descent.

Not all new immigrants could afford such large tracts of land as Myers. Property purchases in rural areas ranged from one- or two-acre plots to two-hundred-acre sections like Myers's, with fifty- and hundred-acre plots being most common. While not all pioneer farms would achieve the impressive levels of production recorded by Myers, most would quickly make significant improvements to their properties and thrive. By 1860, the agricultural census shows a third to a half of African-descent peoples' acreages had been cleared for the production of subsistence and market crops.[39] Production on many farms often rivalled or even surpassed that of their white neighbours' farms. As such, this aspect of the settlement was clearly not indicative of a lowly and wretched population of "fugitives" in need of assistance from white philanthropists or the BAI, but rather an industrious and resourceful group of pioneers who were independently succeeding in their settlement efforts. This early success flew in the face of propaganda by US slaveholders who argued against emancipation, saying that enslaved people lacked the industry and intelligence to thrive independently in the bush of the north.

It would not be until the 1850s that settlement of African-descent people would become a more urban phenomenon within the previously surveyed and settled Dresden townsite. Survey 127 and 128 of Dresden had initially been developed as a predominantly white settlement founded by the white Van Allen family in 1845[40] and was flanked by Fairport, its mainly white sister community to the south..[41] Fairport lay in such close proximity to Dresden that it shared a Main Street which marked the boundary between the two independently founded townsites. Fairport, founded by Irish-born William Wright, had only three business lots owned by people of African descent located along Main St. This lack of Black land ownership in Fairport is likely not indicative of a lack of willingness to sell to African descent people, as Wright often had business dealings with Rev. Henson,[42] and one of Wright's sons married an African-descent woman.[43] That the Van Allen family's properties in Dresden surveys 127 and 128 became owned predominantly by African-descent people was likely a result of timing and economics. With the passage of the 1850 US *Fugitive Slave Act*, large numbers of freemen fled the Northern US for Canada West. Many of them were skilled tradesmen, business owners, industrialists, and professionals seeking urban properties. They arrived at Dresden during a downturn in the economy when its white property owners were anxious to sell. This allowed the new arrivals through partnerships and individual purchases to buy large blocks of Survey 128 and a number of individual properties in Survey 127, more typically consisting of single or double lots, some of which included pre-existing infrastructure. Purchases there began in 1851 and accelerated through the 1850s with many properties being retained even after the American Civil War and emancipation. Ownership by African-descent people here only began to decline in the 1880s.

By the mid-1850s, about 75 percent of the then-existing Dresden surveys were owned by people of African descent. This volume of land purchases, unfortunately, does not create a clear picture of actual settlement numbers as not all landowners settled on their properties. Some properties were purchased by investors like William Goodrich, an Underground Railroad operative and colleague of William Whipper in the William Still network. Despite their ownership of multiple properties at Dresden, Goodrich and Whipper never settled in the community. Conversely, not everyone who was a settler owned land. Some lived and worked on others' properties or

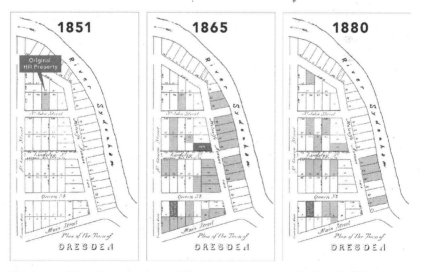

This series of three Survey 127 maps shows the first lot purchase by Dennis Hill in 1851; the settlement at the height of Black ownership in 1865; and the enduring ownership into the 1880s. (*Survey map courtesy Chatham-Kent Land Records; graphics by D. Buchanan*)

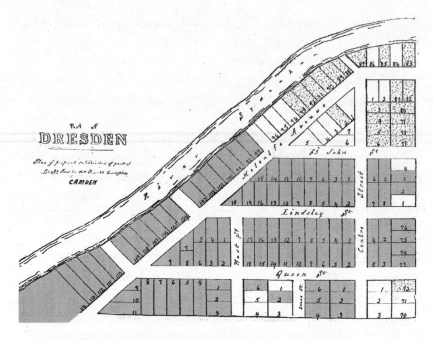

■ Purnell Partnership / William Whipper properties
▨ Charity Brothers properties

Survey 128 of the Dresden showing the extent of Black ownership in the mid-1800s. (*Survey Map courtesy of Chatham-Kent Land Records; graphics by D. Buchanan*)

rented their homes, businesses, or farms. Numbers are also impossible to accurately tabulate through census records, as some settlers stayed so briefly in the Dawn Settlement area that their names were not captured in either the 1851 or 1861 census.

Widespread settlement continued throughout the 1850s, radiating out in every direction from the borders of the BAI grounds, with no clear demarcation point where ownership by people of African descent ended. A clear settlement line is particularly difficult to establish in the area south of the BAI where the former border of Dawn Township (later Camden Gore) met with that of Chatham Township. Here the concentration of settlement by people of African descent continues undiminished into Chatham Township along Concessions 10, 11, and 12.[44] As such we cannot draw an arbitrary line here along the Baseline Road. It is not clear how even the early residents themselves understood when they had left the Dawn Settlement or where they might have perceived they were travelling into another settlement area not understood to be part of Dawn.

To the north, within the Town of Dresden, settlement does diminish dramatically at the river with virtually no Black settlement having established in the earliest surveys of North Dresden.[45] This is likely due to North Dresden having been developed in the mid-1860s, after the main migration from the US had taken place. Yet even here, the Charity brothers bought a two-hundred-acre property beyond the town limits and a smattering of settlers like the Prisby family also appear on properties travelling north into Lambton's Dawn and Euphemia Townships. Even further north at the Village of Oil Springs, evidence also exists of a secondary migration from the Dawn and Chatham Settlements that coincided with that community's oil boom. Tragically, the settlement on the Gum Bed Line at Oil Springs was burnt out by rioting white settlers, incensed by the economic competition presented by African-descent people.[46]

Mappings of settlement concentrations and the attendant difficulty of defining clear boundaries for the Dawn Settlement demonstrates the sheer scale of the nineteenth-century influx of an estimated thirty thousand settlers of African descent into Canada and the prominence of the tri-county area of Lambton, Kent, and Essex as a settlement area. It also hints at the impact and influence of people of African descent on the development of this region, something that is often not recognized in community or Canadian history. Yet, African-descent people emerge in this analysis as a major immigration group who played a significant role in developing rural and urban properties through individual initiative backed by personal resources and skills. This defies an interpretation of Black history as that of a few scattered, failed "manumission colonies" whose survival relied on white philanthropists. Clearly, Black pioneers more often relied on their own resourcefulness to establish themselves, and they made major contributions to the developing agricultural land out of the bush and contributing to the growth of communities like Dresden.

Freeing the Dawn Settlement from the BAI's geography also allows us to free its history from the BAI's timeline and Henson's lifetime. The Dawn Settlement's history emerges from land record evidence as having begun well before Henson's arrival, continuing after Henson's death and the dissolution of the BAI and having an impact to the present day through the enduring presence of decendants. As such, in this new narrative we will unpack not only the rich historical record of Dawn's first settlers but also trace how their descendantscontinued to build on the foundational efforts of their ancestors into the twentieth and twenty-first centuries. It is a rich and proud history in which we will see a two-hundred-year continuum of resistance and contribution running like a golden thread that binds one generation to the next.

Chapter 2

BEYOND *the* UNDERGROUND RAILROAD

Migrations to the Dawn
Settlement in the Fur Trading Era

I N 1826, LEVI AND THOMAS WILLOUGHBY TRAVELLED TO THE land registry office at Sandwich and officially registered the fifty-acre farm they had purchased on the east half of Lot 2, Concession 3, in the newly surveyed Township of Dawn, Lambton County, Upper Canada. Their neighbour Weldon Harris had made the same journey, a year before, to register his adjoining fifty acres. Their land registrations are the first official documentation of people of African descent living in the Dawn Settlement area. Over the next forty years, hundreds more would follow, creating a large and diverse community. They would establish farms, industries, businesses, social institutions, and infrastructure foundational to the development of the area.

This is not the timeline or narrative of the Dawn Settlement we are used to reading about. Usually, histories of the Dawn Settlement begin almost twenty years later, in 1841, when its most famous resident, Josiah Henson, arrived with others to establish a manual labour school called the British American Institute (BAI) to serve a community of formerly enslaved people. The Willoughbys' and Harris's presence here, at a time when Henson was still enslaved in Kentucky, challenges this version of history and has consequences for how we understand the agency and contributions of people of African descent throughout Canadian history. In contrast to the popularized notion that all Dawn's settlers had been Underground Railroad passengers who relied on the British American Institute for survival, these early settlers independently purchased and developed land concurrent with Lambton County's other 147, predominantly white, pioneers.

Harris was so successful that by 1861 his property had been valued at $1,200, rivalling the worth of even larger white-owned farms. Harris grew wheat, oats, buckwheat, peas, corn, and potatoes on his clearing. His livestock were valued at $255, exceeding the average amount for the neighbourhood. His farming operation included five steers, four horses, four pigs, and a milk cow that produced one hundred pounds of butter for sale at market. His orchard and garden produced a further thirty bushels of produce.[1] Levi and Thomas Willoughby's fifty acres were similarly valued at $1,000. Their even more diverse crops included peas, oats, buckwheat, Indian corn, potatoes, a quarter acre of turnips, and three acres of hay. Their fodder crops sustained two steers, two horses, eight pigs, and a milk cow, and they marketed a barrel of pork and one hundred pounds of butter. They also owned a pleasure carriage at a time when only a handful of similar vehicles existed in the neighbourhood, and these were typically valued at between twenty and forty-two dollars while the Willoughbys' carriage had been assessed at sixty dollars.[2]

Harris's and Willoughbys' successful efforts at farming were not unique. Other African-descent people who also settled before Henson and similarly developed successful farms over a lifetime of hard work, using knowledge and skills they had acquired before arriving in what is now Ontario. They carved out a place for themselves and generations of their descendants, some of whom remain in the area, sometimes on the farms their ancestors originally cleared. Their lives and circumstances challenge us to describe these individuals not as "fugitives" or "refugees" (as is the consequence of an overemphasis on the Underground Railroad narrative) but to see them, like their white contemporaries, as pioneers and founders—significant contributors to the shaping of the landscape, communities, and society.[3] That individuals like Harris and Willoughby arrived so early in the area's settlement history also inspires us to look beyond the well-worn UGRR story to discover other possible routes by which they may have come to Dawn.

The Thomas Willoughby Story

The Willoughbys may have arrived even earlier than their documentable presence on the land. One newspaper account suggests they came to the Dawn Settlement area as much as twenty years prior to their land registration when the Anishinaabeg Council of the Three Fires (Ojibwe, Odawa, and Pottawatomi) ceded their land to the British between 1820 and 1823. In 1899, the *Chatham Evening Banner* interviewed Thomas Willoughby on what they believed to be his hundredth birthday.[4] *The Banner's* white reporter may have expected Willoughby to relate stories of life in slavery and of his dramatic escape along the Underground Railroad (UGRR). If so, he would have been disappointed. Thomas instead revealed that he had been born free on the very clearing on the banks of the river he later registered in 1826. According to the 1861 census, Willoughby had, in fact, been a bit younger than one hundred at the time of the *Banner* interview. Still, his birth in 1802 had occurred some forty years prior to Josiah Henson's arrival in the Dawn Settlement. This is remarkably early in Canadian history—the Constitutional Act establishing Upper Canada had only been passed in 1791. Dawn Township, where the families had settled, was then a part of the Western District in British North America and was still sparsely settled. It would be easy to discount the *Chatham Banner* story. Willoughby's advanced age might inspire questions about whether his recall had been of the best and, given the reporter's error in assuming Willoughby's advanced age, his accuracy on other aspects of the story might also be questioned. Yet, the narrative in the *Chatham Banner* has a nagging ring of truth to it. The 1861 Camden Census confirms that Thomas and Levi Willoughby had both indeed been born free in Canada. That their parents had settled on the banks of Bear Creek on unceded territory is plausible in that other early settlers are recorded in local histories as living on the same lands at that time.[5] In 1821, white settler Job Hall, who later officially settled in Dawn's thirteenth concession, had been driven out by Indigenous people.[6] With the signing of Treaty 25 and the 1821 formation of the Canada Company (land sales agents for the British government), those who lacked a deed for the land on which they had settled were asked to leave until such time as a proper survey could be undertaken. They were then permitted to lay official claim to the lands they had previously occupied. This unfolding of events fits well with Thomas Willoughby's account of his early life in Dawn Township. Willoughby maintained that, as a youth, he had left his parents' clearing to live with a man he called Squire McGregor at Chatham, and that at age twenty-one he had returned to register his parents' original clearing. It seems plausible that with their eviction from their original clearing, Willoughby's family would have sought other work and living arrangements for their teenaged son and that he would have returned to reclaim the family's land once he had come of age. Thomas had exceeded his twenty-first birthday by four years at the time he registered his parents' property.[7]

Even if the *Banner* account is unreliable, the 1826 date of the Willoughbys' official land registration and the Harrises' 1825 registration date—and their free-born status—begs a closer examination of early migrations of people of African descent not only at Dawn but in the surrounding counties.[8] Relying on a UGRR narrative to explain the presence, particularly of the formerly enslaved people who appear here prior to Henson, raises important questions about the reasons for their migration and the routes that brought them. At this early date, after all, legal protection under British law was not yet assured. With the creation of Upper Canada, Col. John Graves Simcoe, a man with strong anti-slavery views, was appointed as lieutenant-governor of Upper Canada. Two years later, in 1793, he passed *An Act to Prevent the Further Introduction of Slaves, and to Limit the Terms of Contracts for Servitude within This Province*, which introduced a gradual phasing out of slavery through granting the children of enslaved people freedom after reaching the age of twenty-five. Slavery would essentially remain legal in Upper Canada until the passage of the *British Slavery Abolition Act* on August 1, 1834. This act put an end to slavery throughout the British Empire. The same year Simcoe passed his act to phase out slavery, as pointed out by scholars Thompson and Crook,[9] the original *Fugitive Slave Act* was passed in the US, allowing slaveholders the right to recover escaped slaves in any US state. This made the Canadas seem a more secure destination for those escaping enslavement, but even so, British law did not ensure those who made their way there would be allowed to stay or have their freedom protected. An official declaration that they would be considered free on stepping foot on British soil would not be forthcoming until 1829 under Sir John Colborne.

· · ·

Where the early settlers and, in particular, the freemen travelled to Dawn from at this early date, and what routes they used, cannot be neatly defined by an Underground Railroad route map nor by the notion that they followed the North Star to reach their destination. It is important to place the nine-teenth-century migrations into the longer history of the African diaspora in North America, which is as old as European exploration and settlement. African-descent people's lives are inextricably intertwined with white and Indigenous history and with the development of the continent from its ear-liest days of colonization. The explorer Mathieu da Costa arrived in the New World with Samuel de Champlain in the seventeenth century, and the first enslaved people on the continent were brought to the English settlement of Jamestown in Virginia in 1619. In Canada, free and enslaved African-descent people were involved in building early fortifications in Nova Scotia and throughout the pioneer history of our nation enslaved people can be found not only performing the backbreaking work of clearing land but lending their skills and intellect to a variety of pioneer enterprises. Some came to Canada along astonishing trajectories that often unexpectedly intersect with those of other races and cultures. Census records and family genealogies at Dawn, for instance, make it possible to trace origins of some families to South America,[10] the Caribbean,[11] and one family even claims Malaysian ancestry.[12] Dawn's early settlers more typically reflect the general migration patterns and cultural/racial interactions of the Great Lakes regions during the fur trading era, and a number of historical figures appear at both Detroit and Dawn suggesting close ties of the settlement area with that major fur trad-ing hub.[13] By the mid-1700s enslaved people, including African-descent and Indigenous people, had become "critical among the Detroit labor force that greased the wheels of trade,"[14] and Detroit had become "a lynchpin town in the Great Lakes"[15] because of its strategic positioning at a critical juncture of the main fur trading routes. For early Kent and Essex settlements, including

Dawn, Detroit was an important centre for trade and commerce. The Dawn Settlement area was connected to Detroit through the Sydenham River, one of only two navigable rivers in the County.[16] Early settlers and Indigenous peoples travelled to Detroit by canoe (or by sleigh or on foot when the river froze) to sell furs, potash, and other goods produced on their clearings, and before the establishment of grist mills at upriver at Dawn Mills and downriver at Wallaceburg in the late 1830s and early 1840s people are said to have travelled to Detroit to have wheat milled into flour.[17] The river continued to be a link to Detroit throughout the lumbering boom of the 1850s, '60s, and '70s, with timber cut in the Dawn Settlement first floated downstream in booms, and later being shipped to Detroit in the form of cordwood and barrel staves via steamship and barge. The links between Detroit and Dawn remained into the 1880s as passenger ships continued to travel directly from Detroit to Dresden three times a week.[18]

Tiya Miles's examination of Detroit's history taken from the perspective of its African-descent and Indigenous populations reveals a general movement of people and of specific groups and individuals into the region of the Dawn Settlement during the fur trading era. Richard White, in his book *Middle Ground*,[19] describes the fur trade era as a period during which no one cultural or racial group was dominant and in which there was an intermingling of races and cultures who shared knowledge, skills, and technologies important to their mutual survival. Miles reveals darker aspects of this interaction born of the inequities of power inherent in slavery[20] along with stories of skilled African-descent people who filled a variety of roles, from tanners to ship's captains, that demonstrate that even in enslavement African-descent people were not universally illiterate and unskilled but possessed knowledge, resources, and the ability to travel great distances due to the skills and geographic knowledge they had acquired through the fur trade and military movements or through Indigenous and European interactions. Interracial and intercultural experiences meant some were fluent in French and English as well as Indigenous languages.

By the1830s a Middle Ground–style experience is seen in the Dresden Campground, a large multiracial/multicultural event held on the flats of the Sydenham River (then Bear Creek). It attracted people from a radius of forty miles to what was part religious camp meeting, partsocial gathering, and part trading opportunity. The year the Dresden Campground originated is not documented, but an 1881 account[21] indicates it survived until the 1840s when infrastructure emerged at Dawn that rendered its functions obsolete.[22] This Middle Ground experience seems to explain, in part at least, the rich multicultural/multiracial makeup of many of Dawn's settlers and their descendants. Without taking away the essential "Blackness" of the Dawn Settlement story, we can recognize this racial and cultural diversity as an important feature of early settlement here and in the region, and through its recognition we can come to appreciate a diversity of knowledge and abilities that existed among early settlers.[23]

Indigenous Interactions

Indigenous heritage makes up a large part of the DNA of a number of Dawn's families. This once lost aspect of their personal family histories has recently been revealed through DNA testing. Indigenous people are also increasingly being recognized for their role in the northward migration of African-descent people, particularly during the time of the UGRR. This phenomenon has been noted particularly in the US Midwest and Great Lakes regions by scholar Roy Finkenbine and has been outlined in a recent US National Park Service article.[24] Among the Indigenous groups they identify as assisting in flights from enslavement are the Anishinaabeg, who, as we've seen, were a major presence along Bear Creek at Dawn. "Dramatic and detailed stories" of assistance from the Shawnee or Cayuga people are also noted.[25] Family histories including *Remnants of Forgotten Folk* also show interactions between people of African descent and Indigenous peoples with their ancestors dating back to the seventeenth and eighteenth centuries.[26] At Detroit, Miles's work identifies a number of prominent Detroit traders and military men who can also be found in Fred C. Hamil's history of the Thames River.[27] Among these is the affluent and well-connected Oneida fur and slave trader Sally Ainse (1728–1823). In addition to being involved in the lucrative fur and slave trade at Detroit, Ainse, along with Matthew Dolsen, a former Butler's Ranger,[28] owned a large tract of land that stretched from the Forks (Chatham) to the mouth of the Thames River. Ainse and United Empire Loyalists who moved to the area after the American Revolution, brought their slaves with them. As Hamil notes,

"Between Sarah [Sally] Ainse and a house belonging to Matthew Dolsen...
was a hut belonging to a negro, apparently one of Mrs. Ainse's slaves."[29] At
Detroit Ainse had also traded with the Christian Delaware, who had settled
eight miles upriver from Detroit with the German-born Moravian missionary David Zeisberger. The Zeisberger Moravians and the Christian Delaware
would also move to the Thames near modern day Moraviantown where they
founded a racially diverse polyglot settlement that included French, German,
and Indigenous peoples. By 1803, the Moravians had established a satellite
mission on Bear Creek run by Christian Denke just upriver from Dresden.[30]
Denke's diary demonstrates a Middle Ground–style relationship with the
Ojibwe.[31] While he makes no mention of Black settlers, the Moravians were
known to have served people of African descent as well as Indigenous people in Pennsylvania and, in the absence of Protestant Christian ministers at
Detroit, had also served white people there,[32] yet a more extensive involvement of the Moravians with people of African descent may have existed in the
Dawn Settlement area. The Dresden Campground's name, which is anomalous among the British derived placenames of the area, raises the possibil-
ities that the Moravians may have been involved in its establishment since
the Moravian leader Nicolaus Zizendorf's hometown was Dresden, Germany,
and the curve of its river closely resembles that of Bear Creek.[33]

The Anishinaabeg (Odawa, Ojibwe, and Pottawatomi) who were present
at Detroit also remained a presence on Bear Creek even after the signing
Treaty 25 with the British in 1823,[34] and the permanent Indigenous settlement
of Kitigan lay five miles upstream from where Levi and Thomas Willoughby
and Weldon Harris had settled.[35] These Indigenous groups, like Ainse, traded
in slaves as is evidenced at Detroit. Captured members of rival tribes and
particularly women and children were often a prized "commodity" among
Indigenous groups who either gave them away as gifts or traded them for
goods to other Indigenous groups or European traders.

Detroit was also a "centre for...crafting wartime strategy that pulled in
people of various colours, cultures and creeds" during the French and Indian
War and the War of 1812.[36] Paramilitary groups like Butler's Rangers, who
were also based at Amherstburg, may also account for the migration north of
some early settlers of African descent. Butler's Rangers, founded by loyalist
John Butler, included among their ranks Black soldiers such as Crispus Hall,

the son of Prince Hall, founder of the Black Masonic order. Some Rangers were former fur traders who had intermarried with Indigenous women, and the Rangers are known to have captured and freed enslaved people as a military tactic. These freed people sometimes joined their ranks. Col. William Caldwell established a Butler's Rangers unit at Amherstburg, Upper Canada. He led raids into Ohio, Kentucky, and Pennsylvania. Former Rangers like Matthew Dolsen and Daniel Field also settled in Essex and Kent County as United Empire Loyalists. In a curious intersection of the Rangers' and Moravians' history, Caldwell's group is noted in the Moravian Diaries, in 1813, visiting Fairfield-on-the-Thames (the main Moravian mission), to recruit new members to their ranks.[37]

The early lumber industry also offers a possible explanation as to why the Willoughby family came to the Dawn Settlement area. As we've previously noted, Dawn's lumber industry was connected in its early days to markets in Detroit. Notably, a formerly enslaved man named Benjamin Willoughby operated a lumber mill there. He had been manumitted in Pendleton County, Kentucky, in December 1816. When he was in his thirties, he moved his family to Detroit where he made his fortune in the lumber industry and as an equal opportunity money lender. His daughter Julia would marry William Lambert, a principal figure in the Michigan Underground Railroad.[38] Genealogical work to determine whether the Dawn Settlement Willoughbys were related to the Detroit Willoughbys has not as yet been pursued, so it is not known if they are directly related. Nevertheless, supplying timber to mills in Detroit was a common practice among settlers along Bear Creek (the Sydneham River), and cutting timber was a major occupation of many early settlers who relied on income from lumber, cordwood, and ash,[39] until such time as their land could be sufficiently cleared to sustain themselves through farming. Henson would, by 1850, establish what was perhaps the third sawmill in Dawn Township[40] on the grounds of the British American Institute, and African descent land investor William Whipper and his brother-in-law James Burns Hollensworth would establish a white pine lumbermill at Dresden in the mid-1850s. By the 1860s, providing cordwood to steamships plying the Great Lakes waterways would become an important source of income for those living along the Sydenham River. The manufacture of barrel staves would remain a key Dresden industry into the early twentieth century.

Exactly where the Willoughby and Harris families had previously lived and how they came to settle at Dawn may never be known, but their early presence establishes them as community pioneers and founders. There had been no supportive community or basic infrastructure to assist them on their arrival. Travelling in small groups of family and friends, as they appear to have done, they likely survived and thrived in the undeveloped bush through cooperative relationships with Indigenous people and with the scattering of white neighbours who had concurrently arrived here.

In 1838, the fledgling community that had formed at Dawn, coupled with the Dresden Campground's popularity, likely contributed to the attractiveness of the land located just to the east of the Harris and Willoughby farms as a location for a new manual labour school. Such an ambitious enterprise as the BAI could not have arisen out of uninhabited bush. Distant abolitionists may have supplied cash and advice for its construction, but local people would have been needed to provide the practical labour and skills required for clearing its land and developing its infrastructure. The exact number of people who lived in the area as Henson and his colleagues arrived to establish the BAI is not known. That we have the names of these few early landowners inspires us to rediscover them as early co-founders of the Dawn Settlement. Without their efforts and early activities of lumbering and farming and their co-development of the Dresden Campground, the BAI might never have been founded on this site, and the Dawn Settlement might never have grown to be an important early centre of commerce and abolitionist thought and action.

Chapter 3

The SHARED DREAM
of EDUCATION
The Founding of the
British American Institute

IN 1841, FIFTY-YEAR-OLD JOSIAH HENSON STOOD ON THE
banks of Bear Creek, along with Rev. Hiram Wilson and James Stompf
of the Chatham settlement. The trio had attended an 1840 convention
organized by Wilson and his benefactor, the New York–based British Quaker
James Canning Fuller.[1] The Black convention at London, Upper Canada, had
been organized after an initial conference in Toronto had failed to come to
consensus on how to spent money raised by Fuller for the benefit of formerly
enslaved people. At the successful London gathering, Wilson, Henson, and
Stompf were appointed as a search committee charged with finding a site
for a bold new endeavour—the formation of an educational institute. Their
choice to locate the ambitiously named British American Institute of Science
and Technology on two hundred acres of heavily forested prime land on the
Sydenham River in what was then Dawn Township would mark the beginning of the Dawn Settlement's early promise as a centre for education, one
which its founders hoped would rival that of the Oberlin Institute in Ohio. Its

establishment spurred the growth of the small existing settlement at Dawn and would draw attention to the area from a wide range of African-descent and white abolitionist leaders.

James Canning Fuller had initially set out for London, England, in 1840, to attend the first World Anti-Slavery Convention in a quest to raise money to support Wilson's underfunded Canada Mission, which had been providing education and spiritual services to formerly enslaved people and others at a variety of sites across Upper Canada. On his return from Britain, however, Fuller decided that a $1,700 portion of what he had raised should be set aside for a new project independent of the Canada Mission. He left the decision on what this project should be to the African-descent leaders he had assembled from several settlements across Upper Canada at conventions in Toronto and London, Upper Canada.

At the London convention leaders debated over a three-day period about how to invest the monies Fuller offered before deciding on founding a manual labour school. Wilson, Henson and were tasked with finding an ideal site for the school. They found two hundred acres of undeveloped land on Concession Three of Dawn Township along Bear Creek, available for sale through the Canada Company at a reasonable price of $800.[2] It was covered with rich stands of hardwood, including black walnut, oak, maple, and whitewood,[3] a sure indication of the rich farmland that lay beneath. African-descent settlers had already established themselves in the area that was becoming well known for its Dresden Campground gatherings.[4] Yet, the location was remote enough to not be easily accessible to slave hunters who ventured beyond their jurisdiction and onto Upper Canada soil, as they did in settlements closer to the US border. Henson and Wilson's previous experiences made them excellent choices for searching out the property as both had travelled extensively through the area, and in their previous meeting when Wilson was gathering information for the American Anti-Slavery Society on formerly enslaved people, they had recognized a mutual goal of developing educational opportunities for the formerly enslaved. Henson's life to this point demonstrates his broad knowledge of the geography of the region, his desire to contribute to the uplift of his people, and a spirit of resistance that formerly enslaved people carried with them, particularly in his use of the courts to advance his peoples' interests.

In 1830, Josiah Henson had escaped from a brutal life of enslavement. His flight to freedom was a difficult one. Despite a permanent injury from a severe beating, he carried his two youngest children on his back for much of their travels. On disembarking from the ship that had brought his family along the final leg of their journey, he promised its captain that he would use his freedom well. No one was waiting in Upper Canada to assist Henson and his family. Resourceful, ambitious, and intelligent, the Hensons quickly built a new life for themselves largely through their own initiative. Josiah Henson applied his experience as an agricultural labourer, overseer, and marketer of farm produce to the opportunities he found all around him. He immediately went to work on local farms. One sympathetic white farmer, a Mr. Hibbard, offered Henson a rundown dwelling for his family which they made habitable. Over the next three years, Josiah Henson continued to work for the Hibbards, at first in exchange for housing, food, and wages, and then as a sharecropper. His employers paid for young Tom Henson's schooling, and Tom in turn introduced his father, Josiah, to the rudiments of reading and writing. While, according to Henson's biography, having to be taught by his young son had been an embarrassment to him, Henson put his pride aside and submitted to learning what he recognized to be an essential skill and the key to unlocking the scriptures he'd first come to love while still enslaved and which would assist him in his role as a spiritual leader.

Josiah Henson subsequently left the Hibbards to work for a Mr. Risley. In his three years with his new employer, he became concerned about the lack of progress many formerly enslaved people were making in their lives. At a meeting of a dozen of his peers who shared his ambition to improve themselves, Henson was charged with finding undeveloped land that the group could purchase, and where the crops and livestock they raised and the timber they felled would be their own. In August 1834, Henson set out on foot to investigate an extensive region between Lakes Ontario, Erie, and Huron to find just such a tract of land. Impressed with the fertility of the lands at Colchester (in Essex County), he brought his group to settle on land that had previously been granted to a Mr. McCormick, an absentee landowner. It had the advantage of having been cleared, but it was not, as hoped, available for purchase, so renting from McCormick was their only recourse. On discovering their landlord hadn't made the developments to the property required by the government, the group recognized an opportunity: by failing to improve his land, McCormick had relinquished his rights of ownership. Henson and his group appealed to the legislature and successfully won the right to work the land rent-free. McCormick fought the decision. Like other white land-owners, he may have seen renting the land as an expedient means of making the requisite improvements through the labour of others while also realiz-ing an immediate profit from rents. Such exploitive arrangements often saw tenant evictions once the improvements had been made. As Henson and others observed,[5] this often left early Black pioneers who became involved in such schemes with nothing to show for their years of hard work. McCormick was able to successfully reverse the court decision. Henson and his group remained resolute and launched a second action. The court again granted them free use of the land for as long as they wished to remain there. Still, the knowledge that the land could be sold from under them without warn-ing spurred Henson to continue his search for land that could be purchased outright. These searches likely equipped him with considerable knowledge of available properties in a wide area of what is today Southwestern Ontario.

While at Colchester, Henson had made the acquaintance of white Con-gregationalist minister Rev. Hiram Wilson, then working for the American Anti-Slavery Society (AAS). Wilson's knowledge of the region between the Great Lakes was as extensive as Henson's own, as he had been travel-ling throughout the region for the AAS to gather information on formerly enslaved people who had fled to Upper Canada. Henson found in Wilson a kindred spirit, equally committed to supporting those seeking freedom in Upper Canada.[6] Wilson's life to this point demonstrates his passion and drive to provide education and moral and spiritual "uplift" of formerly enslaved people. His ambitious and self-sacrificial giving to the cause of education in establishing his Canada Mission show him to be more than "a clerical do-gooder."[7]

Hiram Wilson's interest in education of African-descent people had begun during his years at the Lane Seminary in Ohio, where he and a group of fellow white students had committed themselves to teaching African-descent people to read and write. When the school's leadership ordered them to cease this practice, which they had been carrying out during their own free time, they protested in word and action. These "Lane Rebels," as they became known, left the Lane Seminary and travelled north to a new college that had been established at Oberlin, Ohio. Oberlin Collegiate Institute, founded in 1833 was the first educational institution for higher learning in America to admit women and people of African descent. Like the Oneida Institute, the school Wilson had attended as a youth, Oberlin was based on a manual-labour school model. Students who were unable to afford their tuition could work part of the day in lieu of payment. Oberlin would prove to be an important educator of both Black and white teachers and preachers for mission work among formerly enslaved people in the US and Upper Canada.

When he met Josiah Henson in 1836, Rev. Wilson had become one of "The Seventy"—a group of missionaries the American Anti-Slavery Society had chosen to serve the needs of the formerly enslaved in the US and Upper Canada. Wilson exhausted himself and his personal resources over the next fifteen years in work to counsel and distribute aid to formerly enslaved persons in Upper Canada. He would keep his supporters in Britain and America fully informed through his prolific output of reports and letters and in articles to the abolitionist press.[8]

Wilson's 1836 research trip not only introduced him to Henson, but it also inspired him to launch his Canada Mission. In December 1839, he reported to the *Friends of Man* newspaper that eighteen teachers, including himself and his new bride, Hannah, were teaching at Canada Mission sites. These included both women and men working at nearly a dozen locations flung far and wide across the British colony. Eliza Pettengill, from Vermont, taught at Amherstburg; George Bills, of Massachusetts, and Joshua W. Jones, of New York, were stationed at Colchester; William P. Newman, from Richmond, Virginia, who would later be involved in the BAI, taught at Chatham; Henry L. Baltimore, who was described as an "African Prince," taught at London; and Emerson Prescott, of Acton, Maine, taught at Wilberforce (Lucan). A mission was established as far north as Lake Simcoe in the Township of Oro located in a large, unsettled region between Lake Huron and what is now the Regional Municipality of Waterloo, then referred to as the "Queen's Bush". Ari Raymond and his wife, Eliza, both of Boston, faced the challenges of educating in this remote location. Others serving the Canada Mission included Abby S. Chamberlain, of New York City, and Harriet E. Hunter, of Cincinnati, who were stationed at St. Catharines; and Mrs. Maia A. Ells, of

Oberlin, Ohio, and Catherine S. McKenzie, of Vienna, New York, who taught at an unspecified location. Even before the establishment of the British American Institute at Dawn, Wilson had also recruited Henry A. French, of Middletown, Connecticut, to serve in Dawn Township at a Canada Mission outreach centre he had named Hopedale.[9]

Rev. Hiram Wilson worked mainly alone to establish, resource, and recruit staff for the Canada Mission. It was a constant struggle. His own promised wages from the American Anti-Slavery Society were often slow in coming, and he was eventually dropped from the society's list of The Seventy. This was likely not an indication of the society's lack of confidence in Wilson's work but rather of the fractious nature of the abolitionist community and its widely differing opinions on priorities for funding. In February 1837, AAS secretary Elizur Wright praised Wilson's work as being "worth bars of gold," and in September that same year he offered Wilson a one-year appointment to "pursue the work you have laid out." "The fruits you have developed," Wright said, "are richly worth all that they have cost us and what is more, all that they have cost you."[10] Certainly, Wilson was often out-of-pocket in his attempts to finance the needs of the Canada Mission. He was also worn thin from travelling to its sites to encourage teachers and check on progress, as he often went on foot in adverse conditions.

Despite his efforts, by the late 1830s, Rev. Hiram Wilson's critics had become highly vocal in their opposition to his work. Teachers and preachers for his missions were in short supply, and Wilson had relied heavily on the Oneida Institute and Oberlin Institute to supply them. Critics believed needs "back home" should take precedence for these scarce human resources. Money was an especially contentious issue. Wilson's critics believed that American funds raised for the abolitionist cause should not have gone to support what was essentially a foreign mission. To critics, the fact Wilson didn't turn away poor whites and Indigenous people was a particular irritation. If Wilson wanted to do mission work in a British colony for the benefit of British subjects, they argued, he should seek financial help from Britain, not the US.

Despite this opposition, AAS secretary Elizur Wright remained sympathetic. In an effort to relieve Wilson of his personal mission-related debts, Wright invited him to attend the society's 1838 annual convention in New York. There he could raise funds by selling books and appealing directly to anti-slavery philanthropists. It was at this convention that Wilson would meet James Canning Fuller, a man who would become a generous backer, sympathetic friend, and astute mentor. In turn, Fuller found in Wilson a kindred spirit of similar dedication and passion to the abolitionist cause who could bring their shared dream of creating a centre for learning for former enslaved persons now living in Upper Canada to fruition.

The Fuller-Wilson Alliance

James Canning Fuller had been involved in the abolitionist movement in Britain before coming to America in 1833. At Skaneateles, New York, his outspoken abolitionist views had incited a mud-slinging mob to attack him on the streets. Fuller would later be praised for transforming Skaneateles from a community that was openly hostile towards people of African descent to a place where they could "walk without harassment, dignity intact."[11]

In 1838, Fuller became secretary of the Skaneateles Anti-Slavery Society, through which he connected to the American Anti-Slavery Society's wider network. Fuller, was not, however, in lockstep with the views of other society members. Despite having adopted America as his home, he remained critical of US policy and politics and fiercely loyal to his British roots. Rev. Hiram Wilson's appeal to fund mission efforts on British soil must have struck a chord with Fuller. Before throwing his support behind Wilson, however, Fuller would visit the Canada Mission sites and evaluate the worth of Wilson's work for himself. After five weeks of travelling throughout Upper Canada, Fuller unreservedly endorsed Wilson's efforts in the abolitionist press and wholeheartedly threw his personal support behind the mission. Fuller then set out for the first World Anti-Slavery Convention in England, seeking their financial support. His confidence in approaching his former countryman was justified. The British proved financially generous to Canadian missions in general, eventually sending more money to Black settlements in what would become Canada than to any other area.[12] Fuller returned not only with money for Wilson's Canada Mission but also an additional $1,700 he hoped to apply to a new initiative.

While he planned to consult with Black leadership on how to spend the funds he'd raised, James Canning Fuller, like Hiram Wilson, already had a vision for a school that "extended beyond aiding the destitute and providing elementary education…to giv[ing] students advanced training…[that would enable them to] supply…teachers for the Canada Mission's lower schools."[13] Wilson and Fuller anticipated that their new institute would develop to become an Upper Canada version of Oberlin College, as in his sixth annual report on the Canada Mission, he stated, "This institute is not to rival Oberlin or Oneida, but it is necessary because neither of these is safe for the fugitive."[14] The far-sighted partners also anticipated the day when emancipation would come to the US and graduates of their institute would return south to provide leadership for newly freed slaves. While in 1838 this might have seemed like a mad idea, this outcome would be realized after the American Civil War but not by the British American Institute. It would be Rev. William King's Elgin Settlement at Buxton that would send educated leadership to the Southern US after emancipation.[15]

A Common Vision

Henson shared Wilson and Fuller's dream of education and, like Wilson, saw the need for this to be based on the manual-labour school model, similar to Oberlin and Oneida Institutes, ensuring education would be accessible to those who lacked the financial resources to pay tuition. Henson's view appears to have been less grandiose and more practical than his colleague's. He saw the school in Dawn Township as a place "where our children could be taught those elements of knowledge which are usually the occupation of grammar school; and where the boys could be taught, in addition, the practice of some mechanic art, and the girls could be instructed in the domestic arts." Yet Henson also saw it as a place where they could "train up those who would afterwards instruct others."[16]

While Josiah Henson's biography relates that the attendees at the London, Upper Canada, convention needed to be convinced of the priority of education, other attendees, like James Charles (J.C.) Brown, seem to have held similarly strong views of education's worth. Brown would later write, "Education is the greatest blessing to man, strive to encourage it then by promoting its institutions; educate your children, and they will prove a blessing to their country, an honour to themselves and to you."[17]

Education, for many of those who had been denied it while enslaved, held the promise of dignity, honour, and good citizenship, commodities that were elusive throughout J.C. Brown's life. Despite having served in the US Army,[18] Brown had to pay $1,800 for his freedom. He had worked at his trade as a mason, first in Kentucky and later in Ohio. His efforts to live and work peacefully were made impossible by the passage of the 1806 *Ohio Black Code Law* made it impossible for he and other freemen to move freely to conduct business and personal affairs. Brown fought against this tyranny, and eventually moved to Canada, attracted by the equal rights promised under British Law. He helped a group of Ohio freemen in their efforts to purchase land in Biddulph County in order to establish the Wilberforce Settlement at Lucan, named for the famous British anti-slavery activist William Wilberforce. At the time of the Fuller's conventions, Brown was a resident of Toronto.

Despite the London convention's strong representation in favour of education, it took three days of deliberations to come to an agreement on how to spend the funds James Canning Fuller had raised.[19] Rev. Henson would later recall that he already had a plot of land in mind for the educational institute they decided to build. As he, Fuller, and Stompf returned to that location and made plans to purchase the land, it appeared Rev. Wilson, Henson, and J.C. Brown's long-held dreams to find dignity through education were about to come true.

Chapter 4

The SEEDS of DISCORD

Exploring the Political
Landscape of Dawn

I N 1841, JAMES CANNING FULLER SAT DOWN AT HIS WRITING desk in Skaneateles, New York, to write to his colleague Rev. Hiram Wilson at the Dawn Settlement about their new venture there. As he considered his words, his mind was filled with concern, both for his younger friend and for the new enterprise they were undertaking together. Rev. Wilson was about to purchase property for their grandly named new initiative, the British American Institute of Science and Technology. Fuller realized that Wilson could easily falter in these first steps. In his letter Fuller anticipated problems and opposition Wilson might face. His tone at times was warm and personal, reflecting an obvious concern for Wilson's state of financial affairs and health. This concern remained throughout their years of correspondence and went, at times, beyond mere words to practical assistance, as Fuller demonstrated when he tucked twenty dollars from an anonymous donor and five dollars from himself into one of the envelopes he sent his friend.[1] "This is for thy own pocket," he said. "I state this again that there may be no doubt or squeamishness concerning it."[2] Fuller was well aware of Wilson's constant state of personal want and financial indebtedness, born of his dedication to the Canada Mission. Support for the wider mission Wilson still managed continued to be spotty. A new committee of abolitionists, in Rochester, New York, would not relieve him of the burden of the Canada Mission's management until the following year. So now, on the eve of launching the British American Institute, his energies, time, and talents were stretched thin as he continued to travel from Toronto, to check on his Canada Mission sites across Upper Canada. This lack of focus on the new project being undertaken at the Dawn Settlement troubled Fuller: "I'm concerned that thou shouldest travel so much both on thy own account and also of your office, but perhaps there is no help for it," he wrote.[3] His concern may well have been amplified by the knowledge that Wilson's growing responsibilities now included a family: Wilson married his first wife, Hanna Maria (née Hubbard) of Troy, New York, in 1838. She had come to the Dawn Settlement to share in his mission work and was now expecting their first child.[4] Yet the successful launch of the BAI was foremost on Fuller's mind as he wrote his advice to Wilson on practical matters of management for the new enterprise.

By 1840, the early period of racial cooperation in the Dawn Settlement area had given way to rising racial tensions, particularly where competition for land was concerned. This prompted Fuller to write "get some white man from the neighbourhood [to] buy the lot." Fuller was concerned that the land price might go up by $100 or more should a man who was not white, or someone known to be associated with Blacks, apply to purchase it.[5] Fuller also advised that Wilson draft a clear, simple statement of the institute's purpose and include this in the deed, along with the names of the trustees Fuller had instructed him to assemble. In addition to these trustees, Fuller proposed that a second body, an executive committee made up of local people who would manage day-to-day operations, be appointed. This was necessary, given most of the appointed trustees lived far from the institute and would not, for the most part, be able to lend practical, hands-on support for the property's development. There were six trustees in total whose biographies demonstrate the many connections of the Dawn Settlement to the wider efforts of abolitionists on the continent and in England. J.C. Brown was born in Frederick County, Virginia, to a white father and a mixed-race mother. He had been enslaved in Kentucky and, as previously discussed, became involved in establishment of the Wilberforce Settlement before moving to

Toronto.[6] Frederick Stover was also involved in establishing the Wilberforce Settlement in 1830 when the Quaker settlement at Norwich, Upper Canada (near Woodstock, Ontario), the oldest Quaker settlement in British North America, helped facilitate the purchase of Wilberforce's eight-hundred-acre site.[7] Rev. James Roaf (1802–1862) was a white Congregationalist minister who emigrated from Margate, England, in 1837, to Toronto, where he acted as an agent for the Congregationalist Colonial Missionary Society.[8] James Canning Fuller also occupied one of the trustee positions; the British Quaker remained at Skaneateles, New York, throughout his involvement with the BAI. There were two other people of African descent who served in the dual capacity of both trustees and local executive committee members. George Johnson, a previous resident of Toronto, had by 1838 purchased a farm in the Dawn Settlement area.[9] He became the BAI's executive committee treasurer. Peter B. Smith was born in Kentucky and lived in Indiana before moving to Upper Canada in the late 1830s. A blacksmith by trade, by 1844, he had become an African Methodist Episcopalian (AME) deacon and had purchased over three hundred acres of land near Chatham.[10]

Even at this early stage of the institute's development, Fuller hinted at the potential discord among the prospective leadership. Acrimony had already surfaced at the Toronto organizational meeting, forcing a second meeting at London, Upper Canada. Knowing this, and anxious for a harmonious beginning for the BAI, Fuller advised Rev. Wilson that "if any one of the persons named [to a leadership position] is hostile or unfriendly, let that man's name be dropped."[11] The frictions Fuller alluded to, and that would later become so apparent in conflicts between key figures in the BAI's management, are important to understand as they shed light on the conflict that would later derail its development. This conflict often reflects the seeds of discord planted within the very structure of the BAI's board and executive, which also reveals much about the political climate of the time across North America and reflected at times in England.[12] Differing philosophies and practices regarding activism to end slavery and the best means to support freed people resulted in deep rifts that widened over time. This political context can not only help us to understanding the personal conflicts and shifting alliances within the Dawn Settlement but also provide a window onto the intellectual, sectarian, and political diversity that existed among Dawn's citizens.

Tappans vs. Garrisonians

By 1840, the abolitionist movement in the United States had split into two deeply divided camps. The Tappan brothers, Lewis and Arthur, and their largely church-based following, had taken a gradual, political approach to ending slavery. Followers of William Lloyd Garrison, meanwhile, had grown impatient with the pace of reform and advocated more radical solutions; the rhetoric they adopted increasingly condoned violence as a justifiable means to end slavery and manifested itself in the actions of such individuals as John Brown. In March 1841, eight months before the first tree was felled for the British American Institute, a letter from Boston abolitionist Joseph Warren Alden to Rev. Wilson demonstrates the impact this conflict was already having on Wilson's Canada Mission work. Alden wrote that the opposition of the *Anti-Slavery Standard* to Wilson's mission was "just what you may expect from the Garrison party in this country."[13] Rev. Wilson had been firmly aligned with the Tappans due to his position as a missionary of the Tappan-led American Anti-Slavery Society (AAS), and his Congregationalist faith. His reliance on a charity model to support fugitive slaves stood in contrast to Garrisonian views that former slaves should simply apply themselves to working on their own behalf and not rely on what they termed "begging." They were also highly critical of planned colonies or manumission settlements created to support formerly enslaved people. A number of these settlements had sprung up in the US, including Ohio's Carthagena Settlement, near Cincinnati, founded in 1836 by Augustus Wattles, Rev. Wilson's Oberlin colleague. The American Freedmen's Inquiry Commission echoed this sentiment when sent by Abraham Lincoln's government to investigate the state of formerly enslaved people in Canada some years later. It concluded that "the discipline of colonies, though it only subjects the Negroes to what is considered useful apprenticeship, does prolong dependence which amounts to servitude and does not convert them so surely into hardy, self-reliant men as the rude struggle with actual difficulties, which they themselves have to face and to overcome."[14] While the BAI was not a planned settlement, aspects of its operation were reminiscent of the colony model, and the optics of choosing J.C. Brown and Frederick Stover, formerly of the Wilberforce Settlement, as BAI board members surely raised eyebrows in the Garrisonian camp.

Brown had been appointed by a group of African-Americans in Ohio to approach Governor General John Graves Simcoe for the purchase of land on which they could settle. The *Ohio Black Code Law* had been passed to discourage freemen from establishing there, in part because settlements of free people often became refuges for those fleeing enslavemen because they could more easily disappear within these communities and find work and other supports there. The *Black Code Laws* imposed curfews and travel restrictions that made it difficult for tradesmen and labourers to work and feed their families and conduct normal day-to-day activities. Brown was a mason by trade, and these laws no doubt affected his livelihood. With the vision of living in greater freedom, the Ohio group proposed to Simcoe that they purchase eight thousand acres of land where they could establish a planned settlement which would include an educational institute and other infrastructure. When they failed to raise sufficient funds to purchase the land, Simcoe offered them an eight-hundred-acre site near Lucan and a group of Ohio Friends, or Quakers, helped provide the necessary funds. Quaker Frederick Stover would help facilitate the purchase of the smaller property.[15] After Brown and Stover's departure from the Wilberforce project, two financial scandals erupted with fundraisers accused of building up expenses that exceeded the monies they had raised—as had been the case with their agent Israel Lewis—or of having simply refused to turn over the funds that were solicited in the name of the settlement for building a school. Two years before the BAI was established, warnings against Israel Lewis were still being published in the abolitionist press. Regrettably, the assurances that Lewis had not been involved in any wrongdoing drew the name of another principal figure of the BAI, into Wilberforce's troubled narrative by pointing out that theWilberforce's school had been under Wilson's care.[16] In the minds of potential financial supporters of the BAI, these links of Stover, Brown, and Wilson to the Wilberforce Settlement likely raised alarm bells.

The Wilberforce experience appears to have contributed to Brown's growing disillusionment with the colony model, and his subsequent experience at the Dawn Settlement seems to have made him ever more sympathetic to the Garrisonian perspective, resulting in his later alliance with Mary Ann Shadd, the publisher of the *Provincial Freeman*, whose views on colonies and begging expressed in her newspaper clearly reflect the same view. Wilson and Henson meanwhile were heavily reliant on solicited funds to support the BAI and other ventures. Shadd considered it particularly egregious for a white man, like Wilson, to beg on behalf of Black people and had attacked a number of white-led fundraising schemes, believing the white men involved had little understanding of actual needs and that some had even lined their own pockets with funds intended for formerly enslaved people. Members of the Black elite like Shadd also often objected to the tendency of financial appeals to present people of African descent who had migrated north to the Canadas as needy, ignorant, and incapable of fending for themselves. They noted that this image was inaccurate and demeaning and, most egregiously, reinforced Southern slaveholders' propaganda that formerly enslaved people could not possibly survive without the guidance of their "kind" masters. Rising tensions between the two abolitionist camps became increasingly evident at Dawn as Mary Ann Shadd became involved in the heated debates over the BAI's management after 1850, and with its Garrisonian-viewed leadership such as William P. Newman, a teacher and executive committee member; and J.C. Brown and Peter B. Smith, both trustees and executive committee members.

Sectarianism was also a factor in creating tensions. Fuller and Wilson had been altruistic men whose personal values and priorities were deeply informed by their Christian faith. Fuller's belief that all men were brothers seems to have led him to consult with Black leadership and include them, in equal number to white people, as BAI trustees and also to include people of different Christian denominations as trustees and committee members. Consequently, BAI representatives included a mosaic of different Christian denominations, including Society of Friends (Stover and Fuller); Congregationalists (Wilson and Roaf); Methodist Episcopalians (Henson and Smith); and Baptists (Johnson and Newman). Including religious diversity in the BAI management at a time of rising sectarianism was idealistic at best. As a December 1841 letter to Rev. Hiram Wilson from Benjamin F. Haskell[17] of Cornwall, Vermont, demonstrates, sectarianism in the US was already impacting Wilson's missions in Upper Canada. After outlining the religious strife in his community in some detail, Haskell expressed regret to Wilson that he could no longer send funds to support the Canada Mission because Haskell's own home congregation was fighting for its economic survival due to the turmoil.[18]

In addition, the ecumenical nature of the BAI board of trustees had made the institute something of an orphan. Though many faiths were represented, none of their official organizations or mission boards had assumed or would be assigned official sponsorship or oversight of any part of the BAI's operation before 1850, when the Baptists were put in charge of the BAI's church and school. While Fuller had provided the BAI's start-up funds, further development of its infrastructure and day-to-day operations had to be paid for either through fundraising or through the sale of the goods produced by the school's students. Goods production had been minimal in the BAI's early years, forcing reliance on solicited funds. As paid agents[19] of the BAI, Henson and Wilson had been tasked with making charitable appeals to cover the costs of developing the site and caring for those who came there. With no sponsoring church or mission body, Wilson was forced to tap his already stretched Canada Mission network of supporters.

The integrated nature of the board of trustees also created tensions along racial lines. Evidence of this can be found in later criticisms of Wilson's preaching style by BAI executive committee member William P. Newman, who raised allegations that Wilson was not welcomed to preach in Black congregations. White ministers and abolitionists were sometimes criticized for taking a paternalistic tone with people of African descent, something that particularly rankled the educated, freeborn elite.

Divisions also existed between freeborn and formerly enslaved people— the educated and the uneducated. Those with the advantage of education, like Newman, seem to not have always accommodated those with less or no formal education, like Henson, who likely struggled to provide the written accountability of funds Newman required of him. It was not uncommon for those escaping to the north to arrive hungry, exhausted, in ill health, and with few if any resources other than the clothes on their backs. For them, the admonishment of the elite minority to their reliance on missions and other community supports would have seemed out of touch with the reality of their situation. Mary Ann Shadd, who had grown up a free woman with education and economic advantages, indeed seems

Structural problems also plagued the British American Institute. Appointing two bodies to govern the BAI created a geographic disconnect between the day-to-day management decisions of the local executive committee and the more remotely situated absentee trustees, Roaf, Brown, Fuller, and Stover. There was also a lack of a single organizational head who had final say in disputes or decision-making. The confusion this caused is reflected in J.C. Brown's criticisms, voiced in a letter to the *Provincial Freeman*, in which he questioned who had given various individuals the right to make decisions or to act on the BAI's behalf.[20] Fuller himself also lamented that he had not reserved more power for himself, saying: "had the deed been taken in my name as I had wished and I had a right to make that wish, seven eighths of all the trouble that has arisen about the land would have been avoided."[21]

The BAI's structure also effectively sidelined its two most passionate advocates, the Henson and Wilson. While they had been appointed as agents responsible for the institute's financial well-being, they were not given positions as trustees. While Wilson was chair of the executive committee, this position does not appear to have given him any authority over the BAI's trustees, some of whom also sat on the executive committee. Even had he been given greater authority, Wilson lacked expertise and experience in developing and managing a large new institution. Henson for his part does not seem to have been afforded any special powers or special position on the executive committee (other than "agent") during the institute's critical first seven years of development. Although intelligent and resourceful, Henson also lacked the formal education needed to perform administrative functions. Fuller would have been the logical choice to head the BAI, but he chose to remain in the US, where he was too geographically removed from the institute to oversee its day-to-day affairs or to settle disputes as they arose.

Sustainable financing remained the BAI's biggest hurdle, and though Henson and Wilson were tireless in their efforts to raise funds, there still was much working against their efforts. Wilson's Canada Mission experience had already put a fine point on the politics involved in soliciting US funding for projects on British soil. Still, he persisted in his usual methods: writing letters to known, sympathetic donors, and appealing for funds in the abolitionist press. The types of aid Wilson's loyal supporters chose to send could at times be counterproductive. Mission groups sometimes preferred to send goods instead of cash. Bundles of clothing and books they sent were subject to tariffs, and some goods became tied up in customs with cash in short supply and none sufficient ready to release these goods into the hands of their intended recipients. Accusations emerged in the abolitionist press that the missionaries themselves were hoarding the goods or selling them for profit, which likely did little to increase prospective benefactors' confidence and generosity.

The manual labour school model also failed the BAI as a source of predictable income that could ween the institute off charitable support and lead it to self-sufficiency. As Augustus Wattles, Wilson's colleague in Ohio, had predicted, new arrivals were all too happy to remain at the BAI to pursue their studies during the winter months when work was scarce, but in the spring, when their labour was needed most, they often left to seek jobs on neighbouring farms with the objective in doing so was to earn wages they could apply to the purchase of their own property. Henson and Wilson continually found themselves fighting to meet costs, and their fundraising efforts almost immediately took them away from the BAI, leaving its development and care to others who did not necessarily share their vision. Yet despite these obstacles, the BAI began with much promise, and for nearly a decade it would be a shining beacon of hope that drew hundreds to the Dawn Settlement.

Chapter 5

The BRITISH AMERICAN INSTITUTE
The Early Days of Success and Growth

IN LATE NOVEMBER 1841, A SMALL BAND OF DAWN'S EARLY settlers gathered on the newly purchased grounds of the British American Institute. Five inches of snow had accumulated on the ground where they knelt below the spreading arms of an ancient oak. Rev. Hiram Wilson led in offering praise and thanks to God. Then, the group rose to their feet, shouldered their axes, and set to work felling trees. In three days, they constructed a twenty-by-twenty-six-foot log house that would serve as Hiram and Hannah Wilson's first home.[1] Wilson's account of this energetic, yet modest, beginning speaks to the enthusiasm that greeted the inception of the BAI within the Dawn Settlement and signals the initial success of the institute in its early years.

The purchase of two hundred acres of prime land along Bear Creek had been made possible by J.C. Fuller's investment, but now it would be the community at Dawn propelling the project forward. With the BAI's land base secured, Wilson turned to old friends for advice on how to proceed with its development. After all, he had only recently graduated as a seminarian. His first jobs had been conducting research for Oberlin College's white president, Charles Finney, and later for the white abolitionist Lewis Tappan of the American Anti-Slavery Society. While Wilson had set up a large network of small schools and churches as part of his Canada Mission, he had little practical knowledge or experience in developing an educational institution of the scope he, Fuller, and others had envisioned for the bush of Canada West, where there was little or nothing by way of supportive infrastructure. The emerging village of Dresden lacked even a post office and mill, and the nearest community of Dawn Mills, which lay upriver beyond a small rapid, offered only a handful of rudimentary services.

Augustus Wattles, like Wilson, had been a Lane Rebel and a fellow white student at Oberlin College. On graduation, he had remained in Ohio where he established the Carthagena Settlement at Cincinnati. When Wilson wrote to him of his similar plans for developing an educational institute in Upper Canada, Wattles responded in June 1842 with a hearty congratulations and detailed advice. "My heart leaped for joy at the news," Wattles enthused six months after Wilson had already completed his first log building.[2] And yet, Wattles warned of the "hardships and privations" that might prove huge obstacles for those who came to Dawn. For the previous four years, he and his brother John Otis had laboured to bring the Carthagena settlement into existence. Established by the Society of Friends Carthagenahad similarly been envisioned as a self-supporting school and farm where formerly enslaved people could learn new skills. Wattles's letter provided Wilson with richly detailed practical advice for his similar work at the BAI. "Concentrate on clearing and fencing at least 175 acres as fast as possible," Wattles urged. To accomplish this, he advised girdling[3] the trees one year for felling the next. He advised that only when the land had been cleared should building begin. The buildings themselves, he warned, should not be made of log as they would be difficult to keep dry and warm. Wattles suggested instead that the trees felled on the institute grounds be taken to a nearby sawmill and turned into timbers and planks for the construction of frame houses.

To achieve financial stability, Wattles discouraged Wilson from relying on charity, which he predicted would "run dry." Instead, he proposed that the institute aim for self-sufficiency. If enough acreage could be cleared, he suggested, "the Lord and his earth"[4] would provide for a good living from farming. The rich stands of trees on the institute grounds were also seen by

Wattles as a viable source of income. "If a sawmill is on hand and lumber can be taken to the US free of duty," he advised, "the whole improvements could be carried on from the sale of the lumber cut on the school lot."[5] There is little evidence that Rev. Wilson took any of Wattles's advice. It would be Josiah Henson who, two years later, would begin actively investigating the feasibility of erecting a sawmill. It is unknown whether Henson knew of what Wattles advised or had independently arrived at the same conclusion.

Wilson also ignored Wattles's direction on fundraising, and he continued to believe that BAI students could be motivated to work on the manual labour school's property in return for their education and, in so doing, generate funds through the production of goods. This was despite Wattles's observations at Carthagena where the formerly enslaved, once they had gained some basic education, "don't know what they should do with any more [education] and so leave me."[6] Wattles advised encouraging the BAI students to seek paid work off-site, as they were inclined to do, and to have them pay tuition from these wages. This timely advice also went unheeded. Yet, despite this and the economic and other hardships, the BAI enjoyed some admirable initial success. In 1843 the school began with twelve students. By the winter of 1845 that number had swelled to over one hundred.

Wilson's ambitious work to build the BAI became a natural extension of his Canada Mission work as he tapped old friends and supporters in the AAS and his old alma mater, Oberlin, for funds and teachers. William P. Newman, the future BAI leader, who was a Virginia freeman, was one of the Ohio teachers Wilson drew to the Canada Mission. In 1843, Newman wrote, "Just before I left home last fall to go to Canada, I received a letter from St. Catharines requesting me to come over and teach their school."[7] By 1845, he had left his post at that Canada Mission site for a teaching position at the British American Institute.

Early teachers at the BAI had impressive credentials and possessed skills that extended beyond basic subjects. William G. Allen, who had been sponsored by the Oneida Institute, was a talented flute player.[8] Others, like Alfred Whipper, were elite Pennsylvania freemen who had been successful businessmen before becoming educators. Wilson himself served as a teacher and preacher, and by 1838 his wife, Hannah, had joined him in Canada West and began to wholeheartedly share in his mission work.

The missionary life was not a glamorous one. "The grim, tedious, day-to-day fieldwork of anti-slavery... offered little power, prestige or political allure."[9] Devout Christians like the Wilsons were often sustained by their belief that their reward lay in the afterlife. Hannah Wilson appears to have been a particularly devoted missionary and a beloved figure at Dawn, and well she might have been as devotion to the cause seems to have been saintly in its intensity. If Wilson's life had been one of self-privation for the sake of his missionary work, Hannah's was doubly so. She was often left alone to take care of the farm, the household, the children, and her teaching work during her husband's frequent absences for fundraising and Canada Mission work. Her efforts were sometimes subverted by a scarcity of even the most basic necessities. "I am sorry to learn that seed is so scarce for planting," Wilson wrote Hannah from England in 1843. "Trust however, that you will do the best you can."[10] Hannah, at the time, was pregnant with their second child, Lydia. Wilson's wrote his letter to advise her that he had been delayed in England and would not be home for the birth. This fact was a source of anguish for Wilson who told his wife to "get good female help that you can depend upon. Let it cost what it may. Give yourself no trouble about expenses. I will meet them." Beyond this, all the comfort he could offer was to urge Hannah to "lean confidently upon the Lord."[11] Hannah gave birth to four children during the six years she lived at Dawn. John was born in the same year the institute had been founded; Lydia arrived in 1843; Mary, in 1845; and George, in 1847. So, during her short time at Dawn, Hannah had been either pregnant or nursing and, at times, caring for up to three children under the age of six, while carrying out her teaching and other duties. The food scarcity and inadequate housing added to her burden.

The earliest years at the British American Institute were so difficult that by 1842 even the optimistic Wilson would consider abandoning the project. His letter from England to Hannah asked her assistance in impressing on the executive committee that there was an urgency around raising money for provisions for the school's students and staff. His efforts in England were not intended for this purpose but for the construction of a new school building and dormitories. Wilson recognized the urgency of achieving this goal saying, "Something worthy of the cause must be accomplished or the sooner we back out and abandon the work the better.[12]

There had been some early opposition by Dawn's residents to the school as well. Rumours about the BAI and suspicions about its leaders' motivations had circulated in the community. In June 1844, Wilson and Henson called a local convention to address these concerns, and at this Wilson reported "all manner of objection and opposition passed away and left us standing erect in the bright sunshine of popular favor."[13]

By March 1843, following Wilson's fundraising mission in England, a school for young men was organized at the BAI and, despite already being in debt for one hundred pounds, the institute began to grow. By May, student-labourers had cleared and fenced twelve acres and there were three dwellings on the site, a storey-and-a-half school that accommodated sixty students, and a dormitory that housed twenty. By 1844, the school had attracted the attention of white Underground Railroad station master Levi Coffin, who operated on Ohio's UGRR in Cincinnati. Coffin became one of the first of a long line of important visitors who would come to Dawn. One of the BAI's more famous students, Lewis Hayden, who had recently escaped enslavement, also came to the BAI during this period. Hayden would later become a noted lecturer for the American Anti-Slavery Society and would credit the BAI for his development as a person.

By 1845, a surge of community support began to move key projects forward. A report by Wilson to the *American Anti-Slavery Reporter* that year showed that sixty acres had been cleared and were under cultivation and that a framed barn and a two-storey, thirty-by-thirty-two-foot brick building had been erected. Another building, a two-storey, twenty-two-by-thirty-four-foot hewn timber structure, was reported as being under construction and slated for occupation in December of that year. There were now eighty students, with a total of one hundred anticipated to arrive by winter. Wilson believed that if there were more capacity to house students, three times that number could be accommodated.

By 1845, potash was also being produced and tobacco and hemp had been introduced to the school's agricultural production. This project was being advanced by a group referred to as "The Virginians," who likely included the BAI's neighbour John Myers. BAI students turned hemp fibre into rope—a highly marketable product that found an immediate use on the BAI grounds. Bear Creek had blessed the BAI with rich bottom lands that were annually renewed by "the spring freshet." But it also bisected the institute grounds, making it difficult to access fields on the river's north side, so a suspension bridge was proposed. BAI-produced hemp rope was used to construct this bridge, the first to be built across Bear Creek at Dresden. John Myers and others continued to grow the newly introduced hemp crop long after the BAI no longer functioned. By 1861, fully forty-five acres of the Myers farm was devoted to the crop—the single largest acreage of any crop being grown on any farm in the township.[14]

By 1845, the BAI had also begun producing bricks. No evidence has yet been found that a brick kiln existed on the property—a more primitive method of firing in outdoor stacks may have been used. Local clay from the banks of Bear Creek provided the raw material. The clay, refined in a primitive horse-powered milling device,[15] would then be shaped in wooden forms and the raw bricks placed in piles with large quantities of brush. These piles were then sealed with a layer of clay and the brush inside set alight through an opening. Several days later, when the fire had burned out, the outer clay layer was stripped away in order to retrieve the fired bricks.[16] Regardless of the method used, by 1847, the institute had successfully produced a hundred thousand clay bricks.

Other uses of local clay may have been considered as well. A small ceramic jug bearing the inscription *from J. B. to Josiah Henson* has recently surfaced locally.[17] A John Brown who had originally fled slavery to work in the copper mines of Lake Superior and had migrated to Dawn to work at Henson's sawmill is one possible candidate for the J.B. who seems to have gifted Henson the jug. Brown is said to have helped cut the planks Henson took to the Crystal Palace for the Great Exhibition in London, England, in 1851.[18] Regardless of created it, the jug demonstrates the ingenuity of those who had settled at Dawn and suggests that pottery had at least been attempted. This raises questions about what other industries might have arisen on the BAI's resource-rich site if monies could have been found to develop them.

As it was, raising funds for the most basic needs continued to be a major challenge. Despite the confidence expressed in Rev. Wilson by the American Missionary Association's secretary Theodore S. Wright, others, including the BAI's British backers, were not universally assured that Wilson and his various projects were sound investments. DuringWilson's 1843 fundraising campaign in London, which he had undertaken with James Canning Fuller, the Rev. Joshua Leavitt, an American Congregationalist minister and prominent white abolitionist, cautioned British colleagues against supporting the BAI. Leavitt offered that "Wilson has done a great good as a most laborious pioneer...[but] I do not feel confidence in his ability to manage an institution of learning or any other matter involving a large expenditure of money."[19] Wilson pressed forward, and in 1846 he wrote to Charles Birney, a white American politician and abolitionist, outlining his plans to build a three-storey, 100-by-50-foot brick building to be named Clarkson Hall, after the famous British abolitionist. The choice of name seems especially designed to please potential English donors. It is unclear from reports whether this building was ever completed. A frame schoolhouse for women, however, was constructed around this time. Regardless of any disappointments he might have felt over the BAI's progress, by 1845 Wilson would report to Birney that "the manual labour institute at Dawn is in a highly prosperous state and promises fair to be of immediate importance to the coloured population."[20]

By 1845, Josiah Henson had concluded that the practice of burning trees to clear the BAI's land was a waste of a valuable resource. He argued, much as Wattles had, that a sawmill could produce boards for the BAI's own building projects and to be sold for operating capital. Rev. Wilson, on the other hand, continued to rely on US abolitionists, such as Birney, Garrett Smith, and Elizabeth Mountford of the Ladies Anti-Slavery Society of Portland, Maine, to donate goods and cash. Wilson was a prolific writer of persuasive correspondence that made impassioned pleas for money and goods, including Bibles, teaching materials, and clothing. His effusive letters were designed to tug at the heartstrings of his mostly Christian audience and often painted a rather pathetic picture of "the poor and wretched coloured population in Canada" in order to evoke sympathy and support. While this representation of Blacks in Canada may have served to loosen purse strings, it also raised the ire of many free people in Canada who felt denigrated by this characterization. While some formerly enslaved people had struggled in their early years, many had made a success of their lives, becoming fully independent and prosperous. By 1848 even Wilson would concede that the urgency of providing for new arrivals was not what it had once been thanks to the improved support along the Underground Railroad network. In 1849 he

observed that, "I have the pleasure of saying that fugitive slaves are now better furnished with the means of comfort on their way than formerly; hence
their necessities are not as great after they get here. What they most need is
instruction."[21] Still, accounts show a continued need for initial support for
those who arrived sick, injured, or destitute. Setbacks could also befall even
the more established residents. Inclement weather was a factor that led to
crop failures, hunger, and economic hardship for even the most successful
settlers. Even Rev. William P. Newman, who had railed against depictions of
settlers as needy and in want, would make an appeal for funds after multiple
frosts in 1859 resulted in famine. US abolitionists would roundly criticize him
and others for admitting to this in the public forum of the US press.[22] Lewis
Champion Chambers, an American missionary to the Dawn Settlement
would echo Newman in his more private reports that indicated a number of
new arrivals lacked basic necessities like food and clothing.[23]

Chronically underfunded schools and churches of various mission
groups, including Newman's own Baptist congregation, necessitated specific
appeals for donations of teaching materials and Bibles. The number of books
possessed by missions and even the condition of these materials sometimes
appear in reports to sponsoring organizations. Mission sites and churches
were appreciative of the bales of clothing sent for distribution to their members. Collection and bundling of used clothing figured prominently in the
efforts of women's abolitionist groups, but rumours persisted that these
goods were not reaching the intended recipients but were instead benefitting
missionaries or other white people. This suggestion did not sit well with critics of begging and sometimes inspired accusations of fraud.

Fundraising for the BAI also continued to meet the same obstacles the
Canada Mission fundraising efforts had faced. US abolitionists continued
to prefer supporting causes in their own country. Opposition by those who
objected to solicitation of funds and other resources on behalf of formerly
enslaved people became ever more strident in the abolitionist press, and
accountability for funds became a flashpoint of controversy. At the BAI,
fundraising issues would lead to a permanent rift among executive committee members and, in particular, would pit William P. Newman (as BAI treasurer) and James C. Brown (as trustee and executive committee member)
against Henson and Wilson. When Newman arrived at the BAI to teach and

joined the executive committee, tensions between him and the appointed agents, Henson and Wilson, arose almost immediately. Newman had grown suspicious of the white missionary's motives, and in a letter to the *Oberlin Evangelist* dated December 20, 1843, he wrote "respecting brother Wilson and the Canada Mission, the intelligent and thinking part of the world must infer that the part brother Wilson plays in the Canadian mission for the fugitives, after all, is for the benefit of himself."[24] Newman insisted that some $20,000 in funds raised for the BAI had been misappropriated and demanded that Henson and Rev. Wilson provide a full accounting of their activities.[25] The all too recent scandal over Israel Lewis's misappropriation of funds at the Wilberforce Settlement in Lucan and Wilson's involvement there may have played a part in inspiring Newman's suspicion, and as the secretary-treasurer for the BAI's executive committee he would have felt responsible for the organization's financial accountability. By 1843, after having spent the winter reviewing Wilson's records and papers that included receipts and expenditures from Wilson's earliest transactions, Newman had conceded that the expenditures of "brother Wilson…have been for what they were supposed to be for the general good of the colored people, and have been also correctly registered except when Bro. Wilson was absent, or busy and paid out or spent a shilling or two which slipped his memory; and in such cases when he found his purse a little short, he would make an entry of this kind,…'I bought…or perhaps paid the post-boy.' Such being the facts, who can doubt that Bro. Wilson is innocent of what he is charged with?" Newman signed the letter, "Yours in the defense of truth."[26]

Newman would remain adversarial towards Henson, and infighting continued between Newman and other trustees that ultimately led to Newman's resignation.[27] After a brief absence he returned and was reinstated. A protracted conflict then ensued between Newman and Henson that would manifest itself in a highly public war of words in the abolitionist press. Accusations and counteraccusations would be printed for all to see, with Newman's comments becoming increasingly inflammatory and escalating beyond personal attacks of Henson to damning criticisms of the BAI itself. As early as 1848 he would describe the institute as "the curse of our people in Canada."[28] At the height of the conflict, Newman would charge that Henson had threatened to cut his throat if he (Newman) did not desist in his verbal attacks.[29] Henson denied this in a counter-letter. This high-profile conflict between two BAI leaders likely did little to inspire confidence among potential backers at what was a crucial time in the BAI's development. By August 1847, a convention at Drummondville, attended by Newman, discussed the BAI, with the result that convention goers appointed their own committee to audit the Dawn Settlement's books. Later, the convention stated it was "satisfied with the conduct of Mr. Henson, so far as they have heard from him."[30]

That troubles with management and fundraising were not a problem unique to the BAI was highlighted in a July 30, 1848, meeting of teachers and missionaries who gathered at New Hope in the Queen's Bush. Those attending the meeting included Newman, Wilson, and the leadership of other mission sites like Rev. William King of the Elgin Settlement, who discussed common problems of the various Canadian missions. They recommended a more coordinated approach to providing for the "social and moral condition...of the coloured race"[31] and expressed grave concerns about the sustainability of Canadian mission sites. Their findings were publicized through the *Christian Contributor*—the official paper of the Primitive Methodists in Canada—and other abolitionist newspapers and submitted to the American Missionary Association. Their report reveals grave problems at most outreach sites in Upper Canada. "Some stations have been abandoned, the teachers giving up in despair while those that remain are placed in a very precarious condition, their permanency depending on the life and health of the missionaries aided by irregular contributions from a foreign source. There is no promise made for their continuance, should the aid stop, or the missionaries die,"[32] they wrote. An important communication gap was also revealed. "All friends who contribute to these missionaries [are] left in ignorance [of] how the funds are administered, or what good has been affected, there being neither a distinct organization nor annual reports to which they might refer."[33] Consequently, it was recommended that all missions in Canada be organized under one distinct church denomination or missionary association that pledged their continued support and that a coordinated and cooperative approach be taken in the mutual objective of providing for the "social and moral improvement of the coloured people." Annual meetings and reports that involved leadership of the various Canadian sites and their donors and investors were recommended so information could be shared regarding how funds and goods had been used. Rather than any one individual having responsibility for the administration of these public funds, the convention recommended a group of trustees be granted oversight. These measures, they believed, would contribute to the permanence of the mission sites, end competition for funding by various agents, and increase donor confidence.[34]

In the spring of 1847, Wilson suffered a great personal loss that added to the burden of his mission work. Shortly after giving birth to their son George, Hannah Wilson died. Her health had no doubt been compromised from years of deprivation, and she quickly succumbed to an unnamed illness. Her last words are reported to have been: "Jesus can make a dying bed, soft as downy pillows." Indeed, it would seem that after a brief and stark existence at Dawn, Hannah had earned her rest. Rev. Hiram Wilson keenly felt the loss of his wife, as did the people she had served at Dawn and in the wider abolitionist community. In June 1847, John Wilson comforted his brother Hiram by writing "the poor colored people have lost a dear friend. They will strew her grave with flowers and wash them with their tears."[35] Bishop Daniel Payne, who knew Hannah as "Miss Hubbard" when she was a member of his New York Presbyterian Church, visited the BAI in 1851. While walking in the British American Institute cemetery with Josiah Henson, Payne noticed a small fenced-in grave on the riverbank. Henson informed Payne that it was Hannah's grave, and when Payne rushed over to look more closely, he found a rose bush blooming on the gravesite. He gathered some of its petals and leaves to take with him. On a return trip in 1885, he asked Josiah Henson's daughter to help him again find Hannah's burial site; he was dismayed to find no marker, but a rosebush still grew there, and Payne again gathered some petals. Hannah's resting place would never be marked by a stone, and her burial place would be unknown today, but for Payne's description.[36]

After Hannah's death, Rev. Wilson fell ill. He resigned from the executive committee and returned to Ohio to convalesce. On recovery, he returned to the BAI and was reinstated to the executive committee. In July 1847, at the third annual Wesleyan Connexion of Canada meeting at Dawn, Wilson again found himself under Newman's attack, this time facing criticism for his preaching style. Those present had misinterpreted Newman as having said that Wilson was not welcome to preach in Black churches. Josiah Henson and his son Isaac drafted a statement in Wilson's defence. It was signed by the majority of the executive committee that now consisted of Peter B. Smith, James Stompf, George Cary, Thomas Green, Vincent Johnson, and Josiah Henson. The published statement in Wilson's defence set off yet another round of counteraccusations from Newman, who rightly stated that his remarks had been misinterpreted.

Despite the continual setbacks, outside interference, and infighting, the BAI's development continued. In January 1848 a grist mill was designed and built by a millwright from South Carolina at a cost of $3,000—$2,500 of which had been raised and the rest borrowed. The boys' academy under Newman continued to accommodate sixty pupils in the BAI's brick schoolhouse. A wooden two-storey girls' school was erected, but as the *Provincial Freeman* reported, it operated for only one season, its female teacher having left for mission work in Africa and having died en route. In the absence of a female teacher, the girls' school was not revived. In 1849 another devastating and permanent setback occurred as the BAI's brick boys' school sustained significant damage in a violent storm. A major drought and crop failure also forced the BAI's management to go into debt to purchase food for the students.

The stormy relations among the school's leadership escalated as acrimony erupted between the previously allied Wilson and Henson. They would, ironically, after so many years of working together to raise funds to achieve their common vision of a school, come into conflict over a fundraising scheme. Charity had run dry as Wattles had predicted years earlier, and Henson turned his attention to creating infrastructure and industry that held the potential to make the BAI self-sufficient. Despite his status as a "fugitive slave," he had travelled extensively to New York, Connecticut, Massachusetts, and Maine, not only fundraising but bringing others, including the Lightfoot family, out of enslavement. By 1846 he had become convinced that the BAI's timber resources should be developed. He researched mills and markets in New York and found others produced lumber from the same species of trees found at Dawn and that these were commanding high prices. He sought out and found potential markets for Dawn timber in New England. At Boston, he consulted with "some philanthropic gentlemen with whom [he] had become acquainted."[37] This led to an introduction to Samuel Eliot, a Scottish-American medical doctor and abolitionist who had been "kind enough to examine carefully into all my representations [of a sawmill] and to draw up a sketch of them, which was afterwards presented to Amos Lawrence Esq. and others."[38] This resulted in a donation of $1,400 towards the sawmill's construction. That amount was insufficient to complete the project, so Henson borrowed additional funds so the sawmill could be finished. Wilson, who had previously fallen into personal debt to finance the Canada Mission, had grown averse to borrowing money. "Gradual but certain progress with freedom from debt is wiser and better than…premature growth that would involve and encumber us," he wrote.[39] He opposed Henson's acquiring debt in the name of the institute, but Henson moved ahead, believing the proceeds from the sawmill would quickly cancel out any debt. Henson then angered Wilson by approaching Wilson's usual funding sources without his consent, including his white female missionary friend Elizabeth Mountford from Portland, Maine. The depth of Wilson's opposition to Henson's plans is evident in his response to inquiries from the Portland group: "Whatever representations [Henson] may have made…his mill, I am sorry to say, is badly managed and is an unprofitable concern. It had better never have been built."[40]

The BAI's collective setbacks resulted in an amassing of a $58,000 debt (the equivalent of $2.2 million in today's currency), inspiring trustees Rev. John Roaf, George Johnson, and J.C. Brown in June 1848 to call for an investigation into alleged mismanagement of resources. Meanwhile, Wilson would use his platform as a correspondent for Frederick Douglass's *North Star* to attack Newman, intimating he had rented out BAI land to area farmers but that this rent money had not benefitted the school. By 1849 Henson again was charged with mismanaging the BAI's finances and, again, was cleared of any wrongdoing.

In April 1849 James Canning Fuller died, leaving Wilson without his valued mentor and ally. With his devoted wife also gone and his friendship with Henson irrevocably damaged, a discouraged Wilson permanently resigned, and seems to have stayed within the Dawn Settlement for roughly two years at his Hopedale Canada Mission site.[41] He then left Hopedale and travelled to his Canada Mission site at St. Catharines. Previously, some thousand freedom seekers had settled there, and by 1850 this number had swelled by an additional three thousand. At St. Catharines, Wilson became involved with one of the Underground Railroad's most famous conductors,

Harriet Tubman, operating a safehouse for those she and others brought to him. Wilson's new wife, Mary, would also become highly involved in caring for UGRR passengers, and together they would raise Hannah's four children along with a fifth, an orphaned Black child, Alavana Dicken, whom they had adopted. Wilson would die at St. Catharines on April 16, 1864, at the age of 61. He had lived to see freedom achieved through the American Emancipation Proclamation but would never learn the ultimate fate of the institution he had poured so much of his life into at Dawn.

By 1850 the BAI had reached a watershed moment. Its leadership had been radically altered by Rev. Wilson's departure and James Canning Fuller's death. Other trustees had become occupied with other causes. Rev. James Roaf, of Toronto, co-founded the Anti-Slavery Society of Canada.[42] James C. Brown left Toronto, and by 1849 he had relocated to Chatham, joining Mary Ann Shadd at the *Provincial Freeman*. William P. Newman, despite his success in driving out Wilson, also left Dawn, returning to Ohio to further his education and become ordained as a Baptist minister and would serve as pastor of the Union Baptist Church in Cincinnati. Given these changes to BAI leadership and the institute's mounting debt, the remaining trustees, Roaf, Brown, Johnson, and Smith, sought to reorganize the BAI. By 1850, they had divided its management into two distinct areas of responsibility. The BAI's school and church were to be overseen by the Baptist Free Mission Society—a move that seemed in keeping with the recommendations of the 1848 convention at New Hope, which suggested denominational sponsorship as the best method for sustaining churches and schools. By 1850, Rev. William P. Newman and the Rev. Samuel Henry Davis, of Detroit, had taken charge of the BAI church and school under the sponsorship of the Baptists.

Responsibility for the BAI's debts, meanwhile, were linked to the institute's potential income generators—its land and the sawmill Henson had developed. Henson reluctantly assumed management of these with the proviso that trustee Peter B. Smith share responsibility. It was a temporary fix. As Wilson would observe from his vantage point at St. Catharines, "[The BAI] has run down and can hardly be resuscitated again without a miracle."[43] Josiah Henson and Rev. Newman, with their new areas of targeted responsibility, however, seem to have believed the BAI's fortunes could be turned around. They ambitiously set out on mainly separate and sometimes opposing paths to move the institute forward once again. Meanwhile, fate would intervene in Rev. Henson's personal history, catapulting him to a mid-life celebrity that would prove a double-edged sword that both benefitted his fundraising efforts through a new notoriety and, ultimately, worked against the revival of the BAI.

Chapter 6

HENSON'S
RISING STAR
Beyond the Fictional Uncle Tom

A T THREE IN THE MORNING ON AUGUST 1, 1854, FREDERICK Douglass stood in a dark forest clearing in the Dawn Settlement. He was dust covered and bone weary from the jarring wagon ride he had taken from the Chatham train station to Josiah Henson's farm. The journey had been difficult, but his arrival was a joyful one. "Late as it was, our friends here were up and, on the lookout, with fires lighted, busily engaged in the needful preparations for the contemplated celebration," he later reported."[1]

By 1854 Douglass had become something of a celebrity. Enslaved since birth, he had escaped to New York City in 1838, and by 1841 he began sharing his story at abolitionist conventions where he captivated audiences with his powerful oratory style. In 1845 he wrote *Narrative of the Life of Frederick Douglass, an American Slave,* and by December 3, 1847, he had launched his North Star newspaper at Rochester, New York. By the time of his visit to the Dawn Settlement, the *North Star* had become the most influential anti-slavery newspaper in North America.[2] Douglass had come to Dawn, initially, not because of Henson's rising fame but on the invitation of Rev. John Scoble who had recently been sent to the BAI by British donors to manage its affairs. Scoble had calculated that a positive word from an influential and respected voice like that of Douglass would be akin to an endorsement of the institute and Scoble's work.[3] The arrival of Douglass—and Scoble—demonstrates the growing international interest by abolitionists in the Dawn Settlement's development. For Douglass, the prospect of meeting Josiah Henson was an added enticement to travel to the Dawn Settlement. The publication of Henson's slave narrative had launched Henson into a similar celebrity to that earned by Douglass when he had published his own slave narrative. Being cited as one of Harriet Beecher Stowe's inspirations[4] for the lead character in her landmark anti-slavery novel *Uncle Tom's Cabin; or, Life Among the Lowly* had given Henson an almost overnight celebrity as Stowe's novel achieved unprecedented success on both sides of the Atlantic. Douglass would, however, not refer to Henson as "Uncle Tom" in his newspaper article but rather referred to the aging leader by the more deferential title of "Father Henson." Douglass's two-part *North Star* account of his Dawn Settlement visit gives us one of the warmest and most detailed descriptions of Henson ever penned by one of his contemporaries. It paints a picture of a vital patriarch and a gracious host, saying, "Father Henson though well-stricken in years and in labors, advancing toward seventy, was up, bright as a boy and gay as a lark, gave us a cheering welcome to his home in the woods. Pointing to lights peering through the thick bushes and trees around in different directions, he said, 'there lives one son and there another. I have eight children and have only to leap upon a stump and give a hoop to be at once surrounded by them.'…the patriarch would have us take refreshments, though the red streak of day had already appeared on the horizon." The description focusing on Henson's humanity and his family life seems to have been designed to highlight a main point of opposition towards slavery—its destruction of families through the auctioning off of their members. By unfolding the story of Henson's delight in being surrounded by family, and providing him the venerable title of Father Henson, Douglass is not simply creating a character sketch but a powerful argument for the need to eradicate slavery and its attendant destruction of family life Douglass could have instead highlighted Henson's many accomplishments to that point, demonstrated despite his age and before the prominence he'd been given by his association with Stowe's novel. Henson had, after all, become a powerful proponent not only for the development of education through his support of to the BAI but in resistance to slavery as an UGRR conductor. In his British trips undertaken at this time the aging leader's agency and effectiveness in addressing racism and promoting social reform is also evident, as he addressed educational issues that not fit within a narrow self-interest. These accomplishments, recounted in his real-life biography should have earned him a fame similar to Douglass' on his own merits. With the unprecedented success of Stowe's Uncle Tom's Cabin, however, and the identification of Henson as Uncle Tom, his own real-life accomplishments were quickly being overshadowed.

Three years earlier, in May 1851, Josiah Henson had stood proudly among the throngs of people at the Crystal Palace, where the Great Exhibition of the Works of Industry of All Nations, otherwise known as the London World's Fair, was taking place. From the vantage point of his exhibit of lumber products from the British American Institute's mill, Henson would note his important status as the only Black exhibitor. The only other non-white people were, themselves, being exhibited as cultural curiosities in Queen Victoria's widespread empire. Henson, by contrast, had come as an enterprising entrepreneur on a bold marketing venture—showcasing the best of what the BAI's lands and the lumber industry he'd founded there had to offer and, in this role, challenging the racial stereotypes of his day.

As an exhibitor, Henson was among some heady company. Organized by Prince Albert, Queen Victoria's husband, and Henry Cole, British civil servant and inventor, the first World's Fair would attract six million people. The multitude Henson watched file past his exhibit included some of the era's leading scientific minds, industrialists, and cultural icons, including Charles Darwin, Karl Marx, and Charles Dickens. Henson's relatively small exhibit of four polished walnut boards might have gone unnoticed in the immenseness of the event. The massive Crystal Palace, made entirely of steel and glass, housed fourteen thousand exhibitors within its twenty-three acres and included modern marvels from around the world, like Colt's repeating pistols, Goodyear's India rubber, and McCormick's horse-drawn reaper. Yet Henson's exhibit—and Henson, personally—held his own among these impressive offerings, winning a bronze medal and attracting the attention of some of England's leading citizens, including the Queen herself.

Henson's World's Fair marketing venture was a triumphant culmination of two years of hard work that had begun with his adoption of the institute's sawmill project and had been facilitated through another earlier trip to England. Between 1845 and 1849, Henson had singlehandedly raised funds to begin building the BAI sawmill and then had gone into personal debt to complete the project. His sons Isaac and Peter, and trustee Peter B. Smith, a blacksmith, assisted him in the mill's construction. While Henson had invested heavily in the project, he seems to not have viewed it as a personal enterprise but as a resource meant to benefit the institute and the community. Between 1849 and 1850, the mill produced saleable lumber. Henson had contracted a ship's captain to transport its wood products from Dawn to Oswego, New York, then personally met the shipments at Oswego in order to escort them to Boston, where he arranged for their sale. An initial shipment of eighty thousand board feet of good prime black walnut lumber sold for an impressive $3,600 (roughly $137,000 in US currency today).[5] Henson shipped and sold two more lots of lumber in this way. The profit was sufficient to cancel out all the institute's debts to that time. Rather than pay these off, however Henson says he heeded the advice of friends who "insisted that [he] should retain a part of the funds for future use."[6]

During his marketing trips, Henson knowingly faced growing personal peril. He was still, in the eyes of the law, a "fugitive slave." Even in the supposedly sympathetic North there were many who were openly hostile towards Blacks, and, with the passage of the Fugitive Slave Act of 1850, the law now compelled people to assist slavecatchers in their apprehension of "fugitives." Henson faced this danger with characteristic self-confidence—and humour. He would later recall, "When the customs house officer presented his bill to me for the duties on my lumber, I jokingly remarked to him that perhaps he would render himself liable to trouble if he should have dealings with a fugitive slave, and if so, I would relieve him of the trouble of taking my money."[7]

Henson's vision of self-sustainability for the institute had been a lofty one and a goal he had been attempting to achieve amidst increasing challenges. With Fuller's death and Rev. Wilson's resignation, the power struggle over the BAI's management involving Rev. William P. Newman, who was now a Baptist minister, had taken on renewed vigour. Henson believed Rev. Newman's motivations had been sectarian, in that he wished to bring the entire BAI, and not just its church and school, under Baptist control. Henson, like Rev. Wilson and Fuller, had always assumed a more ecumenical approach, accepting assistance wherever he found people of good will with a similar vision. But with Fuller and Rev. Wilson gone, loyalties within the BAI's leadership had shifted. Even Henson's partner in the sawmill's management, Peter B. Smith, was gravitating towards support of Rev. Newman and his Garrisonian-viewed allies. Little wonder that Henson chose to keep his British trip secret even from Smith. In 1849, Henson plotted a solitary course for himself that followed that of Fuller and Rev. Wilson's previous fundraising trips to England.

Henson's travels abroad to raise funds were part of a larger transatlantic migration by North American Black leaders to solicit support in Britain. By the time of the 1840 World Anti-Slavery Convention, formerly enslaved and freeborn people from North America had already begun travelling there to seek support for anti-slavery causes. By 1842, Rev. John Scoble, the secretary of the British and Foreign Anti-Slavery Society (BFASS), had begun organizing these visitors'fundraising tours and facilitating the publication of their slave narratives in Britain. By 1845, Frederick Douglass had sought BFASS support for his speaking tour, and by Henson's arrival in 1849 the BFASS had become "the major clearinghouse for black abolitionists because of the size of the organization, the circulation of its newspaper and the energy of its leaders."[8] Potential English donors had also looked to the BFASS "to pass judgement on Black visitors, and the society…under Scoble…became very serious about that responsibility." And well they might. Scandals over misappropriated funds had marred previous tours, like that of the Wilberforce agent Israel Lewis. Ensuring donors were not defrauded not only protected the donors but helped maintain public confidence and ensured fundraisers "a correct introduction to patrons whose purses might be loosened for reformist causes."[9] The society also provided practical supports procuring lodgings and finding jobs to sustain fundraisers on protracted tours; booking speaking venues; conducting press promotions; printing promotional materials like posters and handbills; and booking local dignitaries to chair meetings.

True to its mandate, the BFASS, provided Henson with twelve individuals to oversee his activities. They included members of the Gurney banking family, Samuels Jr. and Sr.; Rev. James Sherman, a Congregationalist minister; industrialists George and Thomas Sturge; Anthony Ashley-Cooper, Seventh Earl of Shaftesbury; and Scoble, BFASS secretary. All of these men were committed abolitionists. Many were involved in other social and moral reform causes. Four men were further chosen to manage Henson's finances. Samuel Gurney Jr. acted as treasurer of this sub-committee that also included Scoble, Rev. John Branch, and Eusebius Smith. In addition, Samuel Gurney opened important doors for Henson, most notably obtaining an interview with John Bird Sumner, the Archbishop of Canterbury. Henson made the most of these opportunities. His interview with the archbishop had been scheduled as a brief fifteen-minute audience but had turned into an amiable hour-and-a-half exchange in which Archbishop Sumner sat in rapt attention, impressed by Henson's demeanour and speaking abilities. Henson's contact with English society also paid personal dividends. His son Isaac would later be sponsored to study in England. The Archbishop of Canterbury would preside over Isaac's ordination into the ministry.[10]

Henson had understood the importance of establishing his credentials for his first English fundraising trip and had procured many letters of introduction from prominent North American abolitionists prior. These letters of endorsement, and his having won the confidence of Scoble and other BFASS leaders, proved crucial as the conflict with Rev. William P. Newman followed Henson across the Atlantic. Newman had circulated a letter in England that claimed Henson was a cunning fraud and not a recognized representative of the institute. Newman would also travel to England to continue his campaign against Henson. Beyond the sectarian competition that Henson perceived had motivated Newman, wide ideological divisions and the bitterness of four years of infighting likely contributed to Newman's galvanized opposition. That Henson had been so closely aligned with white abolitionists likely made him suspect in the eyes of Newman, who was skeptical about the motivations of white people who offered support for the abolitionist cause. He had good reason to doubt the sincerity and honesty of some white "allies." A former white AAS colleague of Rev. Hiram Wilson, Isaac Rice had given this view credence in his actions as a missionary for the AAS at Amherstburg. He stood accused of grossly neglecting people entrusted to his care and of stealing donations intended for them. [11]

Scoble invited Newman to bring his complaints about Henson to the BFASS committee overseeing Henson's affairs, and Henson was also invited to answer Newman's charges. At the conclusion of this face-to-face confrontation, committee members exonerated Henson, allowing his first British tour to continue. Henson's British backers had been so confident in him that they invited him to return to England in 1851 and encouraged him in two new projects: the publication of his slave narrative and a display of BAI products at the World's Fair, for which they even offered to pay Henson's passage back to England.

Henson's understanding of himself not as a "poor and lowly refugee" but as an important advocate for his people continued to lead him to work tirelessly to better the lot of other formerly enslaved people not only at the Dawn Settlement but in his previous home near Colchester in Essex County. There, he partnered with Henry Bibb who, together with his wife, Mary, had established Canada's first Black-owned newspaper, *The Voice of the Fugitive*. Bibb along with Henson had organized a Black convention that laid the foundations for what would become the Refugee Home Society. This project was an expansion of the Sandwich (Windsor) Mission organized in 1846 by Rev. Isaac Rice and one Rev. Willis, a Black minister. The Rice mission had been backed by AAS leader Lewis Tappan and Wilson's close friend from Oberlin, Hamilton Hill. The 1850 convention led to the formation of the Benevolent Association, which proposed the expansion of the Sandwich Mission through the purchase of a large block of land in Sandwich and Malden townships. These lands were to be resold, at cost, to newly arrived formerly enslaved people. Essex at this time had been at the front line of anti-slavery activity in Canada West, as one of the main crossings for this influx of formerly enslaved people onto British soil. The Refugee Home Society's backers argued that newly arrived formerly enslaved people needed help in securing land— and that land was essential to their independence and prosperity. It was a noble goal, but the society's efforts were controversial. Henson appears to have been too distracted by his many projects and the conflict at the BAI to remain focused on the project. By 1851 he had already dropped out of the Refugee Home Society's leadership; it was at this time the Bibbs became its main spokespersons and promoted its advancement through the *Voice of the Fugitive* and through their connections to prominent men on both sides of the international border. The Bibbs solicited funds to purchase land despite a rising crescendo of dissenting voices. The project had been controversial from its start. Even prior to the 1850 convention, Wilson had warned his friend Hamilton Hill about it. Yet, by 1852, with Henson no longer listed as an officer, George Cary of the BAI's executive committee joined the Refugee Home Society's board of trustees. His future sister-in-law Mary Ann Shadd, a new and increasingly influential voice in Canada West, however, would become a vocal opponent of both the Bibbs and the Refugee Home Society.

Henson, meanwhile, had turned his attention to planning his second trip to England. Plans for the 1851 World's Fair were particularly extensive. They involved choosing a sampling of BAI-produced walnut boards and shipping them to Boston. There, Henson met a Mr. Chickering, a noted maker of Square Grand Pianos who had received the shipment.[12] Together they chose the four best boards from the lot, and Chickering had them carefully packed for transport to England where Henson met the shipment at a London port. Henson then had the boards milled and polished to such a fine mirror finish that he could see his face in them. Since the boards had been transported to England on an American ship, they had fallen under the jurisdiction of the superintendent of the American department of the World's Fair when they arrived at the Crystal Palace. Henson petitioned to have them removed to the exhibition area representing Canada, but the American superintendent refused. Undeterred, Henson hired a sign painter, who, early one morning, according to Henson's biography, painted large white letters on the tops of the boards proclaiming "This is the product of the industry of a fugitive slave from the United States, whose residence is Dawn, Canada"—which was an effective means of creating a "buzz" around what otherwise might have been an obscure exhibit. The American superintendent became so anxious to have Henson's insult removed that he sent the boards to the Canadian exhibit—without charge. The exchange between Henson and the superintendent had attracted a small amused crowd, inspiring Henson to leave the lettering on the boards. It proved a brilliant marketing strategy as many people paused to read the inscription and wonder at the man who stood by the exhibit, day after day. Even Queen Victoria was among those who asked, "Is he really a fugitive slave?" Her aides assured her that indeed he was.

While Henson's efforts have often been understood as fundraising trips, they also reflect Henson's interest and support of the broader reform efforts of his English benefactor, Lord Shaftesbury—as demonstrated in his support of Shaftesbury's activism on educational reform on behalf of the abjectly poor white residents of London's slums. Henson also continued in an advocacy role, challenging British misinformation about Sunday schools in North America, acts which elevate Henson's activities beyond "begging," and places them more in line with moral reformers like William Whipper who showed a similar disregard for complexional differences in social reform issues. A short distance from the Crystal Palace, large numbers of people lived in abject poverty in London's slums—a consequence of the Industrial Revolution. Henson having seen their plight first-hand, would take a "special interest" in the reform issues of Lord Shaftesbury and others who operated Sunday schools and ragged schools—educational efforts aimed at the poorest of the poor. These reformers believed "ignorance" was a major cause of poverty and crime and sought to bring basic education and spiritual and moral uplift at a time when education was economically out of reach for many. Denominational Sunday schools were set up and offered Bible study, religious catechesis, and basic literacy and numeracy skills before worship services on Sunday mornings—a system which Henson would have found reminiscent of Sunday school efforts by missionaries in Canada West. Those considered too "ragged" (because they lacked sufficient clothing, food, and social graces) to attend these schools would, by 1842, be served by the Field Lane Ragged School. In 1844 Anthony Ashley-Cooper, Seventh Earl of Shaftesbury, had formed the Ragged School Union, which integrated social services with these schools' educational initiatives. These were schools of the street, where volunteer teachers used stables and even railway arches as classrooms in order to educate, feed, house, and clothe slum children, and to provide them with religious and moral instruction. In 1851, Henson spoke to students in the ragged schools and addressed fundraising events of benefit to these schools.[13] On one occasion, while attending a fundraising picnic, he would enlighten guests on America's segregationist practices in its Sunday school system.

Henson's return to Dawn from his 1851 trip to England should have been a moment of triumph. The treasures he brought home with him spoke of the great success he had achieved on behalf of his community. These included the bronze medal prize he had earned for his World's Fair exhibit and a life-size portrait of the Queen and Prince Albert and their family. He also bore the good news that an experienced white professional abolitionist and efficient organizer, Scoble, was coming to the institute and would bring the thousands of dollars Henson had raised to pay off the institute's debts. Instead, Henson's homecoming was marked by tragedy and discord. On discovering his wife, Charlotte, was gravely ill, Henson had closed his London office early and barely made it to her side as she died. In his long absence, sawmill workers had gone unpaid and rioted in protest, tearing down the sawmill he had worked so hard to establish. Newman's continual attempts to discredit Henson had made the British investors wary, and they now insisted that their appointed investigator evaluate the BAI's management and present a plan for future development before releasing the funds Henson had raised.

In the meantime, in England, sixty-year-old Scoble had adopted anti-Garrisonian views—the result of a previous tour to the Tappans' American Anti-Slavery Society—which had proved controversial. Scoble seems to have been ripe for a change of scenery and a direct missionary role in Canada appears to have held appeal. Henson for his part welcomed Scoble's involvement having experienced Scoble, through his two English tours, as an effective administrator. Even Scoble's years of experience in the sometimes-fractious abolitionist community, however, could not have prepared him for the opposition he was about to experience at Dawn.

Henson by this time no longer had the universal support of his community. His activities in England had instilled suspicion. New and influential voices, including that of Mary Ann Shadd would now join Newman, J.C. Brown, and others in their positions regarding the British American Institute's management. Running in the background of these developments was Henson's growing celebrity and the jealousy this sometimes inspired. Prior to his 1849 trip to England, Henson had, like Douglass and Henry Bibb, been encouraged and supported by abolitionists in publishing his slave narrative. Some six thousand slave narratives are estimated to have been printed in the years leading up to the American Civil War; but only about 150 were published in pamphlet or book form. These were important tools for countering pro-slavery propaganda and galvanized the anti-slavery movement. They put a human face on enslaved people, revealed the brutality of slavery, and aroused public sympathies amongst their primarily Christian audiences. They were also often endorsed by prominent white leaders who vouched for their authenticity, thus establishing the credentials of their authors and their fundraising efforts.

In 1849, Henson had dictated his narrative to Samuel A. Eliot, a prominent member of Boston's abolitionist community and supporter of Henson's sawmill building efforts. That year, *The Life of Josiah Henson, Formerly a Slave, Now an Inhabitant of Canada, as Narrated by Himself* was published by Arthur D. Phelps in Boston. It focused on the brutality of Henson's life in slavery, his Christian conversion, his dramatic arrival in Canada, and some details of his early life in freedom. Henson presented as a model representative of enslaved people, and his Christian convictions would have been seen as a powerful argument regarding slavery being an affront not only to man but to God. On its own merits it could have positioned Henson to become a powerful abolitionist speaker on a par with Bibb and Douglass. However, it was Harriet Beecher Stowe's linking of Henson's story to that of her protagonist Uncle Tom that would catapult Henson to fame as "the real Uncle Tom" as promoters sought to cash in on the popularity of Stowe's book for Henson's speaking tours. As deep divisions were opening between ideological rivals at the BAI, the fame Henson was gaining through his fictional counterpart would provide additional fuel for his detractors, who used the comparison of Henson to Tom to label him as a fraud. Tom, they pointed out, had died in slavery while Henson obviously now lived in freedom.

Henson and his supporters would find themselves increasingly isolated as, with the closure of the *Voice of the Fugitive* after a devastating fire and the death of Henry Bibb, they lost an important voice that was sympathetic to their viewpoint. Henson's brief involvement with the Bibbs on the Refugee Home Society, in 1850, had introduced him to a kindred spirit in Henry Bibb,[14] but this alignment had also earned him a powerful adversary in the person of Mary Ann Shadd, the vocal and politically active daughter of A.D. Shadd and owner of the *Provincial Freeman* newspaper—a paper she had founded, in part, in direct opposition to the Bibbs' paper.

The Shadds were descendants of a German Hessian soldier and an African-American woman who had nursed him back to health from injuries he'd received in the French and Indian War (1754–1763).[15] The Black Convention and abolitionist movements the Shadds were involved in had championed women's rights. They raised a strong, intelligent, and independent daughter with a strong Garrisonian viewpoint. Mary Ann Shadd would take uncompromising editorial stances against "begging" and planned colonies—and against the Bibb's Refugee Home Society and the British American Institute School.[16] Ironically, Shadd had first come to Canada as one of the hundred delegates of Bibb and Henson's Canadian convention, and the Bibbs had encouraged her to found a school at Windsor. A feud erupted between Shadd and the Bibbs regarding the school. As long as Bibb was alive, Shadd's views expressed in the *Provincial Freeman* were balanced by Bibb's in his *Voice of the Fugitive*, but with Bibb's death in 1854, Henson and others lost this important influential alternative voice who could tell their side of the story. As Shadd became increasingly involved in the controversy over management of the BAI in this time period, she allied closely with Henson's detractors Newman and Brown, and they, would eventually join Schadd's newspaper staff. Exacerbating this was Mary Ann's active role in chairing meetings that were reported on in her paper. At times this meant Henson's voice and that of his supporters were doubly suppressed—first under Shadd's chairing of meetings, and then in how the views expressed at those meetings were presented—or not presented—in the pages of the *Provincial Freeman*. Henson might have had the confidence of British Lords and famous Black abolitionists, like Douglass, and he may have been riding a rising tide of international notoriety, but at Dawn he found himself on the opposite side of the battle lines that had been drawn by new and powerful players intent on wresting the BAI out of the hands of his ally John Scoble. Henson's alliance with Scoble, a white man who presumed a position of authority over the Black community without their consent, would erode his position as a trusted leader in the community and result in his being marginalized from the work of restoring the BAI to its full potential.

Chapter 7

The REV. JOHN SCOBLE and the DECLINE of the BRITISH AMERICAN INSTITUTE

IN AUGUST 1854, THE REV. JOHN SCOBLE OPENED THE *FREDrick Douglass' Paper* to find a glowing account of the speech he delivered at Dawn's celebration of the anniversary of British Emancipation; Scoble's topic had been the British anti-slavery movement.

Scoble's appearance at Dawn, along with that of Douglass, illustrates the growing importance of the Dawn Settlement as an intersection of abolitionist thought and action that transcended borders—and oceans. As the former secretary of the British and Foreign Anti-Slavery Society, Scoble had played a central role in British anti-slavery efforts, making his appearance at Dawn an especially remarkable event. While he had attained notoriety and skill as a professional abolitionist, however, his presence at Dawn would only inflame the increasingly fractious debate over BAI management. Douglass surely understood the significance of Scoble's arrival at Dawn. On July 31, at Scoble's request, he had left Rochester, New York, by train and travelled nearly three hundred miles to the Dawn Settlement to address the Emancipation Picnic and report on the event for his paper. Douglass's coverage proclaimed Scoble's speech to be "strikingly appropriate" and characterized his remarks as "fluent, exact, rhetorical and sometimes truly eloquent."[1] This is consistent with Scoble's reputation for his powerful oratory skill honed during his career as a professional abolitionist in Britain. That career had also resulted in his involvement in France, the US, and the West Indies.

Scoble was born in Kingsbridge, Devonshire, England, on January 16, 1799. He was an ordained Congregational minister. By 1831 he had become a full-time lecturer for the British Anti-Slavery Society, which would two years later become instrumental in the passing of the *Emancipation Act* in Britain.[2] Scoble's career had also made him an expert on the West Indies, the subject matter of his speech. During his time with the British and Foreign Anti-Slavery Society he had conducted research that had advanced West Indian emancipation—the event that was being celebrated at the Dawn Settlement picnic. In British Guiana, his investigations of the West Indian apprenticeship system uncovered violations of the British *Emancipation Act* that had essentially continued to hold supposed freemen in bondage.

Scoble's influential status even in Canada West is evident in a number of his involvements with BAI leadership long before his arrival in the Dawn Settlement. Henson, like Douglass, had had direct and positive experience of Scoble's abilities through their BFASS-managed English-speaking tours. Fellow white Congregationalist Rev. John Roaf had previously corresponded with Scoble regarding his work to establish an anti-slavery society in Toronto. Rev. Hiram Wilson would receive unsolicited advice from Scoble through Lewis Tappan (by way of Charles Marryatt of London, England) that reflected growing and controversial support of the emigration movement to the West Indies among white abolitionists. While those like Scoble often espoused that enslaved people were "brothers and sisters in chains," it did not follow that they supported integration of formerly enslaved people into white society. Scoble, like others, advocated for the formation of segregated colonies in the American West, Africa, the West Indies, and elsewhere for resettlement of manumitted people. Some couched their support for this "solution" in what they saw as the "problem" of where to settle freed people as a concern for their welfare, arguing that freed people would be better adapted to the warmer climates of tropical nations or that racism would always hold them back within white dominated societies. In 1841 Scoble would advise Marryat (who Lewis Tappan had contacted on Wilson's behalf) to encourage West Indian emigration to Dawn's settlers. Scoble, who had become acquainted with Tappan on a trip to America in 1839, had travelled two years earlier, with the BFASS founder and white Quaker abolitionist Joseph Sturge to the West Indies and along with Sturge had published articles on the apprenticeship system in British Guiana and Jamaica. This first-hand knowledge of the region formed the basis of Scoble's argument, neatly laid out by Marryat's correspondence in headings of "Climate, Soil, and Rates of Wages," that conveyed Scoble's opinions of the superior opportunities the Dawn Settlement's people would find there, including "religious instruction, and political privileges." Rev. Wilson was even offered a monetary incentive of "$30 for each adult and child" he delivered to a ship departing Montreal in the fall. The proposal would have been abhorrent to Rev. Wilson, who practiced, as well as preached, integration, believing it to be the only way to overcome the awful prejudices he regularly witnessed. Wilson never acted on Scoble and Marryat's advice.

Scoble's reputation, as a leading activist who had been involved not only in the abolitionist movement in Britain but in France and the US, gave his advice considerable weight. Yet Scoble's actions in this and other situations earned him a reputation as a racist. At the 1840 World Anti-Slavery Convention in London, England, while sitting for the official portrait of that gathering, Scoble had refused to sit next to the Black West Indian delegate. While to the British investors Scoble may have presented as a well-qualified candidate for the position of BAI manager, for community at Dawn these incidents made Scoble's credentials as a champion for their cause suspect from the outset. Henson, for his part, greeted the news that "the English gentleman" would be coming to Canada with enthusiasm, believing that "he intended to benefit the coloured race and to have a splendid school which would be the pride of the neighbourhood."[3]

In 1851, when Scoble arrived at Dawn, he promised BAI trustees that "the spot could be made the brightest spot in the garden of the Lord, if there were only an efficient manager at its head to control it."[4] Their endorsing Scoble as that "efficient head" had the added enticement of released the $7,000 Henson had raised in England from the hands of the British committee charged with the fund's oversight. In 1852, believing he had local support, funds, and the authority to manage the BAI's affairs, Scoble resigned his post at the British and Foreign Anti-Slavery Society and uprooted himself and his family to resettle at Dawn. On the release of the British funds, he solicited trustee Rev. John Roaf's support, travelling with him to visit the BAI's creditors in Canada West and the US and offering them sixty-three cents of each dollar owed.[5] His travels would lead to his involvement in a meeting of the American Anti-Slavery Society in Windsor in January 1852, which he attended along with the AMA's treasurer Lewis Tappan. The AAS's involvement there led to the firing of Mary Ann Shadd, who had been teaching at Windsor at an AMA-funded school. Scoble's involvement in opposing Shadd, who was becoming a force to be reckoned with in Canada West's community of Black elite, would have direct consequences on his ability to effectively lead the BAI out of its problematic management issues.[6] Once the BAI's debts were resolved, Scoble then unilaterally began reorganizing the BAI, attempting to position himself as its sole trustee. By 1853 Rev. John Roaf, George Johnson, and Peter B. Smith had willingly relinquished their trusteeships, but J.C. Brown had refused. Yet Scoble seems to have proceeded as if he had complete authority, ignoring Brown's legal rights as a trustee. Henson, for his part, remained supportive of Scoble, believing in his abilities and his promises.

In 1853 Scoble would further inflame Newman's opposition to him by ending the Baptists' involvement in the BAI church and school. Scoble had likely retained his dim view of Newman, based on his experience of him in England, and had been further incensed by his impression that the Baptists had inappropriately accepted common school funds from the government while also accepting donations or tuitions, thereby treating the BAI's school as both a common school and a private denominational institution.[7] Scoble then pulled down the BAI's deteriorating school buildings, boasting that he would build even grander structures. However, the British investors informed him they "would not incur any pecuniary risks" on the school's behalf.[8] Essentially, after the Henson-raised funds had been released to relieve the debt, Scoble was on his own regarding funds to rebuild the school's infrastructure and to sustain day-to-day operations. Increasing the BAI's agricultural output would become his strategy to fund the institute, but this plan was ill-conceived and ill-fated. Henson would later describe Scoble as a "theoretical farmer" whose plan involved buying "the most expensive cattle in the market, at fancy prices and without any reference to the fact that he had not sufficient fodder to feed them … He also bought expensive farming utensils to work the farm scientifically."[9] Yet, despite his greater experience as a farmer, Henson trusted Scoble's judgement over his own because "I had a kind of respect for the man that almost amounted to veneration."[10]

Henson's trust was not shared by a large and influential segment of the community. In the absence of results, an organized opposition to Scoble's management grew. the sole remaining trustee, J.C. Brown, and a group of educated and influential freemen now based at the Dawn and Chatham settlements began work to wrest control of the BAI's land from Scoble and place it in the hands of Black citizens. Douglass's 1854 *North Star* account hints at the strife that was already brewing, even in the rosy glow of the Emancipation Day anniversary celebrations. Douglass noted that Brown "seized the opportunity that the occasion afforded to offer some objections to the plans and purpose entertained by Messrs. Scoble, Henson and others as to the future management of the affairs of the Dawn."[11] In Douglass's estimation, Scoble, Henson, George Cary, and others had acted in accordance with the original intent of the BAI's mandate and had so satisfactorily responded to Brown's accusations that all attending "appeared to regard the controversy as terminating most favorably in the interest of Dawn."[12] This was a faulty observation.

Meanwhile, in 1854, Newman had moved to Toronto where Mary Ann Shadd had relocated her formerly Windsor-based *Provincial Freeman* newspaper; by 1855 he would assume duties as the paper's volunteer editor while Mary Ann Shadd would take on the more active role of reporting. In July 1854, at the invitation of Dennis Hill, George Cary, and George Johnson, Shadd had travelled directly to Dawn to investigate allegations that BAI affairs were being poorly managed, and, subsequently, her first issue of the *Provincial Freeman* now relocated to Chatham called for an investigation into the BAI. George Cary, formerly Mary Ann Shadd's adversary in the Refugee Home Society controversy, became a supporter of the Provincial Union, the Toronto organization founded to support Shadd's newspaper. Newman had chaired the Provincial Union's inaugural meeting held in the Sayer Street Chapel in Toronto, J.C. Brown, Dennis Hill, and Peter B. Smith had been named vice-presidents. This powerful coalescing of the Dawn Settlement's

Black leadership would result in Brown becoming well-positioned and supported in his bid to oppose Scoble. In the highly public and protracted battle over the BAI's management that would follow, progress of the Institute's
development would languish and it would fail to fulfill its educational mandate for the next thirteen years.

In August 1855 Brown began organizing opposition to Scoble and his
supporters by calling together the first Dawn Convention. He would invite
delegates to attend from across Canada West. Supporters of Henson and
Scoble were not included, and in their absence "former students and all who
had contributed more than five pounds"[13] appointed a committee to launch
a legal challenge to gain control of the BAI. Scoble, who was preparing to
appoint his own new management committee, was not amused.

Mary Ann Shadd now became an important player in the Dawn Conventions. In contrast to Frederick Douglass's descriptions of Scoble's manner
of speaking, Shadd's paper would characterize his speech on a Dawn Convention held at Chatham as "a long egotistical harangue" and note that he
"thought it an honour (that he would) stoop to even consider our cause as
colored people!"[14] Shadd had taken a severe dislike to Scoble based on principle and personal reasons: Scoble would be one of many white missionaries
she would oppose, believing that they should not presume to speak on behalf
of the Black population in Canada West and convinced that they often were
only in abolitionist work for their own benefit or aggrandizement and often
lined their own pockets on schemes that were purportedly for the benefit of
the formerly enslaved. She also had a personal axe to grind concerning her
belief that Scoble had been responsible, through his relationship with Lewis
Tappan, for her dismissal as a teacher in Windsor.[15]

Scoble for his part expressed contempt for Shadd and her newspaper. In
July 1854 he encouraged people to cancel their subscriptions or risk losing
abolitionist support, saying it was edited by unknown persons of no position—something that deeply offended Shadd.[16] In general, he displayed an
attitude of superiority to people he perceived as lesser, including African-
descent and lower-class white people. This likely exacerbated already tense
relations with the Black community. Scoble's dictatorial style also stood in
sharp contrast to the consultative approach that had been previously taken
by Fuller, which particularly rankled Shadd; after Scoble's objections to the

Dawn Convention taking place in his absence, Shadd's paper reported that he demanded that Dawn's people "consult his Lordship, even as to the propriety of our holding a public meeting to consult about our own interest."[17]

Far from positively influencing the community's perception of Scoble, Henson's defence of him led to suspicions about Henson's own motivations. During Henson's time in England, William Wells Brown, a prominent African-American abolitionist stationed in Michigan, had charged that there was a "secret move... in London [England] to induce our unsuspecting people in Canada to go to the West Indies" perhaps alluding to the scheme promoted by Marryat to Wilson, and named Henson as one of the "agents... already in Canada for that purpose."[18] No evidence was given of Henson's involvement. Henson's continued support of Scoble only made his position within the community more suspect.

Meanwhile, Newman had moved back to the Dawn Settlement, had purchased land there, and had begun to volunteer his time as the *Provincial Freeman*'s editor. Brown similarly had relocated to Chatham and joined Shadd's staff further strengthening the *Provincial Freeman*'s effectiveness as a tool for galvanizing public opinion against Scoble and Henson. When a second Dawn Convention was called in 1855, Shadd chaired the meeting, and was named as an agent in charge of raising funds for a lawsuit to wrest control of the BAI from Scoble.[19] Henson's views and those of his supporters expressed at the Dawn Convention are largely missing from the *Freeman*'s report on the second convention. When Shadd, in her role as chair, failed to allow Henson to speak without interference from the crowd, George Cary—who had worked with Henson on the BAI's executive committee and had supported Bibb's Refugee Home Society—would be the one to call for respect and fairness towards the aging Henson. While Cary had become a Shadd ally, he nevertheless used the same title of respect for Henson that Douglass had used, "Father Henson," and urged others to cease in their booing and hissing. Revs. William Newman and H.J. Young (a Methodist Episcopalian Church elder at Chatham) meanwhile would express views, duly recorded in the *Freeman*, that clearly held Henson in contempt.[20] The meetings, held at Dresden, underscored the community's division of opinion over the BAI's purpose and mandate. Rev. Scoble seems to have adhered to a literal interpretation of the BAI's original deed, which said it was intended for Blacks but also for white and Indigenous people. That Rev. Scoble, an accused racist, should defend James Canning Fuller and Rev. Wilson's non-segregationist vision for the school seems ironic and, to his opposition, unbelievable. J.C. Brown, in the spirit of Fuller and Wilson's original intent, believed the BAI was a Black institution that ought to be directed by the Black community.

Ambiguity around Henson's and Brown's roles seem also to have remained, as Henson's responsibility for the BAI's lands and its sawmill, as assigned to him by the original trustees in 1850, do not appear to have been officially revoked on Scoble's arrival. Neither does it seem that Scoble worked immediately to address the fact that Brown was still legally a trustee, with responsibilities and rights in decision-making. It was 1855 before Scoble sought to clarify Henson's role by naming him as a trustee, along with Nero Harding, a woman whom Shadd would only refer to as "Harding's lady," and two other unnamed men she dismissed as "inferior" candidates. Shadd and Brown proposed more suitable candidates, but they were locked out of the meeting Scoble had called to announce his new trustee appointments. The alternative trustees proposed by Shadd and Brown meanwhile included respected, learned, and well-resourced Black leaders from across Canada West. Rev. Thomas Stringer of Buxton was proposed for the position of chairman. He was an American Methodist Episcopalian (AME) minister and important Black leader in Pennsylvania and Ohio before immigrating to Canada and settling at Buxton.[21] He would head an impressive group of fourteen trustees, including Thomas F. Cary (George Cary's brother and Shadd's future husband) and J.O. Bonner of Toronto; Richard Warren of Hamilton; Henry Gray of St. Catharines; Peter O'Banyoun of Brantford; William Hamilton of London; Rev. J.H. Young and James Hansbrow of Chatham; John Myers of Camden Gore; Joseph Mason of Colchester; Coleman Freeman of Windsor; Robert VanVranken also of Buxton; J.C. Brown of Chatham; and Levi Foster of Amherstburg.[22] The quality of the leadership Brown and Shadd chose is undeniable as, for example, Stringer would later become a US senator, during American Reconstruction. Rev. Scoble barred the Stringer-led trustees from holding meetings at the BAI's property, so they met in a warehouse owned by William Whipper, an elite Black abolitionist who had begun investing in Dresden properties. Their second meeting was held at Rev. Young's church in Chatham—a more central location, accessible by rail. The alternative trustees required funds to follow through on the first Dawn convention's resolution to launch a lawsuit against Rev. Scoble. Mary Ann Shadd was appointed official agent and began travelling far afield to places like Niagara and London to raise funds.[23] Shadd, after several months of effort, however, found the dual responsibility of fundraising for her financially struggling paper and the Dawn alternative trustees to be too much, and asked them to appoint their own agent. It is unclear what became of the funds Mary Ann Shadd raised or what further role, if any the Stringer led trustees had after this point. Henson would claim, in his biography, that it was his personal funds that were used in the financing of the lawsuit that was eventually launched—but not until 1863—after the departure of Shadd from the community. It may be that with no legal means to secure control of the BAI, that the members of the Stringer-led "Dawn Committee" turned their attentions and resources to other issues.

Scoble would continue to operate the BAI into the early 1860s, and while doing so continued to engage in broader abolitionist efforts in Canada West. He played a prominent role in 1860–61 in the celebrated extradition case of John Anderson.[24] His successful efforts in the case, however, failed to convince opponents that he had come to Canada West to serve their interests. Local white residents may have referred to him as the "white negro," but many in the Black community continued to believe he was operating the BAI for his own profit. Henson also remained suspect. "The coloured people began to tell me I was in league with him... gaining pecuniary advantages from the cultivation of that splendid tract of three hundred acres of land," he later wrote.[25] Nine years passed before Henson's loyalty to Scoble would end. In confronting Scoble over the lack of any progress in replacing the school building he had pulled down, Henson was taken aback when Scoble replied, "I did not come here for the coloured people to dictate to me." Henson told Scoble he should leave and let the people of Dawn manage the BAI for themselves. Scoble refused to do so, unless he was paid for his expenses and time in managing the institute.[26] He continued at the BAI, erecting a frame house for his family on its property[27] and making a living through farming its land until 1859, when he left for England and placed his son Thomas Clarkson Scoble (named for the founder of the BFASS) in the paid position of the BAI's agent.[28] Scoble's departure would finally precipitate the legal action that Brown and his allies had wanted, charging him with neglecting his duties as trustee, but ironically the suit would also name Brown as a defendant. The BAI's assets would be tied up in the courts throughout the American Civil War and three years beyond, rendered it incapable of providing either education or infrastructure for the Dawn Settlement throughout the 1850s and 1860s. Yet even as the BAI's development was frozen, the Dawn Settlement would enter one of its more dramatic periods of growth as a group of elite Black freemen began to invest in the Dawn Settlement at the community of Dresden.

Chapter 8

"WHO HAS NOT HEARD *of* WILLIAM WHIPPER?"

Exploring the World of the Black Elite

ONE DAY IN MAY 1852, BUSINESS OWNER WILLIAM WHIPPER made a calm and reasoned appeal to an emotionally fraught meeting of his fellow citizens in Columbia, Pennsylvania. Earlier that day, escaped slave William Smith was apprehended by slave hunters Solomon Snyder and Constable Ridgley on Whipper's sawmill property. In the ensuing struggle, Smith was shot dead. His murderers walked away without consequence. The incident shocked and outraged Columbia's African-descent population, many of whom "were in favour, if again attacked of killing and slaying all within their reach, of setting their own houses on fire, and then going and burning down the town."[1] Whipper, a respected leader, appealed for "peace and patience... for their own sakes as well as the innocent sufferers."[2] Whipper's calm is remarkable given how precarious his own situation had become if slave hunters could now enter the property of an elite and monied freeman and act with impunity. The incident would be one of many in a rising tide of violence in Pennsylvania that continued to impact Whipper's life and that of his family and associates. These incidents ultimately led to their histories becoming intertwined with that of the Dawn Settlement. Whipper's involvement at the Dawn Settlement has not been noted in traditional narratives, despite his deep involvement in Underground Railroad, for two reasons. First, his land investments at Dresden were not discovered in primary records until 2002;[3] and second, the accepted UGRR narratives with the notable exception of William Still's 1871 record often do not elaborate on the intense involvement of a small group of elite Black freemen who were major organizers and funders of escape efforts of enslaved people. The existence of this monied, educated group who owned industries, founded libraries, and engaged in political discussion and acts of resistance to slavery and for the advancement of civil rights is, outside of a few isolated individuals, rarely explored in popular accounts of Black history. At Dawn and other Canadian settlements, however, we can see that they were an important force during the 1850s in not only sending hundreds of fugitives from enslavement north, but in building the infrastructure of settlements like Dawn and in advancing the political and social goals they had first forged in the US Black Convention Movement of the 1830s and '40s. Their presence in Canada West settlements like Dawn inspires an understanding that these communities were not passive termini of the Underground Railroad but important and active intersections of abolitionist thought and action where there was a two-way flow of important people and ideas across the US-Canada border and beyond.

Whipper and his colleagues' appearance at Dresden marks shifting attitudes in the US's Black abolitionist community towards emigration. Whipper and many of his colleagues previously had been averse to growing calls to support emigration schemes aimed at resettling free people of African descent in foreign lands. (For more on the emigration movements see Chapter 13.) Such schemes were conceived by white abolitionists who, despite their views on slavery, would not accept Black people as equals in white society. The violent act on Whipper's sawmill property in 1852 was one of a number of growing incidents of violence that played a large part in changing attitudes of Black abolitionists including Whipper, his family, and other associates on emigration to Canada.

Whipper's home in Columbia, Pennsylvania, was by the early 1800s an important industrial and transportation centre on the Susquehanna River that made it in the late 18th and early 19th an attractive place for settlement in general. By 1820, two large groups of manumitted slaves from Virginia established there, creating businesses and investing in real estate. By the 1830s, Stephen Smith and his partner William Whipper had become the most prominent of the Black elite at Columbia by establishing lumber mills and coal yards and acquiring real estate. Their interests in Columbia went beyond business. By the 1830s, as Columbia supplanted Boston as the main route north to freedom for enslaved people from the US South, the bridge across the Susquehanna River at Columbia became the principal crossing from the slave states of Virginia and Maryland to the free state of Pennsylvania.[4] Between 1847 and 1850, Whipper was the "stationmaster" at the Susquehanna bridge where he welcomed "penniless and hungry" people escaping enslavement. The intensity of activity at the Susquehanna bridge crossing is illustrated in Whipper's report that he had greeted as many as seventy refugees in a single night.[5] Initially, Whipper had preferred to set-tle his "passengers" at Columbia, or among other settlements of African-Americans in the Northern US Here they could easily avoid detection and find employment. Formerly enslaved people became so important to the economy of Columbia that Whipper's main opposition to later moving refugees on to Canada came from freemen whose businesses had come to rely on their labour.[6]

Between 1834 and 1835, Columbia would become a dangerous place, not only for those who had escaped there, but for the Black elite as well, as race riots tore through the community. Angry white mobs who saw Black entrepreneurship as a threat to their own interests torched Black businesses and institutions, including the Smith, Whipper and Co. lumber mills, and Whipper's partner Stephen Smith would be subjected to death threats. As Whipper later reported to William Still, their mills were twice attacked in retaliation because their UGRR activities were known. Whipper, married to Smith's adopted daughter Harriet, had moved from Philadelphia to Columbia and managed the operations at Columbia where he became a major sup-porter of the UGRR, pouring thousands of dollars from his personal finances plus borrowed monies into its operation[7] and becoming "stationmaster" at the Susquehanna crossing. The partners would continue to operate their business interests at Columbia together until 1858.[8] Smith would become a major figure among the Black elite in Philadelphia.

The 1850 *Fugitive Slave Act* had dramatically increased the precariousness of those, like Whipper, who were involved in UGRR work. The 1850 act
strengthened the 1793 *Fugitive Slave Act* to appease slaveholders who were
angered by the increased effectiveness of abolitionists' efforts through UGRR
networks like that of William Still and through the legal actions that fought
the return of slaves to their masters. Southern slave states resented Northern
free states' lack of action in curtailing these efforts and saw it as a direct attack
on their economy and way of life. From the slaveholders' perspective, the
hundred thousand escapees during the antebellum period, out of a total population of nearly four million slaves, represented a major economic loss[9] as
each slave had a market value of $1,000 or more (about $35,000 in today's
currency). Hatred of anti-slavery activists escalated the number and severity of violent incidents. In 1838, angry mobs at Richmond, Virginia, burned
a new Anti-Slavery Society newspaper printed by Episcopal minister Rev.
Nathan Stern. By the 1850s, with western expansion, the debate over which
territories should be admitted to the Union as free states and which as slave
states resulted in unprecedented bloodshed in the Kansas Territory, giving it
the unenviable title of Bloody Kansas. As Southern states threatened seces-
sion from the Union if something was not done to ensure slaveholders' rights,
the 1850 *Fugitive Slave Act* was passed. It introduced stiff jail terms for anyone
providing aid to enslaved people attempting to escape bondage. The new law
terrified many. As Whipper observed, "The stoutest hearts quail before the
unjust sovereignty of the law…The white citizens, fearing the danger of a successful resistance…began to talk of the insecurity of…exiles. The fugitives
themselves, whose faith and hope had been buoyed up by the promises held
up to them of protection, began to be apprehensive of danger, and talked of
leaving [Columbia]."[10]

For free African-Americans involved in the UGRR, the law introduced a
particular precariousness. The same Constable Ridgley who was involved
in the 1852 shooting on Whipper's property had previously been employed
by the Baltimore investigative firm of Hays, Zell and Ridgely to abduct the
freeman Archibald Smith of Harrisburg, Pennsylvania. Plantation owner
Richard Emery had lost several slaves through Smith's efforts and sought
to curtail his activities. Ridgely successfully kidnapped the freeman, and,
under the new law, Smith could no longer appear in court to defend his free

status and was directly sold into slavery. The *Fugitive Slave Act* had effectively become a powerful tool that could be wielded by vindictive slaveholders to silence Black anti-slavery activists.

At Columbia Whipper was part of the highly effective William Still UGRR network, which orchestrated the escape of eight hundred enslaved people to Canada West over a period of fourteen years.[11] The level of activity Whipper and others pursued made them a special threat—and target—of slaveholders.

During their lives, Smith and Whipper had themselves risen out of enslavement to become two of the wealthiest Black men in America in their day, and to be important leaders organizing elite freemen not only in anti-slavery activism but in efforts to secure the rights of freemen and to promote education and spiritual and moral development. Stephen Smith was born October 13, 1789, in Cecile County, Maryland, to parents enslaved by a lumberman, General Thomas Boude. Smith learned the lumbering trade from his father, and when he purchased his freedom at age eighteen he established his mill in Columbia. He subsequently built a business empire that included coal and lumber yards, paper and rolling stock in the Philedelphia & Reading Railroad (one of the earliest railroad lines in the US), and real estate. At age twenty-one, Smith met Richard Allen, founder of the African Methodist Episcopal Church (AMEC) and by age thirty-one, he had become an AMEC minister and a major supporter of Allen's Black Conventions Movement.[12] Whipper had also been born into slavery—the son of a house servant, Nance, who was enslaved to his white father. By the 1820s Whipper was living as a free man in Philadelphia, and by 1834 he had opened a free labour and temperance grocery store. In March 1836, he married Stephen Smith's adopted daughter Harriet.[13] Whipper was educated and used his considerable writing talents to encourage free Blacks (much like the Tappans) to peacefully pursue social reforms through political means. He was also a major promoter of education and self-improvement. He was a member of a Philomathean society also supported by Frederick Douglass and Charles Purvis, to promote literacy and learning, and like many moral reformers embraced the temperance movement. On September 15, 1830, he attended Richard Allen's first Black convention in Philadelphia,[14] where he and other prominent Pennsylvanians like A.D. Shadd (a later resident of Buxton in Canada West) would forge the Black Convention Movement's two main goals: the proliferation of education and the securing of civil rights for freemen.[15] While Whipper was an active part of the Black Convention and Moral Reform Movements, he represented a unique and sometimes alternative voice among his contemporaries in his opposition of creating separate "African" or "Black" institutions. Whipper alternatively promoted the achievement of social reforms for all, Blacks and whites, men and women. He believed that by lifting up disadvantaged white people together with people of African descent that a just society could be more readily realized. Integration, for Whipper, was a means of overcoming racism as it allowed people to intermingle and see each other's humanity. Whipper was an influential leader in the racially integrated American Moral Reform Society and acted as editor of its newspaper, The National Reformer. At twenty-four, he penned "An Address on Non-Resistance to Offensive Aggression," which proposed a peaceful political movement for social change, including the eradication of slavery—views that by the 1850s increasingly contrasted with those of William Garrison and his followers. Believing in the importance of education, Whipper established and supported libraries, reading rooms, and schools. In 1835 the anti-Black riots at Columbia were a setback to this work, as angry mobs burned down his schoolhouses. While, according to William Still, he was no orator, Whipper wrote eloquently and was in demand for drafting resolutions and preparing speeches for others.[16]

Whipper and Smith's UGRR work connected them to other abolitionist leaders, including white Society of Friends (Quaker) activists like James R. Shipley, Lucretia Mott, Dillwyn Parrish, and Charles Litton, and prominent Black abolitionists like Frederick Douglass and William Still. Between 1850 and 1855 Whipper became instrumental in reducing Columbia's free Black population by 456 people, encouraging many to emigrate to Canada.[17] After a trip to Canada in the summer of 1853 to check on the progress of those he sent north, Whipper began investigating the possibility of relocating there himself,[18] and at this time a number of his extended family and business partners began investing in or moving to land along the Sydenham River at Dresden in the heart of the Dawn Settlement. Whipper's involvement in the UGRR came at a time when it had evolved into a more organized and sophisticated network than it had been when Henson had escaped enslavement. The Fugitive Slave Act had necessitated greater speed and secrecy in order to transport people across much greater distances to reach relative safety in Canada. Use of new technologies like the railroad and telegraph aided this work. At Harrisburg, Pennsylvania, another Willliam Still collaborator, Joseph C. Bustill of the Fugitive Aid Society, sent his first group of eight fugitives north by train, and by 1857 use of the actual railroad as a means of transport had become so common that Illinois would pass a bill banning African-descent passengers who could not produce a certificate of freedom. Bustill also regularly utilized the telegraph to alert Still of passengers' arrivals.[19] William Goodrich (or Goodridge) who operated further up the rail line from Whipper, and also became a land investor in the Dawn Settlement, owned railroad passenger cars. His use of these resources and the telegraph in his business affairs likely led to their being adapted to his UGRR work. Smith and Whipper also owned a private railcar which they used for business trips. It was reputed to have secreted UGRR passengers in its hidden compartment. Their shipments of lumber were also said to have hidden people among their cargoes.[20]

By the late 1850s Whipper had become associated with George DeBaptiste, then resident at Detroit, who with others operated a marine link of the Underground Railroad on the Great Lakes.[21] Rail passengers were often routed to Sandusky, Ohio, and in winter had been loaded onto sleighs and taken across to the frozen water of Lake Erie to Pelee Island, near Windsor, Canada West, and during the remainder of the year steamships like the *T. Whitney* provided passage.[22] The *T. Whitney*, is reputed to have been owned by Smith and Whipper[23] and was managed by Black abolitionist and physician Dr. Samuel C. Watson. It transported escaping slaves to Amherstburg via Sandusky, Ohio, and Detroit, Michigan. From there Detroit passengers made their way to Canada West settlements, including Buxton, Chatham, and Dresden, utilizing, by 1850, the Grand Trunk Railway into Chatham and also likely utilizing the shipping lanes from Detroit through Lake St. Clair and into Kent County via its two navigable rivers, the Thames, which led to Chatham, and the Sydenham, which led to the Dawn Settlement—as well as overland routes.

Rising fear and prejudice among white people had made travel an increasingly risky affair even for the Black elite, rendering the development of Black-owned transport and accommodation that much more important in the 1850s. Freeman Peter Gallego was a graduate of King's College, Toronto, when he was "shamefully abused" by a steamer captain on Lake Ontario. The would-be restaurant patron had his chair pulled out from under him and was severely beaten by restaurant staff. Others were routinely forced to relinquish their seats on stages or to ride on top of the coach if white passengers objected to their presence inside. Even Josiah Henson, not normally given to criticisms of race relations, told the *British Banner* in 1852 that it was "the invariable rule to refuse association with the white at the dinner table [or] in the salon of the steam vessel."[24] Most devastating perhaps was a case which Rev. William P. Newman recounted in a letter to Augustus Wattles:

> Mrs. Jackson, a lady of intelligence and piety, was last spring, on her way from Chatham to Detroit. She took passage in the steamer *Brothers* which plies between these places. The weather being cold and stormy, and her health very poor, she went into the cabin and the captain came in immediately, and drove her out, and she had to sit on deck in cold winds, heavy rains and dashing waves from seven o'clock in the morning till late at night. She took cold and, in a few days, was no more. Her physicians say prejudice was the cause of her death.[25]

White people who openly associated with people of African descent were also discriminated against. Captain Walter Eberts' passengers had refused to eat with fellow traveller Rev. Hiram Wilson.[26] John Brown Jr. had been ostracized by white society at Chatham because he had greeted people of African descent as equals and had eaten at their tables.[27] As ever greater numbers of freemen arrived in Canada West, alternative Black-owned networks of transportation and accommodation began to emerge. Lodging had become available at Chatham's Black-owned Villa Mansion and William Whipper, by 1853, had established an inn at Dresden; others, including businessmen Francis Moss Turner,[28] Dennis Hill, the Charity brothers, and James Burns Hollensworth were offering rental accommodations.[29] By 1850 it was possible for William Whipper and Stephen Smith to travel in their personal rail coach on the Grand Trunk Railway to Chatham. Abram Reyno operated a stagecoach service that left Villa Mansion in Chatham at 8 a.m. on Tuesdays, Thursdays, and Saturdays, arriving at the hotel of George C. Blakely at Dresden at 4 p.m..[30]

With the incentive of the *Fugitive Slave Act* and more options for safe travel in Canada West, immigration went from a trickle to a flood with hundreds migrating into the Kent Settlements including Dawn, Chatham, and Buxton. The population and sophistication of the Chatham community soon rivalled that at Columbia.[31] As Whipper, Smith, their families, and colleagues in their convention, abolitionist, and business circles liquidated their assets in the US and moved north, they would frequently settle near one another in their adopted homes. Whipper's ship captain Dr. Watson established a medical practice next door to Mary Ann Shadd's *Provincial Freeman* office in Chatham. Members of the Shadd, Smith, and Whipper families resided at Dresden in configurations that were similar to those they had occupied in Columbia. Mary Smith, for instance, lived next door to William and Harriet Whipper in Columbia, and by the outbreak of the Civil War, when Whipper's wife moved to Dresden, Mary had become the owner of a residential property located kitty-corner from Harriet and across the road from Harriet's niece Sarah Whipper Turner. While George DeBaptiste did not settle here, the closeness of his relationship to the Black elite at Dresden is evident in his appearance as a witness at the baptism of his namesake George DeBaptiste Shadd at its British Colonial Church and School Society mission.[32] All of this suggests that the tight-knit community of abolitionists, bound by family and business ties, remained closely associated as they moved north and continued to work together to build infrastructure to support former Underground Railroad passengers—and their own families and friends. They also continued to work together on the goals they had previously forged within the Black Convention Movement.[33] They would continue their work to realize better education and rights of freemen on both sides of the border—as rights of freemen in the US continued to erode and the equal rights promised under British Law in Canada West remained elusive.

It is unknown how many of the hundreds Whipper sent north became Dawn settlers as a result of his actions. The Bradley/Weems family is one of the few examples of people we can say with any certainty escaped along the Still network to the Dawn Settlement and even then we cannot be sure Whipper or his colleagues at Dresden were involved.[34] Whipper was notoriously quiet and modest and was not forthcoming about his activities. By 1853 however, we can trace the investments and settlement of Whipper and his family and colleagues at Dresden in the Dawn Settlement through land records, census, and a scattering of newspaper reports. These reports at times also tell us of the infrastructure they built and their political activities and debates at Dresden and other Kent Settlements, which escalated throughout the 1850s.

In the summer of 1853, Whipper and Smith first travelled to Chatham and Dresden[35] to investigate their former UGRR passengers' welfare and were "much gratified to find them contented, prosperous and happy"[36] and enjoying a relatively peaceful coexistence with whites compared to Columbia. At Philadelphia, the Black Convention Movement had previously discussed emigration to Canadian settlements but would never fully endorse it. Yet the rising violence in Pennsylvania appears to have made the move to Canada a practical consideration for Whipper and others in order to keep family and UGRR passengers safe from the rising violence and the restrictions increasingly imposed on their freedom in the Northern US through the repealing of voting rights in Pennsylvania and the passing of Black Code Laws.

For Whipper, the Columbia race riots and the murder of his employee Smith at Columbia would not be the only violent incidents that directly impacted his family. Not long after the Smith incident Whipper would prevent wholesale slaughter at Columbia in confronting the desperate people, led by Rev. Dorsey, who had fled their masters in Virginia and found refuge in a house in Columbia where they vowed to not be taken alive. Hearing their plan, Whipper sought a meeting and by 9 p.m. found the men "all armed with deadly weapons, awaiting the approach of the intruders." Whipper believed that "had [the slave hunters] come the whole party would have been massacred." He was advised by Rev. Dorsey that the group were resolved to die together rather than be recaptured. Anxious to avoid bloodshed, Whipper patiently negotiated a complex deal in which he provided Rev. Dorsey with two hundred dollars in gold and assurances he would care for his wife and children in order to convince the party to peacefully return to their masters until such time as arrangements could be made for a better planned escape.[37] It would, however, take another violent incident, the Christiana Resistance in Pennsylvania, before members of Whipper's family would be inspired to emigrate to Canada West.

The Christiana Resistance saw the full force of the *Fugitive Slave Act* brought to bear on those who continued to defy the new law. The key player in the resistance, William Parker, had previously been aided in his escape from enslavement by Whipper's UGRR colleague at York, Pennsylvania, William Goodrich. Parker subsequently began operating an UGRR station at Christiana. On September 11, 1851, he was harbouring four enslaved people who had escaped from the farm of Edward Gorsuch in Maryland. Having been tipped off about their whereabouts, Gorsuch had set off to retrieve them, accompanied by a raiding party and a federal marshal. As Parker reported, "Benjamin Whipper [William's brother]...sounded the alarm that 'the kidnappers were at Whitson's and were taking away the girl'"[38] (the girl presumably being one of Gorsuch's slaves). Dozens of neighbours, both Black and white, rallied to defend Parker and his guests. A violent confrontation ensued. Gorsuch was killed. Forty-one resisters were captured. Thirty-one Blacks and some of their white sympathizers were charged with treason. Having managed to escape Christiana, William Parker turned again to William Goodrich and the Still network to spirit him away to safety. In 1851, Parker and Benjamin Whipper can be found relocated together at Chatham. Others of the Black elite heavily involved in both the UGRR and the Black Convention Movement would also appear in the Kent Settlements, including A.D. Shadd at Buxton. By 1852, Whipper's brother Alfred also is believed to have move briefly to Dawn, to teach at the British American Institute for before moving on to Windsor and Chatham. He would later return to Dawn to be married and to teach at the mission school of the Rev. Thomas Hughes.[39] By 1853 Whipper's sister Mary Ann and her husband, J.B. Hollensworth, had also settled in Dresden along with their children. Whipper's nephew James W. Purnell and his wife Julia (Shadd) Purnell would also relocate here. The movement of the elite freemen north to Canada would be greeted with enthusiasm.

Chapter 9

"*And* STILL THEY COME!"

The Black Elite Migration to Dawn

THE MAIN SEASON OF MIGRATION HAD JUST BEGUN ALONG the Underground Railroad's busiest crossing into Canada at Windsor. Henry Bibb tallied the numbers for a report he planned to run in his and his wife Mary's *Voice of the Fugitive* newspaper. Bibb was encouraged by what he saw. Prior to 1850, an estimated 5,500 people had escaped north to Canada on the UGRR. Between then and the time of Bibb's report, the numbers had increased dramatically, with thousands crossing the border over the decade leading up to the American Civil War. What excited Bibb most was not the "three fugitives a day" he had noted[1] but rather the large "numbers of free colored people...arriving...from Pennsylvania, Maryland, the District of Columbia, Ohio, and Indiana." Bibb noted that "10 passed by Windsor to Chatham on the 7th inst. and 20 on the 8th inst. And the cry is 'still they come!'"[2] It was not just their sheer numbers that excited Bibb but the potential the elite freemen in particular represented. Bibb, himself formerly enslaved, was gratified to see free people "casting their lot in with their fugitive brethren here in Canada." Their presence he believed was needed "to lend a hand to advance our interest and position in Canada," something the Black elite were uniquely positioned to do because of their "opportunities for literacy and pecuniary advantages that our more unfortunate brethren have not."[3] As such Bibb understood that this was not only a migration of people, but of resources.

In the Dawn Settlement area, with the British American Institute in serious decline, the influx of freemen would prove especially timely. Little remained in the way of supportive infrastructure at the BAI. Rev. Scoble had closed down its school, and Henson's once promising sawmill would soon lie in ruins, torn down at the hands of rioting unpaid workers. The power struggle over BAI management was about to tie up its land assets and end any meaningful educational efforts there. A dramatic new initiative would be needed so the Dawn Settlement could provide the educational, business, social, spiritual, and industrial infrastructure needed to support its growing population.

Even when the BAI had been fully functional, growth in the Dawn Settlement's emerging community of Dresden had been slow. In 1846, its infrastructure consisted of only one store and four houses.[4] The Dawn Settlement's population still remained largely rural and was mostly confined to the Township of Camden Gore, where some fifty families of African descent lived among the white population.[5] Resistance to African-descent settlers in the area had risen sharply as their numbers grew, making the Black Convention Movement resolution to secure the rights of freemen as relevant in Canada as it had been in the US The influx of freemen as Bibb reported would bring in "many hundreds of respectable colored persons of comparatively good education and comfortable circumstances ... and but a few wealthy persons" who, Mary Ann Shadd also observed, were "more in numbers than Canadians or foreigners are led to suppose"[6] within various communities in Canada West, including nearby Chatham. Yet, it would not be Chatham or other large centres like Toronto that the Whippers were drawn to but the small rural community of Dresden. Alfred Whipper, William Whipper's brother, would be the first to arrive in Dresden from Pennsylvania.[7] He later moved to Chatham, becoming involved with A.D. Shadd's daughter Mary Ann, after she moved the *Provincial Freeman* there in 1855, and other Black elite there, including Dr. Martin Delany, a man of stature similar to that of Frederick Douglass.[8] Alfred would eventually serve as Delany's secretary.[9] A secondary migration also had begun in the 1850s to the Kent Settlements from Toronto and included not only Mary Ann Shadd Cary but her future brother-in-law George Cary, who settled at Dawn and became a member of BAI's executive committee. In Pennsylvania, the September 15, 1830, convention movement had introduced debate about emigration to Canada. William Whipper had been present at the first Black convention, organized by Richard Allen and Stephen Smith (Whipper's business partner). Many Black abolitionists opposed emigration, including emigration to Canada. William Whipper and A.D. Shadd had both become involved in the second Black convention and the crafting of the movement's two major goals: providing education for the uplift of African-descent people and securing the rights of freemen in the US.[10] Throughout the 1830s, William Whipper as secretary of the American Moral Reform Society would take an anti-emigration position, preferring to shelter his UGRR passengers in Pennsylvania or other Northern US free states, but he had not stood in the way of those pursuing the emigration option.[11] By the 1840s, "enthusiasm for resettlement in Canada was growing even among those who had condemned it,"[12] and by the 1850s, even long-time American Moral Reform Society associate Robert Purvis, who had believed that leaving the US was an abandonment of his brothers and sisters in chains, was contemplating emigration to Canada. By 1852 Mary Ann Shadd had become a fierce proponent of moving to Canada, as expressed in A Plea for Emigration; or Notes of Canada West. Whipper's Reform Society was also shifting its focus from issues affecting free Blacks to eradicating slavery and the welfare of freed slaves, and by March 1855 Shadd's Provincial Freeman[13] would report that even Whipper had "decided to pull up stakes and move to Canada."[14] Two years before, on January 15, 1853, Whipper and his partner Smith had already quietly acquired Lot 1, Concession 6, in Camden Township, from a Robert Parker.[15] The property was located on the main road between Dresden and McGee's Ferry, an important crossing on the Thames, and the property was intersected by a small creek that flowed into the Sydenham River—possibly making it attractive as a potential mill site. It would be Smith's only direct purchase of property in the area.[16] His attentions thereafter seem to have reverted to Philadelphia. Whipper retained a low profile on his trips to Canada, rarely appearing in Shadd's reports. A notable exception is his appearance at a meeting on school segregation at Rev. H.J. Young's church at Chatham. Eight hundred people of African-descent, a quarter to a third of its total population, had settled at Chatham by the mid-1850s. The number of prosperous and elite citizens there gave it the reputation as a Black mecca. But it would be Dresden, about twenty miles to Chatham's north, that would be the focus of Whipper's attention and investment and the location in which a number of his associates and family members also invested—and settled—by 1853. Whipper's passion for education may have attracted his attention to Dresden because of the BAI's presence there. In 1852, when Alfred arrived at Dresden, the BAI was still not seen as a failure. Frederick Douglass's glowing endorsement of the institute in his Emancipation Day article and the arrival of Scoble, who was actively addressing the institute's debt issues, would have raised hopes about its future. Even as Frederick Douglass, in 1854, declared "there has not been at Dawn [Institute], that pulling together on the part of prominent persons there, which was essential to the success of the place,"[17] he had continued to maintain that it was "not an entire failure" as it still boasted a "substantial log schoolhouse, now in pretty good condition, the large sawmill and grist mill, ... and the industrious population in the neighbourhood."[18] These would have been encouraging signs to Whipper that the BAI might yet reach its full potential and position the Dawn Settlement as a major centre of education. Financial backing and leadership by a man of Whipper's stature and resources held the potential to turn the fortunes of the institute around, but for reasons that are not documented Whipper chose to remain uninvolved in the growing efforts to wrest control from Scoble. The high-profile and fractious debate may have simply been anathema to Whipper who had a track record of avoiding conflict and of remaining discreet about his activities, likely to avoid attention being paid to his UGRR activities. In 1857, even with mounting evidence that revival of the "Dawn Institute" was a lost cause, Whipper remained interested in the Dawn *Settlement*, and confident of its economic prospects. In a speech he had prepared—but never gave—for the 1857 Emancipation Day picnic at Dresden, he predicted a "bright and glorious future" for the lands along the Sydenham River. He touted the river's potential as a route to American and European markets via the Great Lakes and the Erie Canal and spoke of the land as "this garden of the West ... a paradisiacal Eden to many a weary traveler"—an allusion to both the agricultural potential of the region[19] and its well-established status as a terminus of the Underground Railroad.[20] He saw Dawn's formerly enslaved settlers not as needy fugitives but as valuable human resources and declared they would become to Canada "what Jesus Christ was to the Christian Church"; the rejected stone that would become the cornerstone of Canada's development.[21] His idyllic view of a new Canadian society where people of African descent were major contributors to the nation's development was not unrealistic given that, by 1857, people of African descent had become a major and still growing segment of the population. At Dresden they owned roughly three-quarters of the community's building lots,[22] and at Chatham they were already becoming major developers of real estate, including more than one multi-storey brick business block.[23] Whipper also appears to have believed in promised equal rights under British Law and that the racial cooperation and moral uplift he championed could be realized in Canada West and that harnessing together what he termed "African genius" and "Anglo-Saxon industry" would create social and economic development.[24]

It would not be Whipper, but his nephew James W. Purnell who would make the first major investment in Dresden land in 1853. Purnell had been one of a number of children the childless William and Harriet Whipper[25] had fostered in their Columbia home, and Purnell had also partnered with Whipper in business.[26] At Dresden, Purnell would become involved with William Goodrich, Absalom Shadd, and Dennis Hill in a partnership that would jointly come to own the majority of properties in Dresden Survey 128, the second phase of development of the Dresden townsite by the white VanAllen family. There were five shares divided by the four partners, with two shares held by Purnell.[27] Before they invested at Dresden, many of the partners had become known to each other in Pennsylvania and some were closely related. Absalom Shadd (1815–1857) was Purnell's father-in-law (re: Julia Shadd Purnell) and half-brother to Pennsylvania Black abolitionist and UGRR operative A.D. Shadd (Mary Ann Shadd's father). Absalom's Haitian-born mother, Amelia,[28] was the second wife of African-American Jeremiah Shadd.[29] Amelia, who would settle in Dresden with her son Absalom, the youngest of her three children, was herself a fascinating historical figure. Born in Saint-Domingue (now Haiti) before Haiti became the first Black republic in the Western Hemisphere as the result of the Haitian slave revolt, Amelia was part of an educated, propertied, French-speaking mixed-race elite. On their expulsion from Haiti, in the wake of the revolution, they settled in the

US, where Amelia opened a food business in Delaware which became highly prosperous.[30] Her son Absalom Shadd was a restaurateur in Washington, DC. His Dresden investment monies likely came from the sale of his Epicurean Eating House, located at the corner of 6th Street and Pennsylvania Avenue, which he had purchased from Edward Snow. Snow, who had served a white upper-class clientele with gourmet menu options,[31] sold to Shadd in the wake of the Snow Riots. Shadd then sold the restaurant in the early 1850s for $25,000 (nearly a million dollars in today's currency), which he invested not only at Dresden but in two farms in Chatham Township.[32] When Absalom Shadd died in June 1857, at age forty-two, William Whipper acquired a number of his Dresden properties.[33]

William Goodrich[34] of York, Pennsylvania, William Whipper's associate in the William Still UGRR network, like Whipper, was biracial and had been enslaved from birth. On attaining his freedom he became a barber, and by 1849, at York, Pennsylvania, he had acquired a warehouse, a retail store, real estate, and paper and rolling stock in the Baltimore and Ohio Railroad. That railway line extended to Lancaster, New York, near the US border with Canada West.[35] Goodrich's life was marked by tragedy, and he lost much of his fortune in later years. He and his brother Maurice married twin sisters, and on their wedding trip the two couples had gone rowing on the Susquehanna River. Their boat capsized. William managed to save his wife, but his brother and new sister-in-law were drowned.[36] Goodrich never moved to Canada. His decision not to relocate may have come out of concern for his absence weakening the Still network's effectiveness. Goodrich's land purchases at Dresden may have been a way to support resettlement efforts of people who had been his "passengers" as having these lands and the infrastructure that others would raise meant they would not have to rely on potentially unsupportive white landowners and service providers.

Dennis Hill is the most mysterious of the partners. He was the first to acquire property at Dresden and would purchase a number of additional properties beyond those he bought through the Purnell partnership. His relationship to the Pennsylvania elite before arriving at Dresden is unknown. Hill was born in Maryland, and his wife, Isabella, twelve years his junior, was born in Kentucky.[37] He was described by abolitionist and the Provincial Freeman newspaper's nominal editor Samuel Ringgold Ward as having been highly educated, but how and where Hill had received his education is unknown, as is the exact date of his arrival in Canada West. Hill's connection to the other partners may have been through participation in the UGRR and/or through the Black elite society in Columbia. One possibility is that he was a relation of an Edward Hill,[38] a thirty-five-year-old gardener, also born in Maryland and who lived in Columbia in the same household as UGRR activist James Loney. [39] The Hills were married in Hamilton County, Ohio, on September 12, 1843,[40] but are not recorded in Kent County until the census of 1861, when they are noted in Camden Township living with Rebecca Hill, nineteen, a labourer; Charles, twelve, a labourer; twin girls Adelena and Amelia, six; and a son, Marcelus, nine. While the exact date of Hill's arrival in Canada is not known, he is recorded as *re-entering* the US from Canada at Niagara on January 4, 1851.[41] His travel at this time may explain why he does not appear in either the 1851 Kent County census or the 1850 or 1851 census records for Columbia, Pennsylvania. Hill's first purchase of Dresden land in 1852 confirms his arrival there that year. By 1853, he would join the Purnell partnership in purchasing nintey-five of the 140 lots in Survey 128. Over the next three years he would acquire other properties alone and with Goodrich, James Burns Hollensworth (William Whipper's brother-in-law), and Francis Moss Turner (husband to Whipper's niece Sarah). Hill's partnership with Hollensworth and Turner resulted in the development of a duplex.[42] In May 1854 he independently purchased farmland at Lot 3, Concession 2, in Camden Gore, and on June 20, 1854, he acquired two part-lots from Whipper and Smith that were subdivided from the property they had purchased in Camden Township. Hill sold the Camden Township land to Absalom Shadd just four months later. He made a similar transaction on May 4, 1954, purchasing Lot 1, Concession 7, in Camden Township, and then flipping it to Absalom Shadd on July 20, 1854. The property Hill held longest was the farm he purchased at Lot 3, Concession 2, Camden Gore (roughly a mile west of the BAI and Dresden). Situated near the river, this land was purchased by Dennis Hill in May 1855. He sold part in 1858, and in October 1860 his wife, Isabella, sold an additional portion. Roland D. Hill (relation to Dennis unknown) retained the remainder until June 1862. Dennis Hill's progression towards being a major landowner paralleled his rising political activism. At the time of his purchase in 1852, he had already joined George Cary in protesting developments at the BAI.[43] In 1853 he would launch a landmark court case on the segregation of the Camden and Zone Common School (See Chapter 12).

The Black elite were likely able to make such large purchases of land at Dresden, at a time when racism was on the rise because of a "perfect storm" of economic factors. By the 1850s, a general economic depression had stalled development of the Dresden townsite. Some Dresden Survey 127 lots that the Van Allen's had previously sold or given to select trades-men in order to spur development had since been abandoned or seized by the sheriff to be sold at auction in order to satisfy creditors. Development of the later Survey 128 had also stalled. Freemen arriving with ready cash from the liquidation of their US properties found that white landowners now only cared about the colour of their money. Still the influx of new Black settlers was not welcomed with open arms by all of their new white neighbours. Edwin Larwill, best known for opposing the Elgin Settlement at Buxton through a race riot he incited at Chatham, would introduce a bill to ban Black immigration during his term in the legislature. Between 1846 and 1865 Larwill owned a large industrial lot in Survey 127 near the Sydenham River.[44] At the time of its purchase, the only Black owned prop-erty at Dresden had been the BAI. In 1852 Dennis Hill bought the lot imme-diately adjacent to Larwill's, and by the 1860s Larwill's property would be surrounded on the south and east by James Aray's ashery, Francis Moss Turner's store, and William Whipper's inn. In 1865, Larwill sold his Dresden land. Others, like white business owners George and Martha Webster, were by contrast noted in the *Provincial Freeman* as "friends," and readers were encouraged to patronize their general store and post office.[45] The widow Martha Webster's second husband, physician Dr. T.R. McInnes, treated both Black and white patients. The Irish-born William Wright, founder of the Fairport survey, forged a longstanding business relationship with Josiah Henson.[46] Wright's son-in-law, Alex Trerice, a Scottish descent entrepre-neur owned business properties with Wright interspersed between those of the Charity brothers on Metcalfe Street, would become heavily involved in the affairs of the BAI (Chapter 15). For Whipper these positive interactions would have provided hope that his vision of an integrated and cooperative society was possible.

Not all those who had settled in Dresden would have origins in Penn-sylvania or obvious links to William Whipper and his associates or family. By the mid-1850s, Virginian brothers James and Cornelius Charity had pur-chased twenty-four lots in Dresden's Survey 128 as well as a large number of Chatham properties. Records from Surry, Virginia, suggest that the Charity brothers were of mixed race, and their status as freemen stretched back mul-tiple generations.[47] The Charity family had lived in Surry County since the early 1600s and been taxpayers since the 1760s. By the 1700s most family members are noted to have been skilled tradespeople, farmers, and entrepre-neurs. From 1803 to 1813, Squire Charity, James and Cornelius's grandfather, had even owned slaves—a practice they later abandoned in favour of hir-ing freemen. The Charity brothers' father, Henry, was married to the weaver Mathilda Banks in December 1813.[48] James Charity was a bootmaker. His Maryland born wife, Rebecca, was an able businesswoman.[49] Cornelius, his brother and frequent partner, was also a bootmaker, and his wife, Martha, also from Maryland, was a skilled shoe binder. In Chatham Cornelius oper-ated a shoe and boot store and owned a substantial number of properties, including a two-storey brick building in Chatham that housed offices for the *Provincial Freeman* and the medical practice of Dr. Watson.[50] In Dresden, the Charity brothers acquired prime river-front lots. Cornelius owned seven; one featured a water-powered corn mill. James established a "crockery store" next to the ferry crossing and owned a rental property across from a river-side dock where their two-masted schooner *The Industry of Detroit* is noted as arriving in 1855.[51] They also purchased two hundred acres of undevel-oped land north of the river. By 1860 they sold most of their Kent County properties, some of which were curiously purchased by two Detroit men of unknown race and the white provincial representative for the area, Archie McKellar (who later became a BAI trustee).

Survey 127 saw more modest investment in single lot purchases by indi-vidual investors. William Whipper's first Dresden purchase would be of a previously developed two-storey inn on Survey 127, which was strategically located across from one of Dresden's six docks. Inns were important for pro-viding accommodation and meals to new arrivals while they investigated real estate opportunities. Whipper also bought a large lot at the intersection of Main, Metcalfe, and Water Streets—the most likely location of his flour mill.[52] He would develop additional properties, including a warehouse and a white pine lumber yard which would be managed by his brother-in-law J.B. Hollensworth.

The grocer Mary Smith bought three residential and commercial lots, in Survey 127 and in the Fairport survey of Irish-born William Wright. In Columbia, Pennsylvania, Mary had lived next door to William Whipper with her twenty-eight-year-old husband, also named Stephen Smith,[53] a "car agent." They were people of mixed race; Stephen born in Pennsylvania and Mary (née Petts) born in Maryland, is believed to have been a widow when she arrived at Dresden in 1853 as she came without her husband and in the company of her youngest son, William. Her eldest son, Stephen G. Smith, remained in the US, where he is said to have become a barbering apprentice to the Lee family who were in-laws of William Whipper's partner Stephen Smith.[54] Steven G. Smith later operated a barber shop with his brother William on Dresden's Main Street. Mary was a woman of some means who owned at least three properties in Survey 127 and a pleasure carriage which she loaned to visiting dignitaries. Also accompanying her to Dresden was a young woman named Harriet, who was not her daughter. This appears to be the Harriet listed in the 1850 Columbia census who lived next door to Mary Smith with the forty-three-year-old William Whipper and his thirty-year-old wife, Harriet. Also living with them at this time was a Sarah Whipper, age ten, who appears to be the Sarah who later married entrepreneur Frances Moss Turner at Dresden. The Turners also owned multiple Survey 127 properties, independently and in partnership with Hollensworth and Hill. The properties of Mary Ann Whipper Hollensworth (William's sister) and her husband, James Burns Hollensworth, and those of James W. and Julia Purnell were confined to Survey 128 and the Hollensworths and Purnells are believed to have resided there, immediately north of the BAI property.[55]

Other people unrelated to the Whippers also purchased in Survey 127. Peter Henson's future wife, Isabella Goings (sometimes written Goins), at age nineteen purchased two lots there.[56] Rev. William P. Newman bought a residential property and the land for the First Regular Baptist Church. Rev. Henson bought two properties, one next door to Whipper's inn.[57] In 1856 and 1857 James Aray, along with his son Dr. Amos Aray, purchased two properties. James established an ashery on one.[58] This is not an exhaustive list of the Survey 127 landowners. Some names, like Mount, Johnson, May, Clemens, and others, need further research to confirm their racial identities.

By 1857 Black investors and businesspeople had made significant contributions to the rise of Dresden through the founding of infrastructure and services. By October 6, 1855, the *Provincial Freeman* would report four sail vessels and one steamer docked at Dresden at one time, and streets thronging with teams. William Whipper had established his warehouse and a flour mill, and J.H. (James) Charity had opened his store. Dr. Amos Aray became the first of two African-descent doctors to establish in the community. Dr. Aray, age twenty-three, is said to have been brought to Dresden by Absalom Shadd to provide medical care for his aging mother, Amelia, but would move to Chatham before Amelia's death. White physician Dr. T.R. McInnes would later attend to her medical needs.[59] Dr. Taylor, another Black doctor, later practiced medicine at Dresden. Dr. Taylor's mother and the mother of Rev. Jennie Johnson, Charlotte Poole, were both midwives and "assisted at the birth of many of Dresden's principal citizens…"[60]

James Burns Hollensworth filled many roles in Dresden, including that of real estate agent, property manager, mill manager, restaurateur, and confectioner. In Survey 127 a Black business district seems to have been concentrated along Main Street, Metcalfe Street, and parts of St. John and Queen Streets that thrived for about a decade then slowly shrank over time, with Hollensworth's ice cream parlour—the "Sweet Briar Cottage"—and the Smith barbershop remaining into the late 1800s. Skilled freemen and formerly enslaved people also filled roles as sailors, teamsters, shopkeepers, and ministers. Others provided labour essential to clearing land, developing property, and operating industries. A number were farmers on the land surrounding Dresden.[61]

This sampling of known people of African descent living in the community at this time demonstrates that their application of their resources, education, and talents were a significant contribution to the early development of the community and represent some "firsts" for Dresden, such as first medical doctor, Dr. Amos Aray; first newspaperman, Rev. Josephus O'Banyoun) and first real estate agent and property manager, J.B. Hollensworth. As we'll see in successive chapters, these early settlers also advanced the community's education, its intellectual discourse, social institutions, and spiritual life.

On a lighter note, they brought some new social aspects to frontier life. The well-to-do Amelia Cisco Shadd (Absalom Shadd's mother) would bring her refined, upper-class, "frenchy and polite"[62] ways to the community, and by Christmas of 1855 holidays would include "several beautiful parties"[63] and small luxuries like confections not normally associated with frontier life.

By 1856 Dresden had become a postal village and its first wooden bridge was built across the Sydenham. Dresden was advancing, and its residents of African descent had made significant contributions to its development. Just as Henry Bibb had hoped, by throwing in their lot with formerly enslaved people the freemen had benefitted their advancement—and that of the Dawn Settlement as a whole.

Chapter 10

The INTELLECTUAL MIGRATION

The Ideas and Ideals of the Black Elite Come to the Dawn Settlement

I
N 1854 MARY ANN HOLLENSWORTH PICKED HER WAY ALONG
the dirt track that was Metcalfe Street, paralleling the Sydenham River
in Dresden. Walking here was a far cry from strolling down the streets of
Philadelphia, where as one of the "Philadelphia Elite"[1] she had enjoyed not
only a more developed landscape but participation within a sophisticated
society where she and other women had been encouraged to join political and moral debate that included conversation around universal suffrage.
These and other social reform and abolitionist issues would, however, not
be left behind, nor would the activism of the Black elite in regard to slavery
and civil rights. And especially in the presence of Mary Ann Hollensworth,
Julia Purnell, and Mary Ann Shadd in the Dawn Settlement we can trace a
migration of attitudes regarding "a woman's place" that would continue to
influence later generations of women in the settlement.

Nineteenth-century Victorian society tended to see a woman's sole
sphere of influence as the home, but among some Black and white abolitionists there was a growing conviction that their wives, sisters, and daughters

had an important contribution to make to the various movements to secure freedom and social advancement. While this was not a universal belief among abolitionists, many, including Mary Ann Hollensworth's brother William Whipper, encouraged women's involvement within the racially integrated American Moral Reform Society. Women joined in the political discussions of other abolitionist groups as well, and in at least one case developed their own female-led organization with at least two Dresden women taking part in their proceedings. Mary Ann Whipper Hollensworth and Julia Shadd Purnell, both Dresden residents by 1853 or '54, had been involved in Pennsylvania with an educated and politically astute group of Quakers and abolitionists who had led efforts to secure universal suffrage. Lucretia Mott, a white Quaker whose husband encouraged her involvement in the abolitionist movement, had been among women who were barred from the Philadelphia Young Men's Anti-Slavery Society in 1836. Mott's response was to form the integrated, female-led Philadelphia Female Abolitionist Society.[2] Mott's group at first worked to secure the vote for free Black men and this naturally evolved into efforts for universal suffrage, in essence launching the early women's movement. In 1837, the Philedelphia Female Abolitionist Society had arranged their own national gathering in New York City, and among its delegates were four members of the female auxiliary of the Vigilance Committee of Philadelphia: Mary Ann Hollensworth, Hannah Purnell, Maria Bustill (Robeson),[3] and Grace Douglass (wife of Frederick Douglass).[4] Relationships between Mott in Pennsylvania and Hollensworth and Purnell at Dresden may have endured as Mott later visited Dresden.[5]

The frontier community of Dresden that Hollensworth and Purnell had settled in by 1854 had offered few opportunities for political discourse, for women or men. Yet, the large migration of freemen to Upper Canada would mean an influx of a diversity of intellectual ideas and the migration of representatives of various movements and causes of the antebellum US north to Canadian Black settlements in search of endorsement, financial aid, and manpower for causes ranging from temperance and abolition to emigration schemes and even armed insurrection. (This theme will be further explored in Chapters 13 and 14 in respect to the emigration movements and the John Brown raid on Harpers Ferry.) The small community of Dresden expanded from a terminus of the Underground Railroad to an intersection of abolitionist thought and action in the wider political landscape of nine-teenth century North America.

In September 1855 the indefatigable Mary Ann Shadd, a product of the progressive attitudes towards women in Philadelphia, came to Dresden. Shadd's *Provincial Freeman* newspaper had become a major influence on the political discourse of the Black community throughout Canada West. On arriving at Dresden, Shadd noted the community's advancement in the "industry and progress [that] mark every foot-print made by our people."[6] She continued to watch Dresden's progress with interest and by 1854 enthusiastically noted the imminent arrival of "literary characters" who were activists and writers like herself. That year the thirty-one-year-old William Howard Day, a prominent Ohio newspaperman, activist, and politician,[7] visited Dresden. It was not his first introduction to the Dawn Settlement. During his years as a student of Oberlin University in Ohio, between 1842 to 1847, he had tutored students at Dawn during his summer breaks.[8] By 1855, Shadd announced Day was on his way to Dawn, and by February 1856 he had purchased property at Lot 3, Concession 5 of Camden Gore, just east of the Fairport survey.[9] His purchase of a small Camden Gore farm is puzzling, given he had been more adept with the pen than the plow. However, Shadd, Bibb, Brown, Henson, and others had long promoted land ownership as a pathway to independence. Day had been editor of the *Cleveland True Democrat* (1851 to 1853) and publishing his own weekly newspaper, the *Aliened American* (1853 to 1854), and on its failure had founded, the *People's Exposition* in 1855. This, too, ceased publication, and an ill and demoralized Day had then left Ohio to live at Dawn. His farming career here ended even before the first harvest was over. In truth, he had never truly quit his life as a writer and activist, and at Dresden and Chatham he had readily found issues that invited the application of his "balanced and ready pen."[10] At Chatham Day became involved in the school segregation issue, naming it a contravention of the laws of the province. His presentation of this view to Chatham's town council was ignored. The conditions of Black sailors and boatmen, whom he would have encountered in both Dresden and Chatham, inspired Day to champion reform on lake- and ocean-going vessels. Day became a close ally of Mary Ann Shadd and would join Alfred Whipper, Dr. Martin Delany's secretary, in the 1858 National Emigration convention at Chatham and become an important player in John Brown's "quiet conventions" at Chatham,[11] where the famous raid on the arsenal at Harpers Ferry, Virginia, was organized. By 1859 Day would become a teacher at the Elgin Settlement school, and in 1860 he accompanied Rev. William King to Britain, returning not to Chatham but to the US.[12]

Day and Shadd were not the only newspaper editors to take an interest in Dresden. In 1865 Rev. Josephus O'Banyoun, a Black United Empire Loyalist and the general book steward for the British Methodist Episcopal Church, established Dresden's first newspaper, the *Missionary Messenger*.[13] Subscriptions were seventy-five cents annually for the monthly single-sheet publication. Despite its modest size, it could be found on the exchange lists of major mission publications in the US, such as Philadelphia's *Christian Recorder*.[14] Like Day, O'Banyoun stayed in Dresden only briefly. By June 1866 the paper had folded and O'Banyoun had left for Windsor.[15]

Famous abolitionist speakers who had previously passed through the Dawn Settlement demonstrate Dawn's influence in the development of their talents which they gave back to the wider abolitionist community. In September 1844 Lewis Hayden, who had been enslaved from his birth in 1811 in Lexington, Kentucky, escaped with his wife and son to the Dawn Settlement through the efforts of white abolitionists Rev. Calvin Fairbank and Delia Webster, who were imprisoned for their efforts. When the Haydens arrived safely in the winter of 1844–1845, Lewis attended the British American Institute's school. He would become a noted anti-slavery lecturer for the American Anti-Slavery Society, working out of Boston, and he was active in the UGRR network. Like Day, Lewis also supported John Brown, and when the American Civil War broke out, he formed one of the first Black regiments in the US Army, the 54th Massachusetts Infantry.

Parker T. Smith of the Banneker Institute arrived at Dresden during the American Civil War with a passion for personal improvement and intellectual discourse that he attempted to introduce to the community through Rev. Thomas Hughes's mission church.[16] He left ten months later, changed by his Dawn Settlement experience from a man who merely discussed ideas to one who put those ideas into action for the benefit of his fellow man.[17] While such luminaries quickly passed through the intellectual landscape of Dawn, others had a more lasting impact on the community, contributing to its development as missionaries, teachers, ministers, and organizers of social institutions and mutual aid groups like the Prince Hall Masons Mount Moriah Lodge. Churches and other institutions became important meeting venues for visiting speakers that invited Dawn's people into the wider discourse on issues and to support causes. Visitors recognized the communities of Canada West with populations of Black elite as fertile ground for soliciting funds and saw their populations as potential recruits in the more literal fight for freedom, as in John Brown's appeals in his conventions at Chatham to organize his raid on Harpers Ferry.

In respect to the churches, those like Hughes's mission would promote intellectual debate through contributions of parishioners like Parker T. Smith and Hughes's own erudite style of preaching. Beyond this, missions and churches would foster the all-important educational work set out as a goal of the Black Convention Movement by way of supporting literacy and social advancement through the promotion of moral uplift.

Chapter 11

"I NEVER SEEN GREATER MINDS *to* LEARN"

Dawn's Missionary Influence

I N 1858, REV. LEWIS CHAMPION (L.C.) CHAMBERS LOOKED with satisfaction at the small farm he'd purchased just east of Dresden, along Camden Gore's fifth concession, and where he'd just settled his family including his wife, Ann Maria, a son, three daughters, his aged mother, and other extended family members. It was not the acquisition of the farm's rich land that pleased him so much as the knowledge that he had arrived in the heart of a rich field for ministry to formerly enslaved people in the Dawn Settlement. To Chambers's disappointment, however, in the months that followed, he would find himself with only the gleanings as the harvest had already been long underway and the area crowded with many other mission efforts. At the time of Chambers's arrival, two hundred people of African descent were estimated to be living in the community of Dresden, with seven hundred in the immediate three-mile area around it, and a total of some fifteen hundred in the immediate area beyond this. This concentration had made the Dawn Settlement a magnet for missionary societies. As Chambers reported to his supervisor George Whipple at the American Missionary

Association (AMA), over a dozen missionaries were providing services in the immediate area in and around Dresden, forcing him to take up ministry to the poor, marginalized, and more isolated pockets of settlement that existed in far flung locations from Euphemia Township in south Lambton County to Botany in central Kent County. Struggling along muddy tracks of primitive roads on foot to mission sites that were as much as twenty miles apart and attempting to serve these multiple sites simultaneously often took Chambers away from his family for as long as three weeks at a time. It was a challenging field of ministry and one that he would not remain in long. Barely two years after arriving he would sell his property in Camden Gore and leave for Ingersoll and London, Ontario, where settlers reported not having seen a minister for over three years. Chambers would, in his short time in the heart of the Dawn Settlement, minister to some of the most isolated and poorest of the late arrivals from the Underground Railroad who continued to flood into the area in the years leading up to the American Civil War.

Rev. L.C. Chambers had first arrived in Canada West in 1854 and became involved in Bishop Willis Nazrey's British Methodist Episcopalian Church (BMEC). Chambers was initially introduced to the BMEC at Dresden as a deacon who was "limited to preaching and ministering to Sabbath schools as needed."[1] Not having received a permanent position with the BMEC, in 1857 he applied to the American Missionary Association. The AMA had been formed on September 4, 1846, to provide outreach to people of African descent, Indigenous people, and poor white Americans and operated eight foreign missions, including their Canada Mission sites. George Whipple was in charge of the organization's foreign missions, and in the short period from January 1859 to September of 1860 Chambers would write thirty-three letters from his home in Camden Gore to Whipple in New York reporting on his work. He almost immediately pointed out the presence of some fourteen other missionaries from various denominations and associations who were already providing similar services of teaching and preaching. At least two of these missionaries owned properties within a mile of Chambers: Rev. William Clarke, a white Congregationalist who had been previously known to Chambers had established near Dresden over a decade earlier, and Rev. Thomas Hughes, the white minister of the British Colonial Church and School Society's mission, had arrived in 1858 and purchased property that bordered Chambers' small farm to the southwest. Among the other fourteen ministers of the Christian Gospel were twelve people of African descent and one additional white minister who represented a variety of different missionary organizations or church denominations.[2] This eclectic group of missionaries and teachers had amply filled the void left by the closure of the British American Institute's church and school in 1853. Some of the missions, including that of Chambers, would provide outreach to white people as well, attesting to the general lack of education and church services in the region. While ministers like Hughes would find resistance to integrated worship and education at Dresden, Chambers, who ministered in more remote areas did not. As he testified in his letter of March 19, 1858, "I walked ten miles and preached to a crowded house of both black and white people."[3] where his white congregants revealed they had not heard the Gospel preached in over three years. Chambers addressed gatherings of up to two hundred people held in the woods at Botany in Howard Township. These gatherings, like the Dresden Campground meetings of a generation before, also attracted a mixture of races. Ministering to white people was not officially part of the BMEC's mandate, however, and Chambers had aspired to minister exclusively to the formerly enslaved.

Missionaries like Chambers served by preaching at religious services, performing baptisms and marriages, visiting the sick, and burying the dead. Education and literacy were primary concerns with deacons and others teaching basic literacy and numeracy skills at Sabbath Schools. Learning to read and write was seen as integral to spreading the Gospel, giving people as it did the ability to personally access the Bible and other books that encouraged spiritual and moral advancement. Literacy also provided obvious temporal benefits. Additionally, missionaries funnelled their sponsoring organizations' charity through their outreach sites, providing the less resourced people in their congregations with clothing and sometimes even food.

Dresden provided a base of operations for many missionaries and offered the advantages of support from an established community and facilities to those mission groups who did not own church or school buildings. The Dawn Settlement area's large population included many formerly enslaved people who had been denied the right to learn to read and write and who, as Rev. Chambers letters attest, had not always been encouraged to adopt

Christian lifestyles and morals by their enslavers. Local white residents were critical of those who were considered lax in their moral standards and this made them "a feared people."[4] Chambers impressed this point on his sponsors to solicit funds, pointing out that "those who have the heart to do it [elevate themselves]" could succeed with assistance from the teachers and preachers of the missions, and that they were worthy of such support. "I never seen greater minds to learn. I know what our people want in Canada good men to preach Christ in life, in work and conduct. I pray that I may be a good man," he wrote.

Reports of missionaries to their sponsoring organizations are a rich well of information about conditions of the ordinary people of the Dawn Settlement area and a stark reminder that not everyone there was as fortunate as the elite freemen. Some who had only recently escaped enslavement found themselves in precarious situations eking out livings on what Chambers referred to as "wild lands" that they did not own.[5] Chambers also observed that the behaviours born of the degradation of slavery that made white neighbours fear some new arrivals, also presented challenges to missionaries. Marital infidelity particularly troubled Chambers and a lack of social graces he observed prevented some from advancing themselves. Yet, two of Rev. Chambers's letters give long inventories of many others' whose accomplishments included impressive figures regarding the agricultural production of their farms. Chambers's letters also showed that even the most ambitious who toiled arduously on their farms could suffer setbacks that were beyond their control and could lead to extreme want. His missives between January and August of 1859 regularly tell of the widespread hardship brought on by three years of frosts. As Chambers reported to George Whipple on September 9, 1859, frosts on the August 28 and September 4 in Chatham Township, killed off buckwheat, potatoes, and corn, leaving only a third of the crop for harvest. Chambers concluded that famine was imminent. "Some persons do not want it to be naming those times is so hard ... but it is some bad frost every month this summer so far and I will say more to you. There is not a farmer that has a crop of wheat. The number of bushels among the farms is 10, 18, 20, 30, 40, 60, 70, 80 but who has raised a hundred? I do not know. Well, what the poor will do, I do not know."[6] Additional comments by Chamber in his letter reflects the political sensitivity around the reporting of such events. Earlier, Rev. William P. Newman, who had long been an anti-begging advocate, had himself reported the Chatham Township famine and begged for assistance, but had been greatly criticized in the abolitionist press for doing so. Reporting that former slaves were starving in Canada was seen as strengthening the view of American slaveholders who maintained that their slaves would not be able to fend for themselves if freed. Chambers reporting of the same famine was kept discretely between himself and his AAS sponsors.

The sheer numbers of missionaries at work in the Dawn Settlement and their reporting to separate organizations is striking evidence that the BAI was not responsible for management of missionary activity in the settlement as historians like William and Jane Pease proposed.[7] Quite the contrary, many of the independent missions established in the Dawn Settlement at Dresden operated in a time when the BAI no longer functioned. These independent missions extended services across a wide region. Chambers and Hughes similarly served multiple mission sites in Chatham Township, Thamesville, and McGee's Ferry. Additionally, Rev. Chambers often ventured into remote areas, providing services to landless settlers well south and north of Dresden. Annual reports, correspondence, and session records provided to sponsoring groups of missionaries such as those written by Rev. Thomas Hughes to the British Colonial Church and School Society, by Rev. L.C. Chambers to the AAS, by Rev. John Roaf to the Congregational Union in Britain, and by various other agents to the Baptist Free Mission Society and others provide rich and diverse insights into the daily challenges of this mission work. A few examples of the better documented missions are reviewed below.

First Regular Baptist Church

When Revs. William P. Newman and Samuel Henry Davis were evicted from the BAI by Rev. John Scoble in 1853, they continued to provide a Baptist outreach in private homes.[8] In 1857, a substantial frame Baptist church was erected just over the BAI's property line, on Queen Street in Dresden's Survey 127. The First Regular Baptist Church's building lot was purchased with funds Rev. Newman raised through the Baptist Free Mission Society and appeals he published in the *Provincial Freeman*. Rev. Davis contributed to the church's construction by selling one hundred cords of wood cut from his farm property's rich stand of timber and with additional proceeds from cordwood sales financing the sawing of timber into building materials. It took four years to complete the new building.[9]

Even after First Regular Baptist Church had been constructed, Newman would continue to solicit funds from his mission association and through the *Provincial Freeman*. He maintained in these appeals that his congregation were too few and poor to provide for their own needs—an ironic appeal considering that the *Provincial Freeman* had earlier vehemently attacked others' begging.

The Baptists at Dawn had originally been part of the Canadian Anti-Slavery Baptist Association, which supported a mission area that included Dawn, Chatham, Buxton, Colchester, London, Mount Pleasant, and Detroit, Michigan. Reports of the third annual meeting of the association, on September 2 and 3, 1853,[10] show that the Queen Street church had twenty-one members. By 1857 the construction of the new church had attracted an additional twenty-three members, and by 1858 it had swelled to ninety. That year, Newman resigned as pastor and accepted a post in the US. Davis, now forty-nine, became First Regular's minister. He had been a church elder, and an able and much beloved pastor qualified to both teach and preach through the education he had acquired at Oberlin, Ohio. He had been well attuned to the problems of formerly enslaved people as his previous ministry had been with Detroit's Second Baptist Church, an important station in the Michigan Underground Railroad. In temperament, Davis differed from the fiery Newman. Said to be quiet and easy-going, slow to anger, yet a powerful orator, Davis "commanded [the] respect of his congregation and his Baptist associates."[11] Under his leadership, membership at the First Regular Baptist Church grew to 116 members. On his retirement in 1881, Davis was recognized as "our advisor always, in matters of great consequence," indicating that he had been greatly involved in the day-to-day lives of his congregation, beyond his spiritual and teaching roles.[1213]

First Regular Baptist Church was important for the spin-off congregations that developed from it in neighbouring Chatham Township. Rev. Samuel Lynn, originally a Presbyterian minister from Pennsylvania, had been an elder in Davis's Dresden church. Lynn would go on to establish the Union Baptist Church along Chatham Township's Concession 11. That church appears to have taken on service of an area previously ministered to by Hughes and Chambers. Lynn also owned land in McGee's Ferry (Kent Bridge) in Camden Township where Chambers and Hughes had also been active. Beyond his land ownership there, nothing is currently known about Lynn's involvement in that community.

A young woman's involvement in Lynn's Union Baptist Church and her early formation in Hughes's Dresden mission would give rise to her astonishing career as Canada's first ordained female minister of the Gospel and the creation of yet another Chatham Township church on Concession 11. Rev. Jennie Johnson, then only 16, delivered her first public sermon in School House No. 18, where Lynn's Chatham Township Baptist congregation met. Through preaching missions to young people, Johnson drew a number of new converts to Lynn's church. On October 16, 1909, she became the first ordained woman minister in Canada and established the Prince Albert Baptist Church.[14]

Rev. Jennie Johnson stands with her Prince Albert Baptist Church at its dedication. *(Photo courtesy of the Thompson/Guest family)*

Christ Church (Anglican)

In 1857, the same year the First Regular Baptist Church was built, Rev. Thomas Hughes arrived in Dresden along with mission teacher Jemima Williams. Hughes's mid-life calling and subsequent emigration from England to the Dawn Settlement speaks to his powerful conversion regarding anti-slavery issues and personal spirituality. Hughes was already married, the father of four children, aged eleven, nine, six, and two (a fifth child would arrive in 1860), and was responsible for the care of an aged mother when he left a well-established career in teaching at a private boys' school in England to pursue mission work in Canada West. Reading reports of those who had escaped enslavement and now resided in Canada had deeply moved Hughes. These accounts, which included appeals of reformers like Lord Shaftesbury, advanced in him a vision of elevating former slaves through education and religion in order that they could "walk like Christian men in the light of the Gospel."[15] Having resolved to take personal action, Hughes offered his services to the British Colonial Church and School Society as a teacher, and on arrival at Dresden he had sought full ordination as an Anglican priest under Bishop Hellmuth of the Diocese of Huron.

Church of England clergy in Canada West, in general, appear to have embraced integration of their churches and schools. As Rev. John Gamble Geddes of Hamilton observed, "There are several coloured people belonging to my church and I have them also in the Sunday School … (where) two young coloured women … teach white children of respectable parents."[16] Throughout his time in Dresden, Hughes earnestly sought to ensure that there be "no separate pew among us."[17] It was a vision he would never fully realize in his lifetime.

Hughes arrived in London, Ontario, in 1858, and by 1859, the year of his ordination, he established his mission at Dresden. On arrival Hughes approached the Camden and Zone Common School Board asking to use their schoolhouse for services and classes. He was refused. Hughes briefly held services in private homes until Mary Smith offered him the top floor of her grocery store on the town's Main Street—a location Hughes affectionately referred to as his Upper Room School, an allusion to the location of the Last Supper.[18] It was not until 1867, a full decade after Hughes's arrival, that he began building Christ Church on St. George Street in Dresden. Constructed one block west of the Baptist church, and just outside the boundary of the BAI, it was built with timbers cut from Hughes's farm property on the Concession Five and its bricks were "hand-made from the clay on his riverbank holding."[19] Hughes's congregants provided the carpentry and bricklaying skills. While the cornerstone of the church was laid on June 6, 1867, the church would not be completed until the fall of 1871 Hughes like Chambers had come late to mission work in Dawn, having arrived on the eve of the American Civil War. Yet, this was a time when Hughes's strong voice against segregation was dearly needed to decry the rise in prejudicial treatment that had barred a rising number of people of African descent from full participation in society. Hughes clung to the Biblical imperative that "ye are all one in Christ," and he prayed that local people would cease to "fall in with those prejudices [of society in the US] ... and even carry them to a more disagreeable extent than the native-born Americans."[20] Instilling more enlightened attitudes was an uphill battle. Only one other white family besides his own attended Hughes's new church and sent their daughter to his Sunday school. After being barred from the common school, Hughes also experienced resistance when he sought to purchase a lot to build his church.

Another tragedy impeded Hughes's early mission work. Jemima Williams, the teacher who had accompanied him from London, Ontario, died in Dresden in January 1860, at age twenty-nine.[21] Hughes petitioned to have Alfred Whipper, Williams's brother, who had been teaching in Windsor, come to the mission school to take Williams's place. Other teachers from the West Indies and Pennsylvania, including Aaron Highgate, would later teach at Hughes's school. Highgate would teach there from 1868, until the school's closure two years later. Hughes's personal pastoral efforts would continue beyond that year as would his reports to his British sponsors.

Hughes's preaching style was cerebral and erudite. The Black elite, in particular, seem to have appreciated his preaching and teaching style and likely found the church's theology closer to that of the Episcopal faith they had adhered to in Pennsylvania. Hughes's early church records are filled with the names of many of the Pennsylvanian freemen who relocated to Dresden, including the extended families of the Whippers, Smiths, and Shadds. James Whipper Purnell and William Whipper appear to have owned at least part of the property the church would finally be built on,[22] and James Burns

Hollensworth, Whipper's brother-in-law, and J.H. Hall, a relation of the Shadd family, both Hollensworth and Hall appear as witnesses on church land transfer deeds. Hollensworth had also been the church's lay rector, and Alfred Whipper, as previously noted, had taught at the mission school and would be married in the church.[23] Hughes made at least one pastoral visit to Absalom Shadd's mother, Amelia, and when she died, had officiated at her funeral.[24] The weddings, baptisms, and funerals of the Pennsylvania elite freemen at Hughes' mission attracted important visitors from their extended network of US business and Underground Railroad networks, including George DeBaptiste, the "president" of the Michigan UGRR. DeBaptiste appears at Hughes's Dresden mission attending the baptism of a namesake child, George DeBaptiste Shadd. During the American Civil War, Hughes' reputation drew the writer and lecturer Parker T. Smith of Philadelphia, who settled for ten months in Dresden and became part of Hughes's church. Smith was a member of the Banneker Institute, a literary and debating society in Pennsylvania. He sent frequent letters and reports back to friends and to the *Christian Recorder* newspaper, one of which lauded Hughes's mission and his preaching.[25]

Hughes had high personal standards of morality and service and expected the same from others in leadership roles. In his scathing first entry of what survives of his diary, Hughes criticized the teaching and preaching style of some Black ministers who, to him, seemed too visceral in their delivery and insufficiently informed by scripture. Unlike Rev. John Scoble, however, Hughes did not seem to labour under a sense of superiority in respect to race or class and just as openly criticized white ministers for their unchristian attitudes. He also opposed white public officials whom he judged deficient in their roles or who operated in a manner that was less than principled. His criticisms sometimes went beyond pointed words, privately expressed in his diary, to direct opposition. He once travelled to Chatham to testify against Dresden's white justice of the peace Alexander Trerice in a court case involving one of his parishioners. Hughes had been no less hard on himself. Despite social ostracization, physical hardship, and disappointment, he maintained a continual presence in attending to the sick and dying and others in need.[26] Not even the deplorable roads that, at one point, broke his buggy axle, nor fear for his health during a cholera epidemic that took the life of Rev. Isaac Henson and caused Rev. Josiah Henson to fall seriously ill, prevented Hughes from making his rounds. In addition to his church at Dresden, he would provide outreach at Dawn Mills, Thamesville, McGee's Ferry, and Chatham Township's concession Eleven and build modest but enduring church structures at Dresden, Dawn Mills, and Thamesville.[27]

Hughes's work was often hindered not only by white prejudice but also by the distrust of Blacks who could not accept that a white man was involved with them for reasons other than his own aggrandizement or profit. He was sometimes frustrated by the lack of support he received from the very people he sought to help. His reports to Britain lamented that his efforts to provide education for children were being hampered by their parents' reluctance to pay school fees.[28] In Dawn Mills and Dresden, Hughes was obliged to continue holding separate services for white and Black church members, serving both communities equally. As such, one of Hughes's diary entries—about a funeral at Dawn Mills—is particularly poignant. He noted that while the white community had been resistant to holding integrated services, racial divisions were abandoned when the Cross family's son died. The whole community came together to bury him.

In 1875 Hughes died and was succeeded by a Rev. Beaumont who would describe his church as "the only hope for the coloured people," as other white established houses of worship in Dresden continued to bar entry of people of African descent.[29] It was an exaggerated claim, considering other mission churches like those of the Baptists and BME continued to operate in Dresden and had begun to absorb many of the Anglican Church's Black congregants. The mission declined over time as well because British donors were less inclined to give to missions of the formerly enslaved after the end of American Civil War as with the Emancipation Proclamation the abolitionist cause was considered completed and support no longer needed. By 1879, Beaumont was succeeded, in an ironic twist, by Rev. E.W. Murray, the son of a slaveholder said to have been ruined by the Emancipation Proclamation. Murray served from 1879 to 1881,[30] during which time support for the mission fell off, even though the "numbers, position, circumstances and prospects of the Negroes in British North America had not been materially affected by the American Civil War. [And t]hey were still as numerous, as poor, as much a separate people as before."[31] Dresden's people of African descent also still comprised as much as one-fifth to one-quarter of the settlement's overall population. And yet, by 1876 with Rev. Murray's departure, the flow of grant money from the British Colonial Church and School Society ended altogether.

By 1882, Hughes's vision of "no separate pew" was finally realized; however, the much-diminished Christ Church congregation of fifty-seven families included only seven families of African descent who now attended integrated services.[32] During its years of operation the church Hughes had founded had invested roughly $62,000 (equivalent to approximately $1,324,00 in today's currency) in mission work to the people of the Dawn Settlement and surrounding areas.[33]

The Congregationalists

The Congregationalist Church in Dresden predated the Baptist and Anglican presence in the Dawn Settlement. They erected the first building in the settlement outside the BAI to be exclusively designed as a house of worship. The Congregational Union of England sent its first missionary, Rev. William Clarke, to London, Canada West, in 1837. By the mid-1840s Rev. John Roaf, who had developed a thriving independent church in Toronto and in 1831 had been named a BAI trustee, had become a valuable agent of the mission and had sent regular reports back to England of the Congregationalists' activities in Canada West. In 1846, in the Congregational Union's tenth annual report, he cautioned organizers about the hardship of mission life: "Your agents must be robust men, equally in physical, mental and religious strength. They must labour much, endure much and sacrifice much."

By 1841, in his capacity as British American Institute trustee, Roaf had met the BAI's Congregational co-founder Rev. Hiram Wilson, and by 1845 Roaf had included Wilson's BAI activities in his reports. Wilson may have been one of the six missionaries of the Home Missionary Society that Roaf had established and whose missions he assisted from Toronto. It was perhaps Wilson's departure from Dawn that inspired Roaf to secure the services of Rev. William Clarke, the most senior Congregationalist missionary in Canada West, to provide a continued Congregationalist presence here. Clarke had first come to London, Canada West, in 1837; exactly when he first arrived in Dresden is unclear. According to Samuel Ringgold Ward a Rev. Clarke had been preaching "in a schoolhouse in Dresden Village" before 1852. In May 1854 land records show Rev. Clarke Sr. purchased his farm situated a concession over from the Fairport survey, from former slave and now free landowner William Bradley. Bradley's daughter Maria Weems (or Wiems) is famous for having disguised herself as a boy to escape slavery along the William Still UGRR network.[34] By 1862 Clarke had expanded his holdings by purchasing a neighbouring lot to his original forty acres,[35] and with his three sons cleared the farm's forty acres of bush. His son William Fletcher Clarke would also pursue a career as a minister and in 1844 would become one of the first to be ordained at the new Congregational Academy in Toronto.[36] The movements of Rev. William F. Clarke and his father become difficult to separate after this time, but it appears that the Rev. Clarke, senior, moved to Simcoe in 1846 and that it may be his son who was stationed at Dresden in 1857. In 1860, however, the elder Rev. Clarke is believed to have returned to Dresden to provide services there and in the nearby oil boom town of Bothwell.

It is not certain which of the two Rev. Clarkes (father or son) built the Congregationalist church in 1858, but a number of factors, including the delivery of its opening sermon by the Rev. William King, of the Elgin Settlement at Buxton, and the attentions of the *Provincial Freeman*'s editor Samuel Ringgold Ward to the event of the church's dedication seem to indicate it was established as an integrated church. The *Provincial Freeman* reported the church building was a "creditable structure, pleasantly situated," and capable of seating four hundred people. It had cost $900. Given Clarke's land holdings, its most likely location would have been along the Sydenham River, just east of the Fairport survey on the land the Clarkes had cleared. The Congregational church building no longer exists, and none of its records are known to have survived. The elder Rev. Clarke remained in Dresden until his death at age seventy-seven. He was originally buried in the Anglican Range of the Dresden Cemetery at arm's length of the gravesite of Rev. Thomas Hughes.[37]

The American Missionary Association

While the Baptists, Anglicans, Methodist Episcopalians, and Congregationalists constructed church buildings, other denominations and mission groups, including the American Missionary Association, would not build

a dedicated place of worship. In addition to being an official AMA missionary, Rev. Lewis Champion Chambers remained associated with his British
Methodist Episcopal Church and relied on them at times for meeting space
and occasionally spoke at their established church sites. Chambers and
others also likely used the churches, schools, and halls of other denominations to teach and preach. AMA records show that there were relationships
between the various missions and their leadership established long before
the missionaries arrived in the Dawn Settlement. George Whipple, the AMA's
founder and corresponding secretary, had been a fellow Lane Rebel with Rev.
Hiram Wilson and had corresponded with the senior Rev. William Clarke
and Rev. Chambers. Clarke meanwhile had acted as a sponsor for Chambers
in his bid to become an AMA missionary, and Chambers attended gatherings
of both Black and white Methodist associations. For those missionaries who
never erected a church building, few traces of their presence remain on the
landscape. Still, these men made ambitious contributions particularly in less
concentrated areas of settlement. There they diligently served the poorest of
the poor despite being chronically under-resourced.

When the AMA began supporting Chambers in 1858, he had hoped to
be appointed to serve a church at Dresden, but the settlement was already
ably served by a number of missionaries, including BME ministers. By 1858,
Rev. Chambers was teaching at Sabbath schools in Dresden and Chatham
Township but also had begun ministering at McGee's Ferry, and by 1859 he
had added Botany and Euphemia Township to his preaching circuit. By May
of 1859 his ministry included one hundred scholars and ten teachers providing Sunday school prayer meetings and Bible classes at Dresden at the
same time as he served at McGee's Ferry and in the bush at Botany, fourteen
miles further south in Howard Township. Despite the loss of his mother in
July of 1859, he continued this gruelling schedule. He supplemented his AMA
stipend by farming his small acreage, but this income would not have been
adequate to sustain both his large household and the wider needs of his mission. As a consequence, Chambers, like so many before him, was continually
involved in soliciting funds and, with the famine that had struck the region,
also became involved in appeals for food.

By August 1859, Rev. Chambers was still teaching a hundred scholars at
a Sabbath school in Dresden while simultaneously serving an additional

fifty-eight students in what he described as a fine school located along Chatham Township's Concession 11, and two additional Chatham Township schools on Concessions 10 and 12 that attracted twenty students.[38] By the summer of 1860, Chambers's reports would no longer include news of any work at Dresden or Chatham Township as he had begun confining his efforts to McGee's Ferry and Botany—and even here, numbers were dwindling. He anticipated that those who were leasing land would be evicted from their farms by the fall, and that, without a source of income, they would be forced to move on. By 1860, he had been invited to preach to groups in London, and in Ingersoll, where they had lacked a minister for years and had offered to fund Chambers's transportation costs if he would serve their churches. In the fall of 1860, Chambers sold his Dresden property and moved to London. The British Methodist Episcopalian Church, meanwhile, retained a strong presence at Dresden.

British Methodist Episcopal Church (BMEC)

Rev. Josiah Henson was one of the earliest and most noted Black ministers of the Gospel to arrive in the Dawn Settlement. While still in bondage and unable to read and write, Henson had begun a career as an itinerant preacher. His efforts were aided by the donation of a horse, which allowed him to travel to neighbouring plantations to share the faith he had come to love. In1859, nearly twenty years after he had escaped to Upper Canada, Henson would be formally accepted as a minister of the .

The BMEC was an offshoot of Richard Allen's African Methodist Episcopal Church (AMEC), founded in the US. The AMEC had also established in Upper Canada by 1834. In 1856 Canadian AMEC adherents recognized their unique status and circumstances as British subjects and reorganized as the British Methodist Episcopal Church. In 1855 the BMEC established the Dawn circuit, which included much of Kent County and parts of Lambton. By 1857 this wide geographical area had been divided into two "circuits": the Buxton circuit, which included Buxton, Rond Eau (Rondeau), and Tilbury East Township, in Kent; and the Dresden circuit, which included Lambton County's Euphemia Township and Kent County's Caledonia as well as the mainly French speaking settlement area of Pain Court. By 1861, Dresden advanced to station status with responsibility for ministry to Kent Bridge (formerly McGee's Ferry). They constructed a substantial chapel at Dresden and hired permanent ministers. In 1863, their church building would be valued at $4,000 and its congregation of 255 was led by Rev. Henson along with elders and deacons that included the former BAI trustees Peter B. Smith and Nero Harding as well as W.S. Crosby and Noah Vick,[39] all residents of Dresden. In 1868 the Dresden station was detached from Kent Bridge, where Noah Vick, Josephus O'Banyoun, and others had ministered since 1863.[40]

Rev. Henson was not the only distinguished British Methodist Episcopal figure to serve in Dresden. Bishop Walter Hawkins had also briefly been stationed there. Hawkins, born into slavery in Georgetown, Maryland, in 1809, had experienced years of hardship as a fugitive in Pennsylvania and other northern US states. In Philadelphia, the self-educated Hawkins became a spiritual leader and minister to a congregation of three hundred people. After his arrival in Toronto, around 1837, he attended a BMEC conference and became a BMEC minister, eventually being appointed to serve at Dresden for two years.[41]

Like other missions, the BMEC provided educational services as part of its ministry with twelve teachers reported to have served 125 students at its Sabbath schools in 1857.

Henson served at Dresden until his death at age ninety-two. The original location or locations of Henson's church building(s) are contested in various accounts by later historians.[42] The BME church which Henson is known to have preached in later in life was located on Queen Street, a block West of Hughes's Christ Church and two blocks from the First Regular Baptist Church. The congregation it served was disbanded in 1955, and the building was razed in 1962 to make way for the current Pentecostal Assemblies church. That church currently houses a pulpit and two chairs that were removed from the former BME church and are believed to date to Henson's time.[43]

Other Mission Groups

Occasional glimpses also appear in reports of the abolitionist press of other missionaries who briefly passed through the area including the Rev. Samuel Lowrey who was an evangelical preacher with the Church of God who arrived in Canada West just prior to the American Civil War. Others serving the missions, particularly their teachers are largely missing from the historical record. In time, most of these itinerant missionaries would move on, leaving little trace of their passing through. The accounts that survive remain as testaments to their energetic and often sacrificial efforts to bring hope, support, and education to hundreds of people in the Dawn Settlement and surrounding area.

At least four churches—First Regular Baptist Church, Union Baptist, Prince Albert Baptist, and Christ Church (Anglican)—have continued to serve active congregations for over a century and a half. These churches have persisted as important spiritual and social centres for the Black community, that have supported succeeding generations faced with continued challenges that included a lack of social equity and inclusion.

Chapter 12

DENNIS HILL *and the* FIGHT *to* DESEGREGATE COMMON SCHOOLS

T HE BLACK ELITE WHO WERE SO HEAVILY INVESTED IN the Underground Railroad knew that freedom was an equation with two parts: the eradication of slavery and the securing of civil rights. At Dresden, the same landowners who had brought so many north to freedom recognized not only the need to build well-resourced communities where they could thrive, but to ensure that society made good on its promises of equal rights under British Law. Guided by the goals of securing education and equal rights they forged in the US Black Convention Movement they would continue to work diligently to secure these rights for themselves and the people they had freed. It was an uphill battle as by the1850s these rights were being eroded as "the Black population had increased to the point where whites feared competition over jobs and land as well as the consequences of Black demands for social equality."[1] Undaunted by this prevailing trend, "The Black communities that existed in nineteenth century Kent County paved the way for Black innovation and advancement in education in the region"[2] and would lay the foundations for a continuum of resistance to segregation that would not reach its completion until a century later.

In November 1852 Dawn Settlement landowner Dennis Hill took up his pen to write a long and inordinately respectful letter to Egerton Ryerson, the superintendent of schools for Canada West.[3] "You will please pardon me," Hill wrote, "for the liberty I have taken in appealing to you for redress from the base treatment I have received from the majority of the [directors] of School Section No. 3 in the Township of Camden in the County of Kent."[4] Hill's son, then eleven, had been barred from attending. Hill had reason to expect Ryerson would respectfully listen to his petition and force the reinstatement of his son, as the *School Act of 1843* stated "it shall not be lawful for such Trustees, ... or for any teacher to exclude from any Common School or from the benefit of education therein, the children of any class or description of persons resident within the school district."[5]

While the evaluation of Ryerson's legacy is ongoing due to his problematic approaches to education, he can be found, in his tenure as superintendent of schools for Canada West (a post he held from 1844 to 1876), as recognizing the injustice of segregationist practices which he stated were contrary to the spirit of British Institutions.[6] As early as 1828, complaints had been heard from parents whose children had been banned from schools.[7] By 1842, Lord Sydenham, British North America's first governor general, recognized exclusion from schools as a primary complaint among settlers of African descent.[8] By 1845, an open letter to the Municipal Council of the Western District, printed in the *Chatham Gleaner*, would observe that "there exists such a prejudice, that it has already had the effect of breaking up some schools where attendance of these scholars has been persisted in."[9] The letter's author had offered the "practicable solution" that was modelled on what transpired in Chatham: there, the entire town had been made into one separate school district, and a separate school taught by Black teachers had been established. The writer concluded, "I would earnestly recommend this course wherever practicable, and in all cases to endeavor to allay the irritation the subject produces."[10]

Throughout the 1840s, the "irritation" regarding integration evolved into an overarching opposition to Black immigration in general. Edwin Larwill, during his tenure as Kent County's representative in the legislature from 1854 to 1858, was an unapologetic racist who believed "the Negro is a distinct

species of the human family... far inferior to the European." Disgusted by mis-
cegenation (intermarriage of races) Larwill would, by 1841, oppose school aid
for people of African descent. In 1848 he sought the support of the Western
District Council[11] for a resolution banning Black immigration to Canada
West. And in 1848, he organized opposition to Rev. William King and his
rival in politics Archie McKellar, in their work to form the Elgin Settlement
at Buxton. Larwill did not receive sufficient support to uphold the immigration law he sought or in his agitation against Buxton. He would be ousted in
the next general election by McKellar, largely through the determination of
Buxton's settlers to exercise their voting rights. Still, Larwill's ability to rally
so much support and to be voted into positions of authority shows how systemically entrenched racist attitudes had become among a significant portion
of the white population and the extent to which the community was prepared
to either support or turn a blind eye to Larwill's views. And Larwill was certainly not alone in those views. Fellow Kent County resident Walter McCrae
publicly stated his opposition to the Buxton settlement, calling its settlers a
"horde of ignorant slaves." George Duck, chair of the board of school trustees
for Chatham, espoused that "no respectable board members whose views
were moderate and reasonable" would support integration of schools.[12]

Some school boards had initially accepted Black children, but without the
full support of all parents, both Black and white, integration of these schools
was doomed. Some white parents pressed for segregation by threatening to
withdraw their children. African-descent people also sometimes preferred
separate schools, believing their children would not receive fair treatment at
the hands of white teachers or receive an education geared to their needs. Yet,
separate schools were notoriously unequal. Founded by businessman Israel
Williams in Chatham in 1824, the Princess Street separate school had its start
in a log cabin on one acre of land.. The school building was primitive at best,
and until 1856 its eighty students lacked heat in winter and had no teaching
aides nor sufficient books.[13]

Mary Ann Shadd (herself an educator) was highly critical of separate
schools, as were Henry Bibb, William Whipper, and others, who opposed
them based on broader principles. They believed all separate institutions,
including both schools and churches, served to perpetuate racist attitudes
because they did not expose people to a diversity of races and cultures

and through this experience learn how to live together.[14] Even the Sabbath schools established at white churches often discouraged integration. James Stompf, one of the original BAI search committee members, had initially been reluctant to approach Chatham's Sabbath school to enroll his children, fearing the prejudice they would experience. When others urged him "several times" to enroll his children, he relented and took his "well dressed...three little daughters and son who were bright mulattoes to a local Sabbath school where they were offered a seat on the bench which the white children put their feet on. In the face of this insult, Lewis left the school with his children."[15]

Before Ryerson introduced the *Education Act of 1850*, Canada West had lacked a standardized curriculum and regulated teaching standards. The Sabbath schools whose teachers were not always qualified had previously been the only option for those who had been too poor to afford private schools or tutoring. This was reflected in the general population's literacy levels, which are evident on land deeds of those such as Levi Devin, a contemporary of Rev. Josiah Henson in the Dawn Settlement, who, like some other whites, signed his name with an "X."[16] Missionary schools had grown in number since the time of Wilson's Canada Mission and attempted to fill the gap, but distances to these schools meant they were not universally accessible.

Ryerson, the superintendent of schools, sought reform, believing that quality Christian education should be made universally available, free of charge to the entire citizenry. Ryerson had spent two years touring schools in preparation for drafting the new education act. He found discrimination a disgrace and sought to ensure nothing in his new education act sanctioned or abetted its practice. Ryerson was not fully supported in these views, even within his own administration, who continued to push for segregation as a remedy to the conflicts over integration at local schoolhouses.

Section XIX of Ryerson's *Education Act of 1850* made it mandatory for school trustees to create separate schools for "Protestants, Roman Catholics or Coloured People" should twelve or more families request them. But as Ryerson would later explain, it had not been his intent to empower white residents or boards to impose separate schools on Black residents who did not request them.[17] Instead he had sought to empower those within Catholic and Black communities to create their own fully funded and self-directed schools if they chose. His new act made it possible to divert taxes normally collected for the use of public common schools to new separate school boards allowing the creation of separate schools as an option where the common school was not accepting or supportive of Blacks or Catholics.

Some Black communities that had established their own schools long before the act had been passed were quick to embrace the opportunity to receive tax funds to relieve poor families of the burden of tuitions. On August 8, 1850, the Elgin Association in Buxton was among the first to apply for funding. Yet, ironically, Buxton's school, like most Black founded schools, did not deny anyone entry due to their race or religion. The quality of Buxton's education became so respected, meanwhile, that white parents eventually sought and were granted the right to enroll their children there. At Dawn's British American Institute School, the Baptist Free Mission sought separate school funding only to have Rev. John Scoble judge this as an improper solicitation of government funds for what he viewed as a private school. He consequently ended the involvement of the Baptists at the BAI and closed the school, never to reopen it.

Dawn Settlement residents William Bradley and others were opposed, believing separate Black schools were "an infringement of their rights."[18] Opposition to separate schools also developed for practical reasons. In some cases, large territories were imposed on separate schools, forcing some students to travel up to six miles one way to attend. This posed an unreasonable hardship, especially for young children during winter. The Princess Street School experience also shows that having a separate school did not always mean the Black community were allowed to retain Black teachers. Highly qualified individuals like Aaron Highgate and Alfred Whipper were hired and then replaced by a white teacher, on the excuse that Highgate and Whipper had been unable to produce proof of their teaching credentials.[19] It seems unlikely that Highgate in particular had lacked the appropriate accreditation, given that a Chatham Township superintendent's report had assigned him an A rating as a teacher, while giving some white teachers in the same school district a B.[20]

Unfortunately, Ryerson's *Education Act* made no provision for those who chose to opt out of separate systems. Ryerson believed the right to do so existed but that it did not follow that students had the right to attend any school they wished. In effect, once a separate school district had been established, whether by choice or imposition, all Black families in that school section had to send their children there, regardless of their beliefs on segregation or whether the established school section actually featured an operating school. After the act was passed, "numerous petitions to the Education Department complained of exclusion from the common schools and expressed desires for integration, not segregation."[21] As historian Robin Winks observed, "There were 2,610 schools in Canada West by 1844 instructing 97,000 pupils and the problem of maintaining equal education for a few hundred Negroes received low priority compared to the many other pressing issues that confronted a sprawling frontier educational system."[22]

Ryerson would not intervene with the Camden and Zone Common School Board, despite being requested to do so by Dennis Hill in his November 1852 letter. Inaction was Ryerson's standard response to requests such as Hill's. In addition to the practical considerations Winks outlined, a lack of political will may have played a large part in Ryerson's failure to address legitimate grievances. After all, Ryerson's predecessor, Governor General Sir Charles Metcalfe, had been responsive and direct in dealing with similar issues. When petitioned by excluded families in Hamilton in 1843, Metcalfe had placed the Hamilton police in charge of the common school with orders that "the law... be enforced without distinction of colour."[23] Ryerson, by contrast, believed a law would not change how people felt about racial integration and that strife would continue at the local level. Over twenty petitions much like Hill's had been sent to Ryerson. His typical response had been to request that trustees voluntarily comply. If they did not, he advised the complainants to take the offending trustees to court. "Few did, from fear, ignorance of the law, lack of funds or weary indifference"[24]—but Dennis Hill would. When Ryerson refused to help, Hill did as he had been advised and launched the landmark case *Dennis Hill v. the School Trustees of Camden and Zone*, the first legal challenge to segregation in Ontario.

Most accounts of Hill's case against these school trustees give the impression that his court challenge had been a personal action made solely on behalf of his own family. However, Hill's activities at that time suggest that the Black elite had backed his efforts as a civil rights action on behalf of everyone affected. That Hill was spearheading an action that had a broader intent, beyond his own family's schooling needs, is plausible given Hill's business alliances with the Black elite, many of whom had deeply held convictions on access to education and the rights of freemen, forged in their previous Black Convention Movement involvement and his related rise as an activist involved with Mary Ann Shadd Cary and others at Chatham who were fighting for the same cause. In the Dawn Settlement, Hill would undertake a series of puzzling land transactions with the Black elite before and after the common school suit that suggest they may have provided encouragement and possibly monetary backing of his efforts. When Hill wrote to Ryerson in 1852, he owned two properties in Camden Gore (formerly Dawn Township). By 1853, the year he filed his suit, he had become part of the Purnell partnership and one-third owner of other Camden Township properties he had invested in along with Pennsylvania-based William Goodrich and Stephen Smith. These large and numerous purchases firmly established Hill as a significant ratepayer in the school district. After the suit, Hill abruptly divested himself of much of this land. William Goodrich had been particularly generous in buying out Hill's shares on some of their jointly owned properties.[25] Hill may have needed help simply to defray the costs of his lawsuit. Still, the Pennsylvania abolitionists had invested much towards their dream of establishing a new, more just society in Canada and would not have abandoned these convictions in respect to those they had sent to Canada West. The segregation of public schools, moreover, had the potential to become a slippery slope towards an ever-greater erosion of rights, including the right to citizenship, free movement, land ownership, and the vote. Given Edwin Larwill's lobbying to ban Black immigration, this was a significant existential threat.

Regardless of whether Hill had taken his landmark case before Justice John Beverly Robinson alone or with the help of others, it was clearly a brave and necessary step in the fight for civil rights. Unfortunately, the court ruled against Hill, with the decidedly racist judgement that "the children of the coloured people, many of whom have but lately escaped from the state of slavery may be, in respect to morals and habits, unfortunately worse trained than the white children are in general and that [white] children might suffer from the effects of bad example."[26]

It is not known whether Judge Robinson was aware that Hill was better educated, more affluent, and better travelled than some of his white neighbours and that his children had never experienced slavery. The ruling, in effect, allowed school board trustees throughout Canada West to freely introduce segregated school sections in areas where none had previously existed. This, as W.H. Day had observed at Chatham, was in direct opposition to Ryerson's act. In some areas, school section boundaries were deliberately redrawn to exclude Black neighbourhoods.

The timing for the Dawn Settlement's residents could not have been worse. While in 1852 the trustees of Camden had designated a separate school area centred on the BAI, that institution's school, by 1853, had ceased operation. That school section, operational or not, existed, thereby eliminating the option to attend the common school. Faced with the magnitude of these multiple injustices and intent on having his sons educated, Hill joined Mary Ann Shadd and Rev. William P. Newman in vehement opposition to Rev. John Scoble, the new BAI manager, hoping to wrest control of the BAI's assets and ensure the institute fulfilled its educational mandate. Until 1857, when the Baptist Free Mission built their church and Rev. Thomas Hughes introduced his Upper Room school, education of Black students in the Dawn Settlement area would take place primarily in private homes.

Rev. Hughes's diary provides us with a last heart-wrenching glimpse of Hill and the impact so much personal disappointment, including his son's death, had on him: "I do not believe he can live many days. Poor man, he has actually agreed to sell his farm and made arrangement to emigrate with his family to Hayti. I spoke to him of another land of promise and besought him to think of another voyage."[27]

The fight for equal educational rights would not be won in the Dawn Settlement, and, before success was realized, others would also suffer economically and otherwise in their efforts to achieve desegregation. In Norwich, Solomon Washington had been denied admittance to the common school despite his father, George Washington, having paid common school fees and having been assessed for repairs made to the common school building. George Washington appealed to the district and provincial superintendents, who then informed the trustees that their actions were illegal. The trustees persisted in barring Solomon from attending, while still demanding the payment of school support from his father. An appeal to Ryerson again resulted in the advice to sue. George Washington did so, and in 1854 a judge ruled in his favour, but the cost of the court case led to the loss of Washington's farm.

Hill's case continued to be cited as a precedent for justifying enforced segregation. Yet, the Black community remained resolute, lobbying for change at the local and provincial level. W.H. Day and Mary Ann Shadd would become early allies in this fight, but they did not stay in the region long enough to see its successful conclusion.

In 1858, there was an important challenge against Chatham Township's imposition of two separate school sections. Township council had defined School Section No. 1 in Chatham Township and School Section No. 2 in the Gore of Chatham as encompassing any property owned by a family of African descent, either presently or in the future, *regardless of where it was located*. This was challenged by a Mr. Simmons, who took the township of Chatham to court. The judge's favourable decision stated that Chatham Township's bylaw had effectively excluded from the common school system children of African descent who lived at a remote distance from the schoolhouse.[28] Because the bylaw establishing the two separate school sections did not clearly define a

An integrated school in the Dawn Settlement Area c. 1890. *(Photo courtesy of the Thompson/Guest family)*

distinct territory from any other area of the township, but merely designated any present or future Black-owned property as falling in the section, the judge deemed the bylaw too vague, indefinite, and fluctuating to be legal.[29]

Meanwhile, at King's Ferry, a Sydenham River crossing two miles west of Dresden, local people struggled to make their integrated school a harmonious reality. While their school had been attempting to accommodate a number of neighbourhood children of African descent, the structure mysteriously burned to the ground. In what appears to have been an effort to appease those who did not want their white children sharing a classroom with children of African descent, the replacement structure consisted of two rooms, but it, too, was burned. A third structure, which was again a one-room schoolhouse, finally survived.[30] In Dresden, the Black separate school the Dresden Village Council created in 1873, at the request of the trustees of the Wilberforce Institute (former BAI) was also destroyed by fire. The cause of the blaze remains unknown.[31]

In January 1891 the segregation of common schools was struck down. By 1902 a fine new brick schoolhouse had been built on Concession 2 of Camden Gore a block away from Dennis Hill's former farm property. Union School Section No. 3, Camden, otherwise known as "Mount Pleasant," served Black, white, and Indigenous students from Chatham Township and Camden Gore from its first year of operation until its closure in 1967—finally realizing the dream the British American Institute's founders had envisioned sixty years earlier.

In the Town of Dresden, schools were integrated from at least the 1880s. Dresden's original town hall provided classrooms for students living south of the Sydenham River prior to the Dresden Public and Continuation School being built in 1912. Early photos of the town hall school show it was integrated. On January 26, 1901, when a mass meeting was held in Dresden to discuss school amalgamation into the single site in North Dresden, only one white speaker rose to oppose the new school being integrated.[32] As Rev. Thomas Hughes's comments on Dennis Hill illustrate, however, continuously fighting for the rights and freedoms they had been promised under British law had tired Hill and others, inspiring them to look to more distant shores to achieve the elusive dream of freedom and equality.

Chapter 13

LEAVING *the* PROMISED LAND

The Haitian Emigration Movement

I T WAS THE JULY 4, 1861, INDEPENDENCE DAY IN AMERICA—A fitting time for George Cary to make his final bid for freedom. That day, he finalized the sale of his land located immediately west of the British American Institute to Rev. John Scoble in preparation for joining members of the Cotton Growing Association, formed by a group of Canada West's African-descent people that would sail for Haiti in December. Cary's emigration and that of others, including a handful of people from the Dawn Settlement, was a desperate move born of increasing disillusionment they felt at not being able to achieve full freedom and equality on British soil. George Cary, along with his brother Isaac, were part of a larger emigration movement that caught up thousands of people of African descent throughout North America in similar schemes aimed at resettlement in the Caribbean and Africa.[1]

Born free in Virginia, George Cary, along with his brothers Isaac, John, and Thomas, had emigrated to Canada West in the 1840s. In Toronto they had owned a chain of barber shops, four ice houses, and an ice cream business. Like William Whipper, they were reformers who were "deeply interested in the moral, social and political elevation of all classes."[2] George Cary had purchased his Dawn Settlement property in 1855 and had joined the BAI's management. The following year, his brother Thomas married Mary Ann Shadd and joined them in the frustrating work of attempting to wrest control of the BAI from the hands of Rev. John Scoble. By1861 people of African descent found themselves increasingly segregated and isolated from the main institutions of Canadian life—churches, schools, business and politics,"[3] and denied equal employment opportunities. The extent to which anti-Black racism had taken hold in the area around Dawn is illustrated by a violent incident in the oil boom town of Oil Springs, located in the neighbouring Lambton County. With the drilling of the first commercial oil well there in 1858, Oil Springs had attracted a flood of settlers, including a secondary migration of African-descent people from the Dawn and Chatham settlements who formed a small community just outside of town on the Gum Bed Line[4] where they made their living selling cordwood. Their competitive pricing took business away from local white suppliers, leading to a conflict that culminated in an angry white mob burning down the Gum Bed Line settlement. Instigators of the riot, though they were arrested, tried, and found guilty, would never serve a meaningful sentence.[5] At Dresden eight years earlier, Cary and others had seen their fellow resident Dennis Hill lose his battle against systemic racism in his challenge to desegregation in the common school. The failure of British law to provide promised equal rights and the growing strife with white neighbours dashed hopes that the harmonious, integrated, and progressive community the Carys and moral reformers like Whipper had envisioned could be achieved.

Personal loss may also have played a role in George Cary throwing in with his brother Isaac in encouraging others at Dawn, like Dennis Hill and Rev. William P. Newman, to seek greater freedom and economic opportunities in Haiti. Isaac would successfully recruit 113 emigrants from the region. On January 3, 1856, George Cary's brother Thomas had married Mary Ann Shadd. The Carys were an unconventional couple for their time. Thomas continued to raise his three children by his previous marriage at Toronto, while Mary Ann maintained a home at Chatham while travelling extensively to speak on emigration to Canada and sell subscriptions for her struggling *Provincial Freeman* newspaper. While Thomas would father two more children with Mary Ann, they are not believed to have ever maintained a household together.[6] In 1857 Thomas fell gravely ill, and George brought him to his Camden Gore home to care for him. Mary Ann, who had recently given birth to the couple's first child, a son, Linton, likely assisted George in his vain attempts to nurse her husband back to health. Thomas died, and his body would be buried in the British American Institute cemetery after a long cavalcade had processed it from Chatham to Dresden. George's grief over his brother's death may have been a further demoralizing blow.

This series of events would also curiously align with the coming to Chatham of the fiery abolitionist John Brown. He arrived on April 30, 1858, in the company of thirteen supporters who commenced to hold military drills at what is today Tecumseh Park. Brown invited leaders of the Canada West settlers to join him for a series of three conventions between May 8 and May 10 of 1859. Alfred Whipper, now a teacher at Chatham, would offer his Princess Street Schoolhouse for one of Brown's "quiet conventions." Forty-six people would attend, assisting Brown with working out details of the raid on the US arsenal at Harpers Ferry and even taking positions for Brown's proposed provisional government that he envisioned would, after a successful slave revolt, replace the existing US government and immediately end slavery. Among the Black and white anti-slavery activists who would attend from across Canada West were Dawn residents like James Whipper Purnell and former residents like Osborne Perry Anderson[7] and William Howard Day. Anderson, who had been a farmer at Dawn and an ally of Cary's in the BAI struggle, would be named as a senator of Brown's proposed Congress. Day would draft the constitution for Brown's proposed government.

Not all of the Black leadership were supportive of Brown's plan. Rev. Toyer, whose church had hosted the first quiet convention, had, along with Rev. William King, withdrawn support fearing Brown's rebellion would fail and, similar to Nat Turner's Rebellion in Virginia,[8] would result in disproportionate retaliations. King actively discouraged those at the Elgin Settlement from further participation.[9] Rev. Henson is said to have been visited by John Brown in the Dawn Settlement[10] but would, like King, cite the revolt led by Nat Turner and state similar fears of extreme retaliation. Leadership of Chatham was strong with prosperous Black men like Isaac Holden, chief of Chatham's Black fire brigade, offering Brown's second convention the brigade's building as a meeting space. Mary Ann Pleasance,[11] a highly affluent Chatham property owner, was not invited to his convention because she was a woman but became one of his "secret six" investors, donating $30,000 to Brown's cause and promising more "once the axe was taken to the roots of the tree."[12] Osborne Perry Anderson would march with Brown along with two members of the First Regular Baptist Church at Dresden, Josiah Jones and Isaiah Johnson, who were Chatham township farmers. On reaching Amherstburg, Jones and Johnson and the majority of the other local recruits would turn back but Anderson would continue on with him to Harpers Ferry.[13]

On October 16, 1859, unaware that he had been betrayed to US officials, Brown and his remaining company of twenty-one men made their ill-fated raid on the Harpers Ferry arsenal. Before the day ended, ten of Brown's company lay dead, including two of his sons. Brown was wounded and captured. Others escaped, including Osborne Perry Anderson, who managed to return to Chatham. Previous to his departure, Anderson had moved to Chatham to become a printer at Mary Ann Shadd's *Provincial Freeman*, and on his return he would receive her assistance in publishing "A Voice from Harper's Ferry: A Narrative of Events at Harper's Ferry, with Incidents Prior and Subsequent to its Capture by Captain Brown and his Men." Others in Brown's company were not so fortunate. Six of those captured were hanged. On October 31, 1859, Brown himself stood trial for the murder of four white people, for conspiring with enslaved people to rebel, and for treason. On November 2, after only forty-five minutes of deliberation, a Charles Town, Virginia, court found Brown guilty on all three counts. On December 2, 1859, he was publicly hanged, still convinced that the only way the nation would be washed free of the curse of slavery was by blood.

The Harpers Ferry raid and Brown's capture and execution sent shockwaves through the abolitionist community on both sides of the border and likely had a profound effect on members of the Whipper family who had been present at the quiet conventions. William Whipper told William Still in 1871 that he had not immigrated to the Dawn Settlement because of the outbreak of the Civil War,[14] but land records raise questions regarding whether the events at Harpers Ferry played a role, given in his abrupt cancellation of immigration plans coincided more readily with that event than the outbreak of the Civil War. Whipper has not left any writing concerning his views of John Brown, and though his brother Alfred and his nephew James Whipper

Purnell had been supportive, it is not certain if his views aligned with theirs. Yet, William Whipper, who had begun the process of liquidating his considerable assets in Columbia, was well positioned to provide financial aid, and his affluence and influence would have made him the subject of Brown's recruiting of supporters. While his stance on non-violence makes it doubtful that Whipper would have supported armed rebellion, land records show there may be more to the story than the secretive Whipper divulged to Still. In 1859 Whipper left Columbia, and three 1859 land purchases on Survey 127 identify him as a resident of Dresden.[15] If Whipper had made his home in Dresden, his presence was fleeting as he immediately signed over power of attorney for all his holdings there to his brother-in-law James Burns Hollensworth and subsequent deeds at Dresden show him as a resident of New Brunswick, New Jersey.[16] His wife Harriet's presence at Dresden is meanwhile documented in the church records of Rev. Thomas Hughes's mission, as she attended weddings and baptisms of family members, and in the 1861 census where she is listed as the lone occupant of Dresden house, indicating she may have lived there for at least part of the Civil War years. Regardless, the demoralizing effects of Brown's defeat likely contributed to many giving up on the dream of a Promised Land in Canada, or the end of slavery in America.

By 1861 even Frederick Douglass who had staunchly worked for acceptance of people of African-descent as full and equal citizens had begun to consider emigration as an option and had considered Haiti, the only Black republic in the Western Hemisphere, as a possible emigration site. Emigration as a means of addressing the "problem" of what to do with freed slaves, who were often not accepted in white society, became officially supported in 1816 with the formation of the American Colonization Society and would be promoted by white missionaries and abolitionists on both sides of the Atlantic. Scoble's influencing of Wilson to send Dawn's people to the Caribbean in 1841 shows that this effort had reached Dawn by at least the 1840s. The American Colonization Society would relocate twelve thousand people by the outbreak of the American Civil War. While Black leaders had initially opposed emigration efforts, by the 1830s, some, like Dr. Martin Delany, had begun promoting Black nationalism, proposing emigration schemes that would place African-Americans in colonies abroad in places like South America, Africa, and Haiti. By 1856 Delany had heeded Mary Ann Shadd's vigorous promotion of emigration to Canada; had settled at Chatham, where he moved the Black emigration efforts; and had begun working with the Egba chiefs of Abeokuta, Nigeria, to obtain land for a colony.[17] Delany enlisted the assistance of Shadd in his efforts and employed Alfred Whipper as his secretary as he organized the third North American emigration convention at Chatham. It not only promoted his African emigration scheme but provided a forum for those promoting Haitian emigration. As early as the 1820s, Haitian emigration schemes had been proposed because of Haiti's status as the first (and only) republic founded and led by formerly enslaved people. Inspired in part by the French Revolution, the Haitian began in 1791, when Toussaint L'Ouverture, a former slave, led an effective guerrilla war against the island of Santo Domingo's French colonists. In 1795, L'Ouverture made peace with France and became governor-general of the new republic. He then extended his fight to the Spanish half of Santo Domingo (present day Dominican Republic). In January 1802, an invasion force ordered by Napoleon landed on Santo Domingo and, after several months of furious fighting, L'Ouverture agreed to a cease-fire. He subsequently retired to his plantation, but in 1803 he was arrested by the French, taken to a dungeon in the Alps, tortured, and killed. Soon after L'Ouverture's arrest, Napoleon announced his intention to reintroduce slavery on Haiti, prompting L'Ouverture's former generals to mount a new British-backed revolt. On November 9, 1803, the French were again defeated, and in 1804 General Dessalines became Haiti's first emperor.[18] Following Haiti's independence, the island state was plunged into economic ruin as the French led a European movement to withhold trade and investment. Over a hundred thousand men had died in Haiti's fight for freedom, reducing the workforce needed to sustain the country's plantation-based economy. Haitian leaders began promoting immigration by formerly enslaved North Americans as a means of resolving the labour shortage and encouraged the Black elite in America to invest in the island's crumbling industry and infrastructure.

While the third North American emigration convention at Chatham allowed the Haitian emigration proponents representation, it was not supportive of Haiti as a destination. This reflected the views of a number of other free Blacks in the US and Canada, some of whom pointed out the ironic impediment of racism by Haiti's Black population towards people of mixed race. As Frederick Douglass pointed out, "It would be a sad thing for some of us, who have been hated and persecuted ... for being too black, to go there and be hated and persecuted for being too white."[19] As a former Haitian, Dresden's Amelia Shadd could attest to the rebellion in her homeland having resulted in people of mixed race being persecuted and forced to leave.

By the 1850s a growing number of African-descent leaders and their white abolitionist allies in Canada West had begun to promote Haitian emigration schemes. Some contracted directly with the Haitian government and others were recruited through the efforts of white anti-slavery activist James Redpath—a close ally of John Brown in the free-soil wars in Kansas. Redpath had become the head of the Haitian Emigration Bureau in North American. In 1860 Redpath had visited Haiti and met with its president. He concluded that emigration of North American people of African descent to Haiti would fill both the needs of former slaves for a new homeland and Haiti's need for economic and social development. The Scottish-born Redpath had previously travelled extensively in the US as a newspaper correspondent and abolitionist and during the bloody conflict in Kansas had become a close ally of John Brown's efforts there. After Brown's execution, Redpath had written a lengthy and sympathetic biography, donating a portion of the proceeds from its sales to Brown's widow and family. By the time of his arrival in Haiti, the government there had already begun to recruit thousands of formerly enslaved people from the American South to work on cotton, sugar cane, and palm oil plantations, including a group from New Orleans who had reportedly prospered in Haiti's cotton production. Redpath's ambitious scheme aimed to attract a hundred thousand more. His old friend's son, John Brown Jr., was enlisted as Redpath's sole agent for Canada West and Canada East (modern day Ontario and Quebec, respectively) and Brown subsequently began a campaign to attract five thousand people there.

In December 1860 Brown set out on a three-month tour from Windsor to Montreal with extended stops at the Kent settlements of Dresden, Chatham, and Buxton. Brown spent at least four days in Dresden,[20] where he found a number of disaffected freemen ready for a fresh start. These included George Cary, Rev. William P. Newman, James and Cornelius Charity, and Dennis Hill. On March 22, 1861, John Brown Jr. himself would experience the severity of the prejudice levelled against Blacks and that had spilled over onto their white allies. In a letter to his wife, written from Windsor, he lamented that "in all of Canada West, a [white] man would be read out of what they call 'Good Society' who should ask a Colored man or woman to eat at the same table with him. In consequence of my boarding and lodging at their houses, and in the street and at all places meeting them on terms of social equality, I have scarce been recognized by the white inhabitants here, as belonging to the human family."[21]

Previous to Brown's arrival, a recently widowed Rev. William P. Newman[22] had already pinned his hopes and dreams on Haitian emigration. He had gone to Port-au-Prince, Haiti, to investigate the possibility of developing his own colony of freed people there a full year before Brown first arrived in the Dawn Settlement. In January 1860 Newman, now remarried, wrote a glowing letter from the capital city, published in the *Anglo-African Weekly* of New York City, reporting on the emancipation celebrations held there. He noted the Haitian peoples' love of civil rights and the government's desire for immigration, and he personally pledged to bring several hundred families from Canada to the island state. He had made the boast not yet knowing whether his bid to secure the Haitian government's incentive money to help fund his initiative would be accepted. Newman's proposal to the Haitian government had involved the purchase of the small island of La Gonâve, forty miles offshore from Port-au-Prince. His aim had been to organize a separate Protestant colony as Haiti was overwhelmingly Catholic and decidedly hostile to inroads by other Christian denominations. The Haitian government eventually dismissed Rev. Newman's proposal as mere land speculation.[23] Newman then appears to have attempted to create a settlement in Protestant Jamaica, whose government also was offering incentive money.[24]

A.A. Constantine, the corresponding secretary for the New York–based African Civilization Society, had published his views on Haitian emigration in the same edition of the *Anglo-African* as Rev. Newman's initial glowing report. Constantine had specifically urged Dawn investor William Whipper and his partner Stephen Smith, along with other free people of means, to invest in Haiti, promising rich profits on investments in the cotton and palm oil industries. Whipper and Smith are not known to have heeded Constantine's unsolicited advice.

George Cary was interested in demonstrating, by personal example, that success could be achieved through hard work in farming. Despite being

fifty-seven years of age, he set out for Haiti in the fall of 1861, travelling with
a Mr. Morris and a Mr. Brady and hoping to establish a cotton growing initiative. All three men, however, accepted employment on the Haitian president's sugar plantation—enticed there by the promise of a fifty-cent-a-day
wage. On arrival, they were not paid an hourly rate but for the volume they
produced (i.e., piece work). Many North American immigrants to Haiti
were not acclimatized to its tropical heat. The country was also plagued with
cholera and smallpox epidemics. For George Cary the move to Haiti was
catastrophic. He died within three weeks of his arrival. His travelling com-
panions, Morris and Brady, survived, but for their ordeal were paid a paltry
$3.50 US in total between them.[25]

George Cary's death may have fuelled the vociferous opposition of Mary
Ann Shadd Cary to Haitian emigration. By October 13, 1861, she was using the
pages of the *Provincial Freeman* to defame both Redpath and Brown and was
referring to their agents as "a few coloured Judases." Shadd minced no words
regarding the oppressive climate and the toll of disease in Haiti and reported
on one ill-fated emigration group who had experienced 121 deaths in their
settlement. With the American Civil War now raging and the question having arisen of what to do with slaves who had been freed by the conflict, Shadd,
a fierce proponent of Canadian emigration, continued to urge "send them to
Canada."[26] Other scathing reports appeared on Haiti in the Anglo-American
Weekly. A man identified as J.P. Williams had declared it "not suitable for
coloured Americans" and had warned of the climate, the lack of water, and
the Haitian population's opposition to foreigners.[27] These condemnations
were given greater credence as a number of local people who had relocated
to Haiti quickly became disenchanted and returned to Canada.

The Charity brothers are believed to have returned from Haiti to settle in
San Francisco[28] near Mary Ann Pleasance. Here they again encountered racial
conflict, inspiring Cornelius Charity[29] to again move to British Columbia.
There he became part of the Victoria Pioneer Rifle Corps, a segregated volunteer militia created with the threat of US expansionism and as an offshoot
of the Black fire brigade. The militia drilled its forty-four enlisted men twice a
week. Despite their willingness to defend British soil, members of the militia
were refused the financial backing the government had given to white militias. Adding further insult, white militias and fire brigades had also refused

to march with them. Appeals to address this discrimination were ignored and in 1864, and the unit consequently disbanded. Its former captain R.H. Johnson wrote "their enthusiasm and ardour as far as this colony is concerned have evaporated."[30] Cornelius Charity died on May 31, 1885, at age fifty-five. Despite all his travels and contributions, he had never realized his dream of finding a home where he would be treated with dignity and respect.[31]

Rev. William P. Newman remained in Haiti long enough for his second wife, Sarah Cleggett Newman, to give birth to a son, Charles Edgar Newman, in Port-au-Prince on July 4, 1860. He and his family returned to Cincinnati in 1863, and he began to actively warn others against Haitian emigration. P.T. Smith, in his letter from Canada West, dated August 15, 1861, notes the appearance of Rev. Newman at Dresden where he spoke against Brown and Redpath; outlined the shortages of imported manufactured goods like furniture and apparel, as well as a shortage of staples like flour, corn meal, pork, and rice; and told of the prejudicial treatment he had received not because of skin colour but because of his religion..Soldiers at one point had invaded his church and compelled him to stop speaking. Migration continued to be part of the Newman family's story. Charles, who grew up to be a barber, moved to Appleton, Wisconsin, and then to nearby Kaukauna, to live among a community that included his mother's Cleggett relations and James Burns Hollensworth's daughter, Annie, and son, Arthur. In August 1887, Newman married Annie and they had one daughter, Silverth, before Charles died at age twenty-eight.[32]

Dennis Hill had planned to go to Haiti, but given his pastor the Rev. Thomas Hughes's concerns that Hill seemed near death, it is uncertain whether he made the trip. It would be Hill's wife who would sell their farm in 1862. Support of emigration died out in the early years of the Civil War, [33] and Frederick Douglass cancelled his planned two-month tour to investigate Haiti in favour of throwing support behind recruitment of soldiers for the war effort. (Ironically Douglass would become the US Ambassador to Haiti in June, 1888.) Dr. Martin Delany had been touring Africa for nine months to further plans for his Liberian colony[34] but would return to America and, like so many others in the US and Canada, would take up a new opportunity to fight for freedom by joining the Union Army.

Chapter 14

The STORMS *of* WAR

I N 1863 THE AMERICAN CIVIL WAR HAD ALREADY BEEN RAG-
ing for two years as William Whipper, Frederick Douglass, and fifty of
their colleagues met at a Philadelphia convention of African-American
leaders to discuss recent policy changes of the US administration regarding
military service. Prior to that year, African-Americans had not had the option
to enlist in the US military. Many believed them unsuited for battle, that they
would turn and run if faced with enemy fire. However, as the war dragged
on, and white families grieved their sons' shattered lives and deaths, general
resentment grew towards able-bodied Black men who were not required to
serve.[1] Yet, acceptance of Black recruits was problematic for many white people who refused to live and fight alongside them. A solution was found in
May 1863 when, at the request of Secretary of War Edwin M. Stanton, the
Bureau of Colored Troops was created. This allowed units of Black soldiers
to be formed that were led by white officers. Robert Shaw, the son of a white
Bostonian abolitionist, was charged with raising the first Black regiment for
the Union Army, the 54th Massachusetts Infantry Regiment.

Frederick Douglass had organized his 1863 Philadelphia conference throwing his unwavering support and that of his anti-slavery colleagues behind the
war effort. The powerful call to arms issued by the conference coincides with
the declaration of the Emancipation Proclamation in January of that same
year. With its signing into law all enslaved people in the US, including those

in the South, were declared to be free. For Douglass and his abolitionist colleagues, this meant that the Civil War had become a fight to free Southern
slaves. In Pennsylvania, the northward advance of the Confederate Army in
Virginia was also making the fight one to preserve freedom in the free soil
of the North. For Douglass and other African-descent abolitionists agreeing
to fight was also a means of proving their worth as members of society. As
the recruitment poster produced by Douglass and endorsed by many elite
Black leaders including Whipper proclaimed, "MEN OF COLOR TO ARMS!
TO ARMS!... if we wish to be free in this land...if we would be regarded
men, if we would forever silence the tongue of Calumny, of Prejudice and
Hate, let us Rise Now and Fly to Arms."[2] Older men, like Whipper, who
attended Douglass' conference endorsed his recruitment efforts and having
risked their lives in their abolitionist work now pledged to do all they could
to encourage younger men to risk theirs in service to the Union Army. Some
179,000 Black soldiers would heed the call to arms. By the end of the war,
they would make up 10 percent of the Union Army's total troop strength.

From the beginning, Robert Shaw had extended his US recruiting operations to Upper Canada.[3] Over a thousand Canadian men would wear the
Union blue. Hundreds came from Kent and Essex Counties alone, including at least seventy from Buxton. Communities in Kent County, including
Chatham, Dresden, and the townships of Chatham, Camden, Camden Gore,
and Dover, also sent significant numbers of young men to the battlefields.[4]
Even enlisting men for service was dangerous work as recruitment of soldiers
on British soil for service in a foreign land was illegal. This did not dampen
the resolve of Dr. Martin Delany or Mary Ann Shadd Cary. Shadd Cary
would sign up large numbers of men, sending them to Delany who was now
an officer in the Union Army.

For Shadd Cary, recruiting presented an opportunity not only to serve
the cause of freedom but to address growing personal economic challenges.
In the spring of 1861, she was a widow with two small children. She and her
brother Isaac were struggling to keep the *Provincial Freeman* afloat amid
an economic depression and a lack of widespread support from subscrib-
ers. They would continue to sporadically issue the paper. Mary Ann supplemented her income by writing articles for the *Anglo-African Weekly* of New
York City,[5] but it is questionable whether this provided sufficient income to

support her young family. Shadd Cary's earlier support of Delany's Liberia colonization scheme had earned her his continued friendship and respect. In December of 1863, as Delany obtained sole rights to raise Black troops in the US west and southwest, he invited Shadd Cary to act as his recruiter. She moved to Michigan and in her work with Delany became the first official woman military recruiter in the Civil War. She would be paid fifteen dollars for every enslaved person and five dollars for every freeman that she delivered for enlistment.

Shadd Cary applied herself to her recruiting efforts with characteristic zeal. She began enlisting some of the best and brightest of her circle of business and abolitionist associates in Michigan and among her colleagues in Canada West, as well as formerly enslaved people who had been sent north by the Shadds, and their various colleagues. The recruits she brought to military service were said to be "faultless."[6]

Delany, meanwhile, had become a medical officer in the Union Army and as part of his duties provided health screening for new recruits. He would quickly rise in the ranks, becoming the first Black major of a field regiment in the Union Army, the 104th Regiment, United States Colored Infantry. He would be joined by other Kent County doctors, like Buxton's Dr. Anderson Abbot who also became an officer and a battlefield surgical doctor. Dr. Amos Aray, now thirty-one, who had once practiced medicine in Dresden and then in Chatham, had been involved, like Shadd Cary, with Delany in his Liberian emigration planning. This connection to Delaney led to Aray closing his Chatham practice in September of 1863 to assist Delany with medical screening of recruits. Aray would also attempt to enlist, but to date no records of his military service have been found.[7]

At Dresden, an aging Rev. Josiah Henson, who had himself been a soldier in the 1837 Rebellion, encouraged young men to sign up in Michigan and occasionally provided transportation and other supports to facilitate this. His actions in this regard were, at times, controversial. One family accused him of pocketing bounty money. Henson endured personal loss during the war as his son, Tom, joined the US Navy at California[8] and was declared missing in action. His fate remains unknown.

Many of the Dawn Settlement area's men who served left behind established professions as farmers, sailors, and labourers. One recruit, Samuel

Lowrey, was a minister of the Gospel. A bright young freeman from Tennessee, Lowrey came to Canada West at the age of sixteen and became a schoolteacher. At age nineteen he joined the Church of the Disciples at Dresden and served as a minister. He then moved to the Raleigh Plains near Buxton where he briefly served as an evangelist with the Church of Christ.[9] With the outbreak of the Civil War he returned to Tennessee in April of 1865 to enlist and was subsequently appointed as the chaplain of the 9th Regiment, US Colored Heavy Artillery. "Lowrey would hint to his superior officer that since the enlisted men had not yet received any pay, they might be somewhat appeased by receiving the gift of schooling." As a result, Lowrey was assiged by his commander as a teacher to the men of the 2nd Regiment, US Colored Light Artillery. [10]

Other men from the Dawn Settlement also served but not always in seg-regated units. Born in 1823 in Jordan, Mississippi, George Dunn (who used the surname Madison after his arrival at Dresden) escaped slavery and at age twenty travelled through Illinois to Port Huron, Michigan. In 1862 he moved to Dresden to settle but almost immediately returned to enlist with the 27th Michigan—a white unit, likely indicating he was multiracial and his African heritage had gone undetected. Madison was not the only African-descent man who would join white units.[11] Madison survived the war and returned to Dresden where he married Laura Johnston and raised a family of six. He never collected his soldier's pension despite repeated attempts to claim it.

Those serving in segregated units included Daniel Starks who was only sixteen when he became a drummer with Company One of the 102nd United States Colored Infantry in Michigan. Starks served from November 2, 1863, to April of 1864. Camden Township–born Alexander Clemens, was a labourer when he enlisted on Sept. 9, 1864, age twenty-three, as a private in Company C of the 41st Regiment of the United States Colored Infantry. Clemens served until September 30, 1865, mustering out at Edinburg, Texas. Robert Dudley, originally from Ohio County, Kentucky, joined the 1st Michigan Colored Troops. He was among five men named Dudley from Kent County to join the Union Army, including Ambrose, Greene, Thomas, and George. In June of 2008, their descendants, some of whom still live in the Dresden area, gathered at a small family cemetery on the Countryview Line in the former Chatham Township to witness the unveiling of a Civil

War tombstone erected in recognition of Robert Dudley's service by the US Department of Veterans Affairs.[12] On March 24, 1865, another Chatham Township farmer, Solomon Simmons, enlisted at the mature age of thirty-eight in the 13th Regiment of the US Colored Heavy Artillery in Kentucky. It was a common practice for monied families whose sons were drafted to pay someone else to serve in their stead, and it appears that Simmons had entered into such an arrangement.

African-descent soldiers faced the same or, at times, even greater perils than their white counterparts. If captured they were often harshly treated by the Confederates and in some cases tortured to death.[13] Rates of disease for Black soldiers were also appreciably higher than for white soldiers. Of the 190,000 who served, forty thousand would die, with thirty thousand of those deaths being from infection or disease. Despite these challenges they would prove those who had doubted their bravery wrong, often serving with distinction. Their service, however, would not be equitably rewarded. Many would only be paid $7.00 per month. White soldiers were paid as much as $13.00 per month. "Rather than accept this slap to their honour many refused to accept any pay."[14] Others desperately needed the funds to support the family that waited for their return and who were now without their main breadwinner.

The Civil War was noted for its unprecedented carnage. Horrific wounds were inflicted by artillery, and the conflict took a tremendous toll on the minds of combat soldiers. African-descent soldiers often served on the front lines of some of the most horrific battlefields, and those like Benjamin Grinnage of Chatham Township would pay dearly for their service. Grinnage was just eighteen when he joined the 54th Massachusetts, the second African-American regiment organized in the northern states during the Civil War. He fought beside Frederick Douglass's two sons who were also part of the unit. On July 18, 1863, the 54th Massachusetts took part in the bloody second battle of Fort Wagner. Grinnage was one of the 125 men who were wounded during the frontal attack. Another twenty were killed and 102 went missing in action. These casualties represented 40 percent of the unit. Their bravery and sacrifice would later be immortalized in the award-winning 1989 movie, *Glory*.[15] Grinnage's military service was brief and costly. He had enlisted as a private on April 9, 1863, at Readville, Massachusetts, and had served only three months when he was gravely wounded in the Fort Wagner assault. Four months later, on November 15, 1863, he finally succumbed to his wounds. Another Chatham Township man, Charles Henry Griffin endured the bloody Battle of the Crater, often cited as the Civil War's worst massacre. It resulted in 1,269 casualties. Some soldiers died at the hands of fellow white soldiers who bayonetted them during their retreat, hoping Confederates would not deal so harshly with them for serving with Black soldiers should they be seen killing them. Griffin survived this horror physically unscathed but was hospitalized for what we would now call post-traumatic stress disorder.

It is impossible to imagine the unspeakable suffering men like Grinnage and Griffin endured. That suffering, and their service in the cause of freedom, often was not adequately compensated or recognized. In many cases, Black soldiers received neither the bounty they were promised for signing up nor the wages due to them. This often caused hardship and privation for the families they left behind. Alexander Poole, twenty-three, a Dresden sailor and farmer who enlisted on October 13, 1864, was not provided with any pay until the day he mustered out at Charleston, South Carolina, on September 30, 1865. Even then, he was required to pay the government $27.98 for his uniform and $6.00 for his arms and equipment.[16] The previously mentioned George Madison applied for his soldier's pension but never received it. Madison died in poverty at Dresden in March of 1922 at age ninety-seven.[17]

Throughout the Civil War, the exodus north to Canada continued. Like Harriet Whipper, Parker T. Smith had travelled to Dresden seeking a safe haven, remaining in Dresden for ten months. Smith, a correspondent for the *Christian Recorder*, has left us with a rich account of life in Dresden during his time there. He reported on the construction of the Oddfellows Hall and of the building of a house for the now aged Rev. Josiah Henson. Smith was an intellectual, who had been a member of the prestigious Banneker Institute in Pennsylvania. At the church of Rev. Thomas Hughes, he attempted to encourage others to pursue learning and self-improvement through the debates of the Mutual Improvement Association. His accounts of Dresden in general paint a picture of plenty and peace with descriptions of healthy children playing and smokehouses and larders bursting with food and the population's impressive progress in accumulating property. "I have never lived in a place where I felt so free," he wrote.[18]

During the war, enslaved people continued to make a desperate bid for freedom by travelling north to Union lines as did white refugees whose families and properties had been devastated by war. Some families who were without a male head seem to have banded together for mutual survival. At least one remarkable household at Dresden may reflect this reality. It was headed by an African-descent husband and wife, and included not only their own child but five other children, each possessed of different surnames, nationalities, and racial identities.[19] Unfortunately, no records or oral histories survive that could prove this household was a result of the Civil War migrations. Migration to Canadian Black settlements would continue after the war as those newly freed from slavery discovered "southerners refused to employ them and rather than starve they emigrated to Canada."[20] Yet, the migration would quickly slow and begin to flow in the opposite direction. The Black elite were among the first to return to the US, drawn by the same desire to throw in with those who had not enjoyed their "pecuniary advantages" that had once drawn them to Canada West and in the same way would provide the South with needed teachers, lawyers, and other professionals.

Homesickness would drive others back to major Northern US cities. Parker T. Smith would return even before the war ended. Despite his glowing descriptions of Dresden, Parker had never felt totally at home in his new surroundings and had missed the intellectual life of his former home. As he observed, "A contented mind is a continual feast…unless a person is satisfied there's no use talking of staying in a place."[21] Those who had escaped to freedom in Canada were sometimes drawn south to search for loved ones once left behind in enslavement. Josiah Henson returned to visit his mother's grave but came back to the Dawn Settlement after only a short time away. Others would return south only to find a hostile environment where they could find neither work nor welcome, and they would quickly retrace their steps. At times these migrations split families. Harriet Whipper left Dresden, while a number of her extended family remained. Some of Dawn's residents had spent decades in the settlement, where they had accumulated land, established thriving farms or businesses, and had children who now only knew Canada as their home. The decision of whether to stay or go sometimes split extended family. Lawrence Wallace (previously Lawrence Rozarro) had been born in Charles City, Virginia, in 1806, and had come to the Dawn Settlement in the 1850s. After the Civil War Lawrence's children, Littleton, William, and John, remained in Dresden, while other siblings chose to return to Virginia. In 1991 George Davis, a Dresden Wallace descendant, intrigued by oral histories suggesting there was a lost branch of the family, began a three-year search that led him to Charles County, Virginia, where descendants of the "lost" Wallaces were found to still be living. Two happy reunions followed: the first at Charles County attracted five hundred descendants; and the second, organized by a committee headed by Ruth Dudley of Dresden, a descendant of Littleton Wallace, attracted 450 people. A busload of forty-nine people from Virginia participated in the two-day Dresden celebration that included a pilgrimage to the gravesite of Lawrence Wallace in the Dresden Cemetery that still bears an inscription proudly attesting to his Virginian roots.[22]

Rev. John Scoble would also leave Dresden even as Douglass and his colleagues were recruiting Civil War soldiers. His return to England would trigger charges of "wilful neglect and default" laid by the Canadian attorney general in regard to his responsibilities as manager of the BAI. The resolution of the protracted battle that had raged over the BAI for close to a decade would now be decided by the court. On May 2, 1863, the day-to-day care of the institute's assets was turned over to a local receiver Alexander Trerice.[23] J.C. Brown would also be named in the court case. On April 9, 1865, the American Civil War came to its bloody conclusion, but the battle over the institute would drag on for another three years. These two great conflicts and their imperfect resolutions would have a lasting impact on Dresden and the wider area of the Dawn Settlement.

Chapter 15

The FINAL BATTLE *for the* BAI

Brown and Scoble vs.
Wright and Myers

I N APRIL 1863, ALEXANDER TRERICE WAS READY TO WASH HIS
hands of his responsibility as the British American Institute's court-appointed receiver. To qualify for the position, the successful white businessman, justice of the peace, and future mayor of Dresden had put up $1,000
(about $25,000 today) as proof of his financial stability. Trerice was not
intimidated by large, ambitious projects. Raised in humble circumstances, by
the early 1860s he had already established a carriage works and would later
establish a sawmill and a ship's planning mill; he would also enter into partnerships with a series of other industrialists with whom he built ten ships
that hauled passengers and freight on the Great Lakes and a short rail line
that transported timber to Dresden's mills. At the outset, managing the BAI's
affairs must have seemed a comparatively simple matter. Trerice soon discovered that nothing involving the BAI was simple. Two years into his role as
receiver, he became entangled in the ongoing drama and infighting that had
plagued the institute. In a heated passage in his annual report to the court's
master in chancery, in London, Ontario, he proclaimed, "After this year, I do

not want anything more to do with the place, as it gives me a good deal of trouble and anxiety of mind and all for no profit."[1]

Many others involved with the BAI prior to Trerice could well have expressed the same sentiments. Despite its founders' vision and twenty years of exhaustive fundraising, fractious meetings, and faith, sweat, and hope that had been poured into the venture, there was still little to show for these efforts except for the ruined reputations of so many well-intentioned men. The court documents from that time show, however, that far from marking a failure of the BAI, the court actions in the *Scoble and Brown vs. Wright and Myers* trail were an important transition in which old dreams about the institute would be exchanged for new ones as the community transitioned to a post-war reality in which supports for formerly enslaved people were no longer as critically needed as they once had been.

Despite Trerice's protestations about the BAI's situation, he would continue in his post for another five years: collecting rents from farmers who worked the BAI's cleared land; managing the property's upkeep; depositing receipts into the Commercial Bank of Canada, in Toronto; and filing regular reports to the master in chancery.[2] Finally, on April 12, 1870, as J.C. Brown threatened to launch yet another lawsuit against Rev. Josiah Henson in their ongoing conflict over the BAI, Trerice announced that he "had done with the matter"[3] and walked away, leaving the BAI's new court-appointed trustees to resolve any remaining disputes.

Henson, meanwhile, had remained faithful to his dream of developing the institute but, in the end, was denied any control over its progress. As his lawyers advised, he remained in the background of the *Scoble and Brown vs. Wright and Myers* lawsuit that Trerice, his sometimes collaborator in business deals, had become involved in as receiver. That suit was aimed at wresting control of the institute away from Rev. John Scoble. Even though Rev. Henson had financed the suit, his initiative and leadership in launching the action would neither be appreciated nor the expenses he incurred related to the legal challenge be compensated.

Henson's suit named Scoble and Brown as defendants even though these two men were on opposite sides of the conflict over the BAI lands. In the eyes of the court, both retained legal responsibility for the BAI and both needed to respond to the allegations that the BAI had been mismanaged under their watch. Brown, for his part, had remained diametrically opposed to Scoble, believing that the former career abolitionist had been operating the BAI for his own profit. Brown had also viewed Henson as complicit by virtue of his long defence of Scoble's actions. Brown's suspicions are understandable given that, throughout the 1850s, the BAI had failed to operate as an educational institute, as well as given the fact that the only substantial building Rev. Scoble had constructed on BAI lands had been a frame house intended for his own family's use. Others besides Brown had accused Henson of being in league with Scoble and of benefitting from the institute's assets. Henson insisted that the opposite was true, claiming that he had used his own purse to compensate Scoble for debts he had incurred while operating the institute.[4] By 1861 the attacks on his integrity had inspired Henson to act. He had given Scoble one last chance, pressing him to outline concrete plans for rebuilding the BAI school, to which Scoble had haughtily replied, "I did not come here for the coloured people to dictate to me."[5] Henson felt that Scoble had "greatly deceived" him and told him that if he had no intention of building the school, then he should leave. At this point, Henson was convinced that the greater community of the Dawn Settlement would never have a school until they gained possession of the BAI property. Scoble reportedly refused to leave until his expenses were reimbursed and he was compensated for his time as manager. Henson immediately called a community meeting to explain the situation and offered to pay out of his own funds for a legal action to remove Scoble. The community subsequently granted Henson power of attorney, which allowed him to act on its behalf. In London, Ontario, Henson consulted the law firm of Wilson and Mackenzie who deliberated on the matter for three months. The lawyers then advised Henson to find two debt-free landholders, one white and one Black, willing to be named as informants (i.e., plaintiffs) in the case. If these informants could be found, the lawyers advised they would take the case provided Henson agreed to remain in the background. Henson agreed and subsequently approached his long-time neighbour and prosperous farmer John Myers and his old Irish-born business associate Fairport founder William Wright to take on the role of informants. Both agreed and provided statements to the court.[6]

As the trial was about to unfold, Wright assisted Henson in one final business transaction. Henson and his sons had developed a grist mill on the

BAI property prior to his falling out with Scoble. African-descent farmers were sometimes denied access to white-owned mills. Development of a mill on the BAI property was intended to provide a close, accessible alternative. Once the grist mill was operational, Henson had sought out Wright to take over its day-to-day operations.[7] Wright was understandably hesitant to do so as long as the mill stood on BAI land. Previously, Henson had operated the mill in that location under a gentlemen's agreement with Scoble but had not secured a written contract. When Scoble left for England, he left his son Thomas in charge of the institute and Thomas refused to recognize his father's arrangement that had also allowed Henson to farm BAI land. When Henson attempted to continue his farming operations that spring, Thomas Scoble confronted him. Henson refused to leave the property, and a physical altercation ensued. Henson fled and immediately contacted the authorities. Thomas Scoble was arrested for assault and battery, found guilty of the charges, and compelled to pay the court costs plus a bonus.[8] With no love lost between Henson and Thomas Scoble, attempting to operate the mill on BAI property would likely have led to further conflict. Consequently, Wright and Henson devised a plan to move the mill to Wright's Fairport survey property. When Henson was challenged on how the mill had suddenly disappeared from the institute and reappeared on Wright's land the next day, he replied, with his usual penchant for humour, that ghosts had done it. This spiriting away of the mill became locally infamous as the "Dresden ghost story."[9] Moving the mill had prevented the Scobles from taking over its operation and ensured it would not be tied up in court during the lawsuit, as other assets had been. Wright's Fairport survey property continued to operate as a mill site, under successive owners, well into the mid-twentieth century.[10] Wright would never witness the resolution of the institute's court case. He died at the age of sixty-four, just two years after the suit was launched.[11]

Meanwhile, twenty years had passed since the BAI's founding in 1841 and much had changed on the BAI lands and in the wider Dawn Settlement area. The Civil War had greatly influenced the community's makeup, with many freeman investors having left the settlement, and some having sold off their assets in Dresden and Camden Township. William Whipper would maintain and even expand his ownership of Dresden properties but would never settle in Dresden as many had hoped he would. Some of the BAI's most vocal critics had also left the area. Mary Ann Shadd Cary had moved to Washington, DC. The *Provincial Freeman*'s presses had already fallen silent, and its editorial content no longer stoked debate over the institute's affairs. All the members of James Whipper Purnell's partnership of affluent abolitionist land investors had either returned to the US or had died. New African-descent immigrants were no longer coming in large numbers, and white settlers were increasingly in the majority. The BAI's role in providing infrastructure like its mills was now largely redundant given that these services were now readily available in Dresden and the surrounding area. The BAI's manual labour school model had also become obsolete, and adoption of a new model for funding would not require such a large property. What infrastructure there had been had largely disappeared under Scoble: He had never replaced the school buildings he had razed. The BAI's land also had not been appreciably developed. Only a barn, a granary, and a handful of other small buildings, valued at roughly $225, remained standing, and only eighty acres of the school's land had been cleared.[12] As the court case progressed, the farmer responsible for these improvements was compensated for their worth, and he left the property. The court then solicited bids to rent the land through receiver Alex Trerice.

Initially, there had been strong competition among African-descent farmers in the community to rent the BAI's property. In 1863 and 1864, Egbert Bow and William Wheeler, who owned property in Dresden and Camden Gore, paid annual rents of $305 and $255, respectively, a rate Trerice described as "much more than average rent for similar farms in our locality."[13] In successive years, Trerice would struggle to find renters as farmers became reluctant to invest in improvements to the BAI's land without having a long-term lease that would ensure they could reap rewards for their investment. A small group in the Dawn Settlement continued to be interested in the institute's welfare and worked together on maintenance and improvements to the property. William Bradley, a prosperous local farmer, and George Johnson, a former trustee, as well as Elisha Kersey a farmer who had rented BAI property contributed to the upkeep of the institute's grounds, sometimes working under the direction of Henson's son Peter, and with Trerice's supervision.[14] In this way, a sixteen-acre section of stumps was cleared to facilitate farming, and some of the remaining standing timber was turned into cordwood that was sold "for the benefit of the estate." Work crews also mitigated flood damage and cut and split three thousand rails to fence the site's perimeter. Basic work to maintain the land may have continued, but any progress in returning the BAI to its principal function as an educational institute would stagnate until the court could address the charges of mismanagement against Scoble and Brown, relieve them of their responsibilities, and appoint new trustees who could move the institute forward.

During the court case, Scoble and Brown submitted lengthy written testimonies. In April 1862, Myers and Wright also provided statements that gave a slightly different version of events. In the end, however, Scoble demonstrated that he had simply wanted to be paid and then to leave, just as he had told Henson. The court fulfilled Scoble's wish, and, after declaring him innocent of any mismanagement, they provided him with $4,456.40 in compensation for expenses he had incurred, along with $3,132.54 in compensation for his services plus a reimbursement of $321.70 for his court costs—a total of $7,709.64 (or approximately $170,000 in today's currency). Cash in hand, Rev. Scoble immediately abandoned all claims to the institute and left the community for good. He entered politics in Canada West, running for a seat for Elgin West in 1861, was seated "on petition" and elected in 1863 and again in 1865, leaving office in 1865. He lived in obscurity for the remainder of his life. He died in Hamilton in 1877 at the age of seventy-nine and is buried in the Hamilton Cemetery.[15]

J.C. Brown was also found innocent of mismanagement. By contrast, the court awarded him only $107.27 to cover his court costs. No other compensation was offered.

In November 1865 the court created positions for ten new trustees and began reviewing applications for these positions. Applicants were required to submit a letter of recommendation from a prominent citizen and prove themselves to be debt free. Early contenders for the trusteeships included Rev. Josephus O'Banyon, John Myers, Hayward Day, Isaac Clay, Henry Egbert, and James Oswald.[16] By the time the court finally appointed the BAI's new trustees, none of these individuals were named. Some, like O'Banyon, had moved away, and others, like Myers, had died.[17] In February 1866, Rev. Josiah Henson submitted his application for a trustee position, accompanied by an endorsement from Archie McKellar, the local member of provincial parliament—but he would not be chosen. Henson's controversial status in the community and his ongoing fractious relationship with Brown may have been factors in being overlooked. He had also been mired in debt from his instigating the legal action, and this would have rendered him ineligible on financial grounds. Had he been appointed, serving would have proved difficult as in September 1871 he fell ill with cholera and was grieving the loss of his son Rev. Isaac Henson, who died in the same epidemic.

Henson's former leadership appointment in the BAI by Scoble was neither acknowledged nor revoked during the course of the court case, and throughout the 1860s Henson acted as if he still retained an official role, renting out BAI property as he must have thought was his continued right to do. This resulted in conflict with Trerice's official role as receiver; at one point, Trerice would find that he and Henson had rented the same tract of farmland to two different people. A small faction in the community had continued to oppose Henson and remained suspicious of his activities. When Henson cut cordwood on the boundary line between his farm and the institute, an unnamed individual reported this to the court as a theft of BAI wood. Trerice subsequently wrote a letter to the master in chancery, essentially dismissing the incident as a nuisance complaint.

In the spring of 1870, Trerice was finally told that his role as receiver had officially concluded and that he should not rent out any BAI property for the coming farming season. For reasons that are not clear, Henson then claimed proprietorship over the BAI lands and began to sublet parts of the property. Brown, now a newly appointed trustee, was not amused. As Rev. Thomas Hughes observed at an April 1870 meeting regarding further development of the BAI, Brown became "wild and strange in his talk seeming to be desirous of commencing litigation with Josiah Henson,"[18] Brown would indeed seek legal counsel in London to discover means by which he could bar Henson from any further involvement in the BAI's affairs. The court, meanwhile, had made it clear that the newly appointed trustees now held authority over the BAI lands, and with this Henson ceased any further involvement. He continued to feel he had been ill-treated by what had transpired. On visiting Henson and hearing his side of the story, Hughes concluded Henson had "just cause" to feel that way.[19] He had, after all, poured his time, energy, and personal resources into the BAI's development for years, created its two sawmills and spent countless hours fundraising and marketing the BAI's products. Throughout the court case, he had continued to play a part in the maintenance of the BAI's grounds and had incurred significant debt from the lawsuit that had returned the BAI into the hands of the community—debt for which neither the BAI trustees nor the court would compensate him.

While Henson had not been appointed trustee, in April 1868 his old rival J.C. Brown, who was viewed as a special case, was reinstated as one of the new trustees. This gave Brown the distinction of being the only trustee to continuously serve the BAI from its inception in 1841 to its dissolution in 1871. Other positions were awarded to an impressive roster of African-descent leaders including: Morris Potter, Hayward Day, Isaac Holden, Stanton Hunton, and William Chandler, who would serve with white M.P.P. Archie McKellar and the white missionary Rev. Thomas Hughes. Isaac Holden would act as the new chairman. He was an important African-descent leader at Chatham who had been captain of the town's Victoria Company No. 3 fire brigade whose engine house had been used by John Brown for one of his "quiet conventions." Isaac Holden was a rising economic and political leader in that community. By 1876 he would open and operate a mill and warehouse with Grandison Boyd, next to Chatham's Third Street bridge; he served as grand master of the Prince Hall Masons St. John Lodge No. 9 from 1874 to1879; and in the 1890s, he served as a Chatham alderman. At the time of his appointment Holden had no presence in Dresden, but soon after his appointment he would purchase a single lot on Queen Street. It is not known what enterprise he conducted there.[20] Stanton Hunton was also a former sup-porter of J.C. Brown and a real estate developer. He constructed Chatham's Hunton Block, a large commercial building near the corner of William and King Streets that housed offices and a large meeting hall. William Chandler, the sole Chatham Township–based trustee, owned Lot 20 on Concession 13, and in September 1876 he opened a highly successful business on Wellington Street in Chatham. Chandler would also amass a large number of proper-ties in Chatham Township. Enslaved before arriving at Chatham Township, he had succeeded brilliantly in business without ever having learned to read or write.[21] Two other successful Chatham businessmen, Morris Potter and Hayward Day, rounded out the list of Black trustees.[22]

Of the two white trustees, Scottish-born McKellar appears to have been appointed because of his standing as a local political representative and as someone known to be supportive of African-descent people. McKellar had defeated MPP Edwin Larwill after his violent opposition to the Elgin Settlement inspired its residents to travel en masse to their Chatham-based polling station and cast their votes overwhelmingly for McKellar. McKellar, as the new representative to the Ontario legislature for the riding of Bothwell, was at the height of his political career when he served as BAI trustee.[23] Rev. Thomas Hughes was the sole Dresden-based trustee. His mission activities, unwavering support for integration, and personal integrity had earned him the African-descent community's trust. Under this new leadership, the British American Institute stood poised for restructuring.

Chapter 16

RESTRUCTURING *the* BAI *to* SERVE *a* CHANGING SOCIETY

T HE CIVIL WAR WAS OVER. AN IMPERFECT PEACE HAD SET-
tled over the battlefields and at Dawn's British American Institute.
In Dresden, seventy-seven-year-old James C. Brown could now
rejoice that two of his long-held dreams had been realized: the end of slavery
in North America and the securing of the BAI's assets for the Black community. The Emancipation Proclamation and the Union victory in the Civil
War meant that the quest for freedom and dignity that had absorbed most of
Brown's life seemed more attainable. And in the Dawn Settlement area, as a
result of nearly thirty years of Brown's persistent activism, the BAI could now
finally move forward to fulfill its educational mandate. Brown's reappoint-
ment as a BAI trustee must have seemed a fitting reward for these protracted
efforts which he could now see fulfilled. Restructuring of the BAI, much like
reconstruction in the US, presents as a time of a radically changed social and
political reality in which the actions of remaining Black leaders would continue on the tradition of the Black Convention Movement in establishing
education for the uplift of their people and would contribute to the development of the emerging Town of Dresden.

There would be a bittersweetness to the resolution of the American Civil War and over the battle for the BAI's ownership. Much had been fractured and scarred by these conflicts. Relationships had been severed and new lines of conflict had been drawn. New challenges would also emerge. Still, for African-Americans in the US, the end of slavery and the government's early promises during the Reconstruction period had inspired optimism that things were changing for the better. And in the Dawn Settlement there was a similar optimism regarding the possibility of a revitalization of their educational institute. As US reconstruction began, however, Black elite who had once focused their attention on creating educational opportunities and infrastructure and on fighting for civil rights now turned their attentions southward, seeking to achieve their goals among the much larger numbers of newly freed people in the US South who now had greater need of their talents and resources, and leaving the Dawn Settlement without the resources, ideas, and influence of this important segment of their population. Members of William Whipper's family, including his adopted son William J. Whipper, of Detroit, would head south. Whipper, the lawyer, would move to Charleston, South Carolina, to open a practice with Robert Brown Elliott, becoming the only African-American involved in the revision of the South Carolina Legal Code.[1] The Black Convention Movement's former education goals would be realized between 1865 and 1900, as roughly seventy-five institutions of higher education for African-Americans would be created in the US South. Those educated at the Elgin Settlement's school would be among those who staffed these schools.[2] The Dred Scott decision of 1857 had previously declared African-descent people to not be citizens, but with the end of the Civil War, Blacks now had full rights of citizenship, including the rights to vote and to run for political office. Rev. Thomas Stringer, who had once worked with Mary Ann Shadd Cary at Dawn to create an alternative board of trustees for the BAI, would become one of a handful of African-Americans to sit in the US senate, even in the Deep South state of Alabama. It was a hopeful time.

Then the backlash began. By the 1870s, secret anti-Black societies had been formed, including the Red Shirts[3] and the Ku Klux Klan. A large part of their membership consisted of former Confederate soldiers who had been denied the right to vote or to hold office as a consequence of rebelling against the Union. Resentful of African-Americans' new rights and angered by the loss of their way of life, they had launched a campaign of terror. Their tactics, including torture and murder, would prove effective, and by 1908, the obliteration of the civil rights of African-Americans would become complete as every southern state in the Union passed laws erasing their right to hold political office or to vote. Many African-Americans would continue to live in fear, and to endure the prejudice, exploitation, and loss of basic rights that diminished them to lives of poverty.

In the Dawn Settlement many of the elite families had begun to divest themselves of their properties, and others, including those who had begun their lives in enslavement in the South, made plans to return to the US William Whipper who had acquired Absalom Shadd's properties after Shadd's death now transferred these properties to Shadd's daughters, Isabella Wormley and Julia Purnell. In 1871 the sisters sold this land. The timing of their sales suggest that Absalom Shadd's fortune may have gone full circle. While Shadd had sold his hotel in Washington, D.C., to purchase land in Dresden, his daughter Isabella now sold her father's land just as her husband James Wormley began building their prestigious Wormley Hotel in Washington, D.C.[4] The Shadds were not alone in divesting themselves of their Dresden properties. By the 1870s only a few of William Whipper's business and Underground Railroad associates would remain invested in the Dawn Settlement area (though Whipper would retain a number of his until his death). And while Harriet would return to be with her husband, a handful of his extended family and former elite associates decided to remain, including James Burns Hollensworth, Mary Smith, and Francis Moss Turner. Meanwhile, the British American Institute, the Dawn Settlement's largest and most prominent feature, was about to disappear from the landscape. James C. Brown and the new, mostly Chatham-based trustees, now charged with managing the BAI's assets, faced the challenge of developing its mostly vacant lands into a viable educational institution—even as the community the BAI had been created to serve was undergoing radical changes in its numbers and composition. In the forty years since the BAI's founding, and more than sixty years after it had first been settled, many of the original settlers had aged, and died, and with the end of the American Civil War a number of them would now make the decision to return to the lands of their youth, often to find loved ones left behind. Those who remained would find themselves in the midst of a large new in-migration of white settlers. In 1856 Dresden had been a postal village of five hundred residents, the majority of whom were people of African descent. By 1871, and the village's incorporation, its population had swelled to a thousand residents. By 1882 the population would again double as land-hungry white settlers jumped at opportunities to buy formerly Black-owned lands. By the 1870s the BAI's undeveloped property had become particularly coveted.

The Black community's educational needs were also changing. The model of teaching basic literacy, farming, and domestic skills at a manual labour school had become a relic of the past. The skills traditionally taught in this educational model no longer fulfilled the needs of a new generation who had career aspirations beyond learning basic literacy, lumbering trades, and farming. The BAI's new management needed to create an educational facility that responded to these new needs.

The racially different makeup of the new BAI management also reflected the changing times. The goals and attitudes of the eight new court appointed trustees differed greatly from those of the original six trustees James Canning Fuller and Rev. Hiram Wilson had appointed. The original trustees had mainly been idealistic clergymen whose goals for the BAI's development were directed by their faith and their abolitionist goals. The new trustees were primarily successful businessmen who were perhaps more pragmatically focused on matters of the ledger book rather than their predecessors' preoccupation with the Good Book. This was a fortunate evolution, as the new trustees needed to immediately place the BAI on solid financial footing in order to create a new school and an economically sustainable operating model.

In 1868 the new trustees signalled a radical break from the past by changing the British American Institute's name, through an act of the provincial legislature, to the Wilberforce Institute. The manual labour school model was then scrapped, making it no longer necessary to retain the institute's large property. The new trustees saw that liquating this valuable asset could provide the funds needed to construct a new school building as well as operating funds. To facilitate land sales, the new trustees created Survey 133 of the BAI, including in the survey a reserve strip they called the Wilberforce Reserve.

The Wilberforce trustees in their creation of Survey 133 would honour the BAI's original leadership and leave their own mark on the property through the naming of the roads they had surveyed for the property. Isaac Holden would name two streets, Isaac and Holden, for himself, and Fuller, Wilson, Brown, Chandler, and Hughes would be similarly recognized. Despite his ongoing grievances with the trustees, Henson would also be honoured with the naming of Henson Street.[5] Most of these street names and their original layout in Survey 133 have been retained to this day. Survey 133's streets divided the BAI land base into industrial, residential, and park lots, and these were subsequently offered for sale at public auction. To further facilitate sales, the trustees had added value to these lands through further development. On Wednesday, March 24, 1871, the Wilberforce trustees approached the Camden Township Council (where the BAI lands still officially lay) and obtained five hundred dollars "for the purpose of making a new road in lieu of the old road" that ran through the institute.[6] In May, Rev. Thomas Hughes paid for that road's construction out of the council grant.[7] The development of the BAI lands could not have come at a more fortuitous time for Dresden, which stood on the verge of incorporation as a Village and was anxious to expand its limits to accommodate the influx of new settlers looking for residential and industrial properties on which to establish. The year Canada was created, 1867, Fairport was absorbed into the Dresden townsite, and by 1872 a large segment of the former BAI would also become part of the new Village of Dresden. The all-white Dresden council, headed by the former BAI receiver Reeve Alexander Trerice, set to work in developing these properties following the survey plan the Wilberforce trustees had created. Councillor Dr. T.R. McInnes (Amelia Shadd's former physician) who had been appointed commissioner of roadways, ditches, and other infrastructure, oversaw further development of the site plan.[8]

The portion of the former BAI retained as the Wilberforce Reserve remained under the Wilberforce trustees' ownership and control. This educational reserve was located between the new Village of Dresden's main thoroughfare and the Sydenham River, and its prime lots were situated on high ground above the flood plain and encompassed the former BAI's cemetery. The establishment of this reserve suggests that, for a brief time, Wilberforce trustees had considered continued development of their school on these lands at Dresden. Any plan to do so, however, was abandoned sometime between 1871 and 1873, when the Wilberforce Reserve was also subdivided and sold off, leaving none of the former BAI property for future development.

To further facilitate sales, the new Wilberforce Institute's functions included the ability to grant mortgages. Its trustees were equal opportunity lenders who offered these mortgages to all potential buyers, both Black and white. By holding mortgages the trustees would realize a continuous stream of revenue from payments of interest and principal that would help finance their new school and its operating costs. While loans to white land investors seem only to have been made on former BAI properties, investors of African descent were granted mortgages both inside and outside of Survey 133 of the former BAI grounds. Aaron Highgate acquired a Wilberforce loan to purchase a former Whipper property in Survey 128 of Dresden in what today is Rotary Park. Some would be granted in other communities in Kent County outside Dresden, including Chatham and Buxton.[9]

Henson would become the single largest landowner, by acreage, in Survey 133. After having invested so much in the BAI's development, it was perhaps fitting that he now could direct how a large portion of former BAI land would be developed as his own private property. Henson bought Lot 16 of Survey 133, a forty-acre parcel of farmland along the Sydenham River, which he acquired for about thirty dollars an acre. In January 1871 and again in January 1874, he was awarded Wilberforce mortgages of $11.65 and $100, respectively, on these properties—amounts he would pay back by October 1876, after his return from his final fundraising trip to England. Henson had Lot 16 subdivided and, interestingly, sold part lots to the families of William Wright and Alex Trerice. Julia Wheeler, Henson's daughter, inherited part of Lot 16 on her father's death, and her family retained it into the twentieth century. Other of Henson's properties in Survey 133 were located in a rural area along Henson Street. These never became part of the village or later town of Dresden.

There is a curious historical footnote regarding a structure that existed on this piece of property. In 1871 Rev. Henson appeared before Camden Township Council asking for monetary assistance in repairing what the council referred to as "Henson's Bridge."[10] By-Law No. 583 granted Rev. Henson seventy-three dollars for this purpose, plus another fifty dollars for a road allowance (possibly Henson Street) between Concessions Three and Four of Camden Gore. This bridge may have been the original hemp bridge that had been built for the BAI twenty-five years earlier, as no other bridge is known to have existed over the Sydenham River at Dresden during this time period. The bridge also appears to have been important enough to the wider community to have warranted funds being granted for its repair.[11]

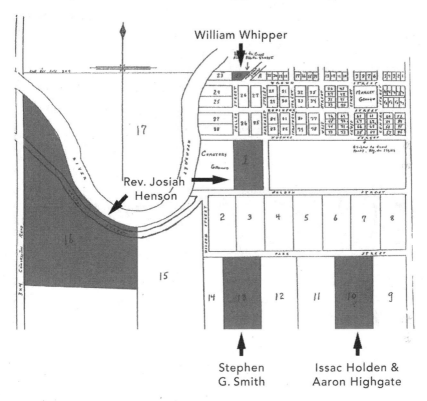

BAI (British American Institute) 1873

Map of the British American Institute grounds after their sale showing Black owned properties. *(Survey map courtesy of CK Land Records; graphics by D. Buchanan)*

Others who purchased land on Survey 133 included Stephen G. Smith, Mary Smith's barber son, who bought Park Lot 13. He received two Wilberforce mortgages as well as a private loan from a James Rankin, each valued at five hundred dollars. All of these loans were to have been repaid by October 1887, when Smith inexplicably resold the land at a $1,200 loss. Trustee Isaac Holden also bought Park Lot 10 in partnership with Aaron Highgate.

William Whipper made his final land purchase at Dresden in the BAI survey, buying Lot 22 with the Wilberforce Institute trustees as his partners. The reason for this partnership and the nature of this joint venture is currently unknown. Lot 22's prime location at the base of Brown Street, however, was adjacent to one of Whipper's previously established Survey 128 properties. In April 1872 this Wilberforce property was transferred to Whipper and his wife for a mere five hundred dollars. Six years later Whipper's widow sold it for $4,375, indicating that a major development had taken place there.[12] What that development was remains unknown. Alexander McVean, a miller of Scottish descent who later developed a factory on the site, maintained that he had based his business on the oldest sawmill site in Ontario, raising the possibility that this had once been the BAI sawmill property and that Whipper and the Wilberforce Trustees may have revitalized it.[13] Another possibility, given the factory's proximity to Whipper's Survey 128 property, was that it had been an expansion of Whipper's white pine lumbermill.

Wilberforce mortgages proved a boon to early white industrialists who represented the majority of new owners, and other aspects of their dealings on the BAI lands suggest white investors were the benefactors of the earlier work of Black developers—a reversal to how the title of "founder" is usually assigned. Alexander McVean arrived from Kingston in 1868, shortly after the BAI lawsuit had been resolved, seeking land to establish his five grown sons in their own enterprises. Perhaps it was no coincidence that one of the lawyers involved in the BAI court case had been John A. MacDonald, Canada's future prime minister, who had been a close political associate of McVean's in Kingston. In 1868, the year the BAI suit had been resolved, McVean set out on foot for Dresden with his eldest son, Sandy, to buy properties for himself, Sandy, and his other sons, James, John, Osgood, and William.[14] First, he purchased a flour mill, which he called the Andes Mill, whose building he brought downriver from Dawn Mills and which he established in Dresden's Survey 127. It would be operated by Sandy. By the 1880s, Alexander McVean would also found the Hub and Spoke and Bending Factory. After Alexander's death it was operated by Osgood and William and subsequently was renamed O. and W. McVean Ltd. though it remained a wood manufacturing plant.[15] James and John McVean also established a chrome plating factory on the site, that supplied chrome trim for Packham parlour stoves.[16] The McVeans' small business empire contributed to Dresden becoming the second largest and most industrialized community in the county, after Chatham, in the late nineteenth and early twentieth century.

Other white investors in BAI land were a real who's who of the community. Future mayor and Great Lakes marine captain Asa Ribble paid a total of $1,870 for three properties. Mayor Alexander Trerice purchased seven properties in total at an investment of $1,590. Charles Prangley, a local miller, purchased a single lot for $1,360. Cyrenus P. and Alex Watson, ship owners and captains, purchased the largest number of properties, buying a total of twelve for $1,267. In about 1871 Cyrenus P. Watson built his brick home on the former BAI Survey133 land on Hughes Street. It still stands today. James Johnson paid two thousand dollars for a large riverflat lot on the bank of the Sydenham opposite the town. It remained as farmland until relatively recently. It is doubtful that these properties could have commanded such good prices if they had not been significantly improved through initial land clearances and the trustees' efforts to survey and improve the property.

In June 1872, the Wilberforce Reserve was also subdivided into ten large blocks, designated Lots A to J, and these overwhelmingly went to white buyers who developed them as an upper-class residential area known locally as Quality Hill. Reeve Alexander Trerice purchased Lot A, where he built his large brick home on the corner of Hughes and North Streets.[17] Trerice had borrowed $480 from the Wilberforce trustees for his six-hundred-dollar purchase. T.R. McInnes, a medical doctor and future mayor; Sibere Clarke, a pharmacist and physician; Charles Prangley, a mill owner; and James W. Sharpe, a lawyer and canning plant owner were among others who purchased the former reserve land. On May 8, 1878, Henson became the only Black landowner on Quality Hill, in his purchase of a part lot for fifty dollars. In August of that same year, he resold the lot to white banker Charles Livingstone for eight hundred dollars. Henson's profitable resale illustrates his shrewdness as a businessman and adds land speculator to his list of talents.

By 1875 ninety-seven town lots and seventeen park lots that had been carved out of the former BAI; Survey 133 had been absorbed into the Dresden townsite by an order of the Kent County Council.[18] Despite the land having been developed by the Black community and purchased by white industrialists and professionals and financed with the assistance of Wilberforce mortgages, local histories have for generations failed to recognize African-descent people among its "town fathers." It would not be until Canada's sesquicentennial year that the Dawn Barn Quilt Trail would recognize William Whipper and the Black elite, and Henson and the BAI trustees among its early founders in two quilt blocks mounted side by side with those representing the early surveys of Dresden and Fairport by their founders the Van Allens and William Wright.

Despite the eradication of the British American Institute and Wilberforce Reserve from the landscape of the Dawn Settlement, people like Brown, who still remained, would see their original dreams of an educational institute realized in the founding of a school, but it would be erected at Chatham. At the opening of that school, the Wilberforce-Nazrey Institute, in October 1888, Rev. Henson's role and that of many others who had been associated with the British American Institute would not even be acknowledged. That day a long roster of dignitaries would deliver their congratulatory speeches at the impressive new brick school's dedication. When Nathanial Murray, husband of J.B. Hollensworth's daughter Ida, rose to speak, he would present a curious piece of revisionist history. Murray portrayed James Canning Fuller as the BAI's sole developer, who had acted on the advisement of leading Black citizens. Rev. Hiram Wilson, Rev. William P. Newman, and—most glaringly—Rev. Josiah Henson were omitted. The lack of recognition of Henson is particularly puzzling, given that the venerable clergyman had recently died. The Wilberforce-Nazrey Institute was a British Methodist Episcopal Church BMEC institution, and Henson was a BME minister, making this a perfect occasion to eulogize him. Murray also only briefly mentioned the BAI's troubles, diplomatically stating that it had failed due to an absence of financial aid.[19] It is as if Murray were purposely trying to distance the Wilberforce-Nazrey from the BAI's troubled and politically charged past and still controversial figures. Murray's account, however, attested that the reconstruction of the BAI had led to the successful realization of its founders' original vision.

From 1869 to 1873, the BAI's final trustees had worked diligently to redirect BAI assets towards this vision at a time when Black education was also going through a major struggle in Kent County. Murray's account was a window onto this post-American Civil War reality. From the time of Dennis Hill's failed efforts to desegregate the common school, that fight had continued. In 1891, through the political pressure exerted by African-descent people at Chatham, public schools would finally desegregate. Even so, systemic prejudice remained deeply entrenched in the public system well into the twentieth century, as evidenced by the findings of the infamous Tanser Report. Completed by Kent County's white superintendent of education H.A. Tanser, the report maintained that there was "a marked superiority of…Whites over the Negroes."[20] Tanser had arrived at this conclusion after applying four types of intelligence tests whose results he elaborated on in his PhD thesis. Such prejudices, endorsed by an official report of the top administrator in the county, underscored the need for separate educational institutions where Black students could reach their full potential free from prejudicial judgement of their abilities. The considerable assets generated from BAI land sales and investment revenues and passionate leadership of the Wilberforce trustees would ensure that just such an institution would arise, at a critical juncture in the efforts to establish appropriate educational opportunities—one that would be ably led and properly financed thanks to the BAI's restructuring.

BAI land sales netted over $20,000, and additional revenues generated mainly from interest payments on mortgages of the land raised this to $36,000 with an additional $10,000 grant being added from the estate of the late Charles Avery of Pennsylvania.[21] By 1873, Avery's Allegheny Institute, which had a similar function and fate to the BAI, had been liquidating its assets, and its trustees had been charged with dispersing these funds in ways that reflected Avery's original vision. Several schools in both the US and Canada became beneficiaries of Avery grants.[22]

None of the funds that were generated would be applied to providing education in the Dawn Settlement area. While the Wilberforce Institute in Dresden was now financially well-endowed and had retained reserve lands in Dresden, its new trustees had mainly been residents of Chatham. Chatham's Black population was larger than Dresden's but faced similar struggles in creating and financing schools. By the 1870s the Princess Street School, which was once a segregated Black private school in a basic log structure, had evolved and now was now housed in a fine new brick schoolhouse. Conditions of public funding, however, required the school to become integrated, and with integration the teaching positions of Aaron Highgate and

Alfred Whipper were given to white teachers on the excuse that Highgate and Whipper had failed to present proof of their qualifications. Another school, the Nazrey Institute established under the sponsorship of the British Methodist Episcopal Church with start-up funds from Charles Avery's estate, had been created on farmland seven miles outside of Chatham. It operated under the same manual labour school model the Wilberforce trustees had just abandoned. The Nazrey Institute was named for Rev.Willis Nazrey who in 1850 had become a minister with the African Methodist Episcopalian Church (AMEC) in New York. In 1852, he was ordained bishop of the AMEC in Canada West, and in 1856 transitioned to become bishop of the new British Methodist Episcopal Church (BMEC) in Canada.[23] In 1869 the Rt. Rev. Willis Nazrey along with the Rev. R.R. Disney, his later successor as BMEC bishop, founded the Nazrey Institute on the Dover and Chatham Townline near present day Oungah. The Nazrey Institute's operating model proved impractical, and its buildings were so poorly constructed that the school's rural site was abandoned in favour of a leased property in Chatham. As the Nazrey Institute's lease was about to expire due to insufficient funds, the Wilberforce trustees in Dresden were making important decisions about the Wilberforce Institute's development, including where to locate its new school building.[24] By 1872 they had approached Dresden's village council to create a separate Black elementary school in the village. No funds would be offered from the BAI land sales. Instead, council's By-Law No. 24 gave council the authority to borrow $4,000 to erect Union School Section (USS) 3 on the corner of Tecumseh and Brock Streets in the old Fairport survey in Dresden.[25] Some of the Wilberforce Institute's Chatham-based trustees were also board members of the Nazrey Institute in Chatham, interested in securing a proper educational institute in their own community. With Dresden's basic educational needs now addressed by USS 3, the trustees, through an Act of Parliament, incorporated the Wilberforce-Nazrey Institute as a single educational body, based in Chatham. Isaac Holden and Morris Potter, former Wilberforce trustees, were appointed to its board. The new corporation was mandated to provide primary and secondary education "proper preparation for matriculation examination in the areas of art, law, and medicine at the university level"[26] education for teachers, and preparatory courses for those entering the field of commerce. One hundred students would be enrolled in the new institute and, true to the original BAI deed, continued to be admitted regardless of their "sect, creed or nationality."[27] Monies generated by the Wilberforce trustees at Dresden allowed for the erection of a substantial brick school and a yearly operating budget of $25,000.

A seventy-seven-year-old J.C. Brown, standing on the steps of the school now named the Wilberforce Educational Institute, at the corner of Princess and Wellington Streets, could look up at the structure with pride, as here at last was a meaningful completion of his life's work. The Wilberforce Educational Institute (and the Woodstock Vocational Institute, a vocational school that also established at Chatham) would continue to serve the needs of people of African descent in the county into the twentieth century.

While the BAI's educational mandate was finally fulfilled, the work of trustee Rev. Thomas Hughes was not. As others turned their attentions to the new Chatham school, he was left alone to address one last remaining issue regarding the BAI's land and its people—and in its resolution would make his final and lasting contribution to the fight against racism and exclusion.

Chapter 17

A TIME *to* DIE
and a TIME *to* MOURN
The Fate of Dawn's Early Leaders

I N FEBRUARY 1874 THE REV. THOMAS HUGHES ENTERED Dresden's Village Council chamber to present a complex plan for reloca-tion of the BAI cemetery. His action was an important final mission for him as trustee of the Wilberforce Institute. He had reason to be confident that the all-white council he was about to appear before would back his pro-posal. Sitting at the head of the council chamber was the new first Reeve of the village, and former BAI receiver, Alex Trerice, and among the councillors was Dr. T.R. McInnes, who had treated his parishioner Amelia Shadd. Other councillors had recently been beneficiaries of BAI land sales and Wilberforce mortgages. Hughes was additionally assured that councillors who were look-ing for workable solutions to the emotionally charged work they had been mandated to undertake—the relocation of all of the community's burial grounds. The ultimate success of Hughes plan also relied on the support of the Black community and his Bishop. The protracted action Hughes was about to undertake provides a fascinating glimpse into both the inter-racial cooperation he was able to broker—and the racial strife that continued to exist in the community and what remains of public records of his transac-tions suggest this was his final attempt to combat racial segregation. Hughes' final actions as a trustee also coincide with a time when the Dawn Settlement was mourning the loss of many key leadership figures.

With its formation in 1871, the Dresden Village Council became legally responsible for the oversight of cemeteries. Passage of Ontario's *Baldwin Act*, which had assigned municipalities this responsibility throughout Ontario, had been inspired by a growing awareness of the need to address public sanitation in order to control disease. In the late 1880s, two major cholera epidemics had swept the globe. In England, cholera's spread had been linked to drinking water contaminants in wells and watercourses. This spurred large urban European centres like London and Paris to invest in massive sewage disposal systems and to order the removal of burial sites to outside city limits. These practices soon spread to North America.[1] In 1871 Dresden's newly minted council, to comply with government requirements, was grappling with how to comply with the law by taking steps to remove burial grounds within the new village limits, including: the Fairport survey's Methodist burial ground and Strangers' Burial Ground; a single burial at Rev. Hughes's church; and the BAI cemetery. One of the council's earliest bylaws had established a new cemetery on the Sydenham River, northeast of Dresden's village limits. Development of the cemetery and its access road took three years. Finally, on February 13, 1874, a notice was given that "parties having friends interred inside the Corporation...have them removed to the New Cemetery."[2]

The BAI cemetery had for thirty years been the burial site for the Dawn Settlement, and was the final resting place of people such as Rev. Josiah Henson's first wife, Nancy; Rev. William P. Newman's first wife, Nancy; Rev. Hiram Wilson's first wife, Hannah; Mary Ann Whipper Hollensworth; and other African-descent pioneers.[3] The order to remove their remains likely sparked a difficult and emotional debate that racial prejudice had the potential to complicate. Historical opposition to integrated burials by white cemetery managers is not an unknown phenomenon in Canada. In Nova Scotia, as recently as five decades ago, it was not allowed for the earthly remains of Black people to be buried alongside the bodies of whites in some cemeteries.[4] Some Canadian cemeteries are known to have included specific sections for non-whites, often located on their fringes. Evidence of the latter trend appears in two burial grounds in the vicinity of the Dawn Settlement area.[5]

The trust and respect Hughes commanded seems to have enabled him to complete a complex set of transactions that lead to creation of the "Anglican Range" on the northern border of the municipal cemetery whose control rested not with local cemetery managers but with the Bishop of the Anglican Diocese of Huron, based at London, Ontario. Land records show that Hughes independently purchased BAI lots that contained the former BAI cemetery from the Wilberforce Institute and 1874 council minutes show that interim financing was arranged with council to purchase the Anglican Range property. Hughes then appears to have designed the layout of the new cemetery so it lay immediately adjacent to the Dresden Cemetery[6] and oversaw the removal of graves from the BAI site and another burial site at his church to the new location. Once the BAI cemetery had been cleared of burials, he sold the land where it had been located and used the proceeds to pay off the loan granted to him by Dresden Village Council to make the initial purchase of the Anglican Range. Hughes's efforts in this regard are not recorded in any detail in council notes or his diaries, and surviving oral history[7] had tended to attribute the establishment of the Dresden Cemetery as a whole to Hughes. Primary records, including land deeds and council notes, do not support this version of events. Hughes's surviving diary pages make only a brief mention of his visit to an unspecified cemetery near the end of his entries. As such, Hughes's motivations and details about what graves were relocated and why he went to such elaborate lengths to develop a separate Anglican Range are undocumented. However, Hughes's diary does show, he was a champion of integration at a time when all of Dawn's churches except his own were segregated. Whether people of African descent had been actively excluded from the Dresden Cemetery or not, the racist attitudes Hughes had witnessed throughout his ministry likely gave him little confidence that the new Dresden Cemetery would be open to all. The deal he struck with the Dresden Village Council and the Bishop of Huron guaranteed his vision regarding racial integration would be respected by placing control over who could be buried together in the Anglican Range in the hands of the Bishop of Huron Diocese, in London, and not a local authority pressured by who might be influenced by any ardent segregationists who existed in the community.

In his original design of the Anglican Range,[8] Hughes created two sections. Range A would become occupied primarily (but not exclusively) by deceased members of Hughes's Christ Church integrated congregation and included his own family plot. Members of his church like Mary Ann (Whipper) Hollensworth, family members of Francis Moss Turner, and close associates like the Smiths and the Campbells are interred there. Range A also originally was the burial location of Rev. Hughes's colleagues in mission work, including white Congregational minister Rev. William Clarke and Rev. Samuel Lynn, founder of the Union Baptist Church in Chatham Township.[9] Archeological evidence suggests Hughes also provided plots for people from outside the community whose circumstances had led to denial of a Christian burial in their home parishes.[10] Plots on the plan for Range B, meanwhile, are curiously inscribed with the names of Dawn Settlement families including Richardson, Smith, Wallace, Davis, Jones, Grinnage, Highgate, Talbot, and Vandyke. While some individuals by these surnames remained associated with Hughes's Anglican congregation, others are more closely associated with Baptist congregations in Dresden and Chatham Townships and along with Rev. William Wright and Rev. Samuel Lynn's burials suggest the Anglican Range may have been created with the assistance or blessing of other ministers. Over time Range B has taken on the appearance of being a Baptist burial ground while Range A has been understood as more specific to the Anglicans. Meanwhile, Hughes's grave in Range A, in its original configuration, was situated on a slight rise that gave his plot a central position that directly overlooked Range B, so that in death, as in life, he was surrounded by the people he had served.

Discrepancies between the names on headstones in Range B and those on Hughes's original plan indicate that BAI graves were likely not exclusively relocated to Hughes's cemetery. The majority of dates on headstones in Range B also tend to fall well after the time of the relocations, suggesting some families did not follow through in using plots that were reserved for them.[11] Some may have preferred to entrust reburial to their own spiritual leaders. Archeological evidence[12] suggests that the burial ground known today as the BAI Cemetery and the Henson Family Cemetery, which lie on opposite sides of Freedom Road[13] near the Josiah Henson Museum, may have received a number of the reburials. Ground penetrating radar and headstone information at the "new" BAI Cemetery and the Henson Family Cemetery together with land records suggest Rev. Samuel Henry Davis's Baptist congregation may have chosen to create what is now identified as the BAI Cemetery[14] as a denominational burial ground. That site includes burials of the Rev. Davis and his family, of Peter B. Smith's family members, Rev. William P. Newman's wife, and other known Baptists. Some headstones date to times before the cemetery was established, indicating a relocation from the original BAI Cemetery likely took place. Ground penetrating radar also reveals so few burials here that it is unlikely that all the original BAI cemetery removals came to this site.[15] Similarly, Rev. Josiah Henson may have provided burial spaces for his BMEC congregation[16] as evidenced by the volume of burials in the Henson Family Cemetery. Ground penetrating radar further reveals some multiple burials in a single shaft, a feature also found in relocated graves in the Dresden Cemetery.[17] No records exist of churchyards being established at Davis's First Regular Baptist Church nor at Henson's BMEC site. Evidence does exist that Davis's church had planned a denominational cemetery on a ten-acre plot on Concession 3 of Camden Gore on a corner of Davis's farm, but the site is not known to have been developed for this purpose.[18] This raises the possibility that both the Henson Family Cemetery and BAI Cemetery were developed as denominational burial grounds at the time of the relocation of the old BAI cemetery. Regardless of where the reburials occurred, the original BAI cemetery was cleared of its burials and its land sold, finally ending Hughes's official duties as a Wilberforce Institute trustee. The Anglican Range Hughes established would remain under the control of the Anglican Diocese of Huron until 1935 when its management reverted to the Town of Dresden. The Anglican Range today is completely encompassed by the Dresden Cemetery and its origins as a separately managed cemetery have long fallen out of living memory.

Rev. Hughes would be called on by Rev. Josiah Henson to help him resolve one remaining BAI-related issue: that of repayment of the debt Henson incurred as a result of legal costs associated with the court case against Scoble and Brown. While Scoble and Brown had recovered their expenses from the court, Henson, for reasons not elaborated on in the public record, remained uncompensated. Wilberforce trustees, with the exception of Hughes, continued to be unsympathetic to Henson's complaint that he had been poorly treated. Hughes would provide what support he could, even as, at age fifty-eight, he lay dying. On April 12, 1876, Rev. Henson came to his bedside. The two ministers may have had their differences in the past, but at their final meeting Hughes would provide Henson with encouragement and a letter of introduction to English friends that would assist Henson in raising funds during a final overseas speaking tour. Henson would reciprocate by honouring Hughes's memory in the new English edition of his autobiography. A grieving congregation buried Hughes in his Anglican Range, erected a pure white obelisk on his grave, and installed a marble plaque above his pulpit at his recently completed Christ Church in Dresden. The plaque remains in its place of honour to this day. Only a handful of African-descent families would remain with the Anglican congregation after Hughes's death. Most would join the area's Black Baptist Churches or Henson's BMEC congregation. Yet, Hughes's vision of an integrated church and society remained. His vision and his work (see Chapter 19) remained as a lasting influence on successive generations.

Henson's final trip to England, in April of 1876, was a triumph that introduced him to a new generation of British audiences and reconnected him with old supporters. His successful speaking tour capitalized on his link to Stowe's famous fictional character. Large crowds of people may have been attracted by the promise they would meet "the real Uncle Tom" of Harriet Beecher Stowe's great work, but it would be Henson who would captivate them with his characteristic delivery of his message that included singing, humour, and his dignified manner of speaking. He and his second wife Charlotte would be presented to Queen Victoria who gifted them with a signed portrait of herself in a gold frame. Rev. Henson's efforts were so successful he was able to pay off his court costs and all of the Wilberforce mortgages he had acquired to buy former BAI land.[19] His mortgage repayments in essence would be his final financial contribution to the educational institute and the community he had worked so hard over much of his forty-plus years as a free man to support.

With the final vestiges of the BAI now removed from the map of the Dawn Settlement and the departure of the important Black abolitionists, Dawn's reputation as a centre for Black education and activism began to fade. As the sun began to set on the abolitionist era, the lengthening shadows of the fictional Uncle Tom grew, obscuring other aspects of Henson's life and of the other internationally connected figures who had once lived at Dawn.

On May 5, 1883, Henson died. His funeral took place at his British Methodist Episcopal Church where he had preached his last sermon just days before, and where Rev. Walter Hawkins and Rev. Samuel Henry Davis officiated at his funeral. Mourners overflowed the small frame building into the yard and the street beyond. The funeral procession of over fifty-two carriages followed by hundreds more people travelling on foot comprised a multiracial group of mourners who bore him to his final resting place on his farm. A January 17, 1882, *Hamilton Spectator* account noted that church bells had rung throughout the Town of Dresden and businesses had closed for the funeral. What details of the funeral that exist, however, fail to paint a complete picture of the remaining community who gathered to honour Henson at his graveside. Included among them were likely many of Henson's forty-four grandchildren and dozen great-grandchildren whose tears Henson had predicted would comfort him as they fell on his coffin. While Dresden now numbered over two thousand people, only a remnant of Henson's abolitionist era contemporaries remained. William Whipper had died in the US on March 9, 1876, and by the time of Henson's death Whipper's widow, Harriet, had sold off most of her husband's Dresden land holdings. Only a small, thriving Black business district remained on the east end of Main Street that included a blacksmith, a grocery store, and a barber shop. James Burns Hollensworth had advanced in years but had continued to reinvent himself with the changing times. Once a land agent and lumber mill manager, he had become a confectioner and restaurateur who operated the town's first ice cream parlour, Sweet Briar Cottage, and an upscale oyster restaurant on Main Street. He had married a third time, to Mary Smith, after the deaths of his first wife, Mary Ann Whipper, and his second wife, Margaret Brown. His daughter Ida, meanwhile, had married prominent Chatham businessman Nathaniel Murray, and they moved to Chicago. His and Mary Ann's two sons, Albert and Ellsworth, had returned to the US. Annie and Arthur, his children by Margaret, had moved to Wisconsin. As Hollensworth aged, he became blind, and after forty years of life in Dresden moved to Kaukauna, Wisconsin, to be cared for by his daughter Annie. He had a massive stroke, lingering in this world for several months until his death on April 9, 1898. Subsequently, his third wife, Mary, moved to Detroit to be with her son William. Mary died in Cape May, New Jersey, in 1914.[20] Mary Smith's son Stephen lived out his life in Dresden as did his wife Jane Levere Smith. Their son Stephen Levere Smith, (who preferred to be known by Levere) like his grandmother and uncle, moved to Detroit where he contracted pneumonia and, tragically, died at age thirty. Levere's remains were returned to Dresden, and he was buried in the Dresden Cemetery's Anglican Range near Mary Ann Hollensworth. Some descendants of Stephen and Jane Levere Smith's daughters continue to live in the Dresden area.

Francis Moss Turner, husband of Sarah Whipper, self-described in his will as a man of "sound mind but weak in body," died in Dresden on November 19, 1865.[21] His widow, Sarah, died thirty-seven years later. [22] James Whipper Purnell left Dresden for Philadelphia to operate a lumber mill he owned with William Whipper. Purnell remained politically active, joining the Pennsylvania State Equal Rights League, and remained a prominent member in Philadelphia's Black society. He died in Philadelphia in February 1880 and is buried in the Olive Cemetery in West Philadelphia.[23] The migrations and deaths of these individuals represented a major loss to the community in the former Dawn Settlement. At Dawn there was no longer an "elite" group of leaders, and the African-descent population tended rather to be made up of a more economically homogenous group who pursued quiet, industrious lives as labourers and skilled tradesmen. Among them was William Kersey, a carpenter; Clem Gordon, a hostler; Arthur and Willard Talbot, blacksmiths; Abel Cockfield and Aaron Highgate, teachers; James Freeman and Jacob Stout, shoemakers; Joseph Lucas, a mason; Moses Lucas and George Washington, sailors; and Hiram Moore and Thomas Taylor, boatmen.[24]

The loss of the Black elite was so profound that little documentation and few photos remained to document their presence and few family members remained to keep their memory alive. Only vague references to their presence would remain in the public record, while the legend of "Uncle Tom" would continue to grow. Henson's death would poignantly show just how profoundly and how quickly Henson's real life became overshadowed. Numerous obituaries would appear in newspapers in Canada, England, parts of Europe, and the US. But few would provide details of Henson's real life. A Cedar Rapids, Iowa, paper was among the few that did, revealing Henson as a family man and mentioning his son Tom's service in the Union Army and the trip Henson had made to his mother's graveside after the Civil War. A

Marysville, Ohio, paper portrayed Henson as "cheerful and jovial" and noted the number of his expansive family, and papers in England placed emphasis on his encounters with British Lords and Queen Victoria. Other newspapers seemed to place little or no relevance on Rev. Henson's life outside of his association with Stowe's popular novel and merely repeated those aspects of Rev. Henson's life that aligned with those of the fictional Uncle Tom. A Chicago, Illinois, obituary even entitled their writeup as the "Obituary of Uncle Tom." Some even used Henson's death notice as an excuse to resurrect the controversy over the legitimacy of the claim that he was Tom.

By the time of Henson's death in 1883, a full generation had grown up not having read a slave narrative while *Uncle Tom's Cabin* continued to reinforce how most people understood the lives of enslaved people. The novel had been translated into several European languages, and sales would remain strong on both sides of the Atlantic into the first half of the twentieth century. Stowe's characters Tom, Topsy, Eliza, and Simon Lagree also lived on in popular minstrel shows. These so-called Tom plays denigrated Stowe's characters and did not honour her novel's original intent. As the *St. Albans Daily Messenger* of Vermont would editorialize in its obituary on Rev. Henson, he "never saw a performance of 'Uncle Tom's Cabin.' He was lucky."[25] On March 12, 1890, eight years after Rev. Henson's death, an *Uncle Tom's Cabin* play came to the Shaw Theatre in Dresden and would likely influence how Henson would be remembered locally.

Contemporary accounts of Rev. Henson given during his lifetime, meanwhile, have left us with conflicting views of the man. These accounts show Henson to be what was once said of General James Wolfe: "a victim of useable history...his character buried beneath the various agendas of his supporters and detractors down through the centuries."[26] Henson's slave narrative had been heavily influenced by abolitionists anxious to use his life story as the representation of the powerful reasons to support the anti-slavery cause. Frederick Douglass would paint him as the kindly Father Henson, a venerated community leader and family man. Rev. William P. Newman, his principal detractor, condemned him as an opportunist and a knife-wielding ruffian. And in more modern times, Rev. Henson has been portrayed both as the spiritual leader of his people, a Black Moses, and as the incompetent manager of a failed settlement. In the 1940s and '50s, Rev. Jennie Johnson

Two portraits of Rev. Josiah Henson taken from his 1858 and 1876 are emblematic of the differing views of him, on one hand as a dominating force in Dawn and on the other as the revered Father Henson.

would recognize the potential of his life for promoting the civil rights cause. And the Black Power movements of the 1960s and '70s would denigrate his memory as "Uncle Tom" became a derisive term to describe people of African descent who lowered themselves to ingratiate themselves to whites. These kinds of "hero" or "villain" extremes, as the historical documentarian Ken Burns once expressed,[27] reduce history to melodrama and fail to create an understanding of the humanity of historical figures and the extraordinary circumstances into which they are thrust. The burial of Henson beneath layers of myth, legend, and political debate have meant much of who he was has been lost. Yet, at Dawn, one can still see those aspects of his life that give us reason to not simply dismiss his role in Dawn's early development as exaggerated or false—or as purely "fictionalized" history. Dawn is where Henson came into his own, purchasing and operating a farm and a store, playing a significant role in the BAI's development, raising an astonishing amount of funds for the BAI and other causes, acting as an Underground Railroad conductor, becoming a remarkable entrepreneur with a tremendous gift for promotion and marketing, and, well into old age, remaining a vital international public speaker capable of transfixing large audiences. While most surviving photographic images show him as a sombre elderly man disabled from a severe beating, one account describes him at around age fifty as having been "a man of splendid physique who...would be a very dangerous antagonist in a personal conflict."[28] He is also portrayed as "a man of great natural ability and sound common sense, and a devout and sincere Christian, not only by profession but in practice of daily life."[29] Henson's sombre portraits belie a keen sense of humour that made it possible for him to make pointed remarks about slavery and racism palatable to his white audiences. On Henson's quick wit, Archie McKellar related the encounter of Henson with the Honourable Edward Blakely in which Henson had remarked, "A white man is just as good as a negro as long as he behaves himself."[30] Though not the sole figure of international historical significance to appear in the Dawn Settlement's history, Henson was very much a representative of the era's massive migration of formerly enslaved people and their efforts to establish new lives and to help those yet held in bondage as well as their fellow settlers. What Henson was assuredly not, as his English biographer John Lobb claimed, was the "founder of a town called Dawn." The honour for founding the Dawn Settlement, which was not a town, must, as this book has shown, fall to a number of individuals—both ordinary people and Black elite—who developed the community. And just as Rev. Henson's arrival at Dawn did not signal the creation of the Dawn Settlement, neither does his death mark its end. Neither can the departure and deaths of the freemen who invested so heavily in creating a space of freedom and equality at Dresden put a coda on the settlement's history, nor can the erasure of the British American Institute's presence from the landscape be seen as the end of the wider Dawn Settlement. In the same fashion that the Dawn Settlement's geography does not have a definitive end neither can an end date be placed on its timeline. While the original settlers at Dawn lay dead and buried, and their lives are often forgotten, the foundational work they successfully began here can be traced along a continuum of contribution and resistance that, as we will see in the following final chapters, extends well beyond the abolitionist period.

Chapter 18

MIGRATION, RESISTANCE, *and* CONTRIBUTION *in a* NEW CENTURY

I N 1910, A SMALL GROUP OF BAPTISTS FILED INTO AN ABAN-doned labourer's shelter at Cooper's Mill in Chatham Township. Rev. Jennie Johnson, the first ordained woman minister in Canada, presided there over a service for the congregation she would continue to serve for the next five years. During that time, she would oversee the construction of a new brick church on the Prince Albert Sideroad, located roughly halfway between Dresden and Chatham. Rev. Johnson's life bridges the abolitionist period with the modern era, and through her career we can trace the continuum of resistance and contribution begun with the abolitionist era and extending into the modern civil rights era, and particular in Rev. Johnson's sense of self as a woman in leadership. This appears as a consequence of her rootedness in a community where women had previously been empowered by Lucretia Mott's early women's movement and the encouragement of William Whipper's moral reform movement.[1]

Born in 1868, the year after Canada became a nation, Rev. Jennie Johnson would live to see Canada's Centennial celebrations. In her early life she had attended the funeral of the Rev. Josiah Henson and lived in a Dresden that was still home to a remnant of the Black elite, including the Smith and Hollensworth families and people who had been born into enslavement. In her later life she would witness the modern US Civil Rights Movement and be uplifted by the impassioned speeches of Rev. Martin Luther King Jr. The ninety-nine-year span of Johnson's life as such was an important transitional period in which the people of Dawn continued to fight for dignity and equality within a society that often sought to push them to the margins. Many people of Rev. Johnson's era would continue in the spirit of resistance and contribution, introduced by their forebears in their lives at Dawn and the places they continued to migrate, into the twentieth and twenty-first century as will be explored in Chapters 18 to 21.

Jennie Johnson was born in Chatham Township to Isaiah Johnson, a formerly enslaved man from Maryland, and Charlotte Butler Johnson. The harrowing story of her father and his brother's desperate flight north ended at Dresden in 1858[2] where the Johnson family became members of Rev. Thomas Hughes's mission church. As a child, Jennie Johnson had felt a strong calling to preach the Gospel. In October 1885, when Rev. Samuel Lynn left the First Regular Baptist Church to form the Union Baptist Church in Chatham Township, Johnson, then still a teenager, began evangelizing the community's young people, bringing many of them into Rev. Lynn's fold. After attending the Wilberforce Seminary in Ohio, Johnson wrote a manual outlining the order of worship for Rev. Lynn's church services. Despite her deeply felt calling, education, and proven service, Johnson's desire to become an ordained Christian minister was not universally accepted because she was a woman. Having grown up in a community with an Abolitionist tradition where women's involvement in public life was supported and women like Mary Smith, Mary Ann Hollensworth, and Mary Ann Shadd had modelled active and effective leadership likely was an influencing factor in Johnson's young life.[3] Despite opposition within her own church community, she persisted in pursuing ordination, and in October 1909, at age forty-, achieved it through the support of the white Free Baptist Church in Galesville, Michigan.

In Johnson's migration story we can also trace the "trajectories of Blackness" that permeate the stories of Dawn's descendants and continued to involve them in major movements on both sides of the US-Canada border.

Rev. Johnson would herself become involved with African-Americans at Flint, Michigan, who were caught up in the Great Migration. The Great Migration was one of the largest and most rapid mass internal movement by any ethnic group in US history. It resulted in a major demographic shift in the US. Prior to 1900, 90 percent of African-Americans had lived in the rural South. By the 1970s, six million mainly rural African-Americans had migrated so that 80 percent of America's Black population now resided in the industrial cities of the North.

In the Deep South, African-Americans faced segregation, a lack of economic opportunities, and extreme violence and murder. The positive northward pull of better paying jobs, particularly in the labour-hungry auto industry, and a better quality of life brought them to industrial centers like Chicago, Illinois; and Detroit, Flint, and Pontiac, Michigan. In Flint Rev. Johnson would establish a Christian centre that provided migrating families with a place to socialize and find spiritual uplift, hot lunches, clothing for children, and guidance and counselling for adults.[4]

Others in the Dawn Settlement area in the early part of the twentieth century also continued to migrate, as their forebears had, in a search for freedom, equality, and economic opportunities. Movements from the Dawn Settlement area sometimes mimicked those of the Great Migration. While in Ontario they did not face the same level of life-threatening aggression their US counterparts did, migration by rural Blacks from the Kent settlements and other areas of Canada was likely inspired in part by systemic racism by the government that at times signalled they were not wanted as citizens. Order-in-Council PC 2011-1324, approved on August 12, 1911, by Prime Minister Sir Wilfrid Laurier's cabinet, is a dramatic example. The changes it proposed to the *Immigration Act* would have, if imposed, ended any new immigration by people of African descent because, as the act stated, they had been "deemed unsuitable to the climate and requirements of Canada." Thankfully, the order never received enough support to become law, but it nevertheless demonstrated that the legacy of racist individuals with links to government like Edwin Larwill remained into the twentieth century.

The changing rural landscape and the need for better economic opportunities would be the main driver of the exodus of the original Dawn settlers' descendants to Canadian urban centres like London, Toronto, and Windsor and the same Northern US industrial centres as their African-American counterparts. Even Rev. Josiah Henson's son Peter would settle in Flint and then Detroit.[5] It is difficult to tease out the extent to which this movement of Canadian Blacks from rural areas to US industrial cities paralleled the Great Migration and how much was simply part of a more general outmigration from rural to urban areas between 1900 and 1970. This was a period of rapid mechanization in agriculture and consolidation of farms into fewer and fewer hands that dramatically reduced the number of labourers needed to produce food and the numbers of farms and farm owners. In the mid-1850s, 90 percent of Canada's general population was rural; by 1931 this had fallen to 50 percent, and by the 1970s only 30 percent of Canadians lived outside major urban centres with less than 3 percent making their living from farming.

As the farm population decreased, main street businesses in small towns, along with agricultural industries and services like mills and farm-equip-ment dealerships also dramatically decreased in number. Rapidly chang-ing technology also contributed to the disappearance of lucrative trades like blacksmithing, and Dresden's four smithies, two of which were owned by people of African-descent, were reduced to one, white owned, by the mid-twentieth century. The shipping industry, a nineteenth-century main-stay of Dresden's economy, declined sharply with the arrival of the railroad in 1882. Rail offered a more direct and efficient means of transporting goods and passengers as trains could operate in winter when ice blocked water-ways. Shipbuilding yards operated by white industrialists like Alexander Trerice ceased operation.[6] Those who had worked as boatmen and sailors, like the Washingtons and Lucases, no longer had a local source of employ-ment. By the late 1880s, railroad construction jobs that had provided 2,500 Canadian Blacks temporary work at a rate of $10 per month plus board had disappeared. Pullman porter was now one of the few railroad positions left open to African-descent people. A handful of men from the former Dawn Settlement area and Chatham Township took up this profession, including William Jones (1874–1965) and two members of the Myers and Richardson families. Jim Myers, grandson of Virginian farmer John Myers, was a member of the porter's union and worked for the CPR, travelling between Toronto and Vancouver. William Isaac Richardson (1902–1989) was a descen-dant of Kentuckian James Richardson, who had migrated in 1855 to the

Dover Settlement in Kent County. William grew up on his father's farm in Chatham Township's Concession Ten, leaving at age nineteen for a six-to-eight-year stint as a porter, which helped him fulfill his ambition to see the world—which for him was the rail line between Toronto and Vancouver.[7] In the early 1960s, William Richardson took his son William Jr. on a trip to retrace his journeys, returning to the grand hotels where he had stayed and an apartment he had once occupied in Toronto's Royal York Hotel. William Richardson Sr. had, after his time with the railroad, returned home to farm, but his job experience had been life-changing. It had taught him a number of personal skills and shown him how to get on in the wider world where, as a man of African descent, he often encountered complex and unspoken rules regarding social interaction with the train's paying white passengers. While Richardson returned home, others, like William Jones, did not, eventually settling in Chicago, Illinois, instead.[8]

In 1880, Dresden's general population peaked at 2,800. Like many small towns in Ontario, the collapse of the lumber industry due to clear-cutting resulted in a period of sharp economic decline. The population plummeted to 1,200 people by 1900. Lumberman and shipper Alexander Trerice fought the inevitable by building the Dawn Tramway, a narrow-gauge railroad that would import wood from the still more heavily forested areas of Lambton County to mills in Dresden. With the declining use of ships for freight, he also transformed his cargo vessel, the *Byron Trerice*, into an excursion boat. These measures only delayed the inevitable economic fallout caused by the decline of traditional lumbering and shipping industries, and by1892 Trerice had gathered the remnants of his fortune and moved to Melita, Manitoba, to farm. He died there in 1900.[9] His body was returned for burial in the Dresden cemetery.[10] The general outmigration from the area to the Canadian and American West included African-Canadians. The genealogy of the Jones-Carter family is peppered with accounts of migration to Montana, Oklahoma, and Missouri. Included in this migration was John Alexander Jones (1887–1943), formerly of Chatham Township, who opened a successful poolroom and barbershop in Kansas City. A Smith family photo album also includes the portrait of an unidentified man with a photographer's mark from Montana.[11]

Others resettled closer to home in places like Windsor, Toronto, Detroit, Flint, Pontiac, and Chicago, as evidenced in the social columns of

204 · IN THE LIGHT OF DAWN

Black-owned and -operated newspapers in the US and Canada. Bethune Binga, who lived in Chatham, wrote a column for the *Chicago Defender* that shows the continued interactions of local people with those who had moved to Chicago, Illinois; and Detroit, Ypsilanti, and Battle Creek, Michigan. The London, Ontario–based newspaper *Dawn of Tomorrow* (published in the early 1900s) and the Toronto-based *Canadian Observer* (1915–1919) record similar interactions in the US and in Canada and between the communities of Dover, Buxton, Chatham Township, and the City of Chatham. Typical *Canadian Observer* social columns note: "Mr. and Mrs. Perkins and Mr. and Mrs. Davis motored up from Detroit (to Dresden) last Sunday, returning yesterday";[12] and "Mr. Garnet Cook of Dresden, Mr. Jimmie Hanson of Cleveland, Mr. Clarence Lucas of Dresden, Miss Norma Lucas of Dresden, Miss Lucil Richardson of Detroit and Odessa Price of Pittsburgh, PA, were the guests of Miss Flora Handsor (of Dover) Sunday."[13]

The decision to migrate was often economic. Clifford Millben of Chatham, for instance, moved to Pontiac, Michigan, in 1914 to work for the Oliver J. Beaudette Company, a supplier of autobodies to the Ford Motor Company. Millben, who had been paid fifty cents per day at Chatham, now earned 22.5 cents *per hour*, working nine hours a day and five-and-a-half days a week.[14] Higher wages, more free time, and the prospect of living among large concentrations of people who shared the same racial identity and enjoyed similar cultural and social pursuits turned larger urban centres in both Canada and the US into magnets. People broke away from the relative isolation and constant toil inherent with mixed farm operations to new urban lives where good pay and regular work hours allowed for leisure activities available through Black social institutions, sports teams, nightlife, and cultural venues.

Career opportunities unimaginable back in the old hometown existed outside the auto industry, in the service sector, private business enterprises, and in culture and entertainment. As a young girl, Hazel Solomon (1919–1999) moved from Dresden to Windsor with her parents, John and Ethel Solomon. She was considerably gifted musically, mastering the piano, organ, and violin. Singing was her most notable talent. After formal instruction in Toronto, Solomon taught music in Windsor before embarking on a professional singing career. She toured across Canada and in seven US states, presenting a program that included arias from Mozart's *Marriage of Figaro*, selections from Dvorak, and "negro spirituals." [15] Dawn's descendants continue into the present generation to excel at careers in entertainment. Andrew Chambers, a Burnett descendant, was part of the cast of the CBC hit series *Degrassi High*. Katherine Highgate, the daughter of Dresden residents Lee Highgate and Sandra (Travis) Highgate, has acted in commercials and music videos and in the Netflix mini-series *Self Made*, the story of Madam C.J. Walker.[16]

Those who left in the early-twentieth century often maintained a strong attachment to the area, and some would eventually be drawn back home.[17] Some chose, on their death, to be buried in the family plot at Dresden. When Stephen Levere Smith died of pneumonia, at age thirty, in Detroit,[18] his body was entrusted to Dresden's white undertaker J.W. Harris, and his funeral was held in his grandmother Mary Smith's church. Levere is buried in the Dresden Cemetery plot near Mary Ann Hollensworth.[19]

Some remained, continuing on family farms that had been established a half century or more before by their forebears. Land continued to represent as it had for Henry Bibb, Rev. Josiah Henson, Mary Ann Shadd Cary and Rev. William King, independence and a dignified way of life. New opportunities presented in agriculture in the twentieth century in the form of innovative crops like tomatoes, flax, and sugar beets, and African-descent people would be among those who pioneered their cultivation. In 1903, when the first tomato cannery was established in Dresden, an S. Talbot applied for and received a grower's contract. Talbot grew an acre of tomatoes, making him the third largest grower of the new crop. Canadian Canners Limited's leading producer at Dresden was the white farmer James Anderson, who received $142.43 per acre for his efforts. Talbot by contrast received $71.02 per acre. An explanation for this discrepancy cannot be found in the *Dresden Times* account where this was reported.[20] If Talbot was being treated inequitably, he had no alternative marketing options. Unlike in the nineteenth century when Black industrialists like the Whippers and Purnells had owned lumber and other industries, none of the twentieth-century industries and processing plants in Dresden were Black owned. Regardless of the reasons for the difference in pay between Talbot and other growers, Black-owned farming operations continued to thrive, sometimes into seven or more consecutive generations.

Not all of the new and innovative agriculturally based industries succeeded. In 1903 Dresden's massive sugar beet plant closed after only two years of operation and traditional industries like the Smith Woolen Mill (later the Burns' Linen and Wool Mill that produced locally made textiles) could not compete against imports brought in by rail from larger plants. Industry closures presented challenges to all farmers, as did the caprices of the markets and weather. Many turned to supplementation of farm incomes with off-farm work or farmgate sales. Tom Jones, of Chatham Township, contracted himself and his team out to do drainage work on neighbouring farms and along township roads. He performed the backbreaking work of digging ditches using a large manually operated dump bucket pulled by his team of horses.[21] The Campbell family sold cordwood to passing ships from their dock on the Sydenham River, known as Campbell's Landing.

Icum Campbell with one of his racehorses. (*Photo courtesy of Thompson-Guest family*)

The Campbells also generated income through entertainment. Charles Campbell, the family's patriarch, had been born enslaved in Kentucky in 1829. After a harrowing escape via Niagara, he arrived in Wallaceburg, at the mouth of the Sydenham River, and had worked at a livery stable there before purchasing a farm in Camden Gore. Campbell had a keen interest in horses but was best known for his musical talents. He began playing the violin at neighbourhood social events and in 1873 formed a small orchestra with his brother Jack. Jack married Delphine Smith, a freeborn woman from Euphemia Township, and together they had seven children: Charles (b. 1869), John (1871), Thomas (1873), Nellie (1875), William (1877), Lavina (1879), and Icum (1889). All were musically talented and eventually joined the family orchestra.

The Campbell Family Band were in demand at house parties and old-time country dances in neighbouring communities, including Starkweather's Corners (Tupperville), Dresden, and Bothwell. The Campbells also operated a dance hall on their farm and were in demand on excursion boats travelling between Dresden and Walpole Island on Lake St. Clair for Sunday school picnics and on dinner cruises between Dresden to Detroit. In the 1940s, Icum Campbell, his wife, Tillie, and brother Tom kept the family's musical tradition alive by playing at local dances. Icum would remain a popular entertainer into

Campbell family band member with instruments. (*Photo courtesy of Calvin Shreve*)

the 1960s. On January 15, 1970, on his seventy-ninth birthday, five hundred people gathered at the Royal Canadian Legion Branch 113 in Dresden to celebrate Icum Campbell Night, honouring the veteran musician who had spent seventy of his seventy-nine years bringing joy to others through his music. People from several US states and across Canada attended.[22]

Breeding, training, and driving horses also was a source of income for many. In the 1880s one of the two horse-drawn buses that took passengers from the Dresden train station to its three hotels was driven by a man of African descent. Others worked as hostlers in hotel stables.[23] The Campbells and others would become respected as racehorse breeders, drivers, and trainers. Standard bred racing in Dresden was established in the 1880s with the introduction of regular Labour Day races and became a major industry in Dresden in the 1980s as Dresden Raceway introduced night racing and para-mutual betting on Saturdays and three weeknights. In its heyday, the Dresden track became known as Southwestern Ontario's "Little Saratoga," attracting capacity crowds from Toronto, London, Windsor, Detroit, and other urban centres. The raceway is located on what was once the northeast corner of Rev. Josiah Henson's farm, and there is a curious connection of Henson to the industry as he once owned a Hambletonian stallion,[24] a foundational breed of trotting horse favoured for harness racing. Rev. Henson, as a minister, likely was not involved in racing. His purchase of the Hambletonian likely reflects his interest in improving farm stock and was used to breed fine carriage horses. The stallion may also have been offered for stud services for those who did wish to race. Henson descendants like Beecher Henson, Josiah's grandson, was a handler and trainer for the white Elgie family's racing stable in the 1930s.[25] Other families became leading breeders, trainers, and drivers at the Dresden Raceway, and Dwayne Guest enjoyed an international career as a sulky driver in Macau where he earned a second-place trophy in the World Driving Championship.[26] At Dresden Raceway during the 2021 Emancipation Day weekend, harness racing legends, including members of the Grinnage, McCorkle, List, Prince, Davis, Simmons, Tanner, and Guest families, were recognized for their contributions to the racing industry.

Skilled trades, like blacksmithing, and the service industry, including shopkeeping, were other areas where Dawn's descendants continued their contribution to community life after 1900. At least two women, the Burkett sisters, continued in the tradition of Mary Smith as independent storeowners. Those who had no land, no trade, and no business turned to factories like O. and W. McVean Ltd for employment, working side by side with white employees as general labourers and skilled tradesmen.[27] Life at the turn of the twentieth century continued to be difficult for many, particularly for widows whose circumstances had forced them to become the family breadwinners while still caring for young children. A fortunate few, like

Rev. Jennie Johnson's mother, had been practical nurses and midwives. For others, the dual disadvantage of sex and race meant they could only find low-paid domestic work in upper-class homes. Some positions required maids or child caregivers to live in. Martha Isobel Jones worked in the home of white hardware store owner and real estate developer J.B. Carscallen, where she remained until her death in January 1922.[28] Even Rev. Jennie Johnson worked for a short time as a young woman in Georgia Place, the stately home of Osgood and Catherine McVean.[29] The McVeans employed a live-in nanny for their large family of young children, as did other well-to-do families, and when hosting clients from the US they would employ the Smith brothers, a Chatham family that specialized in catering high society functions, to serve these events. The Smiths were highly sought after for their stylish catering service. They dressed in white livery and donned white gloves and served their dishes on domed silver trays—giving local affairs a perceived elegance that imitated that seen in 1920s Hollywood movies.[30]

Unfortunately, life also imitated art in other less-positive ways. Among the more popular—and offensive—of early Hollywood offerings was D.W. Griffith's silent film *The Birth of a Nation*. It celebrated the Ku Klux Klan as white knights dedicated to preserving white institutions giving a dangerous endorsement of their terrorist tactics. Many early-twentieth-century mov-ies also tended to relegate non-whites to stereotypical roles and African-American musicians and dancers were often the only African-descent people featured for their talent and sophistication. This heavy cultural influence imported from the US was combined with Canadians' British-influenced culture, which included a degree of class consciousness. People of African descent could only enter Quality Hill's grand homes through the servants' entrance.[31] Yet there remained a pride among upper-class families in linking their name to that of Rev. Josiah Henson.[32] Association with Henson was perhaps seen as desirable because his "Uncle Tom" association had made him Dresden's most famous resident, and because he had been embraced by Queen Victoria and British aristocracy. One oral history credits the McVean family as having nursed a very ill Henson back to health. Another claims that Henson owned a pet crow that perched on his shoulder on his trips to town; as he passed William McVean's home, then located at the corner of Fuller and Holden Streets, the crow is said to have flown from Henson's shoulder to McVean's and to have stayed there until Henson made the return journey home. It has not been possible to verify these oral family histories.

The lives of African-Canadians were often limited by the prejudices of the day, yet they would continue to make contributions to the community, working around, over, or through the barriers put in their path. Stories of direct and open defiance are rare, but a sense of self-worth and pride shines through in stories of ordinary people like "Louise."

There is no written record of Catherine McVean's domestic worker's name but Catherine's descendents believe she may have been called "Louise". As the nurse to the Osgood and Catherine McVean children, Louise grew close to their son Osgoode.[33] When Catherine commissioned a local photographer to take his picture, Louise was tasked with taking him to the sitting. Perhaps because of her close relationship with the boy, or because she wanted a photo of herself, she had dressed in her Edwardian finery, crowned her head with a magnificent plumed hat, and prepared to leave Georgia Place. Catherine McVean, having guessed her intent, stopped her and warned her not to appear in the photographs. Catherine was a formidable woman and likely expected this ended the matter. Yet, when she received the photos, they showed Osgood flanked by Louise looking defiantly into the photographer's lens. The photo remains in the collection of a family descendant, a remarkable documentation of a woman whose clear sense of self-worth had allowed her to boldly stand up to authority. Her story and that of Catherine's response remain the stuff of McVean family legend.[34]

If the world was often unforgiving and even sometimes hostile, family, churches, lodges, and other Black institutions provided a supportive community. Dresden had its own branch of the Prince Hall Masons, the Mount Moriah Lodge #4. Rev. Josiah Henson had been a member. Fraternal orders such as the Masons offered mutual aid and fellowship, but churches were "the cornerstones of communities. Religious institutions…ministered to… spiritual needs, performed social and educational functions and supplied most of their administrators. Religion, indeed, was fundamental to the Black experience: in slavery, it was the only consolation; in freedom, it inspired exultation and gratitude. When they were denied full participation in the regular churches, they were prepared to follow a separate path to Christian salvation." [35] That separate path provided strong ties among individuals and families throughout the region. In Dresden, the strength of the Black church was publicly displayed in the large gatherings that turned out for annual river baptisms that took place on what had previously been the British American

"Louise," a servant in the Osgood and Catherine McVean household with their son Osgoode. *(Photo courtesy of Peggy Shepherd-Johnson)*

212 · IN THE LIGHT OF DAWN

Institute lands on the Sydenham River at the base of what is now Freedom Road. These outdoor gatherings survived into the late 1940s. Through this Black society, and the support it gave, many continued to believe in their own worth, talents, and agency and aspired to excellence in the services they provided within Black institutions and, despite resistance, within the wider sphere of Canadian society. Most remarkable in their service were those who offered their very lives to defend British soil. Military service remains a striking example of the historical continuum of resistance and contribution.

Chapter 19

ANSWERING
the CALL

Contributions to
Community and Military

T HE GREAT WAR HAD BEEN RAGING FOR TWO YEARS WHEN a group of descendants of the original Dawn settlers enlisted in the No. 2 Construction Battalion,[1] the only segregated Black unit in Canadian military history. The unit was created in the early days of the Battle of the Somme, in July 1916. The loss of sixty thousand men in the first day of fighting at the Somme had left the Canadian military looking for a quick source of replacements and as a result a non-combatant Black battalion was formed to fill the ranks. And so the No. 2 Construction Battalion was born. Between September 29, 1916, and January 13, 1917, men from Dresden and the surrounding area signed on in London, Ontario, before joining the ranks of the six hundred other regiment members in Pictou, Nova Scotia. Half the battalion had called Nova Scotia home, others came from other parts of the Maritimes, Ontario, and British Columbia, as well as the United States, Trinidad, Barbados, and Jamaica.[2] Seven Dresden men, James and Joseph Goodwin, William "Rex" Higdon, Leo Ellsworth, Walter Lucas, Clarence Vandyke, and James Wales, became part of the unit. As sappers,[3] the battalion's members supported combat troops by building structures, digging trenches, and laying down minefields. For Private Walter Lucas, a Dresden carpenter, building huts for military headquarters was a continuation of the work he'd done back home. But the fact that he and the other men in the battalion were "non-combatants" did not mean they were not in harm's way.

In Dresden and Chatham Township, the military had actively campaigned to enlist new recruits in the No. 2 Construction Battalion. People of African descent were inflamed by the same patriotic fever as the wider community and encouraged their young men to volunteer, as reported in the *Canadian Observer*:

> A patriotic meeting was held at Dresden, Ontario at the 11th Concession Hall, under the auspices of the Canadian Colored Construction Battalion on Wednesday evening, Oct. 25th. This meeting was largely attended, notwithstanding the bad road and very inclement weather, proving beyond a doubt that Dresden's colored citizens are loyal and true to their king and country, and ready to do their bit in defense of the Empire, of which they are no unimportant part. Loyalty and enthusiasm appeared as the outstanding features of this largely attended meeting. Lieut. L.B. Young, RO in charge at Chatham, explained the nature and purpose of this colored battalion. Dr. Lignore, MD of Truro, NS, also spoke as did Rev. W.H. Wales. The Dresden Citizen's Band[4] furnished music…Young men of color, this is your great opportunity. Grasp it by enlisting in the Canadian Colored Battalion.[5]

Remarkably, the soldiers of the No. 2 Construction Battalion were not the first people of African descent to sign on for military service in what soon became known as a global conflict. Clifford and Owen Highgate of Turnerville and James, Joseph, and Noah Johnson of Dresden were among another 1,400 to two thousand men who served in regular units. Others, despite signing on in the segregated unit, were also deployed with regular units.[6] Private Walter Lucas signed on with the No. 2 Construction Battalion in 1916, and in April 1917, after a stay in England, he was sent to the front with the 186th Battalion. In a letter home, he mentioned other Black soldiers from Dresden he had encountered in Europe. "I and Clarence and Leo Ellsworth,

Jim, and Noah Johnson are here. Jim and John Goodwin were left in England when we came over. John was in hospital when we left; he had taken consumption."⁷ While some successfully joined regular units, many others had been turned away. Success of enlistment in regular units depended largely on the disposition of local recruitment officers. Some officers maintained the same prejudicial viewpoints as their counterparts in the American Civil War, questioning the loyalty and courage of people of African descent. Indeed, the American Civil War was not such a distant memory, as George Madison (formerly Dunn), who had served as an infantryman for the Union Army, was still living in Dresden when recruitment for the First World War was taking place. A letter written by Pte. George Cummings, a young white volunteer from Dresden, reflects the attitudes of that time. "I was surprised at hearing the coloured fellows are enlisting. Well, I think that should make the rest of those white (yellow) fellows feel pretty damned cheap."⁸ Some white soldiers in units that accepted Blacks remained vehemently opposed to sharing meals, accommodations, and other facilities with them. Yet a number of young Black men from Dresden and the surrounding areas persevered,

This group of wwi soldiers enjoying a moment of recreation is believed to depict Dresden men serving with the segregted Construction Battalion. (*Photo courtesy of Barbara Carter and family*)

hoping the way they performed their duties would change these attitudes. Even those who could not serve worked tirelessly to change Canadian military policy towards Black recruits, petitioning the Minister of Militia and Defence to create equal opportunities for service within its ranks.[9] Far from lacking in bravery or initiative, many distinguished themselves. Private Noah Johnson, born in 1893 at Elmstead, Ontario, had been working for Canadian Canners Limited in Dresden at the time of his enlistment. He took his army physical in Dresden on March 10, 1916. Johnson instructed the quartermaster to send $15.00 a month from his assigned pay directly to his mother. Service in the military was more than "just a job" for Johnson, who was awarded a Good Conduct Medal in the field and on his discharge received the British War Medal and the Victory Medal. Johnson continued to proudly wear these on parade with Dresden's Royal Canadian Legion Branch 113 until his death in June 1973 at Veterans Westminster Hospital in London, Ontario.

In November 1917, Rex Higdon was admitted to a field hospital in France where he later remained as part of the hospital staff, attaining the rank of corporal. His series of letters to the *Canadian Observer* reflect a longing for home, interspersed with candid insights into soldiers' lives. Soldiers' letters home, reprinted in the *Dresden Times* and the *Canadian Observer*, are often upbeat accounts of life overseas that masked the grimmer realities of war. Higdon's letters, however, often alluded to the perils they faced. As Higdon wrote:

We have only lost three of [No. 2] members, and they died from some ailment, not from a shell…Sometimes a fellow will think that this bloody war will be over in a short time, then our faith turns to gloom as the end can't be seen. That's when a fellow thinks of the loved ones he has left behind in dear old Canada. The end might seem very near to you, dear readers, for all you have to go by is the papers, but when a fellow sees it in reality, he can tell a thing or two about warfare.

As the war dragged on, Higdon's letters grew ever more sombre.

Last night…I sat up all night with one of my comrades and at 9:50 a.m. [he] departed from our midst to meet his Maker. So, at this hour I am not feeling in the best of spirits as I just received a letter stating that my cousin, James

Goodman, R.E. who I had left in England on my coming to France and later
was invalided to his home in Dresden, had died on November 25th.[10]

James Goodwin had served in Belgium and then in France, where he
was severely wounded. In November 1917 he was discharged and sent home,
where he died of his wounds days after having arrived. Mourners at his
Dresden funeral included white mayor Ben Madden and the entire white
town council, who paraded on foot with Goodwin's casket from his Metcalfe
Street home to the First Regular Baptist Church on Queen Street. In the
eulogy, Rev. J.H. Pennick praised Goodwin as "one of the greatest heroes of
the 2nd Construction Battalion."[11] Goodwin was buried with full honours in
the Dresden Cemetery.

William Isaac Beecher Stowe Henson, son of Mary Henson, also sustained
significant injuries in the war. Known as Beecher or Beech to his friends
and family, Henson was twenty-seven years old when he enlisted in the
Canadian Expeditionary Force in London, on March 15, 1918. His discharge
papers show that he had sustained an eight-inch wound across his abdomen
and had been medically discharged on October 21, 1919.[12] Days away from
Christmas 1918, Mr. and Mrs. Harris Lucas received the devastating news that
their son Private Walter Lucas had died overseas. His funeral was held on
Sunday, December 22, that year, at the British Methodist Episcopal Church
in Dresden.[13] Lucas's cause of death is believed to have been from illness not
combat wounds. Like John Goodwin, many men contracted diseases like
tuberculosis while overseas; Privates William Davis and Donald Campbell
are said to have survived the torpedoing of their ship not long after deploy-
ment from Halifax Harbour. They subsequently arrived safely overseas only
to succumb to pneumonia—resulting from being wet and cold during the
long voyage across the Atlantic to England.[14]

The Great War forever changed society, and how Black soldiers were
viewed. In Dresden, their sacrifices inspired the local Sydenham chapter of
the Imperial Order Daughters of the Empire (IODE) to broaden their service. Formed by Catherine McVean and other wives of leading industrialists and professionals in Dresden, the IODE led the community in support
of local soldiers who were serving overseas. As wives, mothers, and sisters
of servicemen, they were concerned that an ill-prepared Canadian military

had not provided for the comfort and health of their men. They and other women's organizations like the Women's Institute filled this gap by producing thousands of pairs of socks, ditty bags filled with personal care items, and camphorated belts (to combat lice). They also organized massive fundraising efforts in the wider community, using the proceeds to purchase a mobile field kitchen and a machine gun, which they gave to the Chatham, Ontario–based Kent Regiment.[15] In the beginning, the IODE's efforts were exclusively directed towards white soldiers and sailors. On March 9, 1917, thirty-three members of the Sydenham Chapter IODE passed a motion to "send the coloured boys the same boxes upon leaving for the front as the white boys."[16] It may seem, in retrospect, a small, belated gesture extended late in the war, but given the segregation practices of the time, it was a progressive step taken by community influencers with the potential to change attitudes and behaviours in the wider society.

Sadly, recognition that Dresden soldiers of African descent were equally deserving of the community's support did not translate to a steady progression in improved race relations between the First and Second World Wars. Social exclusion continued to be common in the 1920s and 30s. As a long-time Quality Hill resident later recalled with regret, a social code that was never voiced but nevertheless was universally understood would remain a feature of her upper-class neighbourhood.

> I would walk home with a group of friends [from school] and we'd talk and laugh all the way, with no sense of difference between us. But when we got to our front door my white friends were invited in, while my Black friend continued down the hill to her house. No one said anything. We all just knew that was the way it was. It wasn't right. But that was the way it was.[17]

The sacrifices of Black soldiers also failed to elicit respect for their individual dignity and equality after the war as illustrated in the treatment of WWI veteran Daniel Solomon Jr. of Turnerville. Solomon, like so many others, had enlisted in London, Ontario, joining the 1st Depot Battalion (Ontario regiment) on June 11, 1916 and was deployed overseas.[18] On July 12, 1939, two months before the outbreak of World War II, Solomon would become a principal figure in the famous Dresden meteorite story. A large meteor burned through the earth's atmosphere, lighted up the sky, and broke into three pieces, the largest of which, weighing 47.7 kilograms (about 88 pounds), crashed to the ground and was buried into the earth of the Solomon farm. The then-forty-one-year-old former soldier Dan Solomon Jr. dug it out. Solomon and his wife had been raising a family of four children through the lean years of the Great Depression when the meteorite struck. A geologist offered him four dollars for his piece of the meteorite which, considering going rates of pay, must have seemed fair. However, the same day, the geologist resold the meteorite to the London Life Insurance Company for $1,000. Solomon was never offered a cut of the spectacular profit.[19] It would be sixty-five years before Solomon's children and grandchildren would see their patriarch's role in the recovery of the Dresden meteorite recognized. The University of Western Ontario, home to Canada's leading meteor research centre are the present owners of the meteorite and consider it an important part of their collection. On November 10, 2004, they invited Solomon's descendants to attend a special ceremony to honour him and in acknowledgement of the injustice that had been done created a special scholarship for family members who wished to study science at Western. That day, granddaughter Susan Solomon recalled, was the first time she and her siblings were able to touch the famous meteorite their grandfather had recovered over six decades earlier.[20]

Despite experiences such as Solomon's, there were also hopeful signs that the more positive attitudes of white Dawn settlers like the Websters and Rev. Thomas Hughes had also survived into successive generations. Hughes church, which had become integrated would include white parishioners such as white businessman George and Elizabeth Brooker who introduced a Boy Scout and Girl Guide movement at the church in the late 1940s that welcomed all.

Floyd McCorkle was among the scoutmasters of the Anglican Church Scouts, and when the Brookers transitioned the Boy Scouts and Girl Guides into a non-denominational community organization, it continued to be integrated. In 1947, when the Dresden Boy Scouts and Girl Guides hosted their "Cyclorama"[21] for the St. Clair district's six hundred members, the program booklet proudly stated this policy.[22] Dresden children's scouting and guiding experiences were an extension of their school experience, where integration had been a reality for over two generations. Other positive interracial

Rev. Hughes tradition of integration continued into the 20th century with the Anglican Church's Boy Scout Troop, with Scout leader Floyd McCorkle. (*Photo courtesy of the Dresden Archives*)

experiences in this period could be found in the farming community where labour and equipment were shared between Black and white neighbours. As *Maclean's* magazine would report in 1949, farmers working in integrated groups drank from the same jar of water passed around during breaks.[23] Similarly, town industries like O. and W. McVean and Canadian Canners were equal opportunity employers.

Change was also occurring in the Canadian military. When WWII broke out, soldiers were no longer assigned to segregated units. Dawn's descendants would be heavily represented in the air force. Dresden resident Tarrance H. Freeman was one of the first to receive a Royal Canadian Air Force (RCAF) commission as a navigator.[24] Rev. Josiah Henson's great-grandson Cleland "Tex" Henson enlisted in the Canadian Army, 43rd Airborne Command, in Chatham, in 1940, becoming one of Canada's first Black paratroopers. He trained at a base near Winnipeg, served in Britain and Northwestern Europe, and was awarded the Defence Medal, the Service Medal, the France and Germany Star, and the Holland-Belgium Star before being discharged in November 1945. A year after Henson's enlistment, Gordon Millburn of Dresden joined as a paratrooper. Milburn also served in Great Britain, Germany, France, Belgium, and Holland and received the Defence Medal and France and Germany Star.

Most Canadian Black soldiers served in the army. Tex Henson's brother William Jehu Josiah Henson became an infantryman in 1943, training in Halifax and serving in England, France, Belgium, and Germany before his capture and imprisonment. He remained at Fallingbostel, Stalag XI-B until the camp's liberation on June 6, 1945. Like the Hensons, other Black families had more than one son in military service during WWII. Private Clayton Lucas, whose brother had died in WWI, enlisted in the army at age thirty-nine and served behind the lines during WWII for Canada and Great Britain. He died in Dresden in 1948. Dwight Hanson of Rural Route 3, Dresden, was thirty-eight years old when he enlisted in 1942. He served in Great Britain until 1945. His younger brother Lloyd Hanson joined the US Army's 18th Infantry Regiment as a technician, Grade V, and saw active duty in Europe and North Africa. After being discharged, he moved to Chicago. Several men from the Lambkin family, including Earl, Guy, and James, also served in various units of the Canadian army.

Military service was sometimes a tradition passed down through generations. Sherwell Johnson, the son of WWI veteran Noah Johnson, enlisted in November 1940, was wounded in Italy, but subsequently rejoined his unit in France. Corporal Clarence Browning served in the Royal Canadian Army Service Corps from May 1941 to April 1942, in Red Deer, Alberta. His son Master Corporal Larry Browning would follow in his father's footsteps, making the military his career. Lloyd Allan Wallace also had a long career in the Canadian military, serving with Canada's Scots Fusiliers during WWII and the Korean War. Dresden's Royal Canadian Legion Branch 113 maintains records of the service of many others provided in WWI, WWII, and the Korean War, and their descendants continue to gather to honour these men at Dresden's annual Remembrance Day services.[25]

Hugh Burnett, a twenty-year-old carpenter, also enlisted for service in WWII, but after a month in basic training, he encountered health problems and was honourably discharged in November 1940. On returning to Dresden, Burnett had gone to a local café, expecting to enjoy the simple pleasure of a cup of coffee with friends. He was refused service. Tex Henson is also said to have gone to the café in a separate incident and, despite his status as a decorated serviceman with an elite paratroop unit, encountered the same treatment. The recent proliferation of images of one of the most horrific examples of racial intolerance, the Nazi death camps, had not been enough to inspire a change to the status quo regarding segregation at some privately owned businesses at Dresden and elsewhere in Ontario and Canada. Change would not come without a fight. And it would be at Dresden, where Dennis Hill had initially fought segregation of schools a century prior, that the fight for civil rights would again be taken up.

Chapter 20

The NUA STORY
The Continued Resistance to Segregation

I N DECEMBER 1948 A SMALL DELEGATION HEADED BY WILLIAM
Carter, president of the National Unity Association (NUA), appeared
before Dresden Town Council with a proposal for a new bylaw that
would require businesses to serve all people, regardless of race, colour, creed,
or national origin, as a condition of their licence to operate. The NUA's proposal, on this wintry day, would not even be heard.

The council the NUA appeared before in 1948 had been exhausted from
a year of dealing with a number of divisive issues. Outgoing white mayor,
Harold McKim, and a large segment of his all-white council had walked out of
an earlier council meeting over a policing controversy. McKim would finish
out his term on this night but seemed in no mood to enter into discussion on
any new business, and especially not a potentially contentious new debate.
The NUA's request was deferred to the inaugural meeting of the incoming
council in January 1949 and the incoming white mayor Walter Weese. Weese
had only reluctantly returned to the mayor's chair he had previously occupied
knowing he faced a still-divided council and a packed roster of pressing issues.

It was not the first delay NUA members had encountered in their work to
end segregation in private businesses, nor would it be the last. Their efforts,

moreover, were part of a protracted battle against desegregation that had begun at Dresden a hundred years earlier with Dennis Hill's attempt to desegregate the Camden and Zone Common School Board. For the NUA, six years had already passed since its secretary Hugh Burnett had sought redress from government officials after being refused service at a local restaurant. In 1943, Burnett, an honourably discharged serviceman had sat down at a local café, ordered a cup of coffee, and been refused service. The highly decorated "Tex" Henson had been similarly treated as had other Black servicemen not only in restaurants, but in barbershops, and the local pool hall. While the practice of barring people of African descent including servicemen was not unique to Dresden, the NUA's resistance to the status quo would end the segregation practice here.[1]

When Burnett was refused service at Kay's Café, he launched a series of actions reminiscent of those taken by Dennis Hill nearly a century before. Burnett wrote to Minister Frederick Percy Varcoe, of the Canadian Department of Justice, much like Dennis Hill had appealed to Egerton Ryerson. Varcoe's response to Burnett was much like Ryerson's had been to Hill. The minister declared he had no authority to act as Canadian law left proprietors of private businesses free to make decisions on who they served. It would be a provincial matter to introduce the civil rights legislation needed to affect change. Burnett's next step was, again, like Hill's. In 1948, five years after sending his letter to Minister Varcoe, he sued Kay's Café proprietor Morley McKay. That same year, Burnett and a group of men from Dresden, Chatham, Buxton, and surrounding townships who also hoped to end discrimination practices formed the National Unity Association—named in homage to the United Nations, a then new international body that among its earliest actions had passed the Universal Declaration of Human Rights after the atrocities committed by Nazi Germany became apparent post-WWII.

Initially, the NUA quietly engaged in a campaign of education and "moral suasion" to effect change. But sadly, as Jewish labour activist Sid Blum would later observe, "quiet persuasion...usually produce(s) one result: quiet inaction."[2] Early efforts of the NUA had involved a respectful dialogue with restaurateur Morley McKay. In a conversation, which oral tradition says took place in McKay's restaurant's back kitchen, members of the NUA made reasoned arguments for ending the segregation but to no avail. McKay held fast to his belief that his white clients would not support his business if he were to serve Blacks. The NUA diligently researched other options and concluded that a bylaw at the local level might effectively address the issue. They sought further legal advice and also conducted a survey to measure public support. A precedent was discovered in another community, where the police commission had been given responsibility for issuing business licences which had been made dependent on compliance with anti-discrimination policies set by the town council.[3] In 1947 such bylaws were rare, while both personal and systemic forms of racism were common across the province and nation.

Some may have sought to conduct business as usual, but the war and images of the Nazi death camps in particular had graphically shown the ultimate human cost of allowing free rein to hatreds based on people's differences. With society as a whole vowing "never again," the time was ripe for implementing guarantees of universal human rights.

It is important to put the events at Dresden into a wider Canadian and international context. Many Canadians, as recent scholarship argues, continue to be unaware or to distance themselves from racism in their own communities and nation, preferring instead to point to extreme examples in the nineteenth and twentieth century as evidence that these were practices of other nations, as in the American South and South Africa.[4] While the National Unity Association's actions and those of Viola Desmond in Nova Scotia have become better known, there remains a tendency for Canadians to believe practices of racial exclusion never happened in their own communities. That the Ku Klux Klan officially organized in Canada in 1925 suggests, however, that racism was more endemic within Canadian society.[5] By 1930, the KKK boasted 25,000 members in Canada who demonstrated a uniquely Canadian understanding of their mandate by pledging to preserve the "Britishness" of the nation. This meant they sought to preserve a Canada that was white, Anglo Saxon, and Protestant, placing them in opposition not only to people of African descent but to those who were immigrants from Catholic, non-English-speaking European countries who had been arriving in large numbers in the wake of WWI. Documented tactics of KKK groups in Canada survive, including cross burnings in Oakville and Hamilton—and in Dresden, in Quality Hill, the former British American Institute grounds. The Quality Hill incident was attributed to three men from the Wallaceburg

KKK. Since the act was presumably done anonymously and under cover of darkness, it is not known how they were identified. Certainly, there were also Klan sympathizers living in Dresden, but surviving accounts of their activities tend to paint the group as isolated and ineffectual.[6]

In 1947, the Windsor-based Audit Committee of the Interracial Council noted that more subtle, systemic forms of racism played the largest role in negatively impacting the day-to-day lives of African-Canadians and others. A report they created documented "the practice of racial, religious, and nationalistic discrimination and injustice [of a] very subtle nature"[7] in relation to housing, accommodation, and labour practices in most Ontario communities. Real estate agents in Windsor honoured "restrictive covenants" that confined people to "little ghettos."[8] Similar concentrations were evident in Chatham, where people of African descent were largely concentrated in the city's east end, home of a notoriously malodorous deadstock rendering plant, which made the neighbourhood far from a prime residential location. Meanwhile, in 1949, no such clear demarcation between white and non-white neighbourhoods existed in Dresden.[9] Public spaces such as parks and swimming pools were routinely segregated in larger centres,[10] and in many Canadian workplaces hiring practices routinely relegated people who were the object of discrimination to menial, low-paid jobs. There were notable exceptions in the region. Windsor hospitals offered services and employment to all. This was not the case in Chatham. Dresden's Virginia (Cook) Travis would be one of the first nurses of African descent to break through the colour barrier there and become so noted for her excellence that she was promoted to head operating room nurse.[11]

During the 1960s civil rights struggle in the US, images of "whites only" signage were often shown as evidence of overt Jim Crow practices in that nation. While Canadians tend to believe this practice was never employed here, the passage of the *Ontario Racial Discrimination Act* of 1944 demonstrates that it was deemed necessary to legislate against this practice. Even if businesses could no longer "advertise" such a policy, there remained in communities a quiet understanding of where people were welcome and where they were not.

"Canadian courts had historically proven a poor forum for defending individuals against discrimination particularly on privately owned properties."[12]

In 1939, the Supreme Court of Canada had upheld merchants' legal right to refuse service, and as late as May 1959 a case of discrimination was allowed by the court, contrary to Alberta's *Hotelkeeper's Act*, based on a technicality.

Legislative change would come slowly. In 1945 British Columbia's *Social Assistance Act* made it illegal to deny anyone social services based on race, colour, or creed. In 1947 Canada's progressive father of socialized medicine Tommy Douglas passed the *Saskatchewan Bill of Rights*, the first general law prohibiting discrimination. And in 1948 the newly formed United Nations ratified the *Universal Declaration of Human Rights*; by becoming a signatory, Canada committed itself to uphold the declaration's principles within future legislation. The Dominion Elections Act of the same year reflected this commitment. It ensured voters' rights for all citizens. It would not be until 1960, however, that another Western-based progressive, Prime Minister John Diefenbaker, would lead the effort to pass the first *Canadian Bill of Rights*. It would take another twenty-two years before the *Canadian Charter of Rights and Freedoms* was signed into law under the Liberal prime minister Pierre Trudeau.

If anti-discrimination legislation was in its infancy at the time of the NUA's actions, so, too, was the modern Civil Rights Movement. Two years *after* Hugh Burnett launched his lawsuit in Dresden, Viola Desmond, the woman whose image now graces the Canadian ten-dollar bill, challenged racial discrimination in Nova Scotia by refusing to leave the white's only section of a movie theatre in New Glasgow.[13] Nine years after Desmond's action, the celebrated American civil rights activist Rosa Parks would refuse to give up her seat on a Montgomery, Alabama, bus sparking the landmark action of the Montgomery bus boycott. The following year, Dr. Martin Luther King Jr. and sixty African-American pastors and civil rights leaders met in Atlanta, Georgia, to coordinate non-violent protests that made King an icon of the Civil Rights Movement. Viewed on this timeline, NUA members represent some of the earliest modern civil rights activists in North America, yet their contributions have been largely unrecognized within Canadian history.

The "Dresden Story"

When the NUA's petition to Dresden's town council was tabled in December 1948, the organization's president, William Carter, likely had mixed feelings about the delay. On one hand, justice delayed was justice denied. On the other, the deferral to incoming mayor Walter Weese ensured they would be heard by someone who had been a sympathetic ally in the past. In 1947, when Weese was a councillor, he had supported another delegation of Black citizens who had approached council with another petition. "[Mayor Byron] ... introduced Rev. Jennie Johnson who ... addressed the council concerning Rev. Josiah Henson, an earlier negro clergyman, and urging that the town and community take action to commemorate his memory."[14] The *Dresden Times* gave a detailed report of the encounter that reveals much about the times and attitudes of the council and Weese's reaction to what was, in hindsight, a remarkable historic event.

In 1947 Rev. Josiah Henson's name was still not widely recognized. Eighty-year-old Rev. Jennie Johnson, then living in Flint, Michigan, was herself decades away from being seen as an important historical figure in her own right. Her petition to council would not have been readily recognized as the rare opportunity it was. As a spiritual leader and social activist, Johnson was concerned with the uplift of her people. She believed that a publicly owned museum celebrating Henson held potential for engendering greater recognition of the contributions by people of African descent in the past, and that this would result in greater respect for African-descent citizens in the present. To ensure Henson's former home would be used for this purpose, Johnson advocated for its development as a public museum. The building, meanwhile, was already being developed privately by white owner William Chapple. Johnson saw that a municipally owned and publicly directed project would attract the support of African Canadians and their involvement would ensure authentic Black history would be presented. Henson descendants and others had already witnessed a co-opting of their history after a county road crew clearing weeds at the Henson Cemetery during a Depression-era work project had "discovered" his grave. Impressed with Henson's historic link with Beecher Stowe's Uncle Tom's Cabin, local groups who also understood the tourism potential of his gravesite set out to beautify it and erect signage. It is unclear from the public record if they obtained the Henson family's permission or blessing. (The site was then, and still remains, an active family cemetery.)

While Johnson spoke favourably to council about Chapple's efforts, she tactfully and strategically promoted the advantages of a town-owned venture.

She outlined the economic benefits from tourism and promised that a municipally backed museum would attract "many personal belongings of the Rev. Henson and relics of the age in which he lived."[13] This was a generous offer. At her home in Flint, Michigan, Johnson had recently located Henson's gold watch, presented to him by Queen Victoria. The watch's discovery had been recently reported on the CBC's International Service, so council would have been aware of the significance of her offer.

Councillor Weese greeted Johnson and her delegation's presentation with enthusiasm. "I think you have a good idea, Rev. Johnson," he said. "I sometimes think we are a little careless about giving your people credit for their contributions to this community."[16] Weese's comments reflect his conviction that he served all of Dresden's residents, a view that his fellow councillors did not share, as he further reflected on that night. "I seem to be the one always sticking his neck out [for Dresden's Black citizens]," Weese told those gathered at the meeting.[17] Despite Weese's support, council informed Johnson that a committee to explore her idea had already been struck but had "not yet had time to meet."[18] Ultimately, William Chapple would develop his Uncle Tom's Cabin Museum without benefit of the artifacts Johnson had collected. Museum curators since that time have tried in vain to relocate Henson's watch and other precious personal items.[19]

Chapple's efforts to develop Henson's last home as a museum happened more or less concurrently with the advent of the NUA's actions to achieve desegregation. This ironic juxtaposition may be the reason Dresden, and not a larger centre like Windsor or Toronto, would become the focus of anti-discrimination activism in Ontario. Larger centres may have boasted well-organized activist groups working on similar issues, but Dresden held powerful symbolic significance capable of capturing the public imagination and turning the desegregation issue into a popular cause. Exploiting the Henson legacy for its tourism potential while not allowing Dawn descendants to eat at local restaurants was an irony that was not lost on reporter Sydney Katz, who in 1949 was dispatched to Dresden by *Maclean's* magazine editor Pierre Berton at the urging of Toronto civil rights and labour groups. Katz took full advantage of the symbolic value of the situation by entitling his feature story "Jim Crow Lives in Dresden" along with the subtitle "Uncle Tom's head lies uneasily... [as his] descendants can't get a store haircut, a permanent wave, or a restaurant meal."[20]

Community Context in the National Unity Association Action

On March 14, 1949, the NUA again appeared before Dresden council, hop-
ing their petition would finally be heard. Their optimism for success was
buoyed by the knowledge they had a sympathetic mayor at the helm and
by evidence of fellow citizens' goodwill and support. After all, Dresden's
Black population could be seen "working peacefully together"[21] at Canadian
Canners and O. and W. McVean, Dresden's two main employers. William
Carter's uncle, the auctioneer Percy Carter, lived around the corner from
Mayor Weese, and their sons were fast friends. Segregated schools had not
been an issue since the 1880s. And discriminatory practices were confined
to only nine of Dresden's businesses.[22] In addition, an NUA poll that asked
if people were opposed to discriminatory practices circulated to 118 leading
townspeople had resulted in 115 "yes" responses (including that of Mayor
Weese). Unfortunately, agreeing in principle to an ideal did not translate into
the ability or will to take bold action. And, as reporter Sidney Katz observed,
Dresden was an "uneasy and paradoxical" place.[23] Paradoxes in thought and
action were evident at the town council's inaugural meeting in January 1948.
Traditionally, council asked a local minister to offer prayers at the opening
session of a new term. Despite their overwhelming white Protestant composition, in 1948 the council showed an admirable inclusivity of the community's diversity by inviting not one but three ministers to give this traditional
blessing: Rev. Leslie Latimer represented the community's white Protestant
Christian churches; Father A.N. Page, the town's Roman Catholic priest
and its largely European immigrant parishioners; and Rev. W.L. Talbot, the
African-descent minister of First Regular Baptist Church. Katz's insightful
article contains a number of examples of Dresden residents' contradictory
and paradoxical behaviour, including the tendency to refuse service to "even
those who did not look like blacks ... when members of the community knew
their racial heritage."[24]

Mayor Weese, though sympathetic, was the reluctant leader of a divided
council who were tasked with bringing the town and its 1,700 residents
through a crucial point in its development. After two decades of economic
stagnation, due to the Great Depression and WWII, major infrastructure
challenges needed to be addressed. The town's electrical system was plagued

by rolling blackouts, and a river- and well-based water supply was inadequate to meet residential and industrial expansion. Canadian Canners Limited, a highly water-intensive industry, had just constructed a new larger plant, and two new industries—the Greenmelk[25] and National Hardware Specialties,[26] were also placing increased demands on water and hydro delivery systems.

Housing was also a pressing need, due to an influx of five hundred new residents. Even existent housing was assessed as " so lowly that the revenue [from taxes] was not enough to keep one child in school." The post-war baby boom placed further strain on housing resources and also threatened to over-whelm a local educational system that had not been significantly updated since 1912. Dresden's school district had also been expanded and now needed to accommodate an additional 250 new students from the neighbouring communities of Thamesville and Florence. Plans to build the new Dresden District High School added a number of special sessions to already packed council agendas.[27] To pay for the needed infrastructure development, council proposed a mill rate, which Mayor Weese opposed believing it would overburden low wage earners, war widows and struggling returning veterans.

The 1948 policing issue that had divided the previous administration had not gone away, heated debates also erupted over the introduction of a provincial liquor control board to curb the illegal sale of alcohol to minors, and there was also the strangely divisive issue of parking. Little wonder Weese had returned to council at the urging of townspeople "contrary to [his] better judgement…[and with] no desire for the mayor's chair."[28]

In March 1949 the NUA would again present their petition with the backdrop of this pressured and acrimonious atmosphere. While it was wrong to deny basic civil rights to 20 percent of the town's residents, council's preoccupation suggests, beyond a simple condemnation of racism, extenuating circumstances that contributed to their failure to understand that the petition before them needed a timely, positive response. March 1949 council minutes demonstrate this failure to grasp the gravity of the situation as they recorded the delegation's presence in a single line as a "protest against seeming discrimination against coloured people."

Division on a broader range of issues and misinformation circulating within in the community would also serve to muddy the waters regarding the NUA's intentions and motivations in the public's mind. NUA members were accused of having communist ties. Many businessmen opposed greater government controls over their business operations and characterized the introduction of new bylaws as evidence of encroaching communism. In the "McCarthy witch hunt" era, with widely viewed televised Senate hearings from the US whipping up public paranoia in a widespread Red Scare, the mere whisper of a possible communist influence could inspire righteous opposition. Added to this was the small-town tendency to push back against what was seen as big city "outsider" interference in local issues that were "none of their business." As city dailies and the national press descended and activists from out of town became involved, anti-NUA sentiment spiked as townspeople wrongly perceived that it was the group (and not the town's segregationist policies) that were defaming the community's reputation in the eyes of the nation. A number of people failed to understand that discrimination was, in fact, a problem. And if discrimination was not seen as the problem, then it wasn't a leap to conclude that those asking for their rights, no matter how peacefully or respectfully, were troublemakers. Some white residents did however demonstrate obvious racist atttitudes going as far as to openly declare to the press that NUA members did not "know their place" or had become "uppity."

By March 1949,council members had become increasingly entrenched in their positions.[29] Many backed business owners and shared their view that whites would stop frequenting their businesses if they served Blacks. Others feared that if the bylaw did indeed result in lost business, they could be sued. Remarkably, the fact that a number of Dresden businesses which had never practiced segregation were thriving was never highlighted in this debate.

Mayor Weese's comments show a man torn between conflicting values. On one hand, he said, "As Mayor I want [African-descent residents] to feel that I'm their mayor, and this is their council as well as anyone else's. Their cause is just. Race discrimination is something that is most unfair." On the other hand, he realized there was nothing in provincial statute books that allowed municipal councils "to interfere with free enterprise." Weese feared that this lack of provincial legislation would make a town bylaw unenforceable.

At the March council meeting, white councillor Mike Fry, a local grocer, was alone in arguing in favour of the NUA's proposal to pass a bylaw enforcing desegregation. Fry's consultation with lawyers and the Department of

National Health and Welfare in Ottawa confirmed for him that while civil rights issues were a provincial matter, and not within council's purview, that the municipality could still act. Regulation of restaurants was a municipal responsibility. Fry proposed that the existing health directives governing restaurants could simply be amended to adding anti-discrimination regulations. He saw this as an effective solution since restaurants were, in his words, "the chief bugbear" in the debate.

Burnett's lawsuit against Kay's Café had not yet wrapped up, and Weese, knowing its results could have relevance within the council's debate, urged the NUA to be patient until the case concluded. People on both sides of the debate appear to have been running out of patience.

The NUA was in no mood to be counselled to have patience in view of the months of delay they had endured. Weese was worn down by "these cold wars ... [that] are ruining this town," and together with his son, Dresden reeve Douglas Weese, advanced the idea that the four most contentious issues they faced—police governance, parking metres, introduction of a liquor control board outlet, and the NUA's proposed restaurant bylaw—be settled with a public referendum.[30] In April 1949 the decision to go to a referendum had likely already been made when William Carter and the NUA again appeared before town council. Accounts in the *Dresden Times* of this final debate show the degree to which relationships had become strained. Weese pressed Carter to deal directly with the restaurant owners and to "leave council out of it."[31] Carter pushed back and, based on legal advice, attempted to cut through Weese's argument that passing a law was not within council's power by saying, "You can enact any law you want to as long as it isn't contrary to any existing law."[32] Mayor Weese countered by suggesting the NUA was not broadly supported even by other African-descent residents. "There are a number of coloured people who have told me you are killing their cause." Carter fired back, "Like any group, we do have some people who haven't the backbone to stand up and fight." In the midst of this increasingly heated exchange, Councillor Fry rose to his feet. "I'm surprised that the mayor has carried on the meeting like this." Mayor Weese ordered Fry to sit down and restated his position. "We know their cause is just and we are not afraid of the restaurant owners. We're probably afraid of a law unknown in the Dominion of Canada. I haven't much faith in curing moral issues by law."[33] The NUA would not be so easily dismissed. "We'll bring our lawyer down and show you how you can do it, if you'll pay the expenses," NUA executive secretary Hugh Burnett offered. Joe Hanson, another NUA member, encouraged further council debate. Finally, Councillor George Wellman steered the session in the direction it seemed to have been planned to go all along. "The question should go to the Town of Dresden for a vote," he concluded. To which Mayor Weese responded, "It has appeared that every time council introduced an issue this year, it has had insults and inflaming letters. If a cure can be found [through a public referendum], I'll be the happiest man in town." And with that, council voted to include the council's four most contentious issues on a ballot for a public vote the following month. But there would be further delays.

The NUA's faith in their neighbours' support was understandably waning, and they were not convinced a referendum was the answer. They enlisted the support of MPP J.B. Salsberg who approached Mayor Weese with an attempt to discourage him from following through with a referendum. Salsberg met with Weese at his home in Dresden for a half a day. In a letter to the NUA, he noted Weese was convinced 80 to 90 percent of Dresden people would vote against the NUA proposal, yet he would not cancel the vote.[34]

As the town dragged its feet on vote preparations, the attentions of civil rights and union activists at Toronto and a related storm of media attention was about to descend on Dresden and, with it, widespread condemnation of the community's handling of the issue.

Media coverage played an important role in the NUA struggle. The *Dresden Times* was among the first to take an editorial stand. The Bowes brothers, who had only recently purchased the newspaper, made the unprecedented decision to print a front-page editorial with a pro-NUA stand, immediately below their lead story of the heated March 1949 council debate. It was a risky move given the newspaper's reliance on advertising and subscription revenues. Nevertheless, they waded into the debate they acknowledged was something that "people don't talk about, but...that everyone knows exists." The Bowes expected to be "criticized and severely, by some, for bringing the problem into the open," but challenged the silence saying, "Anyone who claims racial discrimination in Dresden does not exist is kidding himself." They went beyond naming racism to assigning it "fairly and squarely on every one of us because unless a majority of us thought that way, the situation could not exist." Yet they stopped short of supporting a bylaw saying the solution to the racist practices lay not in legislation but "in our hearts and minds, and until they change, no lasting solution will appear." Perhaps unaware of the NUA's earlier efforts at dialogue, they concluded that it was "not too late, for representatives of both groups to sit down around a table and talk the problem over in the custom of all free men."[35]

The *Dresden Times* was indeed severely criticized for their stance. A number of townspeople cancelled their subscriptions, and some businesses withheld their advertising.[36] Lines had been drawn and only the bravest continued to step over them. While the *Times* would not abandon their detailed reporting of the ongoing struggle and its owners remained equal opportunity employers, no more front-page editorials or editorials of any kind appeared on the matter in their paper.

The NUA struggle, meanwhile was being taken to the provincial level through the labour movement which, by 1947, had become a major force in anti-racial education and activism. The Canadian Jewish Labour Committee (JLC) in particular, had taken a leading role in opposing racist hiring practices. The JLC was social-democratic, anti-communist, and included members of the Co-operative Commonwealth Federation, a political party whose secretary was David Lewis, who later became leader of the New Democratic Party.[37] Countering racial hatred was important to the unions because racism was a powerful tool in the hands of union busters, who used it to destroy the "brotherhood" union strength was based on. By1949 close ties had developed between labour organizations and the Association for Civil Liberties, bringing together Jewish, Chinese, Polish, Japanese, and African-Canadian people in a coalition dedicated to the struggle for the civil rights.[38]

NUA co-founder Hugh Burnett belonged to a carpenters union, and in July 1949 he became a delegate to the JLC's Race Relations Institute. There, Burnett recounted details of the Dresden struggle. Coalition members took an immediate interest,[39] resulting in Sid Blum, undertaking a two-day trip to investigate Dresden. The labour coalition together with civil rights organizations approached newly elected and sympathetic Premier Leslie Frost asking him to enact provincial legislation. The brief they presented to Frost, coming as it did from a labour perspective, naturally centred that appeal on employment practices. Meanwhile, Toronto allies had approached *Maclean's* editor Pierre Berton, and Sydney Katz's story was also bringing the situation at Dresden to national attention. With "The Dresden Story" now clearly on the radar of activists, journalists, and Ontario's premier, there was a push for additional legislation that would allow municipalities to cancel licences of those businesses who practiced discrimination. It was the very legislation Mayor Weese had felt was needed to address jurisdictional issues, but unfortunately for Weese and the Town of Dresden, it had come too late. The die had already been cast, and Dresden had already come to be seen as "the problem" rather than as a community that needed help on jurisdictional issues in order to broker a local solution. Even now, Premier Frost would not immediately act to introduce the legislation based on a Catch-22 of jurisdictional issues. He believed the "province had no legal power to prohibit racial discrimination in cases where municipalities had refused to pass a by-law."[40] And at Dresden such a bylaw was not about to pass.

In December 1949, a full year after the NUA had initially approached town council with their request for a bylaw to address racism in the service industry and eight months after the council's decision to take the issue to its citizens, the community voted in what was arguably the most important referendum in their history under the glare of growing national media attention. Voters were asked to vote "yes" or "no" to four questions: Do you approve of control of our police by our present police commission?; Do you approve of parking metres in the business section of town?; Do you approve of a liquor store and beer warehouse being established here?; and, finally, Do you approve of the council passing a bylaw restraining any Dresden restaurant owner or owners from refusing service regardless of race, creed, or colour?

Of the town's population of 1,700, 625 people voted. No racial split in the vote was tabulated, so we do not know how many were African-descent residents, who made up 20 percent of the population at that time, voted. The final tally on the last crucial question would be 517 votes no and 118 yeses. Condemnation of the negative outcome was swift and scathing, with the national press editorializing that the vote had brought shame to Dresden and to all Ontario.

The referendum's value as a measure of pervasive racist sentiments in the town is unclear. The bylaw's wording certainly had not presented itself as a vote against segregation, as the NUA poll had more clearly done, and misinformation and old alliances had played a part in swaying the vote to its negative conclusion. Some voters had been sympatico with McKay's sentiment that "no one is going to tell me how to run my business." And with the Red Scare running in the background, the characterization of the new bylaw as communist-style government overreach had gained some traction. Others aligned with views of Councillor Mike Fry, unreservedly supporting the NUA out of an understanding that even if a bylaw didn't work, it had value as a moral statement. To be sure there were still others who voted no as strident resistance to change in the racial status quo. And still others occupied a confused middle ground similar to Mayor Weese's, believing that segregation was wrong but also that legislation would be unenforceable and ineffective in changing the hearts and minds—and the practices—of those who opposed it.

Regardless of what influenced the vote, the effect was the same. Justice had again been denied. In Toronto the NUA's allies brought the outcome directly to the attention of Premier Frost. In January 1950 104 people representing various organizations gathered in Queens Park to again press Premier Frost for legislation. In 1951 Frost created Canada's first *Fair Employment Practices Act*, declaring it to be in accord with the 1948 *Universal Declaration of Human Rights*. Passing of the law did not, as had been predicted, change the practices of offending businesses, much less the hearts and minds of their owners.

At this juncture, Hugh Burnett approached Donna Hill, secretary of the Toronto Labour Committee who wrote and presented a brief to Premier Frost in March of 1954. It had positioned the Dresden case as "the height of experience of Jim Crow in Canada." Frost responded by almost immediately introducing additional legislation that, by April 6, 1954, resulted in the passage of Ontario's *Fair Accommodations Practices Act*, which made it illegal in Ontario for private businesses to practice racial and other forms of discrimination.

In Dresden, most businesses readily complied. For some, the law provided "permission" to suspend practices with which business owners had not necessarily agreed but had "gone along to get along." Others remained more strident in their opposition. Six months after the law was passed, Sid Blum, who had succeeded Donna Hill as secretary of the Toronto Labour Committee, visited Dresden and was appalled to find some restaurants and barber shops continued to openly oppose the new legislation. As Mayor

Weese had predicted, enforcing the new law would not be a simple matter; for the NUA, the protracted battle to ensure compliance now began.

Testing the Law

By 1954, the year of the Dresden Old Boys' Reunion, many feared festivities would be marred by violence born of escalating tensions. In a particularly disturbing development, Hugh Burnett received a note scrawled in pencil threatening that there would be "a place for him in the Dresden Cemetery" should he persist in "bringing trouble." Burnett purchased a gun to protect himself and his family, but his efforts and those of the NUA continued.[41]

In 1954, a Canadian Human Rights Commission was not yet a reality. Forcing compliance with the new *Fair Accommodations Practices Act* relied on a complicated process of collecting complaints, launching investigations to confirm the complaints' validity, informal conciliation efforts, and then formal conciliation—and finally, if this was not achieved, prosecution of the offending party. In the face of the technical and monetary challenges this created, the support of outside groups became crucial to the success of NUA's local efforts. Donna Hill, wife of Daniel G. Hill,[42] had initially helped Burnett and the NUA in her capacity as the secretary of the Toronto Labour Committte, and by July of 1954 Sid Blum had expanded that organization's involvement in the NUA's efforts. Blum reported infractions to the Ministry of Labour, but when they sent out their inspector to investigate, the offending parties were told they had "nothing to worry about" and Blum was told to stop upsetting the community at Dresden. Undaunted, Blum arranged for "testers" and witnesses who could systematically document infractions of the law.

The first round of testing conducted with the NUA resulted in eight complaints being filed and brought to court on September 27, 1954, at Dresden. Justice William Schwenger presided. He concluded that the evidence against Emerson's Soda Bar Restaurant had not been conclusive but recommended the prosecution of Morley McKay, proprietor of Kay's Café. Blum redoubled his efforts, arranging for additional testing.

On October 29, 1954, six months after the *Fair Accommodations Practices Act* had been passed, Hugh Burnett, in the company of Bromley Armstrong, a labour activist;[43] and Ruth Lor, the Chinese-Canadian secretary of the

Student Christian Movement;[44] along with an observing reporter from the *Toronto Daily Star*, tested the Kay's Café. Local residents Joseph Hanson and Mrs. Bernard Carter also tested Emerson's Restaurant. Morley McKay and Annie Emerson were consequently charged and tried. In January 1955 they were found guilty of violating the *Fair Accommodations Practices Act*. They appealed the decision, and in September of 1955 County Judge Henry Grosch overturned the guilty verdict.

An angered Frost and a determined NUA and their labour and civil rights activist supporters arranged another round of testing. The offending restaurateurs, meanwhile had begun circumventing testing efforts by warning each other of testers' presence in town so they could close their doors before the testers entered. In November 1955 Blum countered by arranging for three University of Toronto students, one of whom was white, to do the next round of testing. McKay was again charged. In February of 1956 he was found guilty and ordered to pay $100 plus $600 in court fees. He again appealed, but the original ruling was upheld.[45] McKay then announced his intention to appeal to the Supreme Court of Ontario, but he later dropped the case. Finally, on November 16, 1956, thirteen years after Hugh Burnett had initially been refused service, one final test group entered Kay's Café and were served. It seemed like a Hollywood ending in which a heroic struggle had ended in justice for all. The lights could now come up in the theatre and everyone walk out into the bright light of a new future. But as the national audience left, Dresden's Black and white citizens, whose lives and relationships had been so disrupted, were left alone to work out a way forward. Some business owners, as predicted, had not had their hearts and minds changed and would persist in providing inferior or delayed service to discourage returning patronage from those they now sometimes deeply resented for their activism.[46] Those who had been traumatized by the conflict had no process through which a healing dialogue could occur, and silence became the predominant method of dealing with the pain of past events, leading to an entire generation growing up with no knowledge of the important incidents that had occurred in Dresden.[47]

Mayor Weese would never see the conclusion of the conflict. On January 28, 1950, he died suddenly at age sixty. The more romantic among us might characterize Weese as having died of a broken heart after watching his hometown descend into acrimony and division on so many issues.

For those who had actively led the struggle for civil rights, the after-math was especially difficult. As later recalled by community historian Don "Gummer" Spearman, an eyewitness to the trials, "The protesting blacks were labelled as malcontents, vilified as 'trouble-makers,' wishing to upset a status quo which had existed over a century."[48] Burnett's carpentry business suffered badly. Both he and Carter left the community. Yet, Burnett would go on to challenge non-compliant businesses in other communities, including a marina in Mitchell's Bay, and would strike up a warm friendship with Daniel G. Hill.[49]

Burnett once observed that passing a law would not make "one man love another" but that it would "eliminate the act of discrimination, [and then] we will learn to like one another."[50] On January 1958, Sydney Katz returned to Dresden for a follow-up article. His piece showed that this process would take time. Black patrons were still not frequenting local barber shops, with the exception of Casper Faas's establishment.[51] One barber told Katz, "There's no law against using dull tools, is there?"[52] leading Katz to conclude that "most Negroes and many whites agree…The anti-discrimination law was a good thing. The principle was just. But it won't do everything. God will have to take the prejudice out of men's hearts."[53] At Kay's Café, a quiet under-standing that business carried on as usual continued to his death in January of 1972.[54] Like Carter and Burnett, McKay is buried in the Dresden cemetery.

The NUA's work continued into the 1970s under South African immigrant and NUA secretary Dr. Vincent Smith, a teacher at Dresden's Lambton Kent Composite School. He continued the NUA's work on housing, employment, and education. In 1970 eighteen youths, including students from Dr. Smith's classes, participated in a panel discussion with Dr. Howard McCurdy on "The Present Problems of Black People and the Future Challenges."[55]

In October 1973 Daniel G. Hill, now the Ontario Human Rights Commissioner, arranged a banquet and awards presentation at the William Pitt Hotel in Chatham at which certificates of merit were presented to Philip Shadd, Hugh Burnett, Bernard Carter, Arthur Alexander Sr., Alvin Ladd, Leroy Poole, William Carter, Lorne Ladd, Percy Carter, Michael Fry (the former councillor), Vivian Robbins Chavis, Alvin McCurdy, Joseph Hanson, Frank Richardson, and George McCurdy.[56] At Dresden, the NUA's role in completing the work begun by Dennis Hill a hundred years before would remain unrecognized.

The pain of the years of conflict would be reignited with book reviews of John Cooper's *Season of Rage* in which Dresden found itself again identified as an exceptionality in respect to negative racial relations. A renewed flurry of press coverage of Cooper's book generally painted Dresden as the most racist community in the province. That all of Ontario had required a law to combat similar practices in other communities was lost in the press articles and reviews. That the history of desegregation in Ontario had become known as "The Dresden Story" seems an extension of the "mythology of the Great White North" [57] in which Canadians claim a moral high ground to Americans in respect to our track record on slavery because of a lack of awareness of the historical record. Our historical track record on segregation is similarly an inconvenient truth that many Canadians are not aware of, or which they wish to distance themselves from by claiming "it never happened here" in our time, or in our community. This mythologizing of history and claiming of a moral high ground by expressing that African Canadians never had it as bad here as African Americans did in the US, scholars say tends to cut off any meaningful discussion about anti-Black racism in Canada today. [58] The distancing from segregation as "The Dresden Story" similarly perpetuates a truncation of meaningful discussion on current issues of racism and exclusion.

Two generations of Dresden residents were understandably dismayed at these characterizations of their community as exceptionally racist.that way. After the release of his book author James Cooper offered to spearhead an effort to erect an Ontario Heritage Trust plaque to honour Burnett and the NUA at Dresden residents declined his offer realizing this was something they needed to do themselves Ontario Heritage Trust would involve both white and Black descendants of key historical figures in order toarrive at wording for an Ontario heritage plaque finally allowing the community an opportunity for healing dialogue and to embrace a new identity as an important birthplace of civil rights. In 2010, the Ontario Heritage Plaque, Hugh Burnett and the National Unity Association was unveiled at Emancipation celebrations at the Uncle Tom's Cabin Historic Site (now Josiah Henson Museum of African Canadian History). The plaque was installed later that summer in a community garden near Dresden's downtown.

Chapter 21

The JOURNEY TOWARDS a MORE AUTHENTIC HISTORY

O
N SEPTEMBER 27, 1972, ROSA PARKS, THE MOTHER OF
the American Civil Rights Movement, joined a group of two thousand Prince Hall Masons from sixty Ontario and Michigan lodges
to celebrate Prince Hall Day at Dresden. Their cavalcade of five hundred
cars jammed the length of Concession 3, Camden Gore, as they stopped
to lay wreaths at the grave of the Rev. Josiah Henson. Later, at Dresden
Raceway, Masonic dignitaries presented Parks with their Sojourner Truth
Freedom Award.[1] During the ceremony, Parks would take a seat on the temporary stage next to area resident Marion E. Lambkin, Rev. Josiah Henson's
great-granddaughter. The encounter was reminiscent of the 1854 meeting of
Frederick Douglass and Rev. Henson that had taken place at his Dawn farm
as it linked a Henson who had remained in the Dawn Settlement area with a
noted US Black civil rights activist. Parks's appearance at Dresden was also,
similarly, validation, pointing to the importance of Henson's history internationally and of the iconic stature he had reached. How the large important
event was recorded—and not recorded—in the region's press says much
about the significance, or lack of it, attributed to Black history and current

events involving people of African descent in Canadian society in the immediate wake of traumatic setbacks within the Civil Rights Movement in the
US. The historical re-enactments presented by members of the Masonic
Youth and the speeches given that day tell us, as well, how little progress had
been made in overcoming the historical amnesia around the events of the
National Unity Association and the mythologization of Black history. Efforts
of people to overcome the misrepresentation of Rev. Henson's history that
had begun with Rev. Jennie Johnson's petition to Dresden Council in 1948
would continue through the Masonic gatherings and finally culminate in the
renaming of the Uncle Tom's Cabin Museum established at Dresden to commemorate Rev. Henson's life.

The 1972 Masonic gathering at Dresden was the second of its kind at
Dresden. In 1960 Marion E. Lambkin, Thelma Williams, and other local
Henson descendants had joined Rev. Jennie Johnson alongside two thousand people at Henson's grave. Johnson appears to have remained convinced
that honouring important historical figures like Henson was an important
way to engender greater respect and appreciation for their descendants and
to have continued to champion use of his true history for this purpose.

Interestingly, the first Masonic gathering in 1960 and the second in 1972
bookend major events within the modern Civil Rights Movement in the US.
The first gathering was held just five years after Rosa Parks had refused to give
up her seat on a Montgomery, Alabama, bus, sparking the Montgomery Bus
Boycott and establishing her as the mother of the modern American Civil
Rights Movement. The 1972 gathering fell just three years after Parks's colleague and sometime collaborator Rev. Dr. Martin Luther King Jr. was assas-
sinated and just five years after unprecedented riots ripped apart the city of
Detroit where Parks and the Prince Hall Masons leadership that planned the
Dresden event had been living.[2] The 1972 event also fell roughly twenty years
after the NUA's landmark victory for civil rights in Ontario.[3] While the first
gathering had taken place at a time of rising activism, the second came at
a time of setbacks, when an aging cohort of civil rights leaders like Parks
hoped to inspire a new generation to take up the continuum of resistance.
A program of the day's events is not known to survive so it is not known if
Dr. King was specifically honoured at the event, but the stage decorations
that featured his portrait communicate that civil rights was, at least, a theme

that ran in the background. For white observers in the local press, however, emphasis would be placed on the event's historical content.[4] Grand Masters Robert M. Foster of Ontario and William O. Green of Michigan introduced re-enactments by Masonic Youth portraying nineteenth century Black heroes Prince Hall, founder of the Black Masonic order; Sojourner Truth, an abolitionist and early women's rights activist; and Rev. Josiah Henson. The gathering also recognized Henson descendants, including Marion E. Lambkin, the only Canadian representative; James Henson of Detroit; and Harold Henson of Omaha.

Despite the presence of Parks and so many international guests, the important moment in time represented, and the sheer size of the gathering, the event did not receive widespread coverage. Dresden's *North Kent Leader*,[5] faced with an influx of people into the town that essentially doubled their population, dispatched a reporter and ran three pages of coverage. What was put in and what was left out of the *Leader*'s coverage provides a window onto how Black history was understood and presented in this time period. Remarkably, Parks's presence at the event would be essentially ignored despite the fact that the fifty-nine-year-old, by the 1970s, was internationally famous. The photo of her taken by the reporter that day never appeared in the paper's coverage.[6] The report of her receiving her Sojourner Truth Freedom Award received a brief, one-line mention three quarters of the way down the lengthy continuation, but its wording makes it difficult to discern whether Parks had attended the event or received her award in absentia. A photo of Marion Lambkin taken that day was also left out of the photo coverage, a strange omission considering the *North Kent Leader* was a local paper and Lambkin the only local person honoured that day. The presence of a number of former NUA members went similarly unmentioned.

At the 1972 gathering, Rev. Johnson's notion, first promoted in 1948, that knowledge of the past accomplishments of Rev. Henson and others could generate respect for descendants in the present seems to have been taken up by Grand Master William O. Green of Michigan, who declared, "As a result of the understanding, patience and humility [of Prince Hall, Sojourner Truth, and Rev. Josiah Henson], the world has recognized our rights to claim full benefits of democracy."[7] Green's was a decidedly rosy evaluation of the state of Black civil rights and ignored the mixed regard for Black historical figures in general, and Rev. Henson in particular. By 1972, the Black pride movement's push back against negative portrayals of people of African descent in popular culture had resulted in a number of familiar fictional characters being scorned for their reinforcement of racial stereotypes. The figure of Uncle Tom, as a result of the Tom plays, had led to "Uncle Tom" becoming a negative label for those who ingratiated themselves with white people for the sake of personal gain. For descendants like James Henson, this had resulted in a devaluing of the Henson name that had become personal. "We receive resentment from people in our own community because of what we try to do," he told his audience. "They feel if [I] have a good job, I must be an 'Uncle Tom.'" Yet James Henson would continue to express pride in his ancestor, saying, "If they knew who Uncle Tom was and what he did...then I would say I have been complimented."[8] James Henson's pride endured despite the mythology surrounding Rev. Henson that obscured James' knowledge of his own ancestor's history. He would erroneously credit Queen Victoria, in his speech, as having *given* Rev. Henson the land for the British American Institute and continue to frame Rev. Henson's life in respect to his enslavement and flight to freedom. The information he and others at the gathering needed to more accurately present their own heritage was only beginning to become available. Robin Winks's landmark book *The Blacks in Canada: A History* had only been written the previous year. Daniel G. Hill's *The Freedom-Seekers: Blacks in Early Canada* would not appear for another decade. The Black Abolitionist Papers project, which made key primary sources more accessible, would not see its second volume on Canadian Black history published until 1986. The papers of the noted Ontario Indigenous and Black–history scholar Fred Landon, compiled between 1918 and 1967, while available through London's Western University, Weldon Library, would not be released in book form until 2009.[9] Nineteenth-century resources like the *Provincial Freeman* and *Voice of the Fugitive* were only beginning to be made available on microfilm. Wide circulation of university collections like those at Oberlin were decades away from being widely accessible through the Internet. Even the field of Black history would not be established until 1977 when Daniel G. Hill and Wilson O. Brooks established the Ontario Black History Society and instituted the first Canadian Black History Month.[10]

Local Black historians, despite this absence of resources, nevertheless had begun to reclaim and preserve their heritage in the 1970s and '80s in community histories including at significant Black settlement areas like Chatham and Buxton. Gwen and John Robinson,[11] Arlee Robbins,[12] and Dorothy Shadd Shreve (Segee)[13] would publish their well-researched works at this time. Alex Haley's 1977 book, *Roots: The Saga of an American Family*,[14] and the TV series it inspired, would spur an interest in genealogy among people like The Hanson-Cook family would similarly produce the family genealogy *Precious Memories*. In the 1970s, however, sharing family history was still at times a courageous act as not all agreed with making this personal information publicly accessible. At Dresden, there had been a particular aversion to sharing information as a result of the failed 1948 attempt to have Uncle Tom's Cabin Museum created as a public institution. While Rev. Johnson had promised that if this happened, she would ensure artifacts and information would be provided from the Black community, the council's failure to support public ownership had the opposite effect. Descendants of Dawn's settlers, including the Henson family, would not become involved out of fear that their history would be co-opted for the personal gain of the museum's private owners and possibly misrepresented. Noted Black historian Alvin McCurdy would put a fine point on this concern in a letter to Thelma L. Williams, a Henson descendant: "If I may, I would sincerely advise that no copies of the material that you people [sic] have regarding your area be given to any white people because once they possess this, the people are no longer required."[15] The absence of the involvement by the Black community would ensure the interpretation of history at the museum would be decidedly white-centric and have a heavy emphasis on Henson's fame in relation to Stowe's book and on his meetings with British historical figures. The museum would continue to be branded as "Uncle Tom's Cabin" for its promotional value, given the familiarity of the general public with Stowe's novel. In the mid-twentieth century, the novel was still required reading at many schools on both sides of the Atlantic, giving the Uncle Tom name a familiarity and identification Henson's own name did not have. Marketing concerns would continue to persist as an argument against removing what had become a derisive term for Black museum-goers.[16]

Nevertheless, there had been a sincerity to the efforts of original white museum developer William Chapple to achieve national recognition of Rev.

Henson's history. In the context of the times, Chapple's efforts to preserve Rev. Henson's final home were commendable given that other important Black history sites in the county, like Chatham's John Brown House and *Provincial Freeman* building were being demolished.[17] In 1980 he would be awarded with a provincial citation for his educational and preservation efforts.[18] Those efforts had included the reprinting of Rev. Henson's original slave narrative. Jack Thomson, the museum's second white owner, expanded on Chapple's work, moving the museum site farther north and east of Chapple's site so it was adjacent to the Henson cemetery and adding more buildings and general pioneer artifacts to Chapple's modest collection. Along with local historian and newspaperman Don "Gummer" Spearman, Thomson would embark on research to further flesh out the interpretation of the site, travelling to Kentucky to bring back artifacts of the slave era. It was the first time that the cruelty inflicted on the enslaved would be represented at the museum. Thomson's development of the museum, only a decade after the passage of the *Fair Accommodations Practices Act*, took place in a time when the trust of descendants had not been realized and their involvement was still not forthcoming. Consequently, Thomson sometimes relied on white sources, including Susan Hawes—granddaughter of Henson's former master Amos Riley—who was interviewed during the Kentucky trip to provide insights into Henson's early life.[19] His friend and fellow historical researcher Spearman, meanwhile, had begun to research Rev. Thomas Hughes and the history of Christ Anglican Church, Spearman's home parish. Through his work, documents relating to Hughes's early mission made their way to the Diocese of Huron Archives in London. His writing would also generally support the tourism objectives of the museum in features and special sections of the *North Kent Leader* newspaper where he was editor.[20] Spearman's writing followed in the tradition of other local white historians like T.N. Wells,[21] Robert Brandon,[22] Helen Burns,[23] Alda Hyatt,[24] and Victor Lauriston,[25] who universally presented a slavery-to-freedom narrative and Henson's association with Stowe's book in presenting the Dawn Settlement's history. Later in life, however, Spearman would expand on this history, exploring other topics in his weekly "Mostly from Memory" newspaper columns and in his book, *Landmarks from the Past*.[26] He broke open long tabu subjects of racism and exclusion at Dresden with his accounts of the Dresden meteorite, the Ku

Klux Klan, and the NUA. He attempted to interview local people of African descent, but in the face of continued skepticism about his motives many of his stories relied on information gleaned from other whites. As a result, his Black history mainly portrayed people as servants, or victims of injustice, as in the story of an American Civil War veteran, and made no mention of their contributions as pioneers and community developers and activists. The stories in *Landmarks from the Past* are a mixed bag, on the one hand showing that Henson was much revered and on the other presenting an alternative version of what motivated Henson to escape enslavement that seems steeped in racial tropes.[27]

By the 1972 gathering, the emerging field of Black studies saw scholars beginning to explore a more complex and nuanced history of Black settlement in nineteenth-century Canada. Local Black historians would eagerly glean information from these accounts to better understand their community's place within the broader national and international context and to flesh out their understanding of local historical figures and events. Yet, there seemed to exist two solitudes in respect to historical knowledge, with the general public tending to ignore "Black history" books or not thinking to include these histories within "Canadian history."

At Dresden, the more recent civil rights history continued to remain conspicuously absent from Black histories and from museums' interpretive work.[28] When CBC radio personality Stuart McLean visited Dresden to research his book *Welcome Home*,[29] the lack of progress in the twenty years since Rosa Parks's visit in reclaiming a truer representation of Black history was still apparent. McLean would make the predictable pilgrimage to Rev. Josiah Henson's grave and tour the Uncle Tom's Cabin Historic Site, but he would also interview families who had been involved in the National Unity Association struggle. On his final night in Dresden, a despondent McLean purchased a bottle of whiskey from the local LCBO and sat on a picnic table at the museum grounds after hours, draining the bottle—watching, listening, and waiting. He concludes his chapter on Dresden saying, "I am not sure what I am waiting for."[30] Perhaps McLean sensed the disconnects that remained between the histories that were celebrated and those that were not, and between Black history and community history as there were no public representations of Black history in the town at that time, and the historical interpretations at the museum outside town still remained focused on the "Uncle Tom" and Underground Railroad narratives.

It would be another eleven years after the Rosa Parks visit before Canadians would see the first representation of Black history on a Canada Post stamp. On September 16, 1983, on the centenary of Rev. Josiah Henson's death, he would become the first Black historical figure to be so honoured.[31] Marion E. Lambkin, Henson's great-granddaughter, officially unveiled the Henson stamp, along with Kent MP Maurice Bossy and chairman of Canada Post Corporation André Ouellette, in front of an audience of four hundred people at the Uncle Tom's Cabin Historic Site.[32]

Marion E. Lambkin at the unveiling of the Henson stamp, with MP Maurice Bossy and federal minister of Canada Post Corp. Andre Ouellette. (*Photo courtesy of Barbara Carter and familiy*)

Forty years after the NUA's actions, and a decade after the Rosa Parks visit Mary McCorkle would be appointed as head of the Dresden Police Services Board and Allan Thompson would be invited to apply for a job as the town's first Black police officer. Around this time, Allan's wife, Sandra, would be invited by Betty Spearman (wife of historian Don Spearman) to join the

IODE, and by 1990 she would become the Catherine McVean Chapter IODE president.[33] These were hopeful signs of progress in the community towards greater inclusion.

The reclamation of history that was seen as so integral to Rev. Jennie Johnson and the Masonic gatherings at Dresden would also continue to be pursued by the Henson family and others who sought to have Henson's own name and true history recognized and the name "Uncle Tom" removed from the museum dedicated to his memory. That transition would take many more decades. Public ownership was finally achieved with the sale of the museum to the County of Kent, and, with this shift, representation of the Black community was finally introduced through the appointment of a Community Advisory Board. In 1991, with the further sale of the museum by Kent County to the St. Clair Parkway Commission, Barbara Carter (Marion Lambkin's daughter) would be hired as site manager and as head of the community advisory board she would expand its membership.[34] The board now became an integrated body that included original members James Dudley and Dorothy Shadd Shreve Segee, and others chosen for the specific skills they could bring to an ambitious million-dollar revitalization project that was about to take place. Dave Benson, the white curator of Chatham's Museum, undertook an evaluation of the artifacts displayed. White Kent Genealogical Society members Pat and Rupert Bedford and Ida DeBusschere brought their research capabilities and local history knowledge. I was invited because, as a reporter, I was interested in the history represented and in bringing awareness of the museum's development goals to the broader community. Chatham historians Gwen and John Robinson, together with Dorothy Shadd Shreve Segee, applied their specialized knowledge of Black history ensuring historical accuracy in the provincial and national plaques erected at the site and in the museum's literature. In 2006 Ruth Dudley of Dresden would also join the board as a community representative a role she continued to play when the museum came under the stewardship of the Ontario Heritage Trust under the chairmanship of the Honourable Lincoln Alexander.[35] The advisory board assisted staff in guiding the $1.9 million redevelopment plan made possible by a grant from the Bob Rae NDP government. Urgent preservation that was needed on artifact buildings was addressed, and a thorough re-evaluation of the museum's artifact collection led to a de-acquisitioning of items that had no proven links to Rev. Josiah Henson nor any relevance to the 1850s time frame being portrayed at the site. Buildings that did not fit within the time-line of the history being presented were razed, leaving only Henson House, Harris House, the church, the smokehouse, and a period steam engine in a reconfigured, landscaped site. Henson House was restored to reflect its origi-nal 1850s Black architectural style. This necessitated re-creating the building's front porch and removing the stone fireplace William Chapple had added to its kitchen in the 1940s. An impressive new interpretive centre was cre-ated with displays about Henson's life and times. Even the gift shop, under Barbara Carter's influence, now better reflected Black culture by including African art and books on Black history. An annual Emancipation Day event further highlighted Black culture through music, art, and scholarly histori-cal presentations. The historic sites and monuments board of the Canadian government also erected a new plaque near Henson's grave that finally rec-ognized the cemetery and museum grounds as a place of national historic significance, and the improvements at the site now reflected that status.

On Friday, February 25, 2005, Henson descendant Gayle Salisbury (née Carter)[36] stepped up to the podium in the Uncle Tom's Cabin Historic Site interpretive centre, beside the Honourable Lincoln Alexander, former lieutenant governor and now Ontario Heritage Trust's board chairman. A capacity crowd had gathered to recognize the important milestone of the site's transfer to the Ontario Heritage Trust.[37] A bank of television cameras stood ready to record the event. And as Salisbury delivered her passionate speech about her ancestor Rev. Josiah Henson, the mixed audience listened attentively. Few perhaps realized the dramatic shift the unfolding scene represented. Those standing along the front of the gathering now finally reflected the people whose stories were being told. Lincoln Alexander's pres-ence marked his generation's struggle against racism. Salisbury's was repre-sentative of a generation that was more fully realizing its own heritage and becoming engaged in educating others about it. The museum she and her mother, Barbara Carter, and Ontario Heritage Trust officials now stewarded was more truly a tribute to the life and times of the Rev. Josiah Henson.

Beyond the museum, society had also evolved. Black youth of the baby boom generation had become beneficiaries of the Civil Rights Movement and, unlike generations before them, graduates of the local high school could now choose professions that reflected their skills, interests, and hard work, and not the roles imposed on them by society based on racial distinctions. The academic excellence of people like Salisbury[38] ensured that she and others could go on to careers their parents could never have aspired to. While some continued to farm land their Dawn settler ancestors had originally cleared, others would continue to out-migrate to cities like Windsor, Detroit, and Toronto in search of new opportunities. Salisbury, like the generation before her, accepted a job in Detroit's automotive sector, but her position would be a white-collar one.

Yet, another important step remained to make the transformation at the museum complete. This required the museum staff and Henson descendants to keep up the continuum of resistance to misrepresentation of their history, work that had been started decades before by Rev. Jennie Johnson and her delegation to the 1948 Dresden Town Council. On August 2022 at Emancipation Day celebrations, Barbara Carter would smile broadly as the Ontario Heritage Trust unveiled new signage on Uncle Tom's Cabin Historic Site that finally affixed Henson's real name to the museum that honoured his memory. The former Third Concession that The Josiah Henson Museum of African Canadian History lay beside and which had been previously named Uncle Tom Road was now called Freedom Road. The new names would meet a flurry of criticism from the community at large. Tellingly, these criticisms objected to the name changes because they perceived they changed history. Patient explanations by the museum staff that even Henson himself had objected to being represented by the name Uncle Tom and did not wish to be represented by any other name but his own, turned public opinion around.

Work to recognize, preserve, and celebrate Black history at Dresden had continued in the background of these developments. The Trillium Trail Historical Walk project of 2002 began a trend to incorporate Black history within community historical projects and events. Black history is now integrated with community history at the town's main intersection where the Dawn Barn Quilt Trail includes representations of William Whipper's lands along the Sydenham and the British American Institute and Henson in two of the five large "quilt" squares representing Dresden's founders. The Building Heritage Project, identifying heritage homes in Dresden, incorporated Black history sites like the Whipper Cottage and Charity House. And people of African descent have been represented in spirit walks celebrating the town's heritage.

Much remains to be researched, interpreted, preserved, and shared. A number of artifact buildings are fragile and still unprotected, including original churches of Rev. S.H. Davis and Rev. Thomas Hughes. Their dwindling congregations raise questions about the future of these structures. In the 1990s fire destroyed what had once been William Whipper's inn. Harriet Whipper's Georgian cottage, he Charity brother's rooming house, and J.B. and Mary Hollensworth's restaurant also remain as undesignated historic sites.

As Dawn's descendants continue to out-migrate from the community and elders with important oral histories pass on, family histories and related documents and photos remain at risk. With the steady decrease in the presence of those whose lives are directly linked to that of Dawn's early settlers of African descent, it becomes ever more important and even urgent to instill an appreciation of this history within the community as a whole so others can take up the work to preserve and celebrate this history. It is hoped that this book might spark curiosity and wonder at the accomplishments of early African-descent pioneers and their descendants and lead Canadians to fully appreciate the richness that exists in our diverse and shared journey.

The ROAD AHEAD

> *"We shall not cease from exploration*
> *And at the end of all our exploring*
> *Will be to arrive where we started*
> *And know the place for the first time."*[1]
> —T.S. Eliot

My personal journey of exploration into the Dawn Settlement's history, which began with those first tentative steps next door to Mr. Chapple's museum, has led me back to my own neighbourhood and the present time. And here, after peeling away the layers of mythology and historical amnesia that have hidden or distorted important aspects of the Dawn Settlement's history, I feel I have come to truly know this place where I have lived my entire life for the first time. What I know most clearly is that the Dawn Settlement area, where I continue to make my home, is a special place where we can "sometimes feel the nearness of history—the import of people acting and events unfolding in the past."[2] That nearness is present in a handful of remaining historical buildings and, most keenly, through the presence of remaining descendants of the early African-descent settlers. My arrival back at the place I began, however, is not meant to be an end to exploration. There remains a deep well of historical material from which much more can be drawn. Efforts to map all the African decent people in the Dawn Settlement area has not been exhaustive, and there remain in the land records names that still bear further investigation, in collaboration with other historians and family genealogists—and which would. Some of these investigations would benefit from international collaborations, as is especially the case with respect to Detroit, Michigan; Columbia, Pennsylvania; and even possibly the Caribbean. Local church records still hold more names, that bear investigation for possible UGRR connections. There remain also many unanswered questions with respect to major figures like William Whipper. Perhaps more can yet be found in New Brunswick, New Jersey, to shed further light on Whipper's later movements and activities. At Dresden there is still a surprising lack of photographic documentation of the Black elite's businesses here, and I remain hopeful that future cross-border collaborations with families, museums, and universities might yet result in the discovery of images related to local history. As the Promised Land Project's co-investigators realized, this history and the history of the Canadian Black settlements more generally, would benefit greatly from transcontinental and transatlantic investigations.[3] I hope also that future historians will complete a biography of William Whipper that takes into account his movements on both sides of the Canada-US border, and perhaps one of the Rev. John Scoble that focuses on his international anti-slavery involvements in the US, the Caribbean, France, and, of course, Britain and Canada. Though Scoble is a controversial figure in the Dawn Settlement's history, tracing his international influence and travels further could provide additional insights into the transatlantic links of the abolitionist movement. Additional exploration of the local area's relationship with Detroit, Michigan, in the time of the UGRR and the fur trading era would help us to better understand the life of individuals like Samuel Henry Davis, to discover if the Willoughby family in the Dawn Settlement is linked to the Willoughby family at Detroit, and if other recurring names from Detroit like Weir, Blackburn, and French are more than coincidence.[4] Archie McKellar's partnership with two Detroit men in purchasing the Charity brothers' properties at Dresden also suggests additional Detroit's links that are as yet unexplored and George DeBaptiste's brief appearance at Dresden and the Charity brothers' *Industry of Detroit* ship similarly suggest more remains to be discovered about possible marine links of the UGRR at Detroit with Dresden.

Further local preservation and interpretation of Black history is also needed in respect to family photo collections and oral histories. Here and in other communities where descendants of early settlers remain deeply rooted for generations historians and sociologists could gain valuable insights through intergenerational conversations such as the ones informally undertaken during research for this book, which have revealed marked differences between the experiences and perspectives of the National Unity Association generation, the baby boom generation and the current Black Lives Matter generation. These revealed that individuals who were deeply rooted in rural communities over many generations often have markedly different perspectives from those of younger urban-based people and those who have arrived as part of more recent African diasporas.[5] Additional conversations of this kind could perhaps provide more nuanced and complex understandings of issues of racism, inclusion, and identity.

Local Historical preservation has also been revealed through this project as being urgently needed. Remaining photo collections, writings, and artifact buildings in rural communities such as the Dawn Settlement area are historical resources that are increasingly at risk with the outmigration of young people and the passing of elders and at a time when the importance of these materials is just beginning to be understood. Loss of older generations is also resulting in an uncertain future for historic churches of the Rev. Samuel Henry Davis and of Rev. Thomas Hughes, which still house artifacts and archival materials important to the understanding of local and regional Black history. Fostering an appreciation of a small number of remaining artifact buildings is vital if preservation of these structures as historic sites or appropriately repurposed heritage buildings is to be accomplished. Education on Black history at the local, regional, provincial, and national levels is needed to foster an understanding of their historical worth. Imparting a more nuanced and complex understanding of Black history through public education and school curriculums, however, is still an uphill battle. Many Black History Month efforts still tend to pick the low fruit of well-worn UGRR stories and continue to highlight figures such as those of Henson, Shadd, and Tubman as exceptional; even their stories tend to be presented in such broad strokes that a full appreciation of their historical contributions is often missed by the Canadian public. A casual poll of high school students in my local school district, for example, asked students to name five important Black historical figures. They could only name Henson and Shadd and relied on US history for the names of others. Most had a general idea of who Dr. Martin Luther King Jr. was but were unaware of Canadian Civil Rights figures like Viola Desmond and the National Unity Association members. That most were unaware that early Black pioneers had contributed to development of the community perhaps has had a bearing on at least one case of racial bullying that was recently addressed at a local school. As Rev. Jennie Johnson encouraged, teaching people about the accomplishments and contributions of people of African descent could help to foster respect in the present..

As mentioned in the introduction, there is also a need to document new migrations of the African diasporas such as Caribbean migrant workers, who come to Southwestern Ontario in numbers that rival or exceed those of the nineteenth-century migrations. Inclusion of later migration groups to the area would greatly assist in making Black History more relevant to those who have no ancestral connection to the nineteenth century narratives.

It is my fervent hope that this exploration of the Dawn Settlement's history will have an impact beyond the local area by inspiring other community historians to dig deeper into the accepted Black History of their community and similarly questioning its reduction to a simple UGRR narrative. Grassroots work such as this could play an important role in shifting the collective Canadian consciousness to a new appreciation of African-Canadian history—one that shows the diversity of people of African descent and explores their contributions as pioneers and community builders.

. . .

People have often asked me why the Black history of the Dawn Settlement has mattered enough to me to make it a focus of research for so many years—pointing to what they believe to be the obvious fact that this is not *my* history. And I would submit that I am curious about the history of all my neighbours in my diverse community, and that exploring all of their histories is an important part of a personally important search for Canadian identity. None of the Canadian histories I learned growing up had a particular relevance to my own Flemish-Canadian background and culture, and as such all these histories have had an equal importance to me in answering my personal questioning about what constitutes Canadian identity Or, put another way, I have always asked: What is the common historical narrative that is relatable to us all as Canadian citizens? What binds us together and gives us a sense that we are all connected and can see ourselves reflected in Canadian history—and, by extension, in Canadian society? This seems pertinent to discuss in this afterword in the light of the Dawn Settlement's complex multiracial and multicultural history, and given recent debates about the failure of multiculturalism. The abstract for *Global Perspectives on the Politics of Multiculturalism in the 21st Century*,[6] edited by Fethi Mansouri and former Promised Land lead investigator Boulou Ebanda de B'béri states, "Multiculturalism is now seen by many of its critics as the source of intercultural and social tensions, fostering communal segregation and social conflicts. While the cultural diversity of contemporary societies has to be acknowledged as an empirical and demographic fact, whether multiculturalism as a policy offers an optimal conduit for intercultural understanding and social harmony has become increasingly a matter of polarised public debate." I have not followed this debate closely nor am I well positioned to appreciate historically marginalized peoples' relationship to multiculturalism. Yet having grown up before a time of official multiculturalism in Canada, I have faith that multiculturalism—in its very best sense—is still possible, and believe it to be a work in progress, an ideal, that like freedom is worth fighting for even though it may never be fully realized. Perhaps it is in this area that the Dawn Settlement's continuum of history may yet move forward from its past of multiculturality? My own experience with the introduction of official multiculturalism in Canada gives me hope in this regard.

In the 1950s, I attended the one-room school Mount Pleasant (Union School Section 3) in Camden Gore. The symbols of Canadian identity I encountered in that context tended to reflect the heritage, culture, and values of the British Empire. Our daily morning routine reinforced this through opening exercises that consisted of readings of the Protestant Bible, the singing of Christian religious hymns and of our national anthem, "God Save the Queen." While singing we looked up at a large colourful portrait of a young Elizabeth II, inexplicably flanked by the stark Karsh portrait of wartime British prime minister Winston Churchill. (There were no images of Canadian prime ministers on the walls of our schoolhouse or in our history texts.) The wall was also adorned with a colourful map of the world, with Canada, like a host of other nations, coloured red to denote we were all part of the great British Commonwealth of Nations ruled by the young queen. At times, we sang the 1867 patriotic song "The Maple Leaf Forever,"[7] which leading up to Canada's Centennial year many felt should be our new national anthem. It referenced Canadian history, but its rousing chorus proclaimed "the thistle, shamrock, rose entwine, the Maple Leaf forever!"[8] Those of us sitting in the neat rows of desks singing enthusiastically were an eclectic mix of Indigenous people, French Canadians, people of African descent, and recent immigrants from mainland Europe. Those not sharing the British ancestry of other classmates could find nothing in these symbols of Scotland, Ireland, and England that represented us. As an anthem then, "The Maple Leaf Forever" neither bound us together nor gave us any sense of a shared heritage or personal national identity. Many of us were left puzzled as to how our own cultural heritages fit within this vision of Canada and wondering if we were understood, despite our official citizenship, to be fully Canadian.

Leading up to Canada's Centennial in 1967, many Canadians felt that the country should have its own unique symbols that more clearly signalled we were a distinct national identity. We shed the Union Jack from our flag and came to recognize French as an important founding language and culture, officially honoured and preserved as an integral part of our history and our present reality. By 1980 we adopted "O Canada" as our national anthem. Over time, we began to learn new terms to identify Indigenous peoples and started on a slow path to the realization, one that is incomplete even today, that Indigenous communities are nations within our nation—as recognized by historical treaties. Finally, in October 1971, Canada became the first country in the world to officially adopt a policy of multiculturalism and, with this, a door seemed to open into a hopeful new space where there was room for all, regardless of our diverse migration narratives.

Recent scholarly works, like that by Funké Aladejebi and Michele A. Johnson, have included multiculturalism in their discussions of the "mythology of the Great White North,"[9] framing the value of multiculturalism, or lack thereof, within discussions of racism and exclusion. Perhaps altering perspectives by which this and other works, like that of Adrienne Shadd,[10] have understood early rural Black settlements—transforming our understanding as these from failures of a utopian dream to successes could be similarly applied to this perception of multiculturalism? Multiculturalism currently presents as a kind of utopian dream as well but should perhaps be viewed as a societal ideal, like freedom. Freedom was not realized in the US through the single act of legislating the Emancipation Proclamation; while it ended chattel slavery, freedom and equality were not fully established by one stroke of the pen, and official and unofficial policies that allowed for the continued exploitation of Black labour and segregation persisted for some time after. Also, freedom necessarily includes the presence of equal rights and an absence of fear, violence, exclusion, and intimidation. Sadly, even today this degree of freedom has not been fully realized, yet we do not view freedom as a failed experiment. Similarly, legislating multiculturalism as an official national policy has not resulted in the people of all races, cultures, and creeds in our richly diverse Canadian mosaic to be acknowledged, understood, valued, and celebrated as an important and integral part of Canadian history and society. It has only been a first step, and much work remains—and is likely to always remain—in ensuring equity and inclusion for all.

The history of the Dawn Settlement, and I suspect of most early Canadian Black settlements, shows that from our earliest beginnings Canada has been rooted in what Handel Kashope Wright has called "multiculturality before official multiculturalism."[11] Recognizing this historical reality could be helpful in advancing multiculturalism, as it informs us that we have as a nation always been in the process of working out how to embrace and celebrate diverse migrations of people. The more positive examples from the Middle Ground period show that embracing this diversity has helped our mutual survival. To be sure, this history also tells us that we could do better than our ancestors in ensuring we do not exploit, abuse, or marginalize others. Our failures, however, should not cause us to give up on the ideal of a truly multicultural society. History after all instructs us to have patience in our efforts to progress social change, and in the Dawn Settlement's history we can find numerous examples of the protracted timelines involved. Our histories can also provide us with examples of those who persevered in their quest to achieve freedom and equality despite discouraging evidence that told them their goals were unattainable. Rev. Thomas Hughes remained committed to creating an integrated church and society even though this vision would not be achieved in his lifetime. Rev. Jennie Johnson worked to gain greater dignity and respect for African-descent people through the reclamation of their history, but the museum named for Josiah Henson that she sought to make a public institution honouring Henson would remain known as "Uncle Tom's Cabin" for more than sixty years[12] and the authentic history she would have wished to see shown there is only now emerging from the shadow of Uncle Tom. Recognizing the continuum of resistance in Dawn's two-hundred-year history inspires perseverance and hope. History also tells us that we take for granted concepts like freedom and multiculturalism to our peril, as the precious ground we have gained is being eroded by the current rise of "tribalism."

Historical knowledge, of course, does not magically inoculate us against present or future struggles. If we are to move multiculturalism forward as part of a continuum of the history of resistance to racism and exclusion, we must address unique twenty-first century challenges. Here in the Dawn Settlement area, for instance, immigration policy issues continue to systemically enforce the marginalization of migrating groups like temporary foreign workers. While technically able to immigrate, many of these individuals remain unable to meet the rigorous requirements, language and other, of the immigration points system, effectively keeping them locked in a non-citizen status that prevents their full inclusion into Canadian society. While they remain here, year after year contributing to the success of local agricultural industries, they often continue to live away from their families and home communities, all the while remaining largely on the fringes of Canadian society—and this often leads to vulnerabilities in respect to medical care, workplace issues, and community-building. This is, of course, but one challenge among many affecting both rural and urban people of diverse racial and cultural backgrounds that need to be addressed if Canadian society is to live up to its image of itself as a welcoming and inclusive multicultural nation.

The progressive visions of an integrated society that seeks the uplift of all through mutual support and which espouses a diversity of talents being applied to progressive development of our nation, as articulated in William Whipper's writings, are still worth pursuing. It is too soon to know if the visions of men like him mark the beginning of a continuum of multiculturality to true multiculturalism. And perhaps the tracing of this continuum forward is too ambitious a projection of this history. On a more modest level, it is hoped that this history of the Dawn Settlement represents a small step forward in presenting a truer and more complex and nuanced account of Canadian Black history which, like all our histories, more Canadians will come to realize, *matter*. All are part of our shared inheritance as a nation.

Marie Carter
Dresden, 2023

Acknowledgements

It's said that it takes a village to raise a child. The same could be said about writers of history. Certainly, I owe much to the complex and generous community where I grew up and particularly to my parents, Gus and Alice DeBruyn, for the values and life learnings they imparted that underpin this work. Dresden service clubs, and especially the Dresden Rotary and Catherine McVean Chapter IODE, have encouraged research over the years through a variety of community projects. The Trillium Trail Historical Walk Project proved instrumental in discovering the lost Black history at Dresden. Barbara Carter's initial invitation to join the Uncle Tom's Cabin Community Advisory Board was also foundational. Her continued support and encouragement over the years and the contributions she and her daughters, Gayle, Susan, and Cathy, made in reviewing an early draft, offering insights and family documents and photos, were invaluable.

Gwen Robinson of Chatham has been appreciated for sharing her depth of knowledge and assistance with early research efforts, and for the invitation she extended to the Promised Land Project, a one-million-dollar five-year Community-University Research Alliance (CURA) project that introduced me to coinvestigators Boulou de B'béri, Handel Wright, Nina Reid-Maroney, and others from across North America and the United Kingdom who also encouraged and informed this work. The project provided important opportunities for broader learning and travel, and for presentation of the work to academic audiences.

The support and encouragement of Bryan and Shannon Prince at the Buxton National Historic Site over many years has contributed greatly to the evolution of my work. Bryan's generous sharing of his meticulous research has particularly enhanced the American Civil War, World War I, and the Great Migration chapters of this book. The Princes' historical conferences and after-parties at Buxton Homecoming also introduced me to a wide supportive network of fellow researchers. Dennis Gannon, who I met there, generously shared a wealth of information and files from Washington, D C, and St. Catherines, Ontario, over the years, which advanced the work on Rev. Hiram Wilson. Hilary Neary's gracious and supportive conversations and sharing of files on Rev. L.C. Chambers in advance of publication of her book similarly helped inform the chapter on Dawn's early missions.

Steven Cook and the staff of Ontario Heritage Trust's Josiah Henson Museum of African Canadian History provided important opportunities to present, discuss, and develop work through museum events and projects; such developmental opportunities also arose in writing articles edited by Karolyn Smardz Frost for Ontario Heritage Trust's (OHT) magazine *Heritage Matters* and through their YouTube series, *Discovering Dawn*.

Numerous staff and volunteers guided me to important primary resources at the Weldon Library, London; Chatham-Kent municipal archives in the McGeorge Building, Chatham-Kent Museum and Public Library; Dresden Library; Kent Ancestors (formerly the Kent Genealogical Society); and Fox County (Wisconsin) Genealogical Society. Genealogists Cindy Robichaud and Frank Vink in particular are appreciated, Cindy for additional technical assistance in copying family photos and Frank for sharing his considerable knowledge of early settlers and extinct topographical features in Dover Township that influenced early settlement patterns. Local military expert Jerrel (Jerry) Hind's extensive files, now available through the IODE's Gathering Our Heroes website, were important (along with those of the Royal Canadian Legion Branch 113 and Bryan Prince) in piecing together the lives of WWI and WWII military servicemen.

Dresden families also provided much in the way of insights into history. Members of the Weese family contributed their perspective on their grandfather Walter's life and times. Descendants of the Rev. S.M. Davis, Bill Richardson and Susan Solomon, shared a wealth of personal stories, photos, and genealogical and research files that informed work on twentieth-century life and migration patterns. It is with sadness that I cannot celebrate the publication of this book with Susan, as we'd planned, due to her untimely passing in 2021. Sandra Thompson is owed much for her friendship, good humour, frank observations, and advice shared with me in a series of Wednesday walks during the pandemic as I struggled with doubts, fears, and challenges during what was at times a difficult writing process, to say nothing of the amazing and rare photos she shared from her Thompson/Guest family collection.

A generous grant from the Ontario Arts Council supported the hiring of graphic artist Debra Buchanan who created the maps, and Glenna M. Jenkins who edited my initial press submission. Senior Acquisitions Editors Karen May Clark and Rachel Freedman Stapleton of the University of Regina Press guided my manuscript through to publication with skill, patience, and grace, and Stapleton's generous support throughout the peer review and editing process was especially appreciated. Rachel Ironstone demonstrated meticulous attention and Managing Editor Shannon Parr's sage guidance further assisted the work being the best it could be through its final stages.

My main support through all this has been my husband, Jeffrey, who is appreciated for his belief in my writing, for his editing contributions, and for keeping the home fires burning when I was preoccupied by research, meetings, and deadlines.

Finally, I cannot thank Afua Cooper enough for believing in this project. I am honoured she has made my book part of her Henry and Mary Bibb Black Series of Black Canadian Studies.

My heartfelt thanks to all, both named and unnamed, whose support, ideas, experiences, and knowledge are ultimately part of this book.

Bibliography

Primary Sources

Oral Histories

Oral histories and interviews were conducted with a number of people from the community of Dresden, including various descendants of the Dawn Settlement's original settlers and family members of National Unity Association members, as well as white residents, including long-time residents of the Quality Hill area, McVean family descendants, and descendants of Walter Weese. Also, interviews and correspondence were conducted with American descendants of the Hollensworth, Smith, and Whipper families.

Personal Papers, Letters, and Legal documents

BlackPast Organization. "(1837) William Whipper, 'Non-Resistance to Offensive Aggression.'" BlackPast.org, January 24, 2007. https://www. blackpast.org/african-american-history/1837-william-whipper-non-resistance-offensive-aggression.

Burns, Helen. Historical papers and scrapbook collection. Dresden Archives, Dresden, Ontario.

Brown, John Jr. "Letters to His Wife Wealthy C. Hotchkiss, March, 1861." Rutherford B. Hayes Library.

"New Appointments" [announcement of dissolution of co-partnership of Smith, Whipper, and Co.]. *The Columbia Spy*, May 13,1858.

Payne, Daniel Alexander. *Recollections of Seventy Years*. A.M.E. Sunday School Union, 1888.

Scoble and Brown vs Wright and Myers, court case documents. Weldon Library, Western University, London, Ontario.

Thompson, Sandra, and Alan Thompson. Private collection of photos and scrapbooks. Dresden, Ontario.

Archival Newspapers, Magazines, and Pamphlets

Archives of Canada (Ottawa, Ontario), https://library-archives-canada.ca/.

Archives of Ontario (Toronto, Ontario), www.archives.gov.on.ca.

Biography of Hiram Wilson, Oberlin papers, 1835–1856, Oberlin College Archives.

The Canadian Observer, London, Ontario, 1914–1919, Coherent Digital online, https://www.accessible-archives.com/collections/african-american-newspapers/the-canadian-observer/.

Charlton, R.M. *Charlton & Co.'s County of Kent Gazetteer: General and Business Directory, for 1874–5*. Hunter, Rose, & Co, 1874.

Chatham Gleaner, Chatham, Ontario, 1844–1849. Chatham-Kent Library microfilm collection.

Chatham Planet, Chatham, Ontario, 1891–1922. Chatham-Kent Library microfilm collection.

Chicago Defender, Bethune Binga's Canadian social notes in the January 12, 1935, to December 24, 1936 editions. Library of Congress, Online Catalog, Washington, DC.

The Christian Recorder, Philadelphia, Pennsylvania, 1852–present.

Constitution of the Oberlin Anti-Slavery Society, Oberlin College Archives, McGeorge Building archives, Municipality of Chatham-Kent, Chatham, Ontario re:

    1871 minute books for the Village of Dresden,

    1870 minute books of the Township of Camden

    1948–1954 minute books for the Town of Dresden

Don Spearman Collection, Dresden Archives, Dresden, Ontario; and Dresden Branch, Chatham-Kent Library, Dresden, Ontario.

Dresden News, Dresden, Ontario, 1938–1965. Dresden Library microfilm collection.

Dresden Times, Dresden, Ontario, 1871–1958. Dresden Library microfilm collection.

Frederick Douglass' Paper, Rochester, New York, 1851–1859.

Fred Landon Black History files, Weldon Library, University of Western Ontario archives.

Helen Burns papers on the history of Dresden, Dresden Archives, Dresden, Ontario.

"Lane Seminary, Defense of the Students," reprinted from The Liberator, vol. 5, no. 2, January 10, 1835, 5-6, Oberlin College Archives, www.oberlin.edu/external/EOG/LaneDebates/RebelDefence.htm

The Liberator, Boston, Massachussetts, 1831–1865.

Molly's Creek W.I. Tweedsmuir History, Dresden Archives, Dresden, Ontario.

North Kent Leader, Dresden, Ontario, 19651990 Dresden Archives bound file collection.

The North Star, Rochester, New York, 1849–1851.

The Provincial Freeman, Toronto, Windsor, and Chatham, Ontario, 1853–1857.

Records for Christ Church (Dresden), files of the Chatham-Kent Black Historical Society research room, Chatham, Ontario.

Sketches and land record information of the Anglican Range of the Dresden Cemetery, P. Croyn Memorial Archives, Diocese of Huron, Huron University College, London, Ontario.

Smith, WM.H. *Smith's Canadian Gazetteer*. H. &. W. Rowsell, 1846. Local historical book collection, Chatham-Kent Public Library, Chatham branch. Also available online, in the Internet Archive, https://archive.org/details/smithscanadiangaoosmit/page/n7/mode/2up.

The Voice of the Fugitive, Sandwich/Windsor, Ontario, 1851–1854.

Weekly Anglo African Newspaper, New York, 1859–1860, archives, fonds, and gazettes, https://archive.org/details/WeeklyAngloAfrican.

Wilson, Hiram. "Rev. Hiram Wilson papers." Photocopies of original letters obtained from Oberlin Archives archivist Roland M. Baumann, Dec. 20, 2004, collection of the author. Now available online through Oberlin College Archives, Archival resources, https://oberlinarchives.libraryhost.com/?p=collections/controlcard&id=277.

Various genealogical research materials and maps were also consulted, accessed in the Kent Genealogical Society Research Room, Chatham-Kent Public Library, Chatham-Kent, Ontario; Chatham-Kent Black Historical Society research rooms, WISH Centre, Chatham, Ontario; Buxton National Historic Site archives; Fox County Genealogical Society (via Marjorie Crane).

Genealogical Sources

Archives of the Buxton National Historic Site, North Buxton, Ontario. Family genealogical files and photo files.

Censuses: Various government censuses were consulted, including: 1851 Census of Kent County, 1861 Agricultural Census of Camden Township, 1861 Census of Camden, 1871 Census of Camden, 1871 Census of Chatham Township, 1871 Census of Dresden, 1881 Census of Camden Township, 1881 Census of Chatham Township, 1881 Census of Dresden. "Districts and Sub-districts: Census of 1851, Canada West (Ontario)" can be accessed online at Library and Archives Canada, https://www.bac-lac. gc.ca/eng/census/1851/Pages/canada-west.aspx.

Christ Church (Anglican), Dresden, Ontario, records of births, deaths, marriages, and baptisms, 1858–1887, accessed through files of the Chatham-Kent Black Historical Society.

Crane, Marjorie. President of the Fox County Genealogical Society. Personal communication with the author re genealogical records for the Clegett, Newman, and Hollensworth families. January–May, 2009.

Find a Grave. www.findagrave.com.

Heinegg, Paul. "Free African Americans in Colonial Virginia, North Carolina, South Carolina, Maryland and Delaware." https://freeafricanamericans .com.

Kent Genealogical Society newsletter archive. Edited by Frank Vink, Kent Ancestors research room, Chatham-Kent Public Library.

Robbins, Arlee. Compilation of genealogical notes of Chatham-Kent's Black families. From the Buxton National Historical Site in Buxton, Ontario; and the Chatham-Kent Black Historical Society in Chatham, Ontario.

Robinson, Gwen. Compilation of genealogical notes on the Shadd, Whipper, Hollensworth, and Smith families. From the Chatham-Kent Black Historical Society in Chatham, Ontario.

Maps and Atlases

1888 Dresden Fire Map. Collection of the Dresden Archives, Dresden, Ontario.

"Commission of Essex, Kent and Lambton, 1852." Global Heritage Press map reproduction, Kent OGS research room, Chatham-Kent Public Library, Chatham, Ontario.

Illustrated Historical Atlas of Kent and Essex Counties. Beldon & Co., Toronto, 1881.

Illustrated Historical Atlas of the County of Lambton, Ontario. Beldon & Co., Toronto, 1880.

Map of Chatham's "Old Survey" and the Iredell map of Chatham. Chatham-Kent Black Historical Society files, WISH Centre, Chatham, Ontario.

Map of Upper Canada Black Settlements. Fred Landon Papers, Western University, London, Ontario.

Also consulted were survey maps and related abstracts and deeds of Dresden, Fairfield, Camden Gore, Camden Township, Chatham Gore, Chatham Township, Dover Township, and Kent County, procured from the Ontario Land Record Office, Chatham, Ontario.

Miscellaneous

Afrolumens Project: Central Pennsylvania's Journey from Enslavement to Freedom. "1876 Death of William Whipper." Accessed September 14, 2007. www.afrolumens.com.

Afrolumens Project: Central Pennsylvania's Journey from Enslavement to Freedom. "Chronology of the Underground Railroad Activity in Harrisburg, with Related Activity, Relevant Figures and Events." Accessed September 14, 2007. www.afrolumens.com.

Kansas Historical Society. "Augustus Wattles Collection." Call Number: Ms Coll 533; Unit ID: 40533. Accessed May 8, 2020. https://www.kshs.org/archives/40533.

Delany, Martin Robison. *The Condition, Elevation, Emigration, and Destiny of the Colored People of the United States.* Arno Press and the New York Times, 1993. Available online at the Internet Archive https://archive.org/details/conditionelevatiooooodela.

Secondary Sources

Books, Chapters, Articles

African American Registry. "George DeBaptiste, Michigan Abolitionist born." Accessed, Jan 27, 2005. https://aaregistry.org/story/george-debaptiste-a-michigan-abolitionist/.

"Appointment to the Board." *Heritage Matters*, Ontario Heritage Trust 4, no. 1 (February 2006): 10.

Amadahy, Zainab, and Bonita Lawrence. "Indigenous Peoples and Black People in Canada: Settlers or Allies?" In *Breaching the Colonial Contract: Anti-Colonialism in the US and Canada*, edited by Arlo Kempf, 105–136. Springer Dordrecht, 2009.

Amherstburg Bicentennial Book Committee. *Amherstburg 1796–1996: The New Town on the Garrison Grounds.* Brown & Associates, 1996.

Amherstburg Regular M issionary Baptist Association. *Pathfinders of Liberty and Truth: A History of the Amherstburg Regular Missionary Baptist Association (ARMBRA) and its Auxiliaries and Churches.* Self-published by ARMBA, 1940.

Bearden, Jim, and Linda Jean Butler. *Shadd: The Life and Times of Mary Shadd Cary.* NC Press Ltd., 1977.

Beattie, Jessie Louise. *Black Moses: The Real Uncle Tom.* Ryerson Press, 1957.

Blount, Catherine Meehan. *Remnants of Forgotten Folk: The Sammons-Handsor Cemetery, Dover, Kent, Ontario, Canada, Burials from 1856 to 1959.* Audacious Publications (self-published), 2020.

Bordewich, Fergus M. *Bound for Canaan: The Underground Railroad and the War for the Soul of America.* Amistad, 2006.

Bourhis-Mariotti, Claire. "'Go to Our Brethren, the Haytians': Haiti as the African Americans' Promised Land in the Antebellum Era" *Revue Française D'Études Americaines* 142 (2015): 6–23. https://doi.org/10.3917/rfea.142.0006.

Brandon, Robert. *A History of Dresden.* Observer Press (self-published), 1953.

Brock, Jared A. *The Road to Dawn: Josiah Henson and the Story That Sparked the Civil War.* Hachette, 2018.

Brown-Johnston, Lorraine, and Janice McCaughin. *Precious Memories: The Hanson-Cook Family Tree.* Self-published, in the collection of the Dresden Archives, date unknown.

Burns, Helen Watson. *Dresden Fire Department.* Self-published, 1954.

Carter, Jeffrey, and Marie Carter. *Stepping Back in Time: Along the Trillium Trail in Dresden.* IODE, Catherine McVean Chapter, 2003.

Carter, Marie. *100 Years of IODE: In Dresden, 1914–2014.* IODE, Ontario: Catherine McVean Chapter, 2014.

Carter, Marie. *Building Heritage: A Catalogue of 40 of Dresden's Historic Homes.* IODE, Ontario: Catherine McVean Chapter, 2003.

Carter, Marie. "A New Lens on the Dawn Settlement." In *The Promised Land: History and Historiography of the Black Experience in Chatham-Kent's Settlements and Beyond,* edited by de B'béri, Reid-Maroney, and Wright. University of Toronto Press, 2014.

Carter, Marie, "William Whipper's Lands along the Sydenham." In *The Promised Land: History and Historiography of the Black Experience in Chatham-Kent's Settlements and Beyond,* edited by de B'béri, Reid-Maroney, and Wright. University of Toronto Press, 2014.

Congregational Christian Churches in Canada. "Our Rich Heritage: The Christian Churches in Ontario." Accessed March 17, 2004. www.cccc.ca/about-history.html.

Cooper, John. *Season of Rage: Hugh Burnett and the Struggle for Human Rights*. Penguin Random House, 2009.

Cowan, Hugh. *Ontario and the Detroit Frontier, 1701–1814*. Canadian History Series. Upper Canada Press, 1929.

de B'béri, Boulou Ebanda, Nina Reid-Maroney, and Handel Kashope Wright, eds. *The Promised Land: History and Historiography of the Black Experience in Chatham-Kent's Settlements and Beyond*. University of Toronto Press, 2014.

Delany, Martin Robison. *Official Report of the Niger River Valley Expedition* (1861). Project Gutenberg, 2007. https://www.gutenberg.org/files/22118/22118-h/22118-h.htm.

Drew, Benjamin. *A North-Side View of Slavery. The Refugee: Or the Narratives of Fugitive Slaves in Canada. Related by Themselves with an Account of the History and Condition of the Colored Population of Upper Canada*. John Jewitt and Co., 1856.

DuBois, W.E.B. "The Negro in Philadelphia." In *The Philadelphia Negro: A Social Study, 1820–1896*, 25–45. Schocken Books, 1967.

Dungy, Hilda, and Hattie Hanson. *Planted by the Waters: A Family History of the Jones-Carter Family*. Standard Press, 1977.

Elgie, Kae. *This Land: The Story of Two Hundred Acres in Kent County*. Fountain Street Press, 2019.

Encyclopedia Virginia. "Martin R. Delaney (1812-1885)." Virginia Humanities, accessed March 31, 2022. http://encyclopediavirginia.org.

Glaude, Eddie S. "Pragmatism and Black Identity: An Alternate Approach." *Nepantla: Views from South* 2, no. 2 (2001): 295–316. https://muse.jhu.edu/article/23921.

Hamil, Fred Coyne. *The Valley of the Lower Thames 1640–1850*. University of Toronto Press, 1973.

Hill, Daniel G. *The Freedom-Seekers: Blacks in Early Canada*. The Book Society of Canada Ltd., 1981.

Hodgins, J. George, et al. The Consolidated Acts Relating to Common Schools in Upper Canada; Together with Decisions of the Superior Courts, and the Forms, General Regulations and Instructions, for Executing Their Provisions. With a Copious Analytical Index. Toronto Department of Public Instruction for Upper Canada, 1866.

Hopkins, Leroy T. "Black Eldorado on the Susquehanna: The Emergence of Black Columbia, 1726–1861." *Journal of the Lancaster County Historical Society* 89, no. 4 (1985): 110–132.

Howe, Samuel Gridley. *The Refugees from Slavery in Canada West: Report to the Freedmen's Inquiry Commission.* Arno Press, 1864.

Hudson, J. Blaine. *Encyclopedia of the Underground Railroad.* McFarland and Co. Ltd., 2006.

Johnson, Michele A., and Funké Aladejebi, eds. *Unsettling the Great White North: Black Canadian History.* University of Toronto Press, 2022.

Kashatus, William C. *Just Over the Line: Chester County and the Underground Railroad.* Chester County Historical Society, 2002.

Katz, Sydney. "Jim Crow Lives in Dresden." *Maclean's,* November 1, 1949.

Kelly, Wayne. "Inside Uncle Tom's Cabin." *Heritage Matters* 3, no. 1 (February 2005): 1–2. https://www.heritage-matters.ca/articles/inside-uncle-toms-cabin.

Lambertson, Ross. "The Dresden Story: Racism, Human Rights and the Jewish Labour Committee of Canada." *Labour / Le Travail* 47 (Spring 2001): 43–82. http://www.jstor.org/stable/25149113.

Lauriston, Victor. *Lambton County's 100 years, 1849–1949.* County of Lambton, 1950.

Lauriston, Victor. *Romantic Kent: The Story of a County, 1626–1952.* County of Kent, 1977.

MacLachlan, K. Gordon. *A History of Dawn Township and Its Origin.* Self-published, 1971.

Major, Geraldyn Hodges, with Doris E. Saunders. *Black Society.* Johnson Publishing Co. Inc., 1977.

Manning, Chandra. *Troubled Refuge: Struggling for Freedom in the Civil War.* Alfred A. Knopf, 2016.

McCorkindale, Deirdre. "Weaponized History: The Underground Railroad's Mythologized Legacy in Canada." *The American Review of Canadian Studies,* 53, no. 1 (March 2023): 68–81. https://doi.org/10.1080/02722011.2023.2172886.

McIlwraith, Thomas F. *Looking for Old Ontario.* University of Toronto Press, 1997.

McLaren, Kristin. "'We Had No Desire to Be Set Apart': Forced Segregation of Black Students in Canada West Public Schools and Myths of British Egalitarianism." *Social History* 37, no. 73 (2004): 27–50.

McLean, Stuart. *Welcome Home: Travels in Small-Town Canada.* Penguin Canada, 1992.

Mealy, Todd M. *Aliened American: A Biography of William Howard Day.* 2010.

Michals, Debra, ed. "Lucretia Mott (1793–1880)." National Women's History Museum, 2017. https://www.womenshistory.org/education-resources/biographies/lucretia-mott.

Miles, Tiya. *The Dawn of Detroit: A Chronicle of Slavery and Freedom in the City of the Straits.* The New Press, 2017.

Miles, Tiya. "Native Americans and the Underground Railroad." National Park Service online, December 16, 2020. https://www.nps.gov/articles/000/native-americans-and-the-underground-railroad.htm.

Miller, Win. *Years of Change in Chatham and Kent, 1952–1992.* Chamberlain/Mercury Printing, 1996.

Morley, Jefferson. "The 'Snow Riot.'" *Washington Post*, February 5, 2005, W14. https://www.washingtonpost.com/archive/lifestyle/magazine/2005/02/06/the-snow-riot/0514ba84-54dd-46ac-851c-ff74856fcef4/.

Neary, Hilary Bates. *A Black American Missionary in Canada: The Life and Letters of Lewis Champion Chambers.* McGill-Queen's University Press, 2022.

Nelson, Charmaine A. "Black Cemeteries Force Us to Re-examine Our History with Slavery." *The Walrus*, May 28, 2018. https://thewalrus.ca/black-cemeteries-force-us-to-re-examine-our-history-with-slavery/.

Pease, Jane, and William H. Pease. *Black Utopia: Negro Communal Experiments in America.* Wisconsin Historical Society, 1963.

Pease, Jane, and William H. Pease. *Bound with Them in Chains: A Biographical History of the Antislavery Movement.* Greenwood Press, Inc., 1972.

Pettigrew, Joyce A. *A Safe Haven: The Story of the Black Settlers of Oxford County.* South Norwich Historical Society, 2006.

Price, Edward "The Black Voting Rights Issue in Pennsylvania, 1780–1900." *The Pennsylvania Magazine of History and Biography* 100, no. 3 (July 1976): 356–373. https://www.jstor.org/stable/20091079.

Prince, Bryan. *My Brother's Keeper: African Canadians and the American Civil War.* Dundurn Press, 2015.

Prince, Bryan. *A Shadow on the Household: One Enslaved Family's Incredible Struggle for Freedom.* McClelland and Stewart, 2008.

"Racial Segregation of Black People in Canada." *The Canadian Encyclopedia.* May 28, 2019, last edited September 8, 2021. https://www.thecanadianencyclopedia.ca/en/article/racial-segregation-of-black-people-in-canada. 24/023/06.

Reid-Maroney, Nina. *The Reverend Jennie Johnson and African Canadian History, 1868–1967.* University of Rochester Press, 2013.

Rhodes, Jane. *Mary Ann Shadd Cary: The Black Press and Protest in the Nineteenth Century, New Edition.* Indiana University Press, 2023.

Ripley, C. Peter, ed. *The Black Abolitionist Papers.* Vol. 1: The British Isles, 1830–1865. University of North Carolina Press, 1986.

Ripley, C. Peter, ed. *The Black Abolitionist Papers.* Vol. 2: Canada, 1830–1865. University of North Carolina Press, 1986.

Robbins, Arlee. *Legacy of Buxton.* Self-published, 1983.

Robinson, Gwendolyn, and John Robinson. *Seek the Truth: A Story of Chatham's Black Community.* Self-published, 1989.

Sabathy-Judd, Linda, ed. *Moravians in Upper Canada: The Diary of the Indian Mission of Fairfield on the Thames, 1792–1813.* The Champlain Society, 1999.

Shadd, Adrienne. "The Wilberforce Settlement." Ontario Heritage Trust, 2022. https://www.heritagetrust.on.ca/pages/programs/provincial-plaque-program/provincial-plaque-background-papers/wilberforce-settlement.

Shadd, Adrienne, Afua Cooper, and Karolyn Smardz Frost. *The Underground Railroad: Next Stop, Toronto!* Natural Heritage Press, 2009.

Shadd Shreve, Dorothy. *The AfriCanadian Church: A Stabilizer.* Paideia Press, 1983.

Simpson, Donald George. *Under the North Star: Black Communities in Upper Canada before Confederation (1846).* African World Press, 2005.

Smardz Frost, Karolyn, and Veta Smith Tucker, eds. *A Fluid Frontier: Slavery, Resistance, and the Underground Railroad in the Detroit River Borderland.* Wayne State University Press, 2016.

Smardz Frost, Karolyn. *I've Got a Home in Glory Land: A Lost Tale of the Underground Railroad.* Thomas Allan & Son Ltd., 2007.

Smardz Frost, Karolyn, Bryan Walls, Hilary Bates Neary, and Frederick H. Armstrong, eds. *Ontario's African-Canadian Heritage: Collected Writings by Fred Landon, 1918–1967.* Dundurn Press, 2009.

Smedley, R.C. *History of the Underground Railroad: In Chester and the Neighboring Counties of Pennsylvania.* Stackpole Books, 1983.

Spearman, Don. *Landmarks from the Past: A Pictorial History of Dresden and Area.* Stephen Lane Enterprises, 1991.

Stanford, Eleanor, Martin R. Delany (1812–1885), *Encyclopedia Virginia,* https://encyclopediavirginia.org/entries/delany-martin-r-1813-1885/

Still, William. *The Underground Railroad: A Record of Facts, Authentic Narratives, Letters, Etc., Narrating the Hardships, Hair-Breath Escapes, and Death Struggles of the Slaves in Their Efforts for Freedom, as Related by Themselves or Others, or Witnessed by the Author*, Porter and Coates, Publishers, 1871.

Stouffer, Allen P. *The Light of Nature and the Law of God: Anti-Slavery in Ontario, 1833–1877*. McGill-Queen's University Press, 1992.

Thompson, Cheryl, and Julie Crooks. "Race, Community, and the Picturing of Identities: Photography and the Black Subject in Ontario, 1860–1900." In *Unsettling the Great White North*, edited by Johnson and Aladejebi, 433–454. University of Toronto Press, 2022.

Towell, Ann. *Grease Town*. Tundra Books, 2010.

Towell, Larry. *The World from My Front Porch*. Chris Boot Ltd., 2008.

Trotter, Joe W., and Eric Ledell Smith, eds. *African Americans in Pennsylvania: Shifting Historical Perspectives*. Penn State University Press and Pennsylvania Historical and Museum Commission, 1997.

Wadsworth, W., Carl-George Bank, Katherine Patton, and Dena Doroszenko. "Forgotten Souls of the Dawn Settlement: A Multicomponent Geographical Survey of Unmarked Graves at the British American Institute Cemetery." *Historical Archaeology* 54, no. 3 (September 9, 2020): 624–646. https://doi.org/10.1007/s41636-020-00251-7.

Waters, Rosanne. "African Canadian Anti-Discrimination Activism and the Transnational Civil Rights Movement, 1945–1965." *Journal of the Canadian Historical Association* 24, no. 2 (2013): 386–424. https://doi.org/10.7202/1025083ar.

White, Richard. *The Middle Ground: Indians, Empires, and Republics in the Great Lakes Region, 1650–1815*. Cambridge University Press, 1991.

Winch, Julie. *Philadelphia's Black Elite: Activism, Accommodation, and the Struggle for Autonomy, 1787–1848*. Temple University Press, 1988.

Winks, Robin. *The Blacks in Canada: A History*. McGill-Queen's University Press, 1971.

Winks, Robin W. "Negro School Segregation in Ontario and Nova Scotia." *The Canadian Historical Review* 50, no. 2 (June 1969): 164–191. https://doi.org/10.3138/CHR-050-02-03.

Woods, Esmo. *Pontiac… The Making of a US Automobile Capital, 1818–1950*. Self-published, 1992.

Woodson, Carter G. *A Century of Negro Migration* (1918). Project Gutenberg, 2004. https://www.gutenberg.org/ebooks/10968.

Theses and Papers

Carlesimo, Peter. "The Refugee Home Society: Its Origin, Operation and Results, 1851–1876." Master's thesis, University of Windsor, 1973. https://scholar.uwindsor.ca/cgi/viewcontent.cgi?article=5195&context=etd.

Farrell, John Kevin Anthony. "The History of the Negro Community in Chatham, Ontario, 1787–1865." PhD diss., University of Ottawa, 1955. http://dx.doi.org/10.20381/ruor-8898.

Hooper, Tom. "A Heritage Museum's Institutional History—A Case Study of Uncle Tom's Cabin Historic Site." August 23, 2007.

Reynolds, Graham. "A Narrative of Race in Canadian History." Cape Breton University, 2011.

Simpson, Donald G. "Negroes in Ontario from Early Times to 1870." PhD diss., University of Western Ontario, 1971.

Worner, William Frederic. "The Lancaster Colonization Society." Paper read before the Lancaster County Historical Society XXVI, no. 5 (May 5, 1922).

Zimmerman, David. "William Whipper in the Black Abolitionist Tradition." https://web.archive.org/web/20110720065946/http://www.millersville.edu/~ugrr/resources/columbia/whipper.html.

Miscellaneous: Films, Exhibitions, etc.

Biggs, Julian, dir. *Dresden Story.* National Film Board of Canada, 1954. https://www.nfb.ca/film/dresden_story.

Communities, Culture, Tourism, and Heritage. "Meet the Men of the No. 2 Construction Battalion." Government of Nova Scotia. https://cch.novascotia.ca/stories/meet-men-no-2-construction-battalion.

Preservation Association of Central New York. "James Canning Fuller and Lydia Fuller House." Accessed January 28, 2005. https:// pacny.net/freedom_trail/Fuller.htm.

Syracuse University. "'That Laboratory of Abolitionism, Libel, and Treason': Syracuse and the Underground Railroad." Syracuse University, 2005. Published in conjunction with an exhibition of the same title, organized by and presented at Syracuse University, September 30, 2005–February 10, 2006.

Veterans Affairs Canada. "Black Canadians in Uniform—A Proud Tradition." Government of Canada. Accessed February 5, 2021. https://www.veterans.gc.ca/eng/remembrance/people-and-stories/black-canadians.

Notes

Foreword

1   Kent County was dissolved in 1998 and reformed as the Municipality of Chatham-Kent.

Introduction

1   McCorkindale, "Weaponized History," 70–71.

2   Bordewich, *Bound for Canaan*, 7, for example, refers to "Henson's Dawn colony, one of the terminals of the Underground Railroad, the ultimate safe haven for fugitives."

3   Brock, *The Road to Dawn*, 123.

4   Henson's original slave narrative was published in 1849, just four years after that of Frederick Douglass, by Arthur D. Phelps of Boston but was re-released with revisions at several times during Henson's lifetime.

5   McCorkindale, "Weaponized History," 69.

6   McCorkindale, "Weaponized History," 68.

7   McCorkindale, "Weaponized History," 68.

8   Pease and Pease, *Black Utopia*, 65.

9   Drew, "Dresden; Dawn," in *A North-Side View of Slavery*, 309–314.

10   These portrayals by people such as Benjamin Drew, in *A North-Side View of Slavery*, and of Samuel Gridley Howe, in *The Refugees from Slavery*, often stem from travelling to Dawn during the late 1850s and '60s when the BAI's development had stagnated due to ongoing battles over its management.

11   For more information on the changing geopolitical boundaries of Ontario, see the provincial government's archives for "The Changing Shape of Ontario: The Evolution of Ontario's Boundaries 1774–1912," Ontario Ministry of Public and Business Service Delivery, www.archives.gov.on.ca/en/maps/ontario-boundaries.aspx. Accessed September 10, 2007.

12   Pease and Pease, *Black Utopia*, 64–79.

13   Winks, *The Blacks in Canada*, 178–181.

14   Hill, *The Freedom-Seekers*, 309–314.

15   Rhodes, *Mary Ann Shadd Cary*, 32.

16   Carter and Carter, *Stepping Back in Time*. The Trillium Trail project was a Trillium Grant–funded community project that created historical signage and a companion book for a community walking trail that linked the Josiah Henson Museum of African-Canadian History to the town's parkland and included a series of outdoor plaques describing local heritage sites. Primary research of land records revealed the presence of Black elite figures like William Whipper, William Goodrich, Absalom Shadd, and Dennis Hill as major landowners in the area along the trail, and a plaque dedicated to Whipper and one to his brother-in-law J.B. Hollensworth were included onsite, along with a plaque to the Rev. Josiah Henson and the BAI.

17   Simpson, *Under the North Star*, 340.

18   Miles, Tiya, *The Dawn of Detroit*, throughout her work documents a number of United Empire Loyalists who settled in Essex County as well as Sally Ainse, the Moravian missionaries and Butler's Rangers all of whom appear in histories of Chatham and the Thames River in the late 18th and early nineteenth centuries.

19   Reid-Maroney, "Intellectual Migrations in the Promised Land," in *The Promised Land*, eds. de B'béri, Reid-Maroney, and Wright, 107. For more on intellectual migrations, see Reid-Maroney, *The Reverend Jennie Johnson*, especially "In Their Adopted Land," 9–33, for an excellent analysis of intellectual migrations.

20   The Promised Land was a five-year, million-dollar Community-University Research Alliance project that took place between 1998 and 2015 and looked into the Black Settlement of Chatham-Kent. It brought together an international team of investigators from the U.S., Britain, and Canada. For more information, see *The Promised Land Project, 2007–2012* Final Report, University of Ottawa, AMLAC & S Publication, 2012 or DeB'beri, Reid-Maroney and Wrights, eds., *The Promised Land*.

21   Robbins, *Legacy to Buxton*.

22   Robinson and Robinson, *Seek the Truth*.

23   Reid-Maroney, *The Reverend Jennie Johnson*, 10.

24   References to these areas of settlement can be found in the diaries and reports of various missionaries, including J.C. Chambers and Rev. Thomas Hughes who report holding Sunday school and church services at McGee's Ferry, Botany, and three locations in Chatham Township, and through the mapping of Black-owned properties using land records in Camden and Dover Townships, and through the existence of small rural Black cemeteries that still dot the landscape at Oungah and in Dover Township.

25   Pease and Pease, *Bound with Them in Chains*. The authors entitled their chapter on Rev. Wilson as "The Clerical Do-Gooder: Hiram Wilson", 115.

26   Pease and Pease, *Black Utopia*.

27   Pease and Pease, *Black Utopia*.

28   Shadd, Adrienne, "The Wilberforce Settlement, Ontario Heritage Trust background paper for the Wilberforce Settlement plaque," Ontario Heritage Trust, 2022, https://www.heritagetrust.on.ca/pages/programs/provincial-plaque-program/provincial-plaque-background-papers/wilberforce-settlement.

29   "Historical amnesia" was a term used in the Promised Land Project to describe the profound forgetting of historical events such as exists with histories of racism and exclusion and as demonstrated in the long absence of discussion—until after 2000—of the National Unity Association's desegregation battle at Dresden.

30   George Tait, *Breastplate and Buckskin: A Story of Exploration and Discovery in the Americas*, Ryerson Press, 1953.

31   Interview with Barbara Carter, Bruce's widow, 2021

32   "Dresden's Black History: In the Shadow of Uncle Tom," in Carter and Carter, *Stepping Back in Time Along Dresden's Trillium Trail*, 35–63.

33   Prince's work includes *A Shadow on the Household* and *My Brother's Keeper*.

34   The Trillium Trail Historical Walk, completed in 2002, included the development of historical plaques along a five-kilometre trail that connected the Josiah Henson Museum (then Uncle Tom's Cabin Historic Site) to the Town of Dresden, and which incorporated elements of Black history within community history. The project included a companion book, *Stepping Back in Time: Along the Trillium Trail in Dresden*. Research of the trail resulted in the discovery of William Whipper's "lands along the Sydenham" as he described them in his letter to William Still, published in Still's *The Underground Railroad: A Record*, published in 1872. Still, The Underground Railroad: A Record, https://archive.org/details/DKC0088.

35   For more background on the Promised Land Project, see *The Promised Land Project 2007–2012 Final Report*, Audio-Visual Media Lab for the Study of Culture and Societies (AMLACS) University of Ottawa or de B'béri, Reid Maroney, and Wright, eds., *The Promised Land.*

36   de B'béri, Reid-Maroney, and Wright, eds., *The Promised Land* includes Carter's "A New Lens on the Dawn Settlement" and "William Whipper's Lands along the Sydenham." Her other papers presented at the five symposiums of the Promised Land Project included "Historical Amnesia and the Need for a Continued Legacy at Dawn" (2011) and "'Black Utopia' or Early Multicultural Experiment?" (2012).

37   Cooper, *Season of Rage*. Note: Cooper's book is aimed at young adult readers

38   Katz, "Jim Crow Lives in Dresden".

39   Handel Kashope Wright, "Multiculturality Before Multiculturalism: Troubling History and Black Identity Beyond the Last Stop of the Underground Railroad," in *The Promised Land*, edited by de B'béri, Reid-Maroney, and Wright 40–56.

40   Wright, "Multiculturality Before Multiculturalism," 51.

41   Thompson and Crooks, "Race, Community and the Picturing of Identities," 444–464.

42   In her book *The Dawn of Detroit* (The New Press, 2017), Miles details the exploitation and abuse of African-American and Native American women slaves at Fort Detroit during the fur trade that resulted in mixed race identities.

43   White, *The Middle Ground.*

44   Sources consulted include Census of 1851 for Kent County, of 1861 for Camden, and
      of 1871 for Camden and Dresden, as well as family genealogical works (listed in the
      bibliography) and genealogical files of the Chatham-Kent Black Historical Society.

45   1861 Census of Camden Township.

46   Blount, *Remnants of Forgotten Folk,* xii.

47   Dungy and Hanson, *Planted by the Waters.*

48   Brown-Johnson and McCaughin, *Precious Memories.*

49   Brown-Johnson and McCaughan's *Precious Memories* describes a Daniel A. Cook,
      who the family's oral tradition describes as having an unknown ancestor from
      Malaysia. The family was unable to prove this through additional research; however,
      Daniel is said to have had long straight hair, and family members claim "oriental
      features" in their children. A Malaysian migration is not beyond the realm of
      possibility, as the British in the eighteenth century had indirect rule of some Malay
      sultanates, in the time when the British still participated in the slave trade.

50   Kaukauna, Wisconsin, death record of James Burns Hollensworth, provided by the
      Appleton Genealogical Society's researcher Marjorie Crane.

51   This is seen as still being a somewhat faulty means of identification as it assumes all
      European people were white, which is not the case. At least one family of British
      descent at Dawn included a Black man married to a white Quaker woman. Family
      genealogy, files of the author. (Family does not wish to be named.)

52   Shadd Shreve's *The AfriCanadian Church* is also available online through the Internet
      Archive, https://archive.org/details/africanadianchurooooshre.

Chapter 1. Locating the Dawn Settlement in the Historical Landscape

1   See Chapter 12 for a discussion of this phenomenon in the time of segregation of
      schools.

2   Map of the Elgin Settlement, Buxton National Historic Site or see https://pier21.ca/
      research/immigration-history/immigration-from-united-states-on-underground-
      railroad

3   Pease and Pease, *Black Utopia,* 65.

4   Drew, *A Northside View of Slavery,* 308–314.

5   For a complete discussion of this phenomenon, see Carter, "A New Lens on the
      Dawn Settlement," 176–192.

6   McCorkindale, "Weaponized History," 71.

7   Brock, *The Road to Dawn,* 123.

8   See Johnson and Aladejebi, *Unsettling the Great White North.*

9   Drew's *A Northside View of Slavery* (308) lists the Dawn Settlement under the
      heading "Dawn; Dresden" and describes it at the time of his visit in its stagnated
      state under the contested manager Rev. John Scoble.

10   Howe, *Refugees from Slavery.*

11 Samuel May travelled to the region providing the *Frederick Douglass' Paper* a letter from Lake Erie, dated August 2, 1852, which appeared on August 17, 1852, in which he states that he had concluded not to visit Dawn because of the reports he had heard about the "discordant statements" on its management.

12 Pease and Pease, *Black Utopia*, 65–79; Hill, *The Freedom-Seekers*, 71–74; Winks, *The Blacks in Canada*, 178–181. Note: Hill claims, "The idea of the Dawn took root in the mind of Josiah Henson" (71).

13 A 1957 retelling of Henson's slave narrative by Jessie Louise Beattie was entitled *Black Moses: The Real Uncle Tom*.

14 Rev. Samuel May of the American Anti-Slavery Society expressed the opinion that Henson was not competent to run the institution in 1852 (Simpson, *Under the North Star*, 341).

15 Shadd, "The Wilberforce Settlement" plaque project.

16 Brandon, *A History of Dresden*; Lauriston, *Romantic Kent*; Don "Gummer" Spearman, *Landmarks from the Past*.

17 Pease and Pease, *Black Utopia*.

18 Winks, *The Blacks in Canada*.

19 Hill, *The Freedom-Seekers*.

20 The author's home was on the property once owned by original Dawn settler John Myers, Lot 1, Concession 3, Camden Gore, which lies roughly half a mile south of the former British American Institute grounds.

21 McCorkindale, "Weaponized History," 69.

22 The Promised Land Project (2007–2012) involved twelve co-investigators from Canada, the U.S., and England, in a million-dollar Community-Research Alliance Project, under head investigator Boulou Ebanda de B'béri of the University of Ottawa. A final report was issued in 2012. The five objectives of the project were to protect primary historical materials, make these materials publicly accessible, support new academic research and teaching, promote community development, and use the new knowledge generated by the project to frame current discussions of ethno-racial identity, social justice, and Canadian multiculturalism.

23 For a full explanation of the shifts in geopolitical boundaries related to the Dawn Settlement, see Carter, "A New Lens on the Dawn Settlement," 176–192.

24 Drew, *A North-Side View of Slavery*, 31; *The Voice of the Fugitive*, March 21, 1851, letter from Rev. Hiram Wilson to Rev. J.E. Ambrose; *Scoble and Brown vs. Wright and Myers* court case, 1863 to 1868.

25 Lot 2, Conc. 3, land abstracts and records for Dawn Township and Camden Gore, Chatham-Kent Land Records Office, Chatham, Ontario.

26 1846 Deed to the British American Institute, Chatham-Kent Land Records for Camden Gore, Kent County, McGeorge Building, Chatham.

27 *Scoble and Brown vs. Wright and Myers*.

28 Reference Desk collection, Local History room, Chatham-Kent Public Library, Chatham Branch.

29   William Whipper letter to William Still, printed in Still, *The Underground Railroad*.

30   For a longer discussion of this phenomenon, see Carter, "William Whipper's Lands along the Sydenham," 73–90.

31   Josiah Henson, *"Uncle Tom's Story of His Life": An Autobiography of the Rev. Josiah Henson (Mrs. Harriet Beecher Stowe's "Uncle Tom" from 1789 to 1876* (London, 1876), electronic edition at https://docsouth.unc.edu/neh/henson/henson.html, 125.

32   Letter of D.R. van Allen to the editor of the *Chatham Daily Planet*, March 19, 1901, quoted in Carter and Carter, *Stepping Back in Time*, 24.

33   *Illustrated Historical Atlas of Kent*.

34   Dawn Township (Camden Gore) land abstracts for Concession 3, Chatham-Kent Land Records Office.

35   1834 Population Return for the Western District, Dawn Township.

36   1842 Population Return for the Western District, Dawn Township; Smith, *Smith's Canadian Gazetteer*.

37   1861 Agricultural Census of Kent County, microfilm files, Chatham-Kent Library, Chatham, Ontario.

38   Sharpe was an early white Dresden industrialist who established Dresden's first tomato canning plant. Carter and Carter, *Stepping Back in Time*, 104.

39   1861 Agricultural Census of Kent County.

40   While Wright had purchased his ninety-acre Fairport site two years before the van Allen Dresden survey, he would not register his survey of Fairport until 1854—well after the Dresden surveys had been registered. Survey map of Fairport, Chatham-Kent Land Records Office.

41   By 1867 Fairport had been included into the townsite of Dresden. Map of the townsite of Dresden and Fairport, Chatham-Kent Land Records Office.

42   Wright would be chosen by Henson as the white plaintiff representing the interests of the Black community in the 1860s court case that removed the BAI's white manager, Rev. John Scoble. Henson is also reputed to have operated an early store when he first arrived in the Fairport survey in a building owned by Wright.

43   Photo of mixed-race Wright couple, and family genealogy file, collection of the author.

44   Determined in consultation with Francis Vink, former editor of the Kent Genealogical Society newsletter. Black settlement in Chatham Township existed as far west as the fourteenth concession where Ambrose and Rosina Kersey owned a triangular parcel of land located between the Centre Side Road, Concession 14, and the Baseline Road near present day Tupperville.

45   The Charity brothers did make one major purchase here: a two-hundred-acre block on the eastern side of St. George Street. Land Abstracts for Concession 5, Camden Gore, Chatham-Kent Land Records Office.

46   Towell, Anne, *Grease Town*, Tundra Books, Toronto, 2010; Newspaper clip file on Oil Springs riot, Lambton County Archives, Wyoming.

Chapter 2. Beyond the Underground Railroad

1   1861 Agricultural Census of Kent County.

2   1860 Agricultural Census of Camden Township.

3   Modern scholarship such as that of McCorkindale, Walker, Aladejebi and Johnson
     in *Unsettling the Great White North*, University of Toronto Press, 2021, have similarly
     argued that an overreliance on a romanticized and often fictionalized history of the
     Underground Railroad has distorted our understanding of the true history of early
     Black settlers.

4   "Was a Centenarian," Chatham Evening Banner, April 19, 1899.

5   Brandon, *A History of Dresden*; Lauriston, *Romantic Kent*.

6   Brandon, *A History of Dresden*; Lauriston, *Romantic Kent*.

7   It is not revealed in Thomas's story where Levi or his parents spent the intervening
     years nor what ultimately happened to his parents.

8   At least one settler, James Stompf, arrived at Chatham prior to 1800 as noted on the
     first survey map of Chatham.

9   Thompson and Crooks, "Race, Community, and the Picturing of Identities," 437.

10   Don Juan Barberro in the 1871 Dresden census is shown to have originated in South
     America and to have been of Spanish descent but married to an African-American
     woman and having Ontario-born children.

11   Shadd family genealogical files of the Chatham-Kent Black Historical Society show
     Amelia Shadd, of Dresden, to have come from Haiti.

12   The Brown-Johnson and McCaughan, *Precious Memories*, description of Daniel A.
     Cook cites family oral history which says that Cook, a barber born 1818 in Virginia,
     was of Malaysian descent. Though they were unable to confirm this through their
     research, Cook is said to have had long straight hair and members of the family claim
     that their children have "oriental features." Malaysian ancestry is not beyond the
     realm of possibility because of Britain's extensive marine empire in the eighteenth
     century, which included indirect rule of some Malay sultanates, and slavery was
     practiced in Malaysia in the time before Britain's abolition of the slave trade.

13   Hamil, *The Valley of the Lower Thames*, index has over sixty-five mentions of Detroit
     and over twenty of the Detroit River that point to the long association of Kent
     County settlements along the Thames and Sydenham and their connection to that
     fur trading and military centre.

14   Miles, *The Dawn of Detroit*, 15.

15   Miles, *The Dawn of Detroit*, 15

16   The Thames River connected the Chatham Settlement in a similar way and was the
     larger of the county's two navigable waterways.

17   Hamil, *The Valley of the Lower Thames*, 3.

18   As revealed in steamship passenger and freight schedules printed in various editions
     of the *Dresden Times*.

19   White, *The Middle Ground*.

20 Miles, *The Dawn of Detroit*, discusses the sexual exploitation of Indigenous enslaved women as well as a more general dehumanization of enslaved people and denial of their human rights.

21 *Illustrated Historical Atlas of Kent and Essex Counties*, 55.

22 Middle Ground attitudes and cooperative arrangements may have survived later than this period in pockets of more remote settlement, as is evident in the letters of Lewis Champion Chambers who as a missionary served isolated groups from his home base at Dresden in the less developed areas of Howard Township at Botany. Chambers's letters report white and Black people continuing to gather together in large outdoor church services as late as 1859. Neary, *A Black American Missionary in Canada*.

23 Both positive and negative aspects of this multicultural reality, particularly in relation to slavery in the region, are examined by scholar Tiya Miles in *The Dawn of Detroit*.

24 Miles, "Native Americans and the Underground Railroad."

25 Miles, "Native Americans and the Underground Railroad."

26 In the introduction to *Remnants of Forgotten Folk*, Blount traces her family's roots back to late seventeenth-century Delaware where her early ancestors included both people of African descent and Lenni-Lenape peoples (xii).

27 Hamil, *Valley of the Lower Thames*, 3.

28 Hamil, *Valley of the Lower Thames*, 3.

29 Hamil, *Valley of the Lower Thames*, 13.

30 Denke or Denkey Creek is located upriver from Dresden on the Sydenham River and was the site of Chirstian Denke's Moravian mission to the Chippewa (Ojibway), and an offshoot of the Moravians' efforts at Moraviantown, which is situated along the Thames.

31 "The Dairies of Christian Denke on the Sydenham River," Denke.org, accessed March 22, 2022, https://www.denke.org/CDDiaries.htm.

32 Note: no accounts of people of African descent appear in Christian Denke's diary.

33 There may be other explanations for the Dresden name, given that the district was formerly known by the German name of Hesse, and that others of German heritage including Society of Friends (Quakers) settled in the region including the Lewis family, early Dresden store owners who had ties to the oldest Quaker settlement in Canada, at Norwich, Ontario.

34 As late as 1851, a Chippewa family was still living in Camden Gore and is noted as "Indian" and "Chippeway" (sic) in the 1851 Census of the Gore of Camden and Camden Township.

35 Carter and Carter, *Stepping Back in Time*, 2003, 45.

36 Miles, *Dawn of Detroit*, 95.

37 Sabbathy-Judd, ed., *Moravians in Upper Canada*.

38 For more on Benjamin Willoughby, see Smardz Frost, Karolyn, "Transnationalism along the Detroit River Borderland: The Example of Madison Lightfoot," *Journal of American Ethnic History* 30, no. 13 (Winter), 78–88.

39 Ash from the burning of brush and trees while clearing land was sold to local "asheries" to make a product called pearl ash, which was shipped to the Britain for use in the textile industry.

40 Hamil's *Valley of the Lower Thames* documents only two gristmills and two sawmills as having been established in Dawn Township by 1840, existing at Smiths Mills (Dawn Mills) and Wallaceburg.

Chapter 3. The Shared Dream of Education

1 James's surname, Stompf, seems to have been alternatively spelled Stump or Stumps in various documents. The 1832 Rankin Report of Squatters shows a James Stump living at "the Forks" (Chatham) on McGregor's Creek, near the military reserve. A James Stump also appears in the 1861 Agricultural Census as the owner of twenty-five acres on Lot 1, Concession 6, Camden Gore, about two miles from the institute's property, and it is assumed that he moved there after he had become involved with the institute. Little is currently known about Stump or his origins; however, a December 20, 1843, article in the *Oberlin Evangelist*, titled "The Colored People and the Canadian Schools," describes a man they call James Stumps of Chatham as being "one of the most respectable colored citizens of that place" and identifies him as being an elder in the Church (no denomination is listed). Stompf had four children, three daughters, and a son, who are described as being "bright mulattoes" whom he attempted to enroll in one of Chatham's common schools.

2 Pease and Pease, *Black Utopia*, 64.

3 "Whitewood" is a synonym for softwood, usually from coniferous trees, used for cabinet- and furniture-making.

4 *Historical Atlas of Kent and Essex Counties*, 55.

5 Similar observations were made by missionary L.C. Chambers who provided outreach to tenant farmers (Neary, *A Black American Missionary in Canada.*)

6 All details of Henson's life as retold from Henson, *Uncle Tom's Story of His Life*.

7 Pease and Pease, "The Clerical Do-Gooder: Hiram Wilson," in *Bound with Them in Chains*, 115.

8 Stouffer, *The Light of Nature*, 66.

9 Letter of Hiram Wilson to Elizabeth Montford, November 19, 1848, addressed to Montforth by Wilson from Hopedale Dawn Mills, C.W. (Canada West), Maine Memory Network, Maine Historical Society. Note: some scholars alternatively believe Hopedale was the name Wilson gave to his farm.

10 Letter of E. Wright, American Anti-Slavery Society, New York, to Hiram Wilson, Toronto, September 16, 1837, Hiram Wilson Papers, Oberlin Archives.

11 Samuel J. May, Editorial Correspondence, *The North Star*, April 13, 1849, Accessible Archives online, http://accessible.com/accessible.

12 Ripley, "Introduction," *The Black Abolitionist Papers*, Vol. 1.

13   Stouffer, *The Light of Nature and the Law of God*, 66.

14   Pease and Pease, *Black Utopia*, 66.

15   Robbins, *Legacy of Buxton*, 62. Robbins recounts the story of James T. Rapier who after graduating with honours from Buxton's school assisted hundreds of freed slaves in Alabama and became a member of the state legislature during the Reconstruction period.

16   Josiah Henson, *Truth Stranger than Fiction: Father Henson's Story of His Own Life* (John P. Jewett and Company, 1858), 169.

17   Document 51 in Ripley, *The Black Abolitionist Papers Vol. 2*, 318.

18   Brown had volunteered as a fifer in the company of Capt. George Smith in the battle of Tippecanoe. Ripley, *The Black Abolitionist Papers Vol. 2*.

19   Some documents suggest a portion of Fuller's money had been his personal donation.

Chapter 4. The Seeds of Discord

1   Letter of J.C. Fuller to Hiram Wilson, January 1, 1840, Hiram Wilson Papers, Oberlin College Archives, Oberlin, Ohio.

2   Letter of J.C. Fuller to Hiram Wilson, January 15, 1847, Hiram Wilson Papers, Oberlin College Archives.

3   Information on Wilson provided by Dennis Ganon of St. Catherine's, Ontario in an email to the author.

4   Letter of J.C. Fuller, Skaneateles, NY, to Hiram Wilson, Cayuga, NY, January 15, 1847, Oberlin College Archives.

5   Letter of J.C. Fuller, Skaneateles, NY, to Hiram Wilson, Cayuga, NY, January 15, 1847.

6   Document 51 in Ripley, *The Black Abolitionist Papers*, Vol. 2, 318; Drew, *A North-Side View of Slavery*, 239–248.

7   In an email to Marie Carter, dated December 10, 2022, Dr. Edyth Ann Quinn wrote:

> The first Quaker pioneers in Norwich Township came from Dutchess County, NY, in 1808. Peter Lossing joined his brother-in-law, Peter DeLong, and bought 1,500 acres.
>
> According to Robert Gourley in his Statistical Account of Upper Canada, eleven farmers with their wives and families, comprising eighty-nine persons, arrived in 1811. They were all Quakers, and the names of the husbands were: Peter Lossing, Michael Stover, *Fred Stover*, (emphasis added) Adam Stover, Sears Mold, Sam Cornwell, Sol. Sackrider, Peter DeLong, and Peter M'Lees— all from Dutchess County, NY. Elias Moore came from Nova Scotia, and John Syple from Albany, NY.

Gourlay, Robert Fleming, *Statistical Account of Upper Canada, Vol. 1* (London, Simpkin & Marshall, 1822), 336 n.121.

8   Fleming, *Statistical Account of Upper Canada*, 318 n.1.

9   Ripley, *The Black Abolitionist Papers, Vol. 2*, 318 n.2, says George Johnson moved to Dawn in 1850. This is contrary to land record evidence, which places him on Lot 1, Concession 4, Dawn Township in 1838.

10   Ripley, *The Black Abolitionist Papers*, Vol. 2, 318 n.2.

11   Letter of J.C. Fuller to Hiram Wilson, January 15, 1947.

12   See chapter 7 for a discussion of Rev. John Scoble's involvement with the American Anti-Slavery Society, which led to his adoption of anti-Garrisonian views that likely contributed to his opposition to J.C. Brown, Mary Ann Shadd, and others.

13   Letter to Hiram Wilson from J.W. Alden, March 1841, Oberlin College Archives.

14   Howe, *The Freemen's Inquiry*, 69.

15   Drew, *A North-Side View of Slavery*, 239–248.

16   "Further Testimony Against Israel Lewis," *The Colored American*, August 24, 1839. Accessible Archives online, https://www.accessible.com/accessible/.

17   This is likely Benjamin Haskell Sr., an early merchant in that community.

18   Letter from Benjamin Haskell to Rev. Hiram Wilson, December 14, 1841, Oberlin College Archives.

19   Henson and Rev. Wilson's pay came from the funds they themselves raised.

20   J.C. Brown to the Dawn Investigating Committee, reprinted in the *Provincial Freeman*, May 12, 1855, in Document 51, Ripley, *The Black Abolitionist Papers, Vol. 2*, 316–320.

21   Letter to Hiram Wilson, Dawn Mills, C. W. (Canada West) from J.C. Fuller, Skaneateles, NY, January 15, 1847, Hiram Wilson Papers, Oberlin Archives.

Chapter 5. The British American Institute

1   Pease and Pease, *Bound with Them in Chains*, 21, 132.

2   Letter of Augustus Wattles, Ohio, to Hiram Wilson, Dawn Mills, June 1854, Oberlin College Archives.

3   *Girdling* means removing a strip of bark from the circumference of the tree, stopping the flow of sap to the branches. This kills the tree and allows the wood to dry, making it easier to fell and for waste wood to be more readily burned for ash, which was a marketable commodity sold to local asheries for use in the textile industry.

4   Letter of Augustus Wattles to Hiram Wilson, June, 1854, Hiram Wilson Papers, Oberlin College Archives.

5   Letter of Augustus Wattles to Hiram Wilson, June 1854.

6   Letter of Augustus Wattles to Hiram Wilson, June 1854.

7   William Newman, Oberlin Evangelist, letter, "The Colored People and the Canadian Schools," December 20, 1843.

8   Bordewich, *Bound for Canaan*, 395.

9   Pease and Pease, *Bound with Them in Chains*, 21, 132.

10   Letter from Hiram Wilson to Hannah Wilson, London, England, July 3, 1843, Hiram Wilson Papers, Oberlin College Archives. Their son Charles was a watchman who died in Detroit.

11   Letter from Hiram Wilson to Hannah Wilson, London, England, July 3, 1843.

12   Letter from Hiram Wilson to Hannah Wilson, London, England, July 3, 1843.

13   Letter of Rev. Hiram Wilson to the *Christian Age*, London, 1876.

14   1861 Agricultural Census of Kent County.

15   The history of Christ Church, Anglican, the Rev. Thomas Hughes's mission church at Dawn, describes producing the brick for the church using such a device (Don Spearman, unpublished paper, collection of the author).

16   *Victorian Farm*, a six-episode special that aired in January 2009 on BBC Two, dir. Stuart Elliott, detailed this primitive method of brick firing used in England during the Victorian era.

17   The clay jug is currently in the hands of a private collector in Sombra. The author was asked to examine the jug in an attempt to determine the identity of the J. Brown whose name is inscribed on the vessel. Further work is needed to determine the jug's provenance.

18   Bordewich, *Bound for Canaan*, 266.

19   Simpson, *Under the North Star*, 168.

20   Report of the Rev. Hiram Wilson to Charles Birney, 1845.

21   Letter from Hiram Wilson to the *Liberator* from Dawn Mills, C.W. (Canada West), September 27. Reprinted in the *North Star*, November 10, 1848. Accessible Archives online, https://www.accessible.com/accessible/

22   Rev. Lewis Champion Chambers was chastised for supporting Rev. William P. Newman's assertion that the former slaves in Canada West were starving when Newman's claims were printed in the U.S. abolitionist press.

23   In a series of letters written between 1859 and 1860, Rev. Lewis Champion Chambers describes conditions of famine after three years of severe frosts and also describes people served by his mission as being "nearly naked" and wanting of adequate clothing to attend mission schools. Neary, *A Black American Missionary in Canada*.

24   Letter from William Newman to the *Oberlin Evangelist*, December 20, 1843, "The coloured People and the Canadian Schools."

25   Letter of W.P. Newman, Dawn, C.W. (Canada West), September 10, 1846, *North Star*.

26   Neary, *A Black American Missionary in Canada*, 55.

27   Rev. W.P. Newman, letter to the *North Star*, September 10, 1846.

28   Rev. W.P. Newman, letter to the *North Star*, December 22, 1848.

29   Rev. W.P. Newman, letter to the *North Star*, March 9, 1849.

30   Pease and Pease, *Black Utopia*, 73.

31   *Oberlin Evangelist Opinions of Missionaries in Canada*, August 30, 1848.

32   *Oberlin Evangelist Opinions of Missionaries in Canada*, August 30, 1848.

33   *Oberlin Evangelist Opinions of Missionaries in Canada*, August 30, 1848.

34   *Oberlin Evangelist Opinions of Missionaries in Canada*, August 30, 1838.

35   Letter of John Wilson, Knowlesville, NY, to Hiram Wilson, Dawn Mills, C.W. (Canada West), via Detroit, June 1847, Hiram Wilson Papers, Oberlin College Archives.

36   Payne, *Recollections of Seventy Years*, 319–320. It should be noted that the location of
      Hannah's grave today is not marked, and it is not known if, after the relocation of
      the BAI cemetery in 1973, her remains were reburied next to Nancy Henson in the
      Henson family cemetery or lie in the BAI cemetery across Freedom Road near the
      Josiah Henson Museum of African-Canadian History.

37   Henson, *Uncle Tom's Story of His Life*.

38   Henson, *Uncle Tom's Story of His Life*, 128.

39   Hiram Wilson letter to Elizabeth Mountford, Portland Ladies Anti-Slavery Society,
      Portland, Maine, November 29, 1848, Maine Memory Notebook, Main Historical
      Society.

40   Hiram Wilson letter to Elizabeth Mountford, Portland Ladies Anti-Slavery Society,
      November 29, 1848.

41   The biography of Hiram Wilson, Oberlin Archives website, and other accounts do
      not account for Wilson's whereabouts in the two-year gap between his resignation
      from the BAI and his appearance at St. Catharines, Canada West Letters from
      Hopedale, Dawn Mills, sent to his supporters in Maine, suggest Wilson remained at
      his Dawn Township mission site during this time.

      Henson seems to have borne Wilson no lasting ill will. After Wilson settled at
      St. Catharines, he notes in a letter to his supporter Rev. S.K. Lothrop, dated June 26,
      1855: "I had a visit yesterday from Father Henson who was just down from Dawn on
      his way to Rochester. He is in comfortable health." The remark appears almost as an
      afterthought at the end of a long missive that outlined Wilson's continued needs for
      support in his new field of mission.

42   In Stouffer, *The Light of Nature and the Law of God*, it says Roaf first attempted to
      create a society in Toronto in 1846 and that these efforts intensified after the *Fugitive
      Slave Act of 1850* was passed in the US.

43   Letter of Hiram Wilson to Frederick Douglass's *North Star*, Accessible Archives,
      https://www.accessible.com/accessible.

Chapter 6. Henson's Rising Star

1   "First of August Celebration at Dawn Settlement, Canada West," *Frederick Douglass'
      Paper*, August, 11, 1854.

2   Douglass, *Narrative of the Life of Frederick Douglass, an American Slave: Written by
      Himself* (1845, electronic version, 1999), Documenting the American South, https://
      docsouth.unc.edu/neh/douglass/douglass.html.

3   Rhodes, *Mary Ann Shadd Cary*, xiii, points out that Douglass was seen as a
      representative Black leader whose opinions had a powerful sway and that being
      "anointed" by Douglass could provide a positive boost to the careers of others—a
      boost Scoble, in his new and controversial role, badly needed.

4   While Henson was not the sole inspiration for Uncle Tom, he was credited by Stowe
      for his influence on her composite character in the *Key to Uncle Tom's Cabin* and in

her later endorsement of the British edition of his biography. Harriet Beecher Stowe, *A Key to Uncle Tom's Cabin: Presenting the Original Facts and Documents upon Which the Story Is Founded* (John P. Jewitt and Company, 1853).

5   A figure of US$137,544 was realized by adjusting for inflation from 1850 to 2024 via the CPI Inflation Calculator found at https://www.officialdata.org.

6   Josiah Henson, *Father Henson's Story of His Own Life* (Jewitt and Co., 1858), 177.

7   Henson, *Father Henson's Story*, 177.

8   Ripley, "Introduction," in *The Black Abolitionist Papers, Vol. 1.*

9   Ripley, "Introduction," in *The Black Abolitionist Papers, Vol. 1.*

10   Obituary of the Rev. Josiah Henson, *Leeds Mercury*, January 29, 1881.

11   By 1855 Isaac Rice would lose his backing from the AAS and be disgraced for his drinking and his poor handling of affairs at his Amherstburg outreach. Carlesimo, "The Refugee Home Society."

12   While Henson's 1858 biography identifies his benefactor in Boston as a Mr. Checkering, it is likely he was referring to a Mr. Chickering, a prominent piano manufacturer in Boston at the time. Certainly, as a manufacturer of fine instruments, Chickering would have appreciated the fine walnut boards which were prized for furniture-making. The presence of a Chickering piano in Smith's former home suggests Chickering was known to Black abolitionists in Pennsylvania. (Brochure from the Steven Smith Museum, collection of the Chatham-Kent Black Historical Society). It should be noted that Winks, "The Canadian Canaan," in *The Blacks in Canada*, alternatively claims that it was William Newman who cut and polished the boards for shipment to Boston, and credits Newman with operation of the sawmill. Winks, like other scholars, contests the accuracy of Henson's biographies, saying "Henson's account of the Dawn Settlement was accurate enough but not accurate enough to trust" (196).

13   Henson, *Uncle Tom's Story of His Life*, 141–142.

14   "Henry Walton Bibb," Dictionary of Canadian Biography online, accessed February 2, 2020, http://www.biographi.ca/en/bio/bibb_henry_walton_8E.html.

15   Shadd family genealogical files, Chatham-Kent Black Historical Society.

16   Robinson, Compilation of genealogical notes on the Shadd family.

Chapter 7. The Rev. John Scoble and the Decline of the British American Institute

1   Frederick Douglass, "First of August Celebration at Dawn Settlement, Canada West," *Frederick Douglass' Paper*, August 11, 1854.

2   "Scoble, John," Dictionary of Canadian Biography online, accessed December 12, 2020, http://www.biographi.ca/en/bio/scoble_john_9E.html.

3   Henson, *Uncle Tom's Story of His Life.*

4   Henson, *Uncle Tom's Story of His Life*, 165.

5   Henson, *Uncle Tom's Story of His Life*, 166.

6   Rhodes, *Mary Ann Shadd Cary*, 68.

7   Douglass, "First of August Celebration."

8   Henson, *Uncle Tom's Story of His Life*, 167.

9   Henson, *Uncle Tom's Story of His Life*, 167.

10   Henson, *Uncle Tom's Story of His Life*, 167.

11   Douglass, "First of August Celebration."

12   Douglass, "First of August Celebration."

13   Simpson, *Under the North Star*, 143.

14   *Provincial Freeman*, Aug. 29, 1855.

15   Rhodes, *Mary Ann Shadd Cary*, 105.

16   Rhodes, *Mary Ann Shadd Cary*, 91.

17   Mary Ann Shadd, "The Dawn Convention: White and Coloured Tyrants," *The Provincial Freeman*, September 22, 1855.

18   September 25, 1851, Letter of William Wells Brown "Fugitive Slaves—A Word of Advice," *Frederick Douglass Paper*, Rochester, NY.

19   Rhodes, *Jane, Mary Ann Shadd Cary*, 2023 106.

20   Shadd, "The Dawn Convention: White and Coloured Tyrants."

21   Stringer served as a Mississippi senator and was also instrumental in establishing the BME church in Canada and would find several Black Masonic lodges in various US states on his return there. Notes from Bryan Prince, historian and author, Buxton.

22   Sept. 22, 1855, *Provincial Freeman*

23   Rhodes, *Mary Ann Shadd Cary*, 101.

24   John Anderson was a slave in Missouri who during his escape to Canada had stabbed and killed white slaveholder Seneca Diggs. After Anderson arrived in Canada in November 1853, the Missouri governor had pressed for his extradition. The ensuing celebrated court case heard arguments regarding the eligibility of Anderson to remain in Canada. It was argued initially in Canada but eventually brought to the courts in England for resolution.

25   Henson, *Uncle Tom's Story of His Life*, 169.

26   Henson, *Uncle Tom's Story of His Life*, 169.

27   Scoble is said to have erected the house on the high ground overlooking the flats. He would, however, own two other parcels of land in the wider Dawn Settlement area, on the River Road and the third concession, beyond the BAI borders. These were small acreages, and it is not known what their function was. Chatham-Kent Land Records, land abstracts for Camden Gore.

28   Manitoba Historical Society Archives, "Memorable Manitobans: Thomas Clarkson Scoble (1840–1900)," accessed March 7, 2022, https://www.mhs.mb.ca/docs/people/scoble_tc.shtml. Thomas Clarkson Scoble (born in Devonshire England, June 12, 1840) likely did not remain long at Dawn. Having received a private school education before coming to Canada, he studied civil engineering at the University of Toronto between 1857 and 1860 before embarking on a distinguished career in the military and engineering. T.C. Scoble was involved in a number of major construction projects, including railways like the Grand Trunk and CPR, and the International Bridge at Fort Erie. He also served for a time as the mayor of

Toronto, and in various other posts. He moved to Winnipeg in 1881 and continued his engineering career as well as becoming an author and publisher. In 1889 he was awarded a medal for service in the North-West Rebellion.

Chapter 8. "Who Has Not Heard of William Whipper?"

1   Letter of William Whipper, New Brunswick, New Jersey, to William Still, Philadelphia, Pennsylvania, December 4, 1871, reprinted in Still, *The Underground Railroad*, 688–740.

2   Still, *The Underground Railroad*, 688–740.

3   Carter, "William Whipper's Lands along the Sydenham," discusses Whipper's cryptic reference to his Dawn Settlement holdings as his "lands along the Sydenham." Whipper's discreet nature meant even as late as 1871 he failed to disclose that he still maintained these lands (Still, *The Underground Railroad*, 688–740).

4   Still, *The Underground Railroad*, 688–740.

5   Still, *The Underground Railroad*, 688–740.

6   Still, *The Underground Railroad*, 688–740.

7   Whipper, between 1847 and 1860 as well as for five years during the Civil War, contributed $1,000 annually to support the Underground Railroad. Letter of William Whipper, New Brunswick, New Jersey, to William Still, Philadelphia, Pennsylvania, December 4, 1871, reprinted in Still's, *The Underground Railroad*, 740.

8   "Dissolution of Partnership," advertisement in the *Columbia Spy*, March 20, 1858.

9   Numbers quoted are for 1860, from William J. Switala, *Underground Railroad in New York and New Jersey*, (Stackpole Books, 2006).

10 Still, *The Underground Railroad*, 688–740.

11 *Underground Railroad: The William Still Story*, premiered on PBS February 2012, accessed online April 12, 2022, https://www.pbs.org/show/underground-railroad-william-still-story.

12 Hopkins, "Black Eldorado on the Susquehanna."

13 LeRoy Hopkins email to the author, August 30, 2007.

14 New York's *The Weekly Anglo African* 1, no. 13 (October 15, 1859).

15 Rhodes, *Mary Ann Shadd Cary*, 20.

16 Still, "Sketch of William Whipper," *The Underground Railroad*, 688–740.

17 Whipper wrote that the population of Columbia had been 943, but this reduced to 487 through his efforts. Still, *The Underground Railroad*, 688–740.

18 Still, *The Underground Railroad*, 688–740.

19 "Chronology of Underground Railroad Activity in Harrisburg," accessed September 14, 2007, https://www.afrolumens.org.

20 Conversations with Gwen Robinson, Chatham historian, 2006.

21 For more on DeBaptiste, see Sarah Fling, "George DeBaptiste: Abolitionist and White House Valet," The White House Historical Association, https://www.whitehousehistory.org/george-depatiste.

22 Bordewich, *Bound for Canaan*, 409.

23 The White House Historical Society alternatively states DeBaptiste owned the T. Whitney. An attempt was made to establish who owned the ship through Great Lakes Marine registry, but the ship was not listed (Fling, "George DeBaptiste").

24 In Reynolds, "A Narrative of Race in Canadian History," 30.

25 Letter from W.P. Newman to the *Oberlin Evangelist*, January 3, 1844.]

26 Letter from W.P. Newman to the *Oberlin Evangelist*, January 3, 1844.

27 Letter from John Brown Jr. to his wife, from Windsor, C.W. [Canada West] Friday, March 22, 1861, found at "John Brown Jr. in Canada," *Ohio's Yesterdays*, May 28, 2009, http://ohiosyesterdays.blogspot.com/2009/05/john-brown-jr-in-canada.html.

28 Francis Moss Turner was a Black landowner and businessman at Dresden who had married Whipper's niece Sarah who partnered at times with J.B. Hollensworth, Whipper's brother-in-law, and Dennis Hill, a partner of Whipper's nephew James Whipper Purnell. Chatham-Kent Black Historical Society genealogy files, 1861 Census of Camden Township; Will of Francis Moss Turner and Sarah W. Turner, Chatham-Kent Land Records.

29 Buildings and their uses were determined by cross-referencing land records for the Hollensworth/Hill property and the Charity Brothers property on St. John and Metcalfe Streets, Dresden (Survey 127 and 128), with historic photos worker housing provided to employees of the McVean family of industrialists into the 1940s. Whipper's Inn continued to operate as "Fretz House" (destroyed by fire in the 1980s). Its numbered doors testified to its previous use as an inn, and its architectural features and land record evidence show it had been constructed prior to Whipper's arrival. The Hollensworth/Hill property, built c. 1850 and demolished in the 1950s, property of the Charity Brothers, still extant today, shared similar features identified as Black architectural style by area architectural conservators. According to oral history, these have always been rental properties.

30 "New Line of Coaches! Chatham and Dresden Accommodation," *The Provincial Freeman*, June 28, 1856.

31 Author's comparison of 1861 census and land records at Chatham with 1860 Census of Columbia.

32 Birth records of Christ Church, Anglican, Diocese of Huron V.P. Croyn MemorialArchives, Huron College University, London, Ontario.

33 Rhodes, *Mary Ann Shadd Cary*, 20, lists William Whipper and A.D. Shadd among the leadership of the second Black convention at Philadelphia and their active role in determining its goals.

34 Prince, *A Shadow on the Household*.

35 Smith and Whipper's full itinerary could not be determined, but their purchase of a property at Dresden on an earlier trip suggests they came to investigate the availability of real estate in the community during their Chatham trip in 1853.

36 Still, *The Underground Railroad*, 688–740.

37   Still, *The Underground Railroad*, 688–740.

38   William Parker, "The Freedman's Story: Part I [or II]," *The Atlantic*, February [or March] 1866, *The Atlantic Magazine*, 1866, https://www.theatlantic.com/magazine/archive/1866/02/the-freedmans-story/308737/163.

39   Marriage records of the Rev. Thomas Hughes's British Colonial Church and School Society mission at Dresden, V.P. Croyn Memorial Archive, Diocese of Huron University College, London, ON.

Chapter 9. "And Still They Come!"

1   Henry Bibb, *The Voice of the Fugitive*, June 17, 1852.

2   Bibb, *The Voice of the Fugitive*, June 17, 1852.

3   Bibb, *The Voice of the Fugitive*, June 17, 1852.

4   Smith, *Smith's Canadian Gazetteer*.

5   Smith, *Smith's Canadian Gazetteer*.

6   February 1865, Letter of Mary Ann Shadd from Chicago reprinted in the June 16, 1865, *Provincial Freeman*, Toronto, Canada West.

7   Marriage records of Christ Church, Anglican, Diocese of Huron Archives, show Alfred did not marry until 1861.

8   Rhodes, *Mary Ann Shadd Cary*, xv.

9   Robinson and Robinson, *Seek the Truth*; Delany would later come to prominence as a proponent of Liberian emigration and as a medical officer and recruiter of Black troops for the Union Army during the Civil War.

10   Rhodes, "Introduction," *Mary Ann Shadd Cary*.

11   Winch, *Philadelphia's Black Elite*, 68.

12   Winch, *Philadelphia's Black Elite*, 68.

13   The Provincial Freeman was founded in Windsor in 1853, moved to Toronto in 1854, and to Chatham in 1855 (Adrienne Shadd, "The Provincial Freeman," The Canadian Encyclopedia, June 7, 2023, https://www.thecanadianencyclopedia/en/article/the-provincial-freeman.

14   *The Provincial Freeman*, March 5, 1855.

15   It is currently unknown whether Robert Parker held any relation to William Parker.

16   Smith is mentioned as having purchased a "farm" in a letter of Henrietta Clemens Jourseane, great niece of Stephen Smith, to the Historical Society of Pennsylvania, 1931 (copy in the collection of the Chatham-Kent Black Historical Society). There may be a yet undiscovered second property owned independently by Smith; the acreage of the Camden Township site does not fit that site mentioned in the letter.

17   "Canada and the Coloured People," *Frederick Douglass' Paper*, August 18, 1854.

18   "Canada and the Coloured People," *Frederick Douglass' Paper*, August 18, 1854.

19   In modern times, farm organizations such as the National Farmers' Union (NFU) have cited that the agricultural output of Kent is equal to the total output of the entire province of New Brunswick.

20   Letter from William Whipper, Columbia, Pennsylvania, to A. Highgate, J. Hollensworth, H. Damrell, Wm. Crosby, and David Smith, Dresden, Ontario, reprinted in *The Provincial Freeman*, April 11, 1857

21   William Whipper letter to Highgate, Damrell, Crosby and Smith reprinted in *The Provincial Freeman*, April 11, 1857.

22   See Chapter 1 for more information.

23   Notes on the Murray family and Stanton Hunton, files of the Black Historical Society, WISH Centre, Chatham, Ontario.

24   Letter from William Whipper, Columbia, Pennsylvania, to A. Highgate, J. Hollensworth, H. Damrell, Wm. Crosby, and David Smith, Dresden, Ontario reprinted in *The Provincial Freeman*, April 11, 1857.

25   Whipper genealogical files of the Chatham-Kent Black Historical Society compiled by Gwen Robinson note that the Whippers had had one daughter, who died as an infant.

26   A piece in *The Christian Recorder* dated November 4, 1865, notes Purnell "doing business with his uncle William Whipper as a lumber merchant on Broad St. near Willow, Philadelphia."

27   This may indicate that a fifth "silent partner"—perhaps Whipper, who had a penchant for secrecy—was involved. Whipper became more overtly involved after Goodrich encountered financial difficulties and with Absalom Shadd's early death. Deeds and abstracts for multiple properties in Surveys 128 and 127 of Dresden, Chatham-Kent Land Records Office, Chatham, Ontario

28   Absalom's mother, Amelia Cisco Shadd, is noted in the diary of her minister the Rev. Thomas Hughes of the British Church and School Society Mission. Huron University College Archives, London, Ontario.

29   Some Shadd family genealogists say Amelia was Jeremiah's first wife.

30   Rhodes, *Mary Ann Shadd Cary*, 117–118; Genealogical files of the Shadd family, Chatham-Kent Black Historical Society.

31   Morley, "The 'Snow Riot,'" mentions Absalom Shadd, a free Black man from Canada, having purchased the restaurant of Edward Snow. Snow sold his restaurant in the wake of Washington race riots that became known as the Snow Riot.

32   Notes from the research files of historian Gwen Robinson, descendant of M.A. Shadd, Chatham-Kent Black Historical Society research rooms, Chatham WISH Centre.

33   Various abstracts and deeds to Survey 128, Town of Dresden, from 1853 to 1858, Chatham-Kent Land Records Office, Chatham, Ontario.

34   As previously noted, Goodrich's name is alternatively spelled Goodridge in some accounts.

35   Woodson, "Chapter V," *A Century of Negro Migration*.

36   "Melancholy Boating Accident," Lancaster County Historical Society, newspaper reprint, accessed October 1, 2007, http://archive.olivesoftware.com/Archive/skins/Lancaster/navigator.asp?skin.

37   Transcript of Certificate of Death for Charles T. Hill (son of Dennis Hill and Isabella Hill), Wayne State, Lansing, Michigan, June 22, 1903, states Dennis was born in Maryland and Isabella in Kentucky.

38   Alternatively, Hill may have been the one of a number of skilled tradesmen in the Ohio Valley who had amassed considerable personal wealth. At Chillicothe, Ohio, there resided a Mr. Hill (no first name mentioned) who was a leading tanner and currier.

39   Woodson, *A Century of Negro Migration*.

40   Clerk of Court of Common Pleas, Hailton County, Ohio, Marriage Certificate no. 225, September 12, 1835.

41   Research of Dennis Ganon provided to the author re: National Archives and Records Administration (NARA), Washington, DC, Manifests of Alien Arrivals at Buffalo, Niagara, and Rochester, New York, Records of Immigration and Naturalization Service, Microfilm M1480, Ross 53.

42   This development was confirmed by land records combined with photo evidence from the 1940s of a Black architectural style duplex on the property, which was at that time being used as worker housing by the McVean family.

43   George Cary and Dennis Hill, "Comments on the State of Schools at Dawn," *The Provincial Freeman*, July 1852.

44   Edwin Larwill owned a large commercial lot on the corner of Lindsley and Metcalfe Streets, Land abstracts for Lot 41, Survey 127, Chatham-Kent Land Records Office, Chatham, Ontario.

45   T.R. McInnes, Martha Webster's son, wrote a letter attached to his book of poetry "In Amber Lands," which he donated to the Dresden Library. In it he describes Henson's visits to their home when he was a boy. File on the McInnes family, Burns papers, Dresden Archives, Dresden, Ontario.

46   Brandon, *A History of Dresden*, says Wright rented Henson his former store on his Fairport property, where Henson is said to have done a brisk business and also recounts that Henson and Wright cooperated in removing the BAI grist mill onto Wright's property.

47   Heinegg, "Free African Americans in Colonial Virginia." Other sources say the Charities were slaves, freed by the Hamlin family, hence James's and Cornelius's middle name of Hamlin. It is possible that James and Cornelius were not chattel slaves but indentured as a condition of their apprenticeship as bootmakers.

48   Heinegg, "Free African Americans in Colonial Virginia."

49   Ripley, Peter C. *Black Abolitionist Papers* Vol. 2, p. 263.

50   Hill, *The Freedom-Seekers*, 171.

51   "Dresden Going Up," by "Observer", *The Provincial Freeman*, March 29, 1856.

52   This was later the site of Cragg's Dominion Mill. Local historian Victor Lauriston suggests Whipper built a brick structure on Main Street with Cragg that was later the Shaw Hotel, but records show no involvement of Whipper with the hotel site. He was, however, involved with Cragg at the Metcalfe Street milling site.

53 The relationship of Mary Smith and her husband, Stephen, to William's partner, also named Stephen Smith, has been the subject of investigation by various researchers including local historian Gwen Robinson. Carolyn Beacroft undertook research in Pennsylvania to establish the provenance of Mary Smith's needlework sampler housed at the Chatham-Kent Black Historical Museum, but her search of Pennsylvania census records was inconclusive. Research did confirm that Mary was not, as indicated by local oral tradition, the widow of Stephen Smith (William Whipper's partner) but could not establish Mary's husband's relationship, if any, to Whipper's partner. The use of the names William and Stephen for Mary's children suggests that a close relationship, whether familial or not, existed with the Whipper-Smith partners.

54 Notes and oral history of Gwen Robinson gathered from the Binga family of Chicago.

55 On Queen Street, there is an extant Canadian gothic style house (c. 1880) that is one of only two buildings in the community built in this manner. The peaks of the house, near the roofline, bear symbols reminiscent of God's eyes found on Pennsylvania barns. One symbol is reminiscent of the Masonic logo. It is linked by way of a narrow lane, whose road allowance was granted to the town by William Whipper, to another Canadian gothic house. In the backyard of that house, there is the foundation of a pre-existing house which oral history says belonged to someone involved in the Underground Railroad. The property has always been Black-owned until recently.

56 Goings was the daughter of a prominent family said to trace their lineage back to the original twelve African people enslaved at Virginia in the seventeenth century.

57 Note: there may be more African-descent people who owned properties here, but as of the writing of this book not all the names on the survey abstracts have been identified as people of African descent through genealogical research. Some lots in Survey 127 and 128 in addition to those owned by the Webster and McInnes family are confirmed as white owned.

58 Asheries converted potash (the ashes of burnt wood from the timber industry) into pearl ash, which was shipped abroad and used in the textile industry. The asheries were often located on the banks of a river because of the large amounts of water needed for the conversion process.

59 Advertisement for the medical practice of Dr. Aray in Chatham, files of the Chatham-Kent Black Historical Society; an entry in the diary of the Rev. Thomas Hughes on Hughes's visit to Shadd records McInnes as her attending physician, V. Croyn Memororial Archives, Huron University College.

60 Typewritten transcript of the *Autobiography of the Rev. Jennie Johnson*, dated Dresden, May 1, 1950, from the files of the Chatham-Kent Black Historical Society, 9–10; Dungy and Hanson, *Planted by the Waters*, 38. Johnson did not provide a first name for Dr. Taylor. It is possible that he was the Pennsylvania-born Tisdale Taylor who settled in Survey 128 on property he had purchased from James Burns

Hollensworth's son Ellwood, but this man was listed as a yeoman. Tisdale Taylor remained in Dresden until his death in 1883.

61 It has not been possible to analyze all of the hundreds of names in historic land abstracts to determine everyone's racial identification during the time of this study. Genealogies of individuals with the surnames of Day, Smith, Clemens, Bows, Richardson, Johnson, Jones, Talbot, Lewis, and Wilson are also difficult to track as these are surnames common to both Black and white families in the area.

62 Rhodes, *Mary Ann Shadd Cary*, 3–4. Amelia Cisco Shadd, the second wife of Jeremiah Shadd, was a prosperous businesswoman, part of a privileged class of light-skinned people of African descent from Saint-Domingue (now Haiti), who came to the U.S. after the slave revolt there. She was bilingual (French and English). In her household with Jeremiah, she had luxuries such as fine china, a set of wine glasses and a decanter, and carpets.

63 *The Provincial Freeman*, January 1, 1855.

Chapter 10. *The Intellectual Migration*

1 Winch, *Philadelphia's Black Elite*.
2 Lucretia Mott was an American Quaker, abolitionist, women's rights activist, and social reformer dedicated to elevating the position of women in society. Despite being supported by her husband to attend the World Anti-Slavery Convention in 1840, she would be excluded from their sessions, igniting her efforts to create a separate women's movement. Debra Michals, ed., "Lucretia Mott (1783–1880)."
3 Maria Louisa Bustill Robeson was a Quaker school teacher, the wife of Rev. William Drew Robeson of Witherspoon Street Presbyterian Church in Princeton, New Jersey, and the mother of Paul Robeson the American actor, football player, singer and activist and his siblings.
4 Winch, *Philadelphia's Black Elite*, 121.
5 Reid-Maroney, *The Reverend Jennie Johnson*, 25.
6 M.A. Shadd, "Our Tour," *The Provincial Freeman*, September 1855.
7 William Howard Day (1825–1900) was born free, in New York City, to Eliza and John Day, free people of moderate means. Day attended Oberlin College in 1843, the only student of African descent in his class of fifty. He became a writer and was a highly regarded speaker and activist who led opposition to Ohio's Black Code laws and lobbied the state senate for universal suffrage. Ripley, *The Black Abolitionist Papers*, Vol. 2, 394 n.7. For more information on Day, see Mealy, Todd, Alienated American: A Biography of William Howard Day, 2010, Internet Archive http:/archive.org/detaileds/alienatedamericanb0002meal/page/n3/mode/2up.
8 Mealy, *Aliened America*, 41.
9 Land abstract for Lot 3, Concession 5, Camden Gore, Chatham-Kent Land Records Office, Chatham, Ontario.

10   *Frederick Douglass' Paper*, August 26, 1853, Accessible Archives.

11   Rhodes, *Mary Ann Shadd Cary*, 130.

12   After the American Civil War, Day worked with the Freedmen's Aid Society, in 1866,
        he became an ordained African Methodist Episcopal minister and moved to New
        York City, where he enjoyed a celebrated career in education, religion, and civil
        rights activism until his death ("Day, William Howard," Encyclopedia of Cleveland
        History online, Case-Western Reserve University, https://case.edu/ech/articles/d/
        day-william-howard).

13   O'Banyoun's newspaper predated the first white owned newspaper—the *Dresden
        Gazette*, founded by Alex Riggs in February 1871—by about six years.

14   *Christian Recorder*, May 6, 1865, Accessible Archives, https://www.accessible.com/
        accessible.

15   O'Banyoun is listed as the Windsor delegate for the tenth annual conference of the
        British Methodist Episcopal Church in Hamilton.

16   Nina Reid-Maroney, "A Contented Mind Is a Continual Feast," in *The Promised Land*,
        eds. De B'béri, Reid-Maroney, and Wright, 106.

17   Reid-Maroney, "A Contented Mind Is a Continual Feast," 106–128.

Chapter 11. "I Never Seen Greater Minds to Learn"

1   Neary, *A Black American Missionary in Canada*, 29.

2   Neary, *A Black American Missionary in Canada*, 79.

3   Letter from L.C. Chambers, Dresden, to George Whipple, New York, March 19, 1959,
        quoted in Neary, *A Black American Missionary in Canada*, 79.

4   Neary, *A Black American Missionary in Canada*, 59.

5   Neary, *A Black American Missionary in Canada*, 59.

6   Letter from L.C. Chambers, Dresden, to George Whipple, New York, September 9,
        1869, quoted in Neary, *A Black American Missionary in Canada*, 62–63.

7   Pease and Pease, *Black Utopia*.

8   *History of the First Regular Baptist Church*, Ontario Heritage Trust booklet on the 2011
        unveiling of the First Regular Baptist Church plaque in Dresden, Ontario.

9   *History of the First Regular Baptist Church*.

10   The report was filed by Dresden church member George Johnson, a former BAI
        trustee and executive member.

11   *History of the First Regular Baptist Church*.

12   "S.H. Davis, Dresden" article in files of the Chatham-Kent Black Historical Society.

13   "S.H. Davis, Dresden." Davis died in 1908 at age ninety-seven.

14   In 1925, Johnson moved to Flint, Michigan, to serve people who had come from
        the U.S. South as part of the Great Migration. There she provided outreach at the
        Flint Baptist Association's Christian Centre. Biography of Rev. Jennie Johnson,
        files of the Chatham-Kent Black Historical Society. Reid-Maroney, *The Reverend
        Jennie Johnson*.

15   Don Spearman, *Some Highlights of the History of Christ Church*, unpublished paper, 1981, files of the author.

16   Dorothy Shadd Shreve and Alvin McCurdy, *The Afri-Canadian Church: A Stabilizer*, typewritten version, files of the Chatham-Kent Black Historical Society, 16.

17   Diary of the Rev. Thomas Hughes, Huron University College Archives, London, Ontario.

18   Brandon, *A History of Dresden*.

19   "My London," *London Free Press*, February 20, 2013: "Despite Her Health in 1860 at the Age of 29 Jemima Williams Left Her Mark on Education in the area".

20   Diary of the Rev. Thomas Hughes.

21   Transcription of the Jemima Williams tombstone, files of the Chatham-Kent Black Historical Society research room.

22   Abstract and deed for Lot 40, Block C, Survey 128 of Dresden, Chatham-Kent Land Records. Frances Rogers, *The History of Christ Church*, conversely states that the property was bought from a Mrs. White.

23   Death, birth, and marriage records of Christ Church, Anglican, Huron University College Archives.

24   History of the Union Baptist Church, files of the Chatham-Kent Black Historical Society.

25   Reid-Maroney, "A Contented Mind Is a Continual Feast," 106–128.

26   Diary of the Rev. Thomas Hughes.

27   Hughes's Dawn Mills church survived into the late twentieth century, St. Stephen's still stands in Thamesville and was only recently closed, while Christ Church Dresden still remains an active congregation that is part of a multi-church charge.

28   Simpson, *Under the North Star*, 351.

29   Report of the Colonial Church and School Society for 1875, 60.

30   Rogers, *The History of Christ Church*.

31   Shadd Shreve and McCurdy, *The African-Canadian Church*, 468.

32   Simpson, *Under the North Star*, 354.

33   Shreve and McCurdy, *The African-Canadian Church: A Stabilizer*, 470.

34   Prince, *A Shadow on the Household*; Still, *The Underground Railroad*, 177–187.

35   Land abstract for the east half of Lot 3, Concession 5, Camden Gore, and Lot 2, Concession 5, Camden Gore, Chatham-Kent Land Records, McGeorge Building archives.

36   Rev. Clarke retained some of these properties until 1872 but sold others to a Phillip H. Clarke (possibly a son), to the activist W.H. Day, and to the white reeve of the Village of Dresden, Alexander Trerice.

37   Observations of the author made during the Dresden Cemetery relocation project, 2003.

38   It is not clear from Rev. Chambers's letters whether these were held in church or school buildings of other denominations or in the open air or in homes.

39   This may be an alternative spelling for Nero Harding, the man who served on Scoble's BAI board of trustees.

40 Notes of references to Dawn from minutes of the AMEC/BMEC annual conferences at Toronto, 1855–1868, provided by Hilary Neary, emailed to the author February 6, 2021.

41 Robinson and Robinson, *Seek the Truth*, 25–30.

42 427 Speculation on the locations of the first BME church in various local histories and news reports include a Dresden market sales barn on Cross Street; and a Methodist (later United) Church building on St. George St. The date of the construction of the BME church that Henson last preached in on Queen St. is unknown. None of these structures remain today.

43 Carter and Carter, *Stepping Back in Time*, 41; examinations of the pulpit by local architectural conservancy and antique furniture experts have confirmed the age of the pulpit and chairs, but it has not been conclusively proven that they were used by Henson. The chapel at the Josiah Henson Museum also has a pulpit that is said to have been used by Henson.

Chapter 12. Dennis Hill and the Fight to Desegregate Common Schools

1 Deirdre McCorkindale, "Black Education: The Complexity of Segregation in Kent County's Nineteenth Century Schools," in *Unsettling the Great White North*, eds. Johnson and Aladejebi, 334.

2 McCorkindale, "Black Education," 333.

3 *Dennis Hill v. the School Trustees of Camden and Zone*, Queen's Bench Reports, in Ripley, *The Black Abolitionist Papers, Vol. 2*, 578.

4 *Dennis Hill v. the School Trustees of Camden and Zone*, in Ripley, *The Black Abolitionist Papers, Vol. 2*, 578.

5 *An Act for the Establishment and Maintenance of Common Schools in Upper Canada*, section 33, clause 7, as quoted in McLaren, "'We Had No Desire to Be Set Apart.'"

6 McLaren, "'We Had No Desire to Be Set Apart,'" 35.

7 "Religion and Education," *Multicultural Canada: Encyclopedia of Canada's Peoples*, March 31, 2011, https://www.multiculturalcanada.ca/Encyclopedia.

8 McLaren, "'We Had No Desire to Be Set Apart.'"

9 Letter to the Municipal Council of the Western District, *Chatham Gleaner*, November 18, 1845.

10 Letter to the Municipal Council of the Western District, *Chatham Gleaner*, November 18, 1845.

11 The former Western District today encompasses the Counties of Essex and Lambton and the regional Municipality of Chatham-Kent.

12 *Chatham Gleaner*, November 18, 1845, microfilm files of the Chatham-Kent Public Library, local history room, Chatham, Ontario.

13 Robinson and Robinson, *Seek the Truth*, 88.

14 Glaude, "Pragmatism and Black Identity."

15 December 20, 1843, report of W.P. Newman to the *Oberlin Evangelist*.

16   Illustration of signature of early white landowner Levi Devins in Carter and Carter, *Stepping Back in Time*, 16.

17   "Religion and Education," *Multicultural Canada: Encyclopedia of Canada's Peoples/ Africa-Canadians/Ames. W., St. G. Walker*, https://www.multiculturalcanada.ca/ Encyclopedia/A-Z/a16/6 8. Accessed March 31, 2011.

18   Benjamin Drew, quoted in McCorkindale, "Black Education," 341.

19   Robinson and Robinson, *Seek the Truth*, 88.

20   Report from the Superintendent of Schools, Chatham Township, microfilm MS352 (1846-1870), Ontario Archives interlibrary loan.

21   McLaren, "'We Had No Desire to Be Set Apart.'"

22   Winks, *The Blacks in Canada*, 368.

23   McLaren, "'We Had No Desire to Be Set Apart.'"

24   Winks, *The Blacks in Canada*, 368.

25   Land abstracts for Hill property in Camden Township, Chatham-Kent Land Records.

26   *Dennis Hill v. the School Trustees of Camden and Zone*, in Ripley, *The Black Abolitionist Papers, Vol. 2*, 578.

27   Diary of the Rev. Thomas Hughes entry for Oct. 22, 1861.

28   "In the Matter of Simmons and the Corporation of the Township of Chatham," in *Reports of Cases Decided in the Court of Queen's Bench*, Vol. 11, ed. Christopher Robinson (Henry Rowsell, 1862), 75–79, digitized by Google Books, https://books. google.ca/books?id=q9NIAQAAMAAJ&printsec=frontcover&source=gbs_ge_ summary_r&cad=0#v=onepage&q&f=false.

29   "In the Matter of Simmons and the Corporation of the Township of Chatham," in *Reports of Cases Decided in the Court of Queen's Bench*, Vol. 11, 75–79,.

30   Molly's Creek Women's Institute Tweedsmuir History scrapbook, 1949. Dresden Archives. The separate school at Dresden, at the corner of Tecumseh and Brock Streets, is also listed as having been burned during the 1870s, as were the Hollensworth and Turner businesses. Helen Burns, *History of the Dresden Fire Department* (self-published, 1954), local history collection, Dresden Archives.

31   Burns, *History of the Dresden Fire Department*.

32   Colin Stephen McFarquhar, "A Difference of Perspective: The Black Minority, the White Majority and Life in Ontario, 1870–1919" (PhD thesis, University of Waterloo, 1998), 162; *The (Detroit) Plaindealer*, February 13, 1891.

Chapter 13. Leaving the Promised Land

1   Rhodes, *Mary Ann Shadd Cary*, 139, says that Isaac was a recruiting agent for the Haitain Emigration Bureau and supervised the departure of 116 Black emigrants from Chatham.

2   Shadd, Cooper, and Smardz Frost, *The Underground Railroad*, 72.

3   Rhodes, *Mary Ann Shadd Cary*, 45.

4   The size and scope of the settlement could not be determined as land records are not available for the period when the Gum Bed Line community existed in Enniskillen

Township, Lambton County. The single surviving newspaper report of the riot does not indicate the number of people involved.

5   Newspaper clip file on the Oil Springs Riot, Lambton County Archives, Wyoming, Towell, *Grease Town*.

6   Rhodes, *Mary Ann Shadd Cary*, 136.

7   Previous to moving to Chatham to take a position as printer at Mary Ann Shadd's *Provincial Freeman*, Anderson managed Absolom Shadd's farm near Dresden (Rhodes, *Mary Ann Shadd Cary*, 118).

8   The Virginia slave rebellion led by Nat Turner and his group killed fifty-five white men, women, and children. White mobs, in retaliation, killed 100 to 200 African-Americans.

9   Fred Landon, "Canadian Negroes and the John Brown Raid," *The Journal of Negro History* 6, no. 2 (April 1921): 174–182, https://doi.org/10.2307/2713730.

10   Robbins, *Legacy of Buxton*, 70.

11   Pleasance is known as the mother of civil rights in California. The successful businesswoman who was also active in the Underground Railroad, purchased property in Chatham. Between 1857 and 1859, she moved to San Francisco. She provided John Brown with $30,000 (the equivalent of $900,000 today) for his Harpers Ferry raid.

12   Reputedly, after John Brown's execution, a note with this wording was found in his pocket which is attributed to Pleasance.

13   Dungy and Hanson, *Planted by the Waters: A Family History of the Jones-Carter Family*, 8.

14   Still, *The Underground Railroad*, 109.

15   Deeds to Lots 14, 64, and 65 in Survey 127 in records from 1859 list "William Whipper of the Village of Dresden, gentleman" as the landowner.

16   Land deeds for Survey 127 and 128, Dresden, Chatham-Kent Land Records Office.

17   Rhodes, *Mary Ann Shadd Cary*, 137.

18   Editors of Encyclopaedia Britannica, "Haitian Revolution," *Britannica* online, accessed January 6, 2021, https://www.britannica.com/topic/Haitian-Revolution.

19   Frederick Douglass, *Douglass' Monthly*, May Day, 1859.

20   His length of stay is estimated from dates on letters he wrote from Dresden on March 3, 1861, and March 5, 1861. "John Brown, Jr. in Canada," Ohio's Yesterdays, May 28, 2009, http://ohiosyesterdays.blogspot.com/2009/05/john-brown-jr-in-canada.html.

21   Letter from John Brown Jr. to his wife, from Windsor, Canada West, Friday, March 22, 1861, in "John Brown, Jr. in Canada."

22   Rev. William Newman's first wife, Nancy, died in the summer of 1959, and he was remarried to another young woman roughly four months later.

23   Letter of J. P. Williams to *The Weekly Anglo African*, April 26, 1862. https://archive.org/details/WeeklyAngloAfrican

24   Winks, *The Blacks in Canada*, 164.

25   Letter of J.P. Williams to *The Weekly Afro American*, April 26, 1862,://archive.org/details/WeeklyAngloAfrican|

26   Letter of M.A.S. Cary to *The Weekly Anglo African*, October 13, 1861, http://archive.org/details/WeeklyAngloAfrican|

27   Letter of J.P. Williams to *The Weekly Anglo-African*, April 26, 1862, http://archive.org/details/WeeklyAngloAfrican|

28   There is no census or other documentation to substantiate that the Charity brothers settled at San Francisco, but by local tradition/oral history they are believed to have settled there. M.A. Pleasance is, however, a well-documented presence in that community.

29   James Charity's movements after leaving the Dawn Settlement have not been fully documented. Whether he joined his brother Cornelius in British Columbia is not known.

30   Black Past website, Marshall, Valin C. The Victoria Pioneer Rifle Cops (1861-1865), 2007, https://www.blackpast.org/global-african-history/victoria-pioneer-rifle-corps-1861-1865/

31   Microfilm #B13077 (GSU #1927287) Reg. No. 1885-09-004165, BC Archives microfilm. Note: No record of James Charity was found in BC, and his fate is unknown.

32   Files of Appleton Genealogical Society, courtesy of Marjorie Krane. The migratory tradition continued into the next generation, with Anne's children by her second husband, German barber Otto Kuenke, travelling to Colorado and Montana. All died in their early twenties, except Silverth, who remained at Kaukauna.

33   Hill's wife, Isabella, sold their last property in Camden Gore in April 1862. A census search of the county shows no trace of the Hill family after that point. One member of the Hill family, Charles F. Hill, settled in Detroit, re: transcript of Certificate of Death of Charles T. Hill, son of Dennis Hill of Maryland and Isabelle Hill of Kentucky, Michigan Department of State, Lansing, Michigan, Vital Statistics Division, from the files of Bryan Prince.

34   For more on the African emigration movement and Dr. Delany, see Rhodes, *Mary Ann Shadd Cary*.

Chapter 14. The Storms of War

1   Jerrel R. Hind, "Blacks in the Great War," Gathering Our Heroes, https://www.gatheringourheroes.ca/stories/our-black-canadians-in-ww-i/.

2   Frederick Douglass, Men of Color, To Arms! (1863 Poster). Reprinted in African American Reports: Civil War Recruiting Posters, Sat., Feb. 8, 2014, www.africanamericanreports.com/.

3   Prince, *My Brother's Keeper*, 69 and 78.

4   The exact numbers of Black Union soldiers who were residents of Canada is unknown. Bryan Prince has documented at least 1,100 names (seventy from Buxton) in his database of Civil War soldiers and believes more could yet be documented. Interview with Bryan Prince, March 31, 2022.

5   Bearden and Butler, *Shadd*, 203.

6   Bearden and Butler, *Shadd*, 206.

7   Prince, *My Brother's Keeper*, 135.

8   It is not known how Tom Henson came to be in California.

9   1859 Report from Dawn in the *Anglo-American Weekly*.

10   Bryan Prince email to author, March 19, 2021, re: Civil War soldiers. Black Past alternatively states Samuel R. Lowery organized the Disciples of Christ Church at Chatham after arriving there in 1858, returning to the U.S. in 1862, settling in Fayette Co., Ohio, joining the military as a chaplain with the 40th U.S. Colored Troops, and teaching the 2nd Colored Light Infantry. He later became the first Black lawyer to argue a case before the U.S. Supreme Court. www.blackpast.org/african-american-history/lowery-samuel-r-1830-or-1832-1900/.

11   Some discrepancies exist in accounts of Dunn/Madison's enlistment. Spearman, *Landmarks from the Past*, 28, states Madison was in the 2nd Michigan Cavalry and fought at the Battle of Shiloh. His presence in a white unit is corroborated by notes from Bryan Prince's database on Kent's Civil War soldiers. There was also a George Dunn who enlisted with the 27th Michigan. Descendant Irene Moore Davis has provided information to Prince about an ancestor George Dunn who was a fair-skinned Black man who enlisted in the 17th Michigan. Prince's records support Spearman's account that says a George Dunn applied for and was refused his soldier's pension.

12   Prince, *My Brother's Keeper*, 296.

13   For more on atrocities committed against Black soldiers during the Civil War, see Prince, *My Brother's Keeper*.

14   Prince, *My Brother's Keeper*, 296.

15   *Glory*, directed by Edward Zwick (TriStar Pictures and Freddie Fields Productions, 1989).

16   Database of Kent County Civil War soldiers, files of Bryan Prince, Buxton.

17   Spearman, *Landmarks from the Past*; Dresden Social notes item on George Madison's birthday at Dresden, *The Canadian Observer*, December 4, 1919.

18   Letter of Parker Smith to Jacob C. White, quoted in Reid-Maroney, "A Contented Mind Is a Continual Feast," 107.

19   Marie Carter, "The Dawn Settlement: Black Utopia or Early Multicultural Experiment," presentation to the Promised Land Project's fifth annual symposium, June 15, 2012, Chatham, Ontario.

20   John Ferrell, "The History of the Negro Community in Chatham-Kent, 1787 to 1865" (doctoral dissertation, University of Ottawa, 1955), 453.

21   Report of Parker T. Smith to the *Christian Recorder*, quoted in Reid-Maroney, "A Contented Mind Is a Continual Feast," 106.

22   Wallace tombstone, Dresden Cemetery; Marie Carter, "450 Wallace Descendants Travel Path of Ancestors to Dresden," *North Kent Leader*, August 10, 1994.

23   Trerice, a carriage-maker, was justice of the peace for the community. He would eventually build a small business empire, including shares in his father-in-law

William Wright's sawmill and interests in the construction of a variety of ships at Dresden. Trerice became the Village of Dresden's reeve in 1871 and its mayor when it became a town in 1882.

Chapter 15. The Final Battle for the BAI

1   John Scoble papers, 1861–1869, microfilm documents of the *Myers and Wright v. Brown and Scoble* lawsuit, Archives of the University of Western Ontario, London.

2   John Scoble papers, 1861–1869, *Myers and Wright v. Brown and Scoble.*

3   John Scoble papers, 1861–1869, *Myers and Wright v. Brown and Scoble.*

4   Contrary to Henson's biography, Scoble claimed the opposite was true and that Henson had borrowed money from him. Henson, *Uncle Tom's Story of His Life*, 169.

5   Henson, *Uncle Tom's Story of His Life*, 169.

6   William Wright had immigrated from Armagh, Ireland, in 1818, settling in Elgin County, Upper Canada. He purchased Lot 17, Concession 9 of Chatham Township, in 1840, and developed the townsite of Fairport in 1846. Brandon, *A History of Dresden*, says Wright rented his original store to Josiah Henson who successfully operated it for a time. Close ties between the Wrights and the Black community are borne out by photographic evidence of the marriage of one of Wright's sons to a woman of African descent (Wright family photos, files of the author). Wright died in 1863, two years after the court case began.

7   Henson's biography does not identify Wright by name but indicates he enlisted the help of a "local man." Brandon, *A History of Dresden*, and Lauriston, *Romantic Kent*, say Henson removed the mill to Wright's property with his assistance.

8   Henson, *Uncle Tom's Story of his Life*, 172.

9   Brandon, *A History of Dresden*. Dresden historian and genealogist Helen Burns's handwritten history of Dresden in the files of the Dresden Archives maintains that the mill was moved at night to avoid a lawsuit and not for the altruistic reasons of benefitting the Black community as Henson had stated. No citation is given for this assertion.

10   After Wright's death, the mill came into the ownership of the Taylor Milling Company of Chatham. It remained an active mill site under various owners until the late 1970s. The mill's silos were still extant in 2023 on Dresden's Water Street, across from a house believed to have been built by Wright c. 1860.

11   Wright left no will, leaving his twelve children by his first two marriages and his third wife to battle over the his considerable land and business assets in the Fairport survey—including the mill. Land records for the Fairport survey, Chatham-Kent Land Records Office, Chatham.

12   Document #5, *Scoble and Brown v. Wright and Myers*; court documents state George Cary was charged $175 in annual rent for the property that he had occupied for sixteen years. The court judged that his buildings on the institute grounds were worth about $225.

13   *Scoble and Brown v. Wright and Myers.*
14   It is not clear from court notes whether the court or Trerice had appointed Peter Henson to his role.
15   Scoble wrote a series of articles supporting the MacDonald-Cartier government regarding confederation. After leaving office, he disappeared from public life. After taking his family to England for an extended stay in 1871, he returned to Hamilton. Henry J. Morgan, ed., *Canadian Parliamentary Companion/Guide* (John Lovell, 1864); Larry Lamb, *Encyclopedia of Canadian Legislators, Judges and Office Holders* (unpublished), Sarnia, Ontario.
16   Not all names of the applicants are listed as some were illegible in the court documents.
17   John Myers died on September 4, 1868, at age sixty.
18   Diary of the Rev. Thomas Hughes, V.P. Croyn Memorial Archives, Diocese of Huron, Huron University College, London, Ontario. Also accessible online at https://www.uwo.ca/huron/promisedland/hughes/index.html.
19   Diary of the Rev. Thomas Hughes, entry dated May 2, 1870.
20   "Chatham's Early Black Community" educational walking tour, Chatham-Kent Black Historical Society (Gwen Robinson, researcher); Chatham-Kent Land Records Office, abstracts for Survey 127, Dresden.
21   "Last Will and Testament of William Chandler," files of the Chatham-Kent Black Historical Society.
22   Information on Morris Potter and Hayward Day's business or other interests could not be found in local records.
23   McKellar's riding encompassed parts of Kent and Lambton Counties, including Dresden, Camden Gore, and parts of Dawn Township. He would later be voted out of office, then reinstated in 1871. He resigned from the Legislature in 1875, and for the remainder of his career served as a sheriff in Hamilton. He died there in 1894 but is buried in Chatham's Maple Leaf Cemetery. "Margaret A. Evans," Dictionary of Canadian Biography online, accessed March 14, 2005, www.biographi.ca/en/bio/mckellar_archibald-12E.html; Correspondence of author with Mark Epp, Government Archives of Ontario, March 11, 2005; Database of early Canadian politicians, maintained by Sarnia historian Larry Lamb.

Chapter 16. Restructuring the BAI to Serve a Changing Society

1   Major, Geraldyn Hodges, *Black Society*, Johnson Publishing Co. Inc., Chicago, 1977, 177.
2   Robbins, *Legacy to Buxton* 62.
3   Lesser known, but reputedly better organized than underground organizations like the Ku Klux Klan, the Red Shirts were named for their highly visible scarlet shirts. They were an anti-Republican paramilitary group that used violence to achieve their political goals.
4   James Wormley's hotel opened in 1871. It was a five-storey building located at 1500 H Street, NW, Washington, DC. Wormley was free-born and spent time in Europe

training as a chef. His hotel, much like his father-in-law's, was a hub for local and foreign government officials alike.

5   Henson Street was more commonly referred to by the twentieth century as the River Road and was closed in the 1980s due to riverbank erosion. While Concession 3 was officially renamed Uncle Tom Road during the renaming of roads for emergency (911) service, Henson's name would not be reassigned to any street or road in the district. Uncle Tom Road was renamed Freedom Road in 2022.

6   Minutes of the Corporation of the Township of Camden, March 29, 1871, McGeorge Building archives for the Municipality of Chatham-Kent.

7   Minutes of the Corporation of the Township of Camden, May 11 and March 12, 1871.

8   Minutes of the Corporation of the Township of Camden council meetings, May 11 and March 12, 1871.

9   Wilberforce mortgages for the villages of Dresden, Chatham, and Buxton, Chatham-Kent Land Records Office.

10   Camden Township council minutes for 1871, McGeorge Building archives, Municipality of Chatham-Kent.

11   Camden Township council minutes for 1871. A c. 1900 postcard in the Dresden Archives collection at Dresden shows the Sydenham River looking west from today's bridge. There is no label on the photo and except for a tangle of wood and rope in the river in the distance, there are no apparent subjects. While the photo needs further examination to confirm this is a collapsed suspension bridge, confirmation of this would support the theory that the BAI bridge survived into the late 1800s when Henson sought its repair.

12   Other parts of the property were eventually transferred to Whipper's lawyer, Don Juan Barberro, for fifty dollars. Harriet L. Whipper sold her interest in the property to James W. Sharpe and associates for a mere $550. Chatham-Kent Land Record Office, abstracts for Survey 133.

13   Alexander McVean referred to the sawmill on his property as the "oldest establishment of its kind in Ontario" in the *Dresden Times* in 1889. Carter and Carter, *Stepping Back in Time*, 69.

14   McVean also had a daughter, Sarah, who owned a home on Hughes Street (Helen McVean, McVean family history).

15   Carter, *Stepping Back in Time*, 70; Land records of Survey 133, Dresden.

16   James and John also operated the Big Axe hardware store on Dresden's St. George Street.

17   The Concession Four is Dresden's main thoroughfare. It is named North Street south of Main Street and St. George Street north of Main.

18   Included in this redefinition of town boundaries were the eastern half of Lots 3 and 4 of Concession 5 of the Gore of Camden, including Park Lots 2 through 14, which include the Highgate property. Chatham Kent Land Records Office.

19   "Wilberforce-Nazrey Institute, dedication of the New Building on Monday— Admirable Address of Bishop Tanner, DD," *Christian Recorder*, October 4, 1888, Accessible Archives, https://www.accessible.com/accessible/.

20   Harry Ambrose Tanser, "The settlement of Negroes in Kent County, Ontario, and a Study of the Mental Capacity of their Descendants" (PhD thesis, University of Toronto, 1939). Report conducted by the superintendent of schools, Chatham, Ontario, as part of work towards becoming a Doctor of Pedagogy, and can be found in the local history room, Chatham-Kent Public Library, Chatham branch.

21   Avery was a noted philanthropist whose $800,000 estate was dispersed to a number of charities, including for "the education and elevation of the coloured people of the United States and Canada." Stanton Belfour, "Charles Avery: Early Pittsburgh Philanthropist," Western Pennsylvania History: 1918–2022, Penn State Libraries Open Publishing, https://journals.psu.edu/wph/article/view/2680/2513.

22   Liberty Ferda, "Past and Present Good," *Pitt Magazine* (Winter 2018), https://www.pittmag.pitt.edu/news/past-and-present-good.

23   "British Methodist Episcopal Church," Wikipedia, accessed March 26, 2013, https://en.wikipedia.org/wiki/British_Methodist_Episcopal_Church.

24   "Wilberforce-Nazery Institute, dedication."

25   Burns, *History of the Dresden Fire Department*, 8.

26   Robinson and Robinson, *Seek the Truth*, 90–91.

27   Robinson and Robinson, *Seek the Truth*, 90–91.

Chapter 17. A Time to Die and a Time to Mourn

1   This phenomenon is also evident in other municipalities in the area, including at Chatham's Maple Leaf Cemetery.

2   1871 to 1875, Dresden Town Council Minute Books, Chatham-Kent Municipal Archives, McGeorge Building.

3   Tombstone of Mary Ann Whipper Hollensworth, Dresden Cemetery. Some burials were also made in small family cemeteries on farms, not all of which are publicly recorded (interview with cemetery mapping project committee members of the Kent Branch of the Ontario Genealogical Society, 2007).

4   Segregation "even after death" for African Nova Scotians, Nina Corfu, CBC News, February 08, 2017, www.cbc.ca/news/canada/nova-scotia/segregated-cemeteries-camp-hill-african-nova-scotians-black-communities-1.3971054.

5   Blackburn Cemetery, northeast of Dresden, and Oldfield Cemetery in Dover Township are both believed by genealogists to contain unmarked burials of people of African descent on the periphery of their grounds.

6   Hand-drawn sketch of Ranges A and B of the Anglican cemetery, Huron University College Archives.

7   Oral history of Dresden Cemetery was shared with the author by town historian Don "Gummer" Spearman in the 1980s.

8   Sketch of Range A and B, Anglican Range, Dresden Cemetery, Huron University College Archives.

9   The Dresden cemetery's Anglican Range was relocated in 2003 due to riverbank
     erosion, and this has resulted in a different spacing and configuration of the graves.
     Previously Rev. Samuel Lynn's burial plot lay immediately west of Rev. Hughes's
     burial plot; Rev. Clarke was buried two paces north of Hughes; and Mary Ann
     Whipper lay within a few feet of Hughes. Rev. Hughes's grave continues to face
     Range B, as it did in the original burial configuration. Diane French of the Kent OGS
     and Marie Carter were historical consultants on the 2003 relocation project.

10   2002/2003 Dresden cemetery relocation project, conversations between the author,
     one of the local historical consultants, and the project osteologist gave the author
     access to confidential information that included evidence of burials that would have
     been controversial to include on "holy ground" in their day.

11   Survey of the site by author and various descendants comparing maps with the
     current headstones. A full GPR survey would be necessary in order to determine the
     number and placement of burials in the site.

12   Wadsworth, Bank, Patton, and Doroszenko, "Forgotten Souls of the Dawn Settlement."

13   Formerly the third concession of Dawn Township or Camden Gore.

14   The origins of the site's designation as the BAI Cemetery could not be determined
     from land records, and its naming happened prior to the establishment of the
     museum. Even if it is a denominational cemetery, its designation as a BAI cemetery
     still is an accurate assignation given it cotains burials of people who have close ties to
     key personalities involved in the BAI including Rev. Samuel Henry Davis, Rev. W.P.
     Newman and Peter B. Smith.

15   Wadsworth, Bank, Patton, and Doroszenko, "Forgotten Souls of the Dawn
     Settlement."

16   Attempts to locate the deed to the BAI Cemetery on the Uncle Tom Road in local
     land records showing its establishment as a cemetery were unsuccessful.

17   Marie Carter, "No Final Resting Place," talk given at Uncle Tom's Cabin Historic Site,
     Dresden, August 2018. Osteologists' notes, Dresden Cemetery relocation project,
     show multiple burials in a single shaft as a feature of reburials. One grave contained the
     remains of one white adult and a dozen white children under the age of five. Multiple
     burials in a single grave likely reduced the expense borne by families. The Baptists
     previously purchased property further south on the third concession as a cemetery
     ground prior to the new BAI Cemetery being established. This was never developed.
     Rev. S.H. Davis, his family, and other Baptists are buried at the new BAI site. Many
     tombstone dates at the new BAI site fall after the 1874 removal of the old cemetery,
     leading the author to believe that this was not strictly a BAI burial ground, though
     some burials there include those who, like Davis, were associated with the BAI.

18   Land abstracts and deeds to Lot 1, Concession 4, Camden Gore designates the lot as
     "cemetery" in its description.

19   Henson's Wilberforce mortgages were paid on this return from his October 1876
     British fundraising trip. Mortgage listings, Chatham-Kent Land Record Office,
     abstracts for Survey 133, British American Institute, Dresden.

20 Genealogical records of the Chatham-Kent Black Historical Society; the Fox County Genealogical Society, Wisconsin; and Smith family genealogists.

21 "Last Will and Testament of Francis Moss Turner," November 1863, Chatham-Kent Black Historical Society.

22 "Last Will and Testament of Sarah Whipper Turner," files of the Chatham-Kent Black Historical Society.

23 Funeral announcement for J.W. Purnell, *The Christian Recorder*, February 5, 1880.

24 Dresden listings in the 1881 Soutar's Kent County Directory, collection of the local history room, Chatham-Kent Public Library.

25 *St. Albans Daily Messenger*, www.newspapers.com.

26 Earl John Chapman and Ian MacPherson McCulloch, eds., *A Bard of Wolfe's Army: James Thompson, Gentleman Volunteer, 1733–1830* (Robin Brass Studio, 2010).

27 Piya Chattopadhyay, "Ken Burns Turns His Lens on Benjamin Franklin and Delivers a Lesson for the Present Day," The Sunday Magazine, CBC Radio, 22:23, https://www.cbc.ca/player/play/audio/1.6406940.

28 Letter of Registrar McKellar to the *Dresden Times*, March 14, 1910.

29 Letter of Registrar McKellar to the *Dresden Times*, March 14, 1910.

30 Letter of Registrar McKellar to the *Dresden Times*, March 14, 1910.

Chapter 18. Migration, Resistance, and Contribution in a New Century

1 For an excellent analysis of the societal influences at Dawn of Johnson's youth, see Reid-Maroney, *The Reverend Jennie Johnson*, 9–33.

2 Dungy and Hanson, *Planted by the Waters*, 36.

3 Reid-Maroney, *The Reverend Jennie Johnson*, 9–33.

4 Dungy and Hanson, *Planted by the Waters*, 36–38.

5 Henson family Bible, notes of births and deaths, collection of Henson descendant Barbara Carter.

6 Twenty ships were built in Dresden between the 1850s and 1880s. Carter and Carter, *Stepping Back in Time*, 83–92.

7 Interview with William Richardson of Toronto, March 8, 2022.

8 Dungy and Hanson, *Planted by the Waters*, 29.

9 Carter and Carter, *Stepping Back in Time*, 71.

10 Carter and Carter, *Stepping Back in Time*, 71.

11 Photo album, private collection of Calvin Shreve, formerly of Dresden, now living in Toronto.

12 Social notes, Notes from *The Canadian Observer*, August 25, 1917, from the files of Bryan Prince, Buxton.

13 "News Items from All Parts of the Dominion," Notes from *The Canadian Observer*, August 25, 1917, from the files of Bryan Prince, Buxton.

14 Woods, *Pontiac*, 109.

15   Genealogical research notes of Susan Solomon, family genealogist, Chatham, Ontario; clippings from the scrapbook collection of Sandra and Alan Thompson, Dresden, Ontario.

16   Interview with Lee Highgate, May 3, 2022.

17   Dungy and Hanson's *Planted by the Waters* includes two examples of those who returned to the area to farm.

18   "Obituary of Stephen L. Smith," *Dresden Times*, September 18, 1911.

19   Genealogical notes of Lisa Finch (Smith descendant), Detroit; Dresden Cemetery relocation notes, collection of the author.

20   An article in the *Dresden Times*, February 25, 1904, notes Anderson contracted for two acres for $284.95 and Talbot for one acre for $71.02. No explanation was given as to whether the price paid was based on acreage or tonnage per acre, and the report does not list levels of production.

21   Dungy and Hanson, *Planted by the Waters*, 24.

22   *North Kent Leader* bound files for February 13, 1970, and January 15, 1970, Dresden Archives.

23   Soutar's 1881 Kent Directory, Chatham-Kent Library.

24   Will of the Rev. Josiah Henson, Chatham-Kent Land Records.

25   Elgie, *This Land*, 433.

26   Guest drove for the Macau Racing Club. Photo exhibit, Dresden Raceway Emancipation Day celebration; and scrapbook collection of the Thompson-Guest family, Dresden, Ontario.

27   Katz, "Jim Crow Lives in Dresden."

28   Dungy and Hanson, *Planted by the Waters*, 19.

29   Interviews with Scott Shepherd and Peggy Shepherd Johnson, descendants of Catherine and Osgood McVean, 2006 and 2020.

30   Interview with Margaret Rigsby, now deceased, owner of the former James McVean home and neighbour to Osgood McVean, June 2003.

31   Interview with Margaret Rigsby, 2003.

32   McVean family history and clip file, provided to McVean descendants during the Trillium Trail Project.

33   Interviews with Scott Shepherd and Peggy Shepherd Johnson, Osgood McVean descendants, 2006, 2021, and 2022. The name of Osgood's nanny was not known. Attempts to identify her were aided bySusan Solomon and Sue Highgate Anderson who found a Bothwell area photo of a nanny, identified as "Flossy" Morris Harris, who was similar to Louise in dress and features, but it was not conclusively determined that Flossy and Louise were the same woman.

34   Interviews with Scott Shepherd and Peggy Shepherd Johnson, 2006, 2021, and 2022.

35   Shadd Shreve, *The AfriCanadian Church*, 68.

Chapter 19. Answering the Call

1   "Meet the Men of the No. 2 Construction Battalion," Nova Scotia: Communities, Culture, Tourism, and Heritage, https://cch.novascotia.ca/stories/meet-men-no-2-

construction-battalion. It was not possible to glean an exhaustive list of Blacks from Dresden. Representative names were taken from the IODE website, *Gathering Our Heroes* at https://www.gatheringourheroes.ca. Notes and conversations with Jorrol (Jerry) Hind, military historian and *Gathering Our Heroes* site developer.

2   "Meet the Men of the No. 2 Construction Battalion."

3   The term sapper is derived from the French word sappe for "spadework" or "trench," and became connected with military men who dug tunnels to undermine fortifications during the seventeenth century. "Sapper: Military Engineering," *Britannica* online, https://www.britannica.com/technology/sapper-military-engineering.

4   The Dresden Citizen's Band was an all-white band that included residents of Quality Hill in Dresden including William McVean. Photo of Dresden Citizen's Band, c. 1900, Dresden Archives.

5   *The Canadian Observer*, November 4, 1916.

6   In 1910 the *British Manual of Military Law* allowed any "negro or person of colour" to enlist, but they could not hold a rank above warrant officer. This changed in 1914. For more information on enlistment practices in regular units, see J.R. Hind, "Our Black Canadians in WWI," Gathering Our Heroes, https://www.gatheringourheroes.ca/stories/our-black-canadians-in-ww-i/.

7   Memorial books of the Dresden Branch 113 Canadian Legion listing for Walter Lucas.

8   *Dresden Times*, December 7, 1916, microfilm files, Dresden branch of the Chatham-Kent Public Library.

9   Letter from Arthur Alexander to the Minister of Militia and Defence, Nov. 4, 1916, from the files of Bryan Prince, Buxton.

10 Letter from Rex Higdon to *The Canadian Observer*, January 15, 1918

11 Royal Canadian Legion Branch 113, Memorial Books of WWI soldiers, Private James Goodwin's listing.

12 Discharge Certificate of William Isaac Jacob Beecher Stowe Henson, Western Ontario Regiment, collection of Barbara Carter, Henson descendant.

13 Dresden social column, *The Canadian Observer*, December 21, 1918.

14 Royal Canadian Legion Branch 113 Memorial Book.

15 Marie Carter, *100 Years of the Catherine McVean Chapter IODE, Formerly the Sydenham Lodge, 1914 to 2014* (Catherine McVean Chapter IODE, 2014).

16 Carter, *100 Years of the Catherine McVean Chapter IODE*, 11–12.

17 Interview with Margaret Rigsby, long-time resident of Quality Hill, summer of 2003. Rigsby, a professor of history in Toronto, cried when she recounted this story.

18 Dan Solomon, enlistment certificate, Regiment No. 3138291, from the collection of Susan Solomon, Chatham, Ontario.

19 Spearman, *Landmarks from the Past*, 47–48.

20 Interview with Susan Solomon, 2020.

21 Cyclorama was a large-scale, multi-day gathering of Scout troops from various locations across the district.

22   Scrapbook of the late George and Elizabeth Brooker, Cyclorama program booklet,
     Scout-Guides collection, Dresden Archives.
23   Katz, "Jim Crow Lives in Dresden."
24   Freeman, though not listed as having origins in Dresden, is buried in Dresden
     cemetery. "Freeman, Tarrance H." Gathering Our Heroes, https://www.
     gatheringourheroes.ca/hero/freeman-tarrence/.
25   Names in this account have been taken mainly from the memorial books of the
     Dresden Legion Branch 113, but research by Jerrel (Jerry) Hind, researcher of
     the Gathering Our Heroes website, shows these records are not exhaustive. My
     apologies to any families whose extraordinary service has been omitted through lack
     of documentation.

Chapter 20. The NUA Story

1   Numerous businesses in Dresden did not follow this practice, as documented in
     Sydney Katz's November 1, 1949, *Maclean's* article, "Jim Crow Lives in Dresden," and
     revealed in interviews with local residents. Refusing to serve coffee to Black veterans
     was also not unique to Dresden. Matthias Joost, Government of Canada War Diaries
     Team, in an email to the author dated January 25, 2011, stated that servicemen at
     Windsor were similarly refused service.
2   Lambertson, "The Dresden Story."
3   J.B. Salisburg, MPP for St. Andrew, letter to Hugh Burnett, NUA collection, Buxton
     National Historical Site archives.
4   Deirdre McCorkindale, "Black Education: The Complexity of Segregation in Kent
     County's Nineteenth Century Schools," in *Unsettling the Great White North*, eds.
     Thompson and Crooks, 344–367.
5   For a more complete discussion on racial segregation as it was practiced in a number
     of areas of society and various communities across Canada, see Henry-Dixon,
     "Racial Segregation of Black People in Canada."
6   Interview with Margaret Rigsby, summer 2004. Rigsby recalled a group dressed in
     white sheets who appeared on the front porch of a young African-descent man at
     his Hughes Street home. Rigsby recalled with amusement that when he confronted
     them, baseball bat in hand, they scattered. Spearman, *Landmarks from the Past*, 34,
     also notes "the Kluckers" were formed under their "Grand Wizard 'Mr. Al Cohol.'"
7   *Report of the Windsor Audit Committee of the Interracial Council*, National Unity
     Association papers, Buxton National Historic Site.
8   *Report of the Windsor Audit Committee of the Interracial Council*.
9   Katz, "Jim Crow lives in Dresden."
10   Henry-Dixon, "Racial Segregation of Black People in Canada."
11   Interview with Lee Highgate, son-in-law of Virginia Cook, May 2, 2022. Virginia's
     achievements are today recognized in a display at the Chatham Kent Health
     Alliance's Chatham location.

12 "1953–1959 the Supreme Court of Canada," Canada's Human Rights History online, https://historyofrights.ca/encyclopaedia/main-events/1953-59-supreme-court-canada-civil-liberties/.

13 Desmond, the owner of a small chain of hairdressing shops, was on a business trip when her car broke down in New Glasgow, Nova Scotia. While repairs were being completed, she went to the local movie theatre. Weary from a difficult day, she decided not to climb to the "coloured section" in the balcony, taking a seat on the "whites only" main floor. An usher asked her to leave, but she refused. Police were called, and she was forcibly dragged, sustaining a broken hip, but was not taken to hospital. She was immediately incarcerated, sentenced to a fine and thirty days in jail. In 2018 Desmond's portrait was placed on the Canadian ten-dollar bill.

14 1947 Town Council Notes, Chatham-Kent Municipal archives, McGeorge Building.

15 *Dresden Times*, November 4, 1948, microfilm files, Dresden branch of the Chatham-Kent library. Note that this was the second meeting of Johnson with Town Council. The first held between Johnson and a selected committee met on Monday, August 24, 1948 (*Dresden Times*, August 26, 1948, microfilm files of the Dresden Branch of the Chatham-Kent Library). It was chaired by white mayor Harold McKim and members of a committee that included four local ministers, three of whom were white, plus Rev. Talbot and Percy Talbot of Dresden, and a Fred Robertson of Chatham. This is likely the committee that Mayor McKim refers to when dismissing Johnson's delegation at the November meeting.

16 *Dresden Times*, 1947, microfilm files, Dresden branch of the Chatham-Kent library.

17 Weese is also known locally for welcoming the trade of Black residents at his grocery store, and descendants report he provided credit to all families that could not afford groceries during the 1930s.

18 *Dresden Times*, 1947.

19 Author's conversations with various site managers, including Arthur Pegg and Barbara Carter, between 1980 and present.

20 Katz, "Jim Crow Lives in Dresden."

21 Katz, "Jim Crow Lives in Dresden."

22 Katz, "Jim Crow Lives in Dresden."

23 Katz, "Jim Crow Lives in Dresden."

24 Lambertson, "The Dresden Story," 45.

25 The Greenmelk converted alfalfa into vitamin pills.

26 The National Hardware Specialties plant produced chrome-plated home products and auto parts.

27 Information gleaned from multiple issues of the *Dresden Times* from 1940 to 1956. Newspaper microfilm files of the Dresden branch of the Chatham-Kent Library; and Dresden Town Council minutes, 1947 to 1952, McGeorge Building archives.

28 Walter Weese, "Open Letter to the *Dresden Times*," *Dresden Times*, April 24, 1947.

29 1949 Dresden council minutes (bound file), 253, McGeorge Building archives, Municipality of Chatham-Kent.

30   *Dresden Times*, April 1949, microfilm, local history section Dresden branch of the Chatham-Kent Library.

31   *Dresden Times*, April 1949.

32   *Dresden Times*, April 1949.

33   Weese seems to have been misinformed on this point, as by 1948 a number of communities had already passed anti-discrimination bylaws. *Dresden Times*, April 1949, microfilm, local history section Dresden branch of the Chatham-Kent Library.

34   Letter to Hugh Burnett from J. Salsberg, NUA papers, Buxton National Historic Site.

35   Front page editorial, *Dresden Times*, December 16, 1948.

36   Conversations with the late Don "Gummer" Spearman, editor, *North Kent Leader*.

37   Lambertson, "The Dresden Story."

38   Lambertson, "The Dresden Story," 13.

39   Lambertson, "The Dresden Story," 12–13.

40   Lambertson, "The Dresden Story," 16.

41   Note to Burnett from anonymous source, National Unity Association papers, Buxton National Historic Site.

42   Daniel G. Hill became Ontario's first Human Rights Commissioner and is the author of *The Freedom-Seekers*. Donna and Daniel Hill are the parents of Lawrence Hill, author of *The Book of Negroes* (HarperCollins, 2011), and of Canadian folk singer Dennis Hill.

43   Armstrong remained a staunch activist for civil rights throughout his life. Bromley Armstrong, *Bromley, Tireless Champion for Just Causes: Memoirs of Bromley L. Armstrong* (Vitabu Publications, 2000).

44   Ruth Lor Malloy is an international social justice activist. She returned to Dresden in 2023 to promote her autobiography, *Brightening My Corner: A Memoir of Dreams Fulfilled* (Barclay Press, 2023).

45   Lambertson, "The Dresden Story," 21–22.

46   Sidney Katz, "Backstage in a Racial Sore Spot: *Maclean's* Revisits Dresden," Maclean's, January 18, 1958, 3.

47   Casual interviews with white residents born after 1954 revealed that, even in the generation immediately after the NUA action, most never knew it had happened.

48   Spearman, *Landmarks from the Past*, 33.

49   NUA papers, Buxton.

50   Biggs, dir., *Dresden Story*.

51   Casper Faas was a Dutch immigrant. In a 2015 interview, his widow, Wilma, proudly recounted her husband's conviction that everyone should be served regardless of race, colour, or creed.

52   Katz, "Backstage in a Racial Sore Spot," 3.

53   Katz, "Backstage in a Racial Sore Spot."

54   Personal experience of the author, who in 1968, being unaware of the "quiet understanding" that existed, invited a Black friend to Kay's Café for a milkshake but was not able to obtain service after a half hour wait. The waitress remained busy with customers in another part of the restaurant.

55   Letter of Daniel Hill to Vincent Smith, January 1970, NUA papers, Buxton.

56   Letter of Daniel Hill to Vincent Smith, January 1970, NUA papers, Buxton.

57   Johnson and Aladejobi, eds., *Unsettling the Great White North.*

58   McCorkindale, "Weaponized History."

Chapter 21. *The Journey Towards a More Authentic History*

1   Rosa Parks was given the title First Lady of Civil Rights by the U.S. Congress to recognize her role in the Montgomery Bus Boycott. In 1979 she was awarded the Presidential Medal of Freedom and the Congressional Gold Medal.

2   The Detroit riots were among the most destructive riots in American history. The rioting resulted in forty-three deaths, 1,189 injuries, 7,200 arrests, and the destruction of over four hundred buildings.

3   A full listing of the day's program was not given in the newspaper, and no program has been found.

4   Photo negative collection of the *North Kent Leader*, Dresden Archives.

5   The *North Kent Leader* was established as a weekly community newspaper in 1964.

6   Surviving negatives show a photo was taken of Parks sitting beside Lambkin on the stage. Photo negative collection of the *North Kent Leader*, Dresden Archives.

7   *North Kent Leader*, September 27, 1972, bound files, Dresden Archives.

8   *North Kent Leader*, September 27, 1972, bound files, Dresden Archives.

9   Smardz Frost, Walls, Neary, and Armstrong, eds., *Ontario's African-Canadian Heritage.*

10   "February Is Black History Month," Government of Canada website, accessed March 13, 2022, www.canada.ca/en/canadian-heritage/campaigns/black-history-month/.

11   Robinson and Robinson, *Seek the Truth.*

12   Robbins, *Legacy of Buxton.*

13   Shadd Shreve, *The AfriCanadian Church.*

14   *Roots: The Saga of an American Family*, eight-episode miniseries, produced by David Wolper, aired January 23 to 30, 1977, on ABC Network.

15   Handwritten note, collection of Barbara Carter, Henson descendant.

16   Observations of the author as an advisory board member during the museum's revitalization under the St. Clair Parkway Commission. During the revitalization "the Cabin" was renamed Henson House and "Old Uncle Jimmy's House" was renamed Harris House, but the Uncle Tom's Cabin remained the main identifier of the historic site as a whole.

17   Miller, *Years of Change*, 208.

18   Miller, *Years of Change*, 208.

19   Spearman, *Landmarks from the Past*, 36.

20   Survey of bound files of the *North Kent Leader*, 1964 to 1991, Dresden Archives.

21   As publisher of the *Dresden Times*, T.N. Wells wrote a brief history of the settlement on June 16, 1904.

22   Robert Brandon, Dresden's postmaster, published his *History of Dresden* to coincide with the Old Boys Reunion of 1950.

23   Helen Burns was a noted genealogist, local historian, and granddaughter of the town's first clerk, C.P. Watson, whose home, now occupied by Helen's son, is the oldest surviving house built on BAI land. Burns's history of Dresden was not published; however her other histories of Dresden's fire department and its agricultural society were.

24   Alda Hyatt wrote and self-published *A Centennial History of Dresden* in 1967.

25   Victor Lauriston is a noted county historian who wrote the first comprehensive history of Kent County.

26   Spearman, *Landmarks from the Past*.

27   Spearman's *Landmarks from the Past* included two chapters of Black history: "The Role of Blacks" and "Did He Jump or Was He Pushed," 17–34.

28   The Chatham-Kent Black Historical Society would be the first to include the NUA's story in its Black Mecca exhibit at the WISH Centre in the late 1990s.

29   McLean's *Welcome Home* included Dresden among several small towns across Canada with unique heritage or cultural practices. In it, McLean notes how various communities valued and preserved their cultures and histories.

30   McLean, *Welcome Home*, 57–131.

31   Other Canadian stamps have since been issued, featuring A.D. Shadd in 2009 and Mary Ann Shadd Cary in 2024.

32   *North Kent Leader*, September 21, 1983.

33   Catherine McVean Chapter IODE papers, Dresden Archives.

34   Hooper, "A Heritage Museum's Institutional History."

35   "Appointment to the Board," 10.

36   Salisbury is the daughter of Barbara Carter and granddaughter of Marion Lambkin.

37   The trust is mandated to support, encourage, and facilitate the conservation, protection, and preservation of the heritage of Ontario. "Mandate of the Ontario Heritage Trust," Ontario Heritage Trust online, https://www.ontarioheritagetrust.com/pages/about-us/our-mandate.

38   *1972 Yearbook*, Lambton-Kent Composite School, Dresden.

Afterword: The Road Ahead

1   T.S. Eliot, "Little Gidding," in *Four Quartets* (originally published 1941; Gardners Books, 2001).

2   Miles, *The Dawn of Detroit*, 2. Note: This quote was originally used to point out that the city of Detroit's present issues have roots in its past history.

3   The Promised Land's team of co-investigators originally included Olivette Otele, from England, and eleven other researchers from across the US and Canada.

4   The repetition of these names was noted by Karolyn Smardz Frost, during her time researching her book, *I've Got a Home in Glory Land*.

5   In my interviews with three local families this difference in perspectives and attitudes was remarked on by the interviewees themselves. Two mentioned they found it difficult to relate to urban cousins in Canada and particularly to urban African-Americans. Marked differences appeared in relation to racial intermarriage and styles of confronting injustice. These differences were also generational.

6   Boulou Ebanda De B'béri and Fethi Mansouri, eds., *Global Perspectives on the Politics of Multiculturalism in the 21st Century: A Case Study* (Routledge Research in Comparative Politics, 2014).

7   "The Maple Leaf Forever" was written in 1867 by Alexander Muir (1830–1906) of Toronto.

8   These refer to the emblems of England (the rose), Scotland (the thistle), and Ireland (the shamrock).

9   Johnson and Aladejebi, *Unsettling the Great White North*, 3.

10   Shadd, "The Wilberforce Settlement," 2022.

11   De b'Béri, Reid Maroney, and Wright, eds., *The Promised Land*, 40–61.

12   Rev. Johnson saw this as an outcome of developing the home of Rev. Josiah Henson into a public museum when heading a delegation to Dresden Town Council in 1949. See Chapter 20 for more.

Index

[tk]

336 · IN THE LIGHT OF DAWN

Marie Carter is a lifelong resident of Dresden, Ontario, where she researches and writes about the history of her community, the former Dawn Settlement area. Her eclectic career has included graphic artist, reporter-photographer for community newspapers and church press, and rural organizer of outreach to migrant agricultural workers.